MULTIPLE CHOICE QUESTIONS IN COMPUTER SCIENCE

MULTIPLE CHOICE QUESTIONS
IN
COMPUTER SCIENCE

ELA KUMAR
Asst. Professor
Dept. of Computer Engineering
YMCA Institiue of Engineering
Faridabad, Haryana

TECHSAR™
NEW DELHI

Published by

I.K. International Pvt. Ltd.
4435-36/7, Ansari Road, Daryaganj
New Delhi - 110 002 (India)
E-mail : tech_info@techsarworld.com
Website: www.techsarworld.com

ISBN: 978-81-906757-7-2

Reprint 2024

Published/Printed by Krishan Makhijani for I.K. International Pvt. Ltd., 4435-36/7, Ansari Road, Daryaganj, New Delhi - 110 002.

Dedicated to

all the students

who are in pursuit of exciting career

PREFECE

Computer science and technology has become lifeline of the modern industrial and social development. Our civilization is thousands of years old, but computer is just of sixty. In spite of its negligible age compared to the age of human existence, it has captured not only the activities but also, the consciousness of human beings. The stage has arrived where it has become difficult to imagine any action of human begins not involving computer in one form or the other. You are using your mobile phone, viewing television, driving your car or monitoring the progress of the production in your plant, the involvement of computer in all these activities can be easily visualized and felt. Even the book you are reading has been produced using computer at various stages of its production. Advancements made in the area of computer research has made it possible for computers to act and behave intelligently almost like we human beings and, the day is not far when computer would perhaps be able to practically replace us.

Widespread use of computers has increased the demand of experts and professionals in the field of computer science and technology in particular and almost in every other field requiring use of expert systems in general.

In the era we are living, mere completing a professional training and possessing a degree is not sufficient to grab a suitable employment. We need to qualify a competitive examination conducted by various agencies separately for this purpose. These examination generally comprise objective type questions of the subject opted or required. Hence, practice to solve and attempt multiple-choice questions has become a necessity for the aspiring individuals and qualified professionals in almost all the areas. Although, prima facie, answering objective type questions appears easier compared to subjective type ones, because likely answers are given up front and correct answer belongs to one out of the four/five alternative answers given, yet answering these requires not only thorough understanding of the subject but also, practice and familiarity with various possible questions. Keeping the above requirement in mind, it was felt that a book covering the full length and breadth of the subject is essential for helping the aspiring individuals.

I hope the book will serve the purpose for which it has been designed and developed. Sincere efforts have been done to include all varieties of the questions and certain level of difficulty of questions has been maintained, however, comments from the readers regarding any aspect to increase the utility of the book are always welcome.

Ela Kumar

ACKNOWLEDGEMENTS

First of all, I would like to thank almighty God, the source of all positive energy, for bestowing me the spirit of writing this book.

It is obvious that writing a book on any subject and of any from involves enormous task, and in this endeavour, many people have lent their helping hand for the successful completion of the project. It is difficult to name each and every individual here, however, I acknowledge all the persons who have put their direct or indirect efforts in completing this task.

I express my deep sense of gratitude to Dr. Ashok Kumar, Director and Prof A. K. Sharma, Head of Department (Computer Engineering), YMCA Institute of Engineering, for their continuous support and encouragement. I am also thankful to my other colleagues of Computer Engineering Department, YMCAIE, specially Dr. C.K. Nagpal, Shri Naresh Chauhan, Shri Manjeet, Shri Harish, Shri J.P. Sharma, Shri Dharamveer, and Shri Mukesh Garg.

I would like to thank my parents for inculcating the habit of doing everything sincerely, honestly, finishing that in a timely fashion and making time for maintaining health. I convey my gratitude to my in-laws, specially my father-in-law, for his blessings. I also want to acknowledge my sisters, brother and other family members. Finally, I would like to express my deep appreciation to my husband Milind, for never failing to encourage me for the accomplishment of this task. I am indeed indebted to my son, Kumar Adwet, for his patience and for allowing me to remain busy with the project for long, without disturbing me.

Ela Kumar

CONTENTS

1. Computer Fundamentals 1-26
2. Digital Electronics and Microprocessor 27-59
3. "C-Programming" 60-68
4. Data Structure and Algorithms 69-90
5. Computer Organization 91-122
6. Parallel Processing 123-145
7. Theory of Computation 146-172
8. Operating System 173-190
9. Compute Graphics and Multimedia 191-204
10. Database Management System 205-243
11. Object Oriented Programming 244-247
12. Computer Networks 248-275
13. Artificial Intelligence and Neural Networks 276-288
14. Internet Technology 289-310
15. Software Engineering 311-333
16. Data Communication 334-347
17. Information Technology 348-352

1

Computer Fundamentals

1. Natural language processing is a feature of.
   (*a*) First generation computer
   (*b*) Second generation computer
   (*c*) Fifth generation computer
   (*d*) Fourth generation computer

2. 'PARAM' is a supercomputer developed by
   (*a*) Japan
   (*b*) America
   (*c*) India
   (*d*) United Kingdom

3. In a computer system the result of data processing can be reported through.
   (*a*) Control unit
   (*b*) Output device
   (*c*) Secondary memory
   (*d*) Arithmetic unit

4. The programming languages can be divided into two major categories .... level and .... level language.
   (*a*) Machine level and assembly level
   (*b*) High level and low level
   (*c*) Ist level and IInd level
   (*d*) Primary level and Secondary level

5. COBOL language is specially meant for .... people.
   (*a*) Business people
   (*b*) Organisation people
   (*c*) Common people
   (*d*) Beginerr's people

6. Which of the following is are invalid character constant.
   (*a*) 'K'
   (*b*) 'K 51'
   (*c*) 'n'
   (*d*) ' '

7. In C++ or C given the declarations.
   Char ch;
   int i, j, k;
   const char c = 'A';
   float Val
   Which of the following assignments are illegal?
   (*a*) Ch = C;
   (*b*) C = ch;
   (*c*) Val = 23.27
   (*d*) i = j = 25;

8. DOS allows division of disk space into different portions called PARTITIONS.
   (*a*) True
   (*b*) False
   (*c*) Sometime true
   (*d*) Can't be said

9. ATTRIB is an internal DOS command.
   (*a*) True
   (*b*) False
   (*c*) It is not DOS command
   (*d*) It is external DOS command

10. A microprocessor is a complete CPU on a single chip.
    (*a*) True
    (*b*) False
    (*c*) Partially True
    (*d*) Can not be determined.

11. 'C' is
    (*a*) Machine language
    (*b*) Assembly language
    (*c*) High level language
    (*d*) Natural language

12. For x = 9 , y = 5 , z = 3 the answer of if (x > y) && (y > z) statement will be.
    (*a*) True
    (*b*) False
    (*c*) 5
    (*d*) 2

13. Indicate correct order of evaluation of processing expression A + B – C × D
    (*a*) A + (B – C × D)
    (*b*) A + B – (C × D)
    (*c*) (A + B – C × D)
    (*d*) None of the above

14. 'Type – Casting' is used for
    (*a*) Taking the output in specific format
    (*b*) Convert an expression to be of specific type
    (*c*) Give the input from specific type device
    (*d*) It is not used

15. Consider following expressions.
    (*i*) int x = 10;
    float y;
    y = (float) x + 3.9;
    (*ii*) int z
    z = (int) 3.1415;
    Which of the following are valid 'type cast' expression(s)?
    (*a*) Only (*i*)
    (*b*) Only (*ii*)
    (*c*) Both (*i*) and (*ii*)
    (*d*) None of the above

16. The contents of variable 'val' will be
    float val;
    val = 7/3;
    (*a*) 2
    (*b*) 2.00 00 00
    (*c*) 2.333 333
    (*d*) None of the above

17. The operator precedence in an expression can be overruled by the usage of
    (*a*) parenthesis
    (*b*) quote
    (*c*) statement seperator
    (*d*) None of the above

18. Indicate which is not the characteristics of algorithm.
    (*a*) Input
    (*b*) Effectiveness
    (*c*) Infiniteness
    (*d*) None of the above

19. The symbol used to add description comment to the flow chart is
    (*a*) INPUT symbol
    (*b*) START symbol
    (*c*) PROCESSING symbol
    (*d*) ANNOTATION symbol

20. Match the following.

(*a*)	□	(*i*)	Start
(*b*)	()	(*ii*)	Annotation
(*c*)	⬭	(*iii*)	Processing
(*d*)	—— [	(*iv*)	Connector

21. A derived data type is a combination of other already known types.
    (*a*) True
    (*b*) False

(*c*) Partially true
(*d*) None of the above

22. A two-dimensional array of character is known as an array of strings.
(*a*) True
(*b*) False
(*c*) Sometime true
(*d*) None of the above

23. Which of the following is basic data type?
(*a*) Array
(*b*) Character
(*c*) Structure
(*d*) Union

24. The fastest memory is
(*a*) Hard disk
(*b*) Virtual memory
(*c*) Cache memory
(*d*) Magnetic tape

25. Which is not the correct size of hard disk?
(*a*) 610 MB
(*b*) 680 MB
(*c*) 1.2 GB
(*d*) 2.4 GB

26. The declaration of function in calling program is known as
(*a*) Prototype
(*b*) Passing argument
(*c*) Reference
(*d*) None of the above

27. Error which is diagnosed by compiler is
(*a*) Semantic error
(*b*) Logical arror
(*c*) Syntax error
(*d*) None of the above

28. Transistors are basically
(*a*) Monostate devices
(*b*) Bistate devices
(*c*) Tristate devices
(*d*) None of the above

29. The base of octal number system is.
(*a*) 2
(*b*) 8
(*c*) 10
(*d*) 16

30. A hexadecimal digit can replace —— bit binary number.
(*a*) 2
(*b*) 4
(*c*) 6
(*d*) 8

31. The binary equivalent of decimal 18 is.
(*a*) 111011
(*b*) 110001
(*c*) 100100
(*d*) 010010

32. Number of bits in an ASCII number.
(*a*) 6
(*b*) 7
(*c*) 8
(*d*) None of the above

33. 2's complement of 11011 is.
(*a*) 00101
(*b*) 10110
(*c*) 00100
(*d*) 01111

34. Which of the following is not a essential part of computer system.
(*a*) Address bus
(*b*) Multi bus
(*c*) Data bus
(*d*) Control bus

35. In a demand driven architecture.
(*a*) The instruction is executed if data is available

(*b*) Instruction is decoded then data is searched
(*c*) Data is not required
(*d*) Compiler is operated when demand is there

36. Term 'MAR' stands for
(*a*) Memory Access Register
(*b*) Memory Address Register
(*c*) Memory Access Rate
(*d*) Memory Address Rate

37. In a computer system an instruction has 5 bit opcode field. It can support maximum
(*a*) 5 instructions
(*b*) 10,0000 instructions
(*c*) 32 instructions
(*d*) Any number of instruction

38. 'Program counter' holds.
(*a*) Address of next instruction to be executed
(*b*) Instruction to be executed
(*c*) Data
(*d*) None of the above

39. The correct instruction execution sequence is.
(*a*) Execute, fetch, decode
(*b*) Execute, decode, fetch
(*c*) Decode, fetch, execute
(*d*) Fetch, decode, execute

40. The length of time required to go through one machine operation is called
(*a*) Machine cycle
(*b*) Clock cycle
(*c*) Read cycle
(*d*) Write cycle

41. A system has 32K memory to hold instruction. The size of MAR is.
(*a*) 5 bits
(*b*) 10 bits
(*c*) 15 bits
(*d*) 20 bits

42. The input device OCR stands for.
(*a*) Operand Clock Recognition
(*b*) Optical Character Recognition
(*c*) Operand Clock Register
(*d*) Opcode Character Register

43. In a magnetic tape storage media, the inter-block gap is 0.25 inch, the recording density is 1600 dpi, fifteen 80 character records are written per block, how many such records will fit on a 2400 ft tape.
(*a*) 2000 records
(*b*) 43200 records
(*c*) 1000 records
(*d*) None of the above

44. 8086 has
(*a*) 32 bit data bus, 32 bit address bus
(*b*) 64 bit data bus, 32 bit address bus
(*c*) 16 bit data bus, 20 bit address bus
(*d*) 16 bit data bus, 24 bit address bus

45. The main difference between 486 SX and 486 DX family is
(*a*) 486 SX contains cache controller but 486 DX does not have
(*b*) 486 SX has numeric coprocessor but 486 DX does not have
(*c*) 486 DX has numeric coprocessor but 486 SX does not have
(*d*) 486 DX has cache controlled but 486 SX does not have

46. Consider following figure. Indicate which input device is shown.

(a) Mouse
(b) Joystick
(c) Light pen
(d) Keyboard

47. 'EPSON stylus color 500' and 'HP DJ 590 are
(a) Keyboards
(b) Inkjet printers
(c) Dot matrix printer
(d) None of the above

48. Match the following (Resolution of monitors)

Monitor type	Resolution
(a) Monochrome	(i) 320 × 200
(b) CGA	(ii) 720 × 650
(c) EGA	(iii) 640 × 480
(d) VGA	(iv) 640 × 350

49. 'CGA' stands for
(a) Centre Graph Access
(b) Colored Graph Access
(c) Centigrade Graphic Adapter
(d) Color Graphics Adapter

50. 'POST' stands for
(a) Power Operated Soure Tablet
(b) Power On Self Test
(c) Power Operated Service Tax
(d) None of the above

51. Indicate which is not a computer package.
(a) LOTUS
(b) PASCAL
(c) CAD
(d) DBASE

52. Find the odd term out.
(a) MS - DOS
(b) C ++
(c) UNIX
(d) WINDOS - 95

53. 'Multi programming' is.
(a) Having many processor in computer system
(b) Concurrent residency of many programs in main memory
(c) Parallel processing
(d) None of the above

54. In the file organization, the access of records is slowest in.
(a) Indexed sequential file organization
(b) Sequential file organization
(c) Direct file organization
(d) Relative file organization

55. The file organization in which each record has at least one pointer type field is
(a) Sequential file organization
(b) Random file organization
(c) Linked file organization
(d) None of the above

56. 'Coral ring' is
(a) An astronomical ring
(b) A type of jewellery
(c) A file organization
(d) An economic term

57. Indicate which is not a system program
(a) Compiler
(b) Assembler
(c) Interpreter
(d) None of the above

58. Indicate which is not 'Flynn's categorization of high performance computer.
(a) SIMD
(b) DIOD
(c) MISD
(d) MIMD

59. 'Buffering' is used for.
(*a*) Memory management
(*b*) I/O management
(*c*) Processor management
(*d*) None of the above

60. Spooling handles the overlapped processing of I/O and processing of same job.
(*a*) True
(*b*) False
(*c*) Partially true
(*d*) None of the above

61. 'Surfing' is the term used for
(*a*) Washing cloth with 'surf'
(*b*) Seeing the sites on internet
(*c*) Working with computer
(*d*) None of the above

62. Term 'WWW' stands for
(*a*) Working With Word star
(*b*) Working With Workstation
(*c*) World Wide Web
(*d*) None of the above

63. A programming methodology used with internet are
(*a*) C ++ programming
(*b*) HTML programming
(*c*) GUI programming
(*d*) None of the above

64. 'Hamming Code' is used in.
(*a*) Programming code
(*b*) Data communication
(*c*) Auto cad
(*d*) None of the above

65. 'MODEM' stands for
(*a*) Mode emulator
(*b*) Modulator-demodulator
(*c*) Maximum emulator
(*d*) None of the above

66. 'BPSK' stands for
(*a*) Bits per second keying
(*b*) Baud per second keying
(*c*) Binary phase shift keying
(*d*) Bytes per second keying

67. Content addressable memory is one in which
(*a*) Data is searched directly without giving address
(*b*) Address is given and contents are read
(*c*) Address is applied and contents are stored
(*d*) None of the above

68. Indicate which is not the type of digital nodulation.
(*a*) Phase modulation
(*b*) Pulse code modulation
(*c*) Delta modulation
(*d*) Phase shift modulation

69. 'Vedio teleconferencing' mean
(*a*) Sitting together and seeing video film
(*b*) A conference organized in TV studio
(*c*) Seeing the conference on television
(*d*) Sitting at distance and conferencing with the help of computer network

70. In the 'Information theory' the information content of a message is measured by
(*a*) I = pk log 1/pk
(*b*) I = pk log Pk
(*c*) I = log 1/pk
(*d*) I = log pk
(Where pk is the probability of ocurrence of event)

71. The baud rate.
(*a*) Is always equal to bit transfer rate
(*b*) Is equal to twice the bandwidth of an ideal channel
(*c*) Is not equal to signalling rate

(*d*) Is equal to one half the bandwidth of an ideal channel

72. The code which provides parity check is
(*a*) Baudot
(*b*) ASCII
(*c*) EBCDIC
(D) CCITT - 2

73. Full duplex operation
(*a*) Requires two pair of cables
(*b*) Can transfer data in both directions at once
(*c*) Requires modems at both ends of the circuit
(*d*) All of the above

74. The RS – 232 C interface
(*a*) Interconnects data sets and transmission circuits
(*b*) Uses several different connectors
(*c*) Permits custom wiring of signal lines to the conductor pins as desired
(*d*) All of the above

75. Time division multiplexing
(*a*) Can be used with PCM only
(*b*) Combine fine groups into a supergroup
(*c*) Stacks 24 channels in adjacent frequency slots
(*d*) Interleaves pulses belonging to different transmission

76. Satellites used for inter-continental communication are known as
(*a*) Comsat
(*b*) Domsat
(*c*) Marisat
(*d*) Intersat

77. In order to reduce quantization noise in analog to digital conversion.
(*a*) Increase the number of standard amplitudes
(*b*) Send pulses whose sides are more vertical
(*c*) Use an Rf amplifier in the receiver
(*d*) Increase the number of samples/record

78. To permit the selection of 1 out of 16 equiprobable events the number of bits required is
(*a*) 2
(*b*) $\log_{10}$ 16
(*c*) 8
(*d*) 4

79. A file is attached to the cpp file using a
(*a*) Include directive
(*b*) Define directive
(*c*) It is automatically included
(*d*) None of the above

80. A project file
(*a*) Examines the contents of the files in the project
(*b*) Contains instructions for compilation and linking
(*c*) Contains definitions for C ++ variables
(*d*) None of the above

81. A pointer is.
(*a*) The address of a variable
(*b*) An indication of the variable to be accessed next
(*c*) A variable for storing address
(*d*) The data type of an address variable

82. The type of variable a pointer points to must be a part of pointers definition, so that.
(*a*) Data type don't get mixed up when arithmetic is performed on them

(*b*) Pointers can be added to one another to access structure members
(*c*) The compiler can perform arithmetic correctly to access array elements
(*d*) None of the above

83. In a linked list
(*a*) Each link contains a pointer to next link
(*b*) An array of pointers points to links
(*c*) Each link contains data or a pointer to data
(*d*) Both a & c

84. Inheritance is way to.
(*a*) Make general classes into more specific classes
(*b*) Pass arguments to object of classes
(*c*) Improve data hiding and encapsulation
(*d*) None of the above

85. An array element is accessed using.
(*a*) A first in first out approach
(*b*) The dot operator
(*c*) A member name
(*d*) An index number

86. Element double array [7] is which element of array
(*a*) The sixth
(*b*) The seventh
(*c*) The eighth
(*d*) Can't say

87. A function's single most important role is to
(*a*) Give a name to a block of code
(*b*) Accept arguments and provide a return units
(*c*) Help organize a program into conceptual units
(*d*) None of the above

88. A structure brings together a group of
(*a*) Items of same data type
(*b*) Related data items of different type
(*c*) Integers with user defined names
(*d*) None of the above

89. A relational operator
(*a*) Assigns one operand to another
(*b*) Fields a Boolean result
(*c*) Logically combines two operator
(*d*) None of the above

90. In a for loop with a multistate-ment loop body, semicolon should appear following.
(*a*) the for statement itself
(*b*) The closing brace in a multistatement loop body
(*c*) The test expression
(*d*) The last expression

91. The && and ll operators
(*a*) Combine two Boolean values
(*b*) Combine two numeric values
(*c*) Combine two character values
(*d*) None of the above

92. Dividing a program into function.
(*a*) Is the key to object oriented programming
(*b*) Makes the program easier to conceptualize
(*c*) Makes the program run faster
(*d*) None of the above

93. An expression
(*a*) Usually evaluates to a numerical value

(*b*) Indicates the emotional state of the programmar
(*c*) Always occurs outside a function
(*d*) None of the above

94. In C ++ a function contained within a class is called.
(*a*) A member function
(*b*) An operator
(*c*) A class function
(*d*) A method

95. 'STACK 'is a.
(*a*) LIFO structure
(*b*) FIFO structure
(*c*) LILO structure
(*d*) None of the above

96. Size of an integer in bytes is
(*a*) 1 bytes
(*b*) 2 bytes
(*c*) 3 bytes
(*d*) 4 bytes

97. 'CRAY X-MP' is name of.
(*a*) Vector computer
(*b*) Super computer
(*c*) Array computer
(*d*) None of the above

98. 'Compiler' is.
(*a*) A device
(*b*) Software
(*c*) Communication channel
(*d*) None of the above

99. 'Manchester machine 'is.
(*a*) Data flow computer
(*b*) Von neumann computer
(*c*) A latest computer
(*d*) None of the above

100. Hashing is used for.
(*a*) Computing address of a record in a file
(*b*) Storing key value in the record
(*c*) Deleting a record in a file
(*d*) Updating a record in a file

101. A half byte is also called as
(*a*) Data
(*b*) Nibble
(*c*) Half byte
(*d*) Word

102. The difference between a Television and monitor is
(*a*) Monitor can not display TV signals
(*b*) Monitor can not directly display a clear picture
(*c*) Monitor can not give a steady picture
(*d*) None of the above

103. A fast access small capacity semiconductor memory is
(*a*) PROM
(*b*) RAM
(*c*) Scratchpad
(*d*) ROM

104. To enter the zeros in a register is called
(*a*) Rerun
(*b*) Reset
(*c*) Fill zero
(*d*) None of the above

105. A set of information that defines the status of resources allocated to a process is
(*a*) Process control
(*b*) Process
(*c*) Register unit
(*d*) None of the above

106. How many bytes are there in 1011100101101110 numbers
(*a*) 1
(*b*) 2
(*c*) 4
(*d*) 8

107. The decimal equivalent of 2^{12} is
(*a*) 4096
(*b*) 1024
(*c*) 1000
(*d*) 16

108. The value of 8192 in K units is
(*a*) 8×10^3K
(*b*) 8.192 K
(*c*) 8K
(*d*) All of the above

109. Binary coded decimal represent each digit as
(*a*) Byte
(*b*) Nibble
(*c*) Bit
(*d*) All of the above

110. The ASCII code for T is
(*a*) 1010100
(*b*) 1011010
(*c*) 1011100
(*d*) 1011111

111. In boolean algebra, the 'θ' sign stands for the .... operation
(*a*) AND
(*b*) OR
(*c*) NAND
(*d*) NOR

112. The number of output signals of a gate can be
(*a*) One
(*b*) Two
(*c*) Three
(*d*) More than 10.

113. The number of truth table entries of 7 input gate are
(*a*) 64
(*b*) 16
(*c*) 128
(*d*) 000111

114. An AND gate has 7 inputs. The 1 output is produced by input
(*a*) 0000000
(*b*) 1111111
(*c*) 0001111
(*d*) 1110000

115. The following register stores 92_{10}. What is the decimal equivalent of final O/P word if ENABLE = 0?

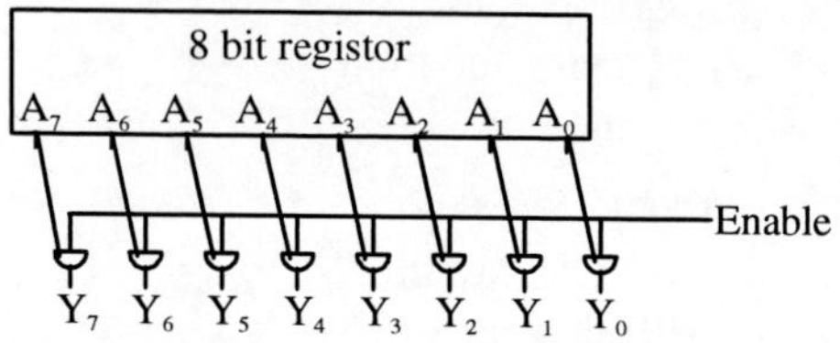

(*a*) 0
(*b*) 4049
(*c*) 1010011
(*d*) 92

116. In above question the output when ENABLE input is 'I' will be
(*a*) 92
(*b*) FF
(*c*) 00
(*d*) 4049

117. The boolean equation of following GATE circuit is

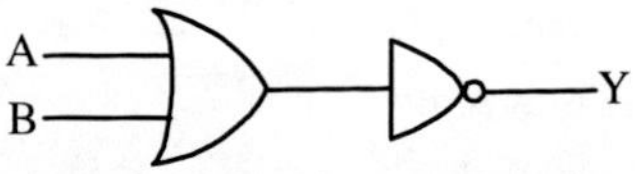

(*a*) y = A + B
(*b*) y = AB
(*c*) y = $\bar{A}$B
(*d*) y = $\overline{A + B}$

118. The output of following figure, if both inputs are high is

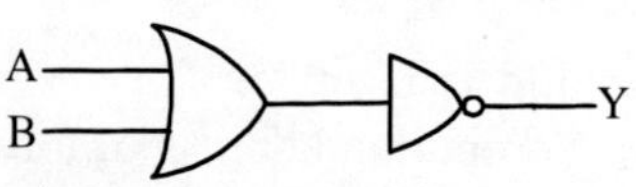

(*a*) high
(*b*) low
(*c*) Neither high nor low

(*d*) All of the above

119. The boolean equation of following circuit is

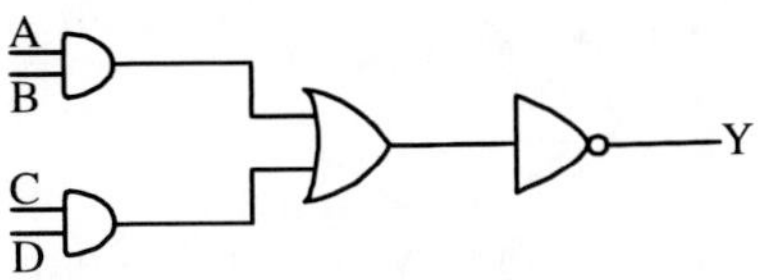

(*a*) $y = \overline{AB} + \overline{CD}$

(*b*) $y = A\overline{B + CD}$

(*c*) $y = \left(\overline{A + B}\right)\left(\overline{C + D}\right)$

(*d*) $y = \overline{AB + CD}$

120. An XOR recognizes word with an .... number of 1's
(*a*) even
(*b*) odd
(*c*) low
(*d*) high

121. De M-organ's second, theorem says that NAND gate is equivalent to a bubbled .... gate
(*a*) AND
(*b*) NAND
(*c*) XOR
(*d*) OR

122. The XOR gates are ideal for testing parity because even parity words produce a .... parity and odd parity words produce a .... parity
(*a*) low, high
(*b*) high, low
(*c*) odd, even
(*d*) even, odd

123. The output of following circuit for low and high A, will be

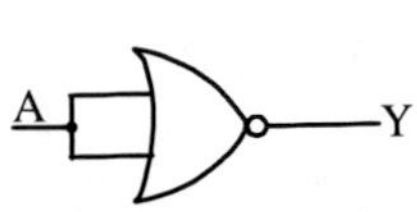

(*a*) low, low
(*b*) low, high
(*c*) high, high
(*d*) high, low

124. In following circuit, consider all inputs X and Y are high, which of Z output are high

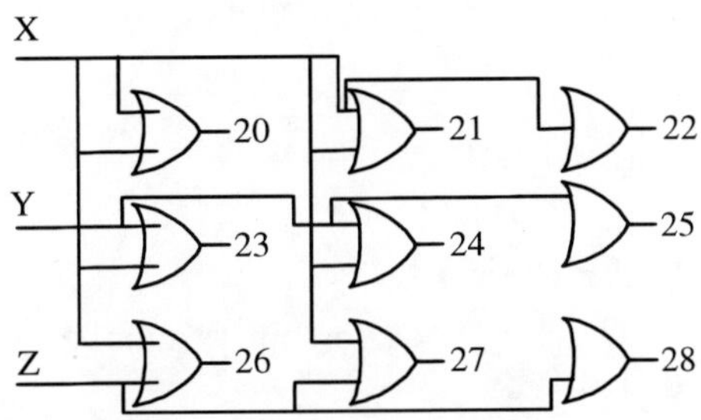

(*a*) Z_0, Z_1, Z_2
(*b*) all
(*c*) Z_0
(*d*) None of the above

125. In above figure, if all inputs are high except x_1 and y_2, which z output is high
(*a*) z_3
(*b*) z_5
(*c*) z_4
(*d*) z_6

126. In following circuit, what is the value of y, if A, B, C, D value is 0101
(*a*) y = 0
(*b*) y = 1
(*c*) y = not defined
(*d*) both

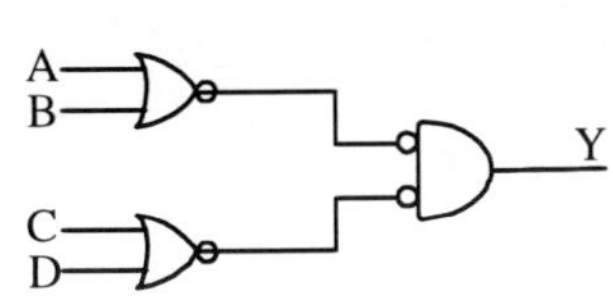

127. In the above circuit, if the value of ABCD is 1111, what will be the value of y.
(*a*) y = 0
(*b*) y = 1
(*c*) y = not defined
(*d*) None of the above

128. The grey code equivalent of binary number 10011 is
(*a*) 11010
(*b*) 01001
(*c*) 11111
(*d*) 10010

129. The grey code for binary number, 10101 is
(*a*) 11010
(*b*) 01001
(*c*) 11110
(*d*) 10010

130. 1's complement of 0000 11110010 1101 is
(*a*) 11110000 0010 1101
(*b*) 1111 00001101 0010
(*c*) 1111 1100 1010 1100
(*d*) 1001 00101010 1100

131. The LSI integrates method more than .... gates per chip
(*a*) 75
(*b*) 100
(*c*) 1000
(*d*) 10000

132. Basic technologies for manufacturing digital Ic's are bipolar and MOS. Bipolar technology is preferred for .... and ...., whereas MOS technology is used for LSI
(*a*) SSI, MSI
(*b*) MSI, LSI
(*c*) SSI, LSI
(*d*) ECL, DTL

133. The most widely used logic family is
(*a*) DTL
(*b*) ECL
(*c*) TTL
(*d*) MOS

134. Logic families which are preferred for LSI and those have low power consumption have
(*a*) NMOS, PMOS
(*b*) MSIPMOS, CMOS
(*c*) NMOS, CMOS
(*d*) None of the above

135. The 7400 series contains variety of SSI and .... chips
(*a*) LSI
(*b*) MSI
(*c*) MOS
(*d*) MOSFET

136. Standard TTL has multiple emitter input transister and a .... output
(*a*) totempole
(*b*) bipolar
(*c*) register
(*d*) transistor

137. The optimum temperature range for 7400 series is
(*a*) 1000°C
(*b*) 80°C
(*c*) 10°C
(*d*) 90°C

138. A TTL device which can sink up to 16mA and can source up to 400 nA is called as
(*a*) low power
(*b*) high power
(*c*) standard
(*d*) schottky

139. Instruction and data during execution resides in the

(*a*) Auxiliary memory
(*b*) Processor memory
(*c*) Cache memory
(*d*) Primary memory

140. RAM is
(*a*) Read write memory
(*b*) Volatile memory
(*c*) Random access memory
(*d*) All of the above

141. Which of the following term is not associated with the magnetic tape
(*a*) EOT
(*b*) BOT
(*c*) IBG
(*d*) None of the above

142. Magnetic disks
(*a*) Are read only devices
(*b*) Have data recorded in form of magnetized and non magnetized spots
(*c*) Sequential access device
(*d*) All of the above

143. A magnetic disk having 80 tracks, 15 sectors per track, storing 512 bytes per sector will have a storage capacity of
(*a*) 720 KB
(*b*) 600 KB
(*c*) 1.4 MB
(*d*) none of the above

144. The storage capacity of a Optical Disk is determined using
(*a*) Number of recording surface, number of tracks per surface, number of sectors per Track.
(*b*) Number of tracks on disk
(*c*) Number of sectors and bytes per sector
(*d*) Number of recording surface, number of tracks per surface, number of sectors per track, and number of bytes per sector.

145. Memory is organized into hierarchical way because
(*a*) CPU cannot access main memory directly.
(*b*) Main memory cannot store large amount of data.
(*c*) Use of auxiliary storage increases speed of computation.
(*d*) None of the above

146. Data backup is taken
(*a*) To safeguard data in case of catastrophic eventualities
(*b*) To use the data set again and again.
(*c*) To supply data at high rate.
(*d*) None of the above

147. Which device uses laser beam technology to read and write data.
(*a*) Magnetic devices
(*b*) Optical devices
(*c*) Charged device
(*d*) None of the above.

148. Which of the following is not fitting with others
(*a*) Trackball
(*b*) Joystick
(*c*) Mouse
(*d*) Web Cam

149. Tick the odd one out
(*a*) Windows
(*b*) DOS
(*c*) LINUX
(*d*) GOOGLE

150. Special purpose keyboards are meant for
(*a*) Quick and easy entry of user data

(*b*) All kinds of applications
(*c*) Checking accuracy of data at the time of data entry
(*d*) All of these

151. Electronic card reader:
(*a*) Reads graphic data existing on cards
(*b*) Reads encoded data on an electronic card
(*c*) Converts drawing and pictures into digital forms
(*d*) None of these

152. Hand Hold scanners
(*a*) Are used to scan large amount of data
(*b*) Are more versatile then the normal scanning devices
(*c*) Input data when they are brushed over the matter to be read
(*d*) Input data when they are passed near the scanning area.

153. Which of the terms are not associated with display devices:
(*a*) CGA
(*b*) TGA
(*c*) VGA
(*d*) EGA

154. Output printed through a printer is referred to as:
(*a*) Soft copy output
(*b*) Hard copy output
(*c*) Temporary output
(*d*) Volatile output

155. Plotters are very useful in application such as:
(*a*) Financial accounting
(*b*) Word processing
(*c*) Computer aided design
(*d*) All of these

156. High quality, high speed, high volume, and non-impact are terms associated with:
(*a*) Laser printers
(*b*) Dot matrix printers
(*c*) Inkjet printers
(*d*) Plotters

157. Point the odd one out:
(*a*) Sound
(*b*) Animation
(*c*) Graphics
(*d*) WWW

158. Which of the following cannot be classified as system software
(*a*) Linux
(*b*) Windows 2000
(*c*) MS Dos
(*d*) Oracle

159. Which of these cannot be considered as an element of Multimedia computer
(*a*) CD ROM
(*b*) Speakers
(*c*) Microphone
(*d*) Network card

160. Which of the following checks the syntactic correctness of a source program:
(*a*) Interpreter
(*b*) Compiler
(*c*) Interpreter and compiler
(*d*) None of the above

161. High level languages are characterized by:
(*a*) English-like statement
(*b*) Translator for machine code
(*c*) Portability of programs
(*d*) All of the above.

162. Which of these cannot be classified as a third-generation language
(*a*) COBOL
(*b*) PROLOG

(*c*) FORTRAN
(*d*) LISP

163. OS that permits multiple programs to be run simultaneously using a single processor is referred to as
(*a*) Multitasking
(*b*) Multithreading
(*c*) Multi user
(*d*) Multi processing

164. DOS commands that is used to quit the command interpreter
(*a*) EXIT
(*b*) CLOSE
(*c*) QUIT
(*d*) None of the above

165. DOS command that is used to rename a file:
(*a*) MOVE
(*b*) REN
(*c*) ERASE
(*d*) RD

166. Microsoft windows 2000 is an up gradation of
(*a*) Windows 98
(*b*) Window NT
(*c*) Window NE
(*d*) None of these

167. Which type of icons cannot be deleted from the desktop
(*a*) Folder icons
(*b*) System icons
(*c*) Program icons
(*d*) Document icons

168. Which of the following is a system icon
(*a*) MS-Word
(*b*) Window explorer
(*c*) My computer
(*d*) None of these

169. Which control do windows use for viewing text beyond the screen
(*a*) Status Bar
(*b*) Task Bar
(*c*) Title Bar
(*d*) Scroll Bar

170. Which type of folder view displays complete information about a folder
(*a*) List view
(*b*) Large icons view
(*c*) Details view
(*d*) None of the above

171. The menu that displays a list of options when a particular item is right clicked is referred to as:
(*a*) Main Menu
(*b*) Sub Menu
(*c*) Context Menu
(*d*) None of the above

172. Which O/S utility rearranges discontinuous files and free space on computer to move files on contiguous memory space and free space in continuous block
(*a*) Disk clean up
(*b*) Patch
(*c*) Logical addressing
(*d*) Defragmenter

173. Linux has strong similarities to:
(*a*) Window NT
(*b*) Unix
(*c*) Window XP
(*d*) None of these

174. LITO is a
(*a*) Loader
(*b*) Disk partioning utility
(*c*) Command interpreter
(*d*) None of the above

175. KDE utilities and application include
(*a*) KOE-Edu
(*b*) KDE-Games

(*c*) K-Office
(*d*) All of the above

176. Which of the following contains all the configuration files that are local to your machine:
(*a*) User
(*b*) Var
(*c*) Etc
(*d*) Config

177. Which one of the following is spread sheet package
(*a*) MS Word
(*b*) MS Power point
(*c*) Windows
(*d*) None of the above

178. A workbook with ready-made formats, content and formulas that can be used as base is
(*a*) Spread sheet
(*b*) Template
(*c*) Wizard
(*d*) None of the above

179. An equator that performs operations on work sheet data
(*a*) Hyperlink
(*b*) Formula
(*c*) Argument
(*d*) None of the above

180. Function in spreadsheet, which returns the interest payable for a given period on an investment is
(*a*) IPMT
(*b*) NPER
(*c*) PMT
(*d*) None of the above

181. An area on the screen which contain entire chart and all of its elements is called as:
(*a*) Plot area
(*b*) Chart area
(*c*) Data Table
(*d*) None of the above

182. This type of object maintain a link with source document, so that any changes done in source document are automatically reflected in destination document
(*a*) Unpicked object
(*b*) Embedded object
(*c*) Dependent object
(*d*) None of the above

183. It can be used to navigate from one sheet to another within same or different worksheet
(*a*) Arrow key
(*b*) Enter key
(*c*) Hyper link
(*d*) None of the above

184. In MS Word the toolbar, which contains icons for changing the look style of text
(*a*) Reviewing toolbar
(*b*) Standard toolbar
(*c*) Formatting toolbar
(*d*) None of the above

185. In mail merge the file that contains the form letter is called as
(*a*) Data source
(*b*) Record
(*c*) Field
(*d*) Main document

186. A series of word commands that have been grouped as a single command
(*a*) Macro
(*b*) Menu
(*c*) Function
(*d*) None of the above

187. Tool used to print a standard piece of text at top and bottom of each page
(*a*) Title

(b) Message box
(c) Header and footer
(d) None of the above

188. Linux has strong similarities to
(a) Windows NT
(b) UNIX
(c) Windows XP
(d) None of the above

189. Pilot testing refers to
(a) It is testing through dry running
(b) It is performed before unit testing
(c) The testing performed in the pilot project
(d) None of the above

190. E-term, E-prime prose refers to
(a) Method of writing English poetry in an electronic format by dropping verbs is, am, are etc.
(b) English written on compact disc
(c) Writing poetry on electronics
(d) No such term exits

191. Hypertert refers to
(a) Document having the facility of referring to another text
(b) Document having largest number of "Hyper" word.
(c) Document written with Hyper extension
(d) None of the above

192. Thumbnail sketch refers to
(a) Miniature sketch of a page showing placement of text and graphics used in page design
(b) A sketch made on a touchscreen
(c) A computer printoutput on a water
(d) None of the above

193. Mirrored page is
(a) Pages making up a two page layout, with page number located on the outside edge of each facing page
(b) A multimedia presentation containing mirror images
(c) A web page containing information about mirrors
(d) None of the above

194. "Man page" format is
(a) A handy format provided by VMS or UNIX for dumping print document online
(b) A home page created by man
(c) Format provided by metropolitan area network
(d) None of the above

195. On screen bullet means
(a) A heavy dot, filled square that calls attention to important points
(b) A computer game
(c) None of the above

196. Which of the following is not a proper guideline followed in multiple window management
(a) Don't obliterate the user work
(b) Avoid window clutter
(c) Give user control over frames
(d) None of the above

197. What is guidance level documentation?
(a) A type of documentation designed to lead user through a procedure one step at a time from designated starting state to an ending state
(b) A documentation created by guidance team
(c) A conceptual level documentation

(*d*) None of the above

198. The different form of index information is
(*a*) Print index
(*b*) One line index
(*c*) Keyword searches
(*d*) None of the above

199. $a^2 - b^2$ is a prime number (a, b, $\in N$)), then
(*a*) $a^2 - b^2 = 1$
(*b*) $a^2 - b^2 = 3$
(*c*) $a^2 - b^2 = a + b$
(*d*) $a^2 - b^2 = a - b$

200. Let the function of $R \to R$ be defined by $f(x) = 1$ if x is rational and -1 if x is irrational then $f(x)$, $f(1.272727)$, $f(-x)$ respectively are
(*a*) 1, –1, –1
(*b*) 1, –1, 1
(*c*) 1, 1, –1
(*d*) 1, –1, 1

201. Let $Y = \{y \mid y$ is multiple of $6\}$ and $X = \{x \mid x$ is a multiple of $4\}$. If $Z = XUX$ and ZEZ then z is a multiple of
(*a*) 2
(*b*) 4
(*c*) 8
(*d*) 16

202. Which of the following relation is neither reflexive nor symmetric nor transitive on human being?
(*a*) is a brother of
(*b*) is a sister of
(*c*) is a friend of
(*d*) is a mother of

203. Let A = {+, –1} and B = {00, 01, 10 11}. How many elements do $(A \times B)^3$ have?
(*a*) 512
(*b*) 4
(*c*) 64
(*d*) 256

204. The truth table of $(P \wedge q) \vee (q \wedge r) \vee (v \wedge P)$ is
(*a*) 00010111
(*b*) 01010101
(*c*) 11101000
(*d*) None of the above

205. If U = P {1, 2, 3, 4}, then truth sets of the # A^C = # A proposition, is
(*a*) {A$\subseteq$U : # A = A^C}
(*b*) {A$\subseteq$U : # A = 2}
(*c*) {A$\subseteq$U : # A = ϕ}
(*d*) None of the above

206. Use universal quantifiers to state that the sum of any two rational number is rational, these are
(*a*) $(\forall_a)Q(\forall_b)Q((a + b)$ is a rational number)
(*b*) $(\forall_{ab})Q((a + b)$ is a rational number)
(*c*) $(\forall_a)R((a + b)$ is a rational number)
(*d*) None of the above

207. The chromatic number of the following graphs is :

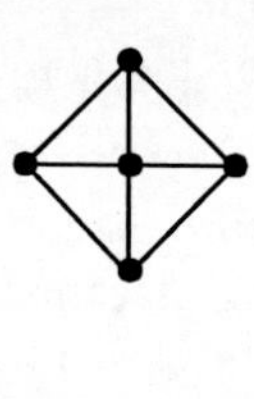

(*a*) 2
(*b*) 3
(*c*) 5
(*d*) 8

208. The set of letter in AARDVARK is

(a) {A, R, D, V, K}
(b) {A, A, R, D, V, A, R, K}
(c) {A, R, D, K}
(d) None of the above

209. Empty set is equal to
(a) ϕ
(b) U
(c) R
(d) None of the above

210. Write an explicit formula for the sequence 2, 5, 8, 11, 14, 17 ......
(a) $a_n = (n + 1)$
(b) $a_n = (n + 1)/2$
(c) $a_n = 2 + 3\ (n - 1)$
(d) None of the above

211. Write 107 integer as a product of powers of primes
(a) $10^2 \cdot 7$
(b) $5^2 \cdot 72$
(c) 107
(d) None of the above

212. Which of the following are statements?
(a) Is 2 a positive number?
(b) $X^2 + X + 1 = 0$
(c) Study logic
(d) None of the above

213. Write the statement "working hard is sufficient for me to be awake" in terms of P, q, r and logical connectives:
(a) $\sim r \rightarrow P$
(b) $P \rightarrow q$
(c) $a \rightarrow P$
(d) $r \rightarrow P$

214. Let S be the product set {1, 2, 3} × {a, b}. How many relations are there on S?
(a) 2^4
(b) 2^{36}
(c) 2^{18}
(d) None of the above

215. Let lg(X) = $\log_2$(X). Then lg(16) is:
(a) 10
(b) 7
(c) 4
(d) 9

216. If A = {1, 2, 3, 4, 5, 6, 7, 8}. Then product (2, 6)0(3, 5, 7, 8) 0 (2, 5, 3, 4) is
(a) (2, 8, 7, 4, 6)
(b) (1, 7, 8, 3, 2)
(c) (2, 7, 8, 3, 4, 6)
(d) (1, 5, 7, 8, 3, 2)

217. The maximal and minimal elements of the poset are:

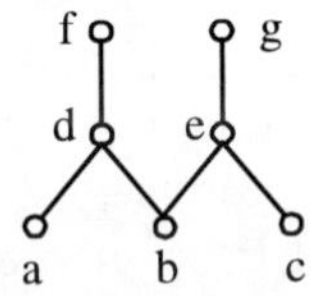

(a) Maximal f, g; minimal a, b, c
(b) Maximal c; minimal a
(c) Maximal g; minimal a
(d) None of the above.

218. If a finite set A has n elements, then the power set of A has
(a) n elements
(b) 2n elements
(c) 2^{2n+1} elements
(d) None of the above.

219. The intersection of sets is associative i.e., if A, B and C are any three sets then $A \cap (B \cap C)$ is
(a) $(A \cap B) \cap C$
(b) $(A \cup B) \cap C$
(c) $(A \cap B) \cup C$
(d) None of the above.

220. Union of sets is a commutative operation i.e. if X and Y are any sets then $(A \cup B)$ is equal to
(*a*) $(A \cap B)$
(*b*) $(B \cup A)$
(*c*) $(B \cap A)$
(*d*) None of the above.

221. If A = {a, b}, B = – {2, 3} and C = {3, 4}, then $A \cap (B \cap A)$ is
(*a*) {(9, 2), (9, 3), (9, 4), (b, 2), (b, 3), (b, 4)}
(*b*) {(9, 3), (b, 3)}
(*c*) {4, b, 2, 3, 4}
(*d*) ϕ

222. $A \cup B = A \cap B$ if and only if
(*a*) A is empty set
(*b*) B is empty set
(*c*) A and B are non-empty set
(*d*) A or B are empty sets

223. The function f : IR → IR given by $f(X) = X^2$ is
(*a*) Onto
(*b*) One-One
(*c*) One-one and onto
(*d*) None of the above

224. If A = {2, 3, 4, 5}, B = {3, 4, 5} and C = {2, 5}, then null set is
(*a*) A – B
(*b*) B – C
(*c*) $B \cap C$
(*d*) $(B \cup C) - A$

225. Let f(X) = 2, $g(X) = X^2$; (fog)(4) is equal to
(*a*) 16
(*b*) 32
(*c*) 20
(*d*) 128

226. If A and B are two sets, then $A \cup (A \cap B)$ is equal to
(*a*) B
(*b*) A
(*c*) $A \cap B$
(*d*) $A \cup B$

227. If f(X) = (X), then $f^1(0)$ is
(*a*) 0
(*b*) 1
(*c*) X
(*d*) None of the above

228. If $A \cup B = A \cap B$ then
(*a*) A = ϕ
(*b*) B = ϕ
(*c*) A = B
(*d*) $A \subset B$

229. If f(X) = X + 5 and $g(X) = X^2$, then gof is
(*a*) $X^2 + X + 5$
(*b*) $X^2 (X + 5)$
(*c*) $X^2 + 5X + 5$
(*d*) $X^2 + 10X + 25$

230. Enumerate the elements in the $\{X \in R \mid X^2 - 3X + 2 = 0\}$
(*a*) {2, 1}
(*b*) {–2, 1}
(*c*) {–2, –1}
(*d*) None of the above

231. Let A = {+, –1} and B = {00, 01, 10, 11}. The elements of A × B are
(*a*) {00, 01, 10, 11}
(*b*) {+00, +01, +10, +11, –00, –01, –10, –11}
(*c*) {+, –, 00, 01, 10, 11}
(*d*) None of the above

232. The largest set of propositions generated by P and q with the property that no two elements are equivalent is

(*a*) 2
(*b*) 2^5
(*c*) 2^4
(*d*) None of the above

233. Let A be a set and r a relation on A, then r is called .... if and only if ara is defined for all a∈ A
(*a*) reflexive
(*b*) antisymmetric
(*c*) transitive
(*d*) None of the above

234. The function f(X) = –2X on R, the set of real numbers, is
(*a*) subjective
(*b*) bijective
(*c*) injective
(*d*) None of the above

235. A .... is an undirected graph whose components are all trees
(*a*) cycle
(*b*) tree
(*c*) forest
(*d*) (n –1)n/2

236. If A = {1, 2, 4, a, b, C}, then A∈ A is
(*a*) true
(*b*) false
(*c*) can't be said
(*d*) partially true

237. If A = {3, 7, 2}, what is |A|?
(*a*) 7
(*b*) 3
(*c*) 2
(*d*) 8

238. $A \cup U$ is equal to
(*a*) A
(*b*) U
(*c*) A^1
(*d*) None of the above

239. The least common multiple of the integers 32, 27 is
(*a*) 864
(*b*) 150
(*c*) 625
(*d*) 725

240. The disjunction of P and q for the following assertion is :
P : I am rich
q : I am happy
(*a*) I am rich or I am happy
(*b*) I am rich and I am happy
(*c*) I am neither rich nor happy
(*d*) None of the above

241. I will become famous or I will not become a writer, then

I will become a writer

∴ I will become famous, is written as

(*a*) $(f \vee W) \wedge W \rightarrow f$

(*b*) $(f \vee W) \wedge W \rightarrow f$

(*c*) $f \vee W \wedge W \rightarrow f$
(*d*) None of the above

242. Find a cycle starting at vertex 6.
(*a*) 6, 4, 1, 6
(*b*) 6, 4, 3, 4, 1, 6
(*c*) 6, 4, 3, 2, 1, 6
(*d*) None of the above

243. Let a = {1, 2, 3, 4, 8} = 8; aRb if and only if a = b. Find the matrix of aRb

(*a*) $\begin{bmatrix} 1 & 0 & 0 & 0 & 0 \\ 0 & 1 & 0 & 0 & 0 \\ 0 & 0 & 1 & 0 & 0 \\ 0 & 0 & 0 & 1 & 0 \\ 0 & 0 & 0 & 0 & 1 \end{bmatrix}$

(*b*) $\begin{bmatrix} 1 & 0 & 1 & 0 & 0 \\ 1 & 0 & 0 & 0 & 0 \\ 1 & 0 & 0 & 0 & 0 \\ 1 & 0 & 1 & 1 & 0 \\ 1 & 0 & 0 & 0 & 1 \end{bmatrix}$

(*c*) $\begin{bmatrix} 1 & 0 & 0 & 0 & 1 \\ 0 & 1 & 0 & 0 & 1 \\ 1 & 0 & 1 & 1 & 0 \\ 0 & 1 & 1 & 1 & 0 \\ 1 & 0 & 0 & 0 & 0 \end{bmatrix}$

(*d*) None of the above

244. Let f be the mod 10 function. Calculate f (417)
(*a*) 7
(*b*) 8
(*c*) 3
(*d*) 5

245. Let $f_2(n) = 2^n$. Compute $f_2(5)$
(*a*) 1024
(*b*) 32
(*c*) 8
(*d*) 4

246. Which of the following functions f : R → R are permutations of R?
(*a*) f is defined by f(*a*) = a – 1
(*b*) f is defined by f (*a*) = a^2
(*c*) f is defined by f(*a*) = e^a
(*d*) None of the above

247. Let A = {1, 2, 3, 4, 5, 6, 7, 8}. The permutation (6, 4, 2, 1, 5) is
(*a*) even
(*b*) odd
(*c*) Data Insufficient
(*b*) None of the above

248. Let A = {1, 2, 3, 4, 5}. Let f = (5, 2, 3) and g = (3, 4, 1) be permutations of A. Compute $f^{-1}0g^{-1}$ and write the result as the product of disjoint cycles.
(*a*) (3, 2) 0 (3, 5) 0 (3, 1) 0 (3, 4)
(*b*) (1, 3) 0 (1, 5) 0 (1, 2) 0 (1, 4)
(*c*) (2, 1) 0 (2, 2) 0 (2, 3) 0 (2, 4)
(*d*) None of the above

249. Let U = {a, b, c, d, ... y, z} and A = {a, e, c, 0 4}. Compute $f_A(y)$
(*a*) 3
(*b*) 0
(*c*) 2
(*d*) 1

250. Let A = B = C = R and let f : A → B, g : B → C be defined by f(*a*) = a – 1 and g(*b*) = b^2. Find (fog) (2)
(*a*) 3
(*b*) $(X - 1)^2$
(*c*) (y – 2
(*d*) y^4

251. Let A = B = the set of real numbers. Let R be the relation < and S be the relation >. Describe RUS
(*a*) {}
(*b*) R X R–Δ
(*c*) $\{(X, y) | y \le X\}$
(*d*) None of the above

252. Let A = {1, 2, 3, 4} and R = ϕ. Determine that the relation A ∧ R is (are):
(*a*) irrefilexive
(*b*) symmetric
(*c*) asymmetric
(*d*) antisymmetric
(e) All of the Above

253. Find the relation determined by following digraph

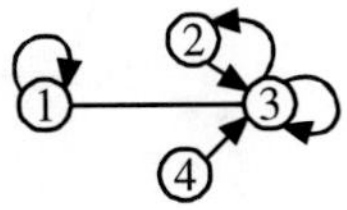

(*a*) R = {(1, 1), (1, 3), (2, 3), (3, 2), (3, 3), (4, 3)}
(*b*) R = {(1, 3), (4, 3), (3, 2), (2, 3)}
(*c*) R = {(1, 1), (3, 3), (3, 2)}
(*d*) None of the above

254. Let A = {1, 3, 4, 7, 9}, B = {2, 4, 6, 8}; aRb is defined if and only if b < a. Find the range of R
(*a*) {2, 4, 5, 8}
(*b*) {2, 4, 6}
(*c*) {2, 4, 6, 8}
(*d*) None of the above

255. If A = {3, 7, 2}, what is |P(A)|?
(*a*) 2
(*b*) 3
(*c*) 4
(*d*) 8

256. A Boolean expression generated by X_1, X_2............ X_n has .... different minterms.
(*a*) 2^{K+1}
(*b*) 2^K
(*c*) K(K – 1)/2
(*d*) (K + 1)(K)/2

257. If the statement S : $A \cap B = A$ if $A \subseteq B$, then its dual, S*, is
(*a*) S* : $A \cap B = A$ if $A \supseteq B$
(*b*) S* : $A \cup B$ if $A \supseteq B$
(*c*) S* : $A \cap B = A$ if $A \subseteq B$
(*d*) None of the above

258. Let D_{30} = {1, 2, 3, 5, 6, 10, 15, 30} and let the relation | be a partial ordering on D_{30}. The g | b of 10 and 15 is
(*a*) 1, 3
(*b*) 1, 5
(*c*) 1, 3, 5
(*d*) None of the above.

259. How many maximum edges excluding self loops, does a simple undirected graph of eight vertices have?
(*a*) 7
(*b*) 8
(*c*) 28
(*d*) 14

260. Solve the following sets of recurrence relations and initial conditions.

S(K)–10S (K–1) + 9S (K–2) = 2

S(r) = 3, S(1) = 11
(*a*) $1 + 2^K + 9^{K-}$
(*b*) $3 + 8^K$
(*c*) $2 + a^K$
(*d*) None of the above

261. The truth table of $\sim (P \wedge q)$ is
(*a*) 1110
(*b*) 0101
(*c*) 0001
(*d*) None of the above

262. The sets V, W and Z has 3, 4, 5 elements respectively. Determine the number of elements in VXWXZ
(*a*) 12
(*b*) 20
(*c*) 15
(*d*) 60

263. If Translation T is defined by (X, Y) → (X + 7, Y – 4), then the value of (5, 4) is
(*a*) (12, 0)
(*b*) (–2, 8)
(*c*) (2, –8)
(*d*) (0, 12)

264. R is relation in the natural numbers defined by X + 2y = 10. The domain of R is
(*a*) {2, 4, 6}
(*b*) {1, 3, 5, 7}
(*c*) {2, 4, 6, 8}
(*d*) None of the above

265. The range of the function f(X) = 1/(2–Cos 3X) is
(*a*) [1/3, 1]
(*b*) [1/3, 1]
(*c*) [1, 3]
(*d*) [1, 3]

266. Which one of the following is not a function?
(*a*) (a, c), (b, a), (c, b)
(*b*) (a, b), (b, c), (a, c)
(*c*) (a, a), (b, a), (c, a)
(*d*) (a, b), (b, c), (c, a)

267. For a constant function
(*a*) Domain contains only one element
(*b*) Range contains only one element
(*c*) Domain and range contains only one elements
(*d*) None of the above

268. $A \cup A = A$ is called
(*a*) Identity law
(*b*) DeMargan's law
(*c*) Idempotent law
(*d*) Complement law.

269. If A = {1, 2, 3}, B = {X, Y, Z}, then the number of injections from A into B
(*a*) 3
(*b*) 6
(*c*) 9
(*d*) 27

270. For the sets A and B, B – A is a subset of
(*a*) B
(*b*) $\overline{B}$
(*c*) A
(*d*) $\overline{A}$

271. Chromatic number of the following graphs is

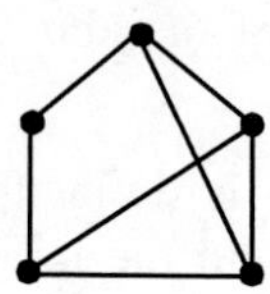

(*a*) 2
(*b*) 1
(*c*) 3
(*d*) 4

272. $\overline{\overline{A}}$ is equal to
(*a*) $\overline{A}$
(*b*) A
(*c*) $\cup$
(*d*) None of the above

273. Which of the following statements is the negation of statement "2 is even or –3 is negative"?
(*a*) 2 is even or –3 is not negative
(*b*) 2 is odd or –3 is not negative
(*c*) 2 is even and –3 is negative
(*d*) 2 is odd and –3 is negative

274. Let A = {1, 2, 4, 6, 8}, B = {2, 4, 5, 9}, Compute B – A
(*a*) {5, 9}
(*b*) {1, 6, 8}
(*c*) {2, 4}
(*d*) None of the above

275. If f(X) = X + 3 and g(X) = X^2. Find gof
(*a*) $X^2 + X + 5$
(*b*) $X^2 (X + 3)$
(*c*) $X^2 + 3X + 3$
(*d*) $X^2 + 6X + 9$

276. If f = (1, –1), (2, –3), (3, 1). Then f^2 is
(*a*) {1, 1}, (2, 9), (3, 1)}
(*b*) {(1, –1), (2, 3), (3, 1)}
(*c*) {(1, –1), (2, 9), (3, 1)}
(*d*) None of the above

277. If f(X) = log XC, g(X) = X^3, then f(g(*a*)) + f(g(*b*)) is
(*a*) f(g(*a*) = g(*b*))
(*b*) g[f(ab)]
(*c*) g(f(*a*) + f(*b*))
(*d*) 3f (ab)

278. If A, B and C are sets, then A – (A ∩ C) is
(*a*) (A – B) ∩ (A – C)
(*b*) (A – B) ∪ (A – C)
(*c*) {ϕ}
(*d*) ∪

279. If X = {2, 3, 8, 9}, y = {3, 4, 5, 6}, then X ∩ Y is
(*a*) 3
(*b*) {2, 8, 9}
(*c*) {4, 5, 6}
(*d*) {2, 3, 4, 5, 6, 8, 9}

280. If A {1, 2, 3, 4}, B = {2, 4, 6, 8}, C = {3, 4, 5, 6} then (A ∩ B) ∩ C is
(*a*) {2, 4}
(*b*) {ϕ}
(*c*) {1, 2, 3, 4, 5, 6, 8}
(*d*) {4}

281. The elements in the $\{X \in C \mid X|^2 + 1 = 0\}$ are (is):
(*a*) {1, 2}
(*b*) {3, 4}
(*c*) {1, –1}
(*d*) None of the above

ANSWERS

1. (*c*)	2. (*c*)	3. (*b*)	4. (*b*)	5. (*a*)	6. (*b*)	7. (*b*)
8. (*a*)	9. (*b*)	10. (*a*)	11. (*c*)	12. (*a*)	13. (*b*)	14. (*b*)
15. (*c*)	16. (*b*)	17. (*a*)	18. (*c*)	19. (*d*)	20. (*a*)	21. (*a*)
22. (*b*)	23. (*b*)	24. (*c*)	25. (*a*)	26. (*a*)	27. (*c*)	28. (*b*)
29. (*b*)	30. (*b*)	31. (*d*)	32. (*b*)	33. (*a*)	34. (*b*)	35. (*a*)
36. (*b*)	37. (*c*)	38. (*a*)	39. (*d*)	40. (*a*)	41. (*c*)	42. (*b*)
43. (*b*)	44. (*c*)	45. (*c*)	46. (*b*)	47. (*b*)		
48. a.- ii, b-i, c-iv, d-iii		49. (*d*)	50. (*b*)	51. (*b*)	52. (*b*)	53. (*b*)
54. (*b*)	55. (*c*)	56. (*c*)	57. (*d*)	58. (*b*)	59. (*b*)	60. (*a*)
61. (*b*)	62. (*c*)	63. (*b*)	64. (*b*)	65. (*b*)	66. (*c*)	67. (*a*)
68. (*a*)	69. (*d*)	70. (*a*)	71. (*b*)	72. (*b*)	73. (*d*)	74. (*a*)
75. (*d*)	76. (*d*)	77. (*a*)	78. (*d*)	79. (*a*)	80. (*d*)	81. (*c*)
82. (*a*)	83. (*d*)	84. (*a*)	85. (*b*)	86. (*c*)	87. (*c*)	88. (*b*)
89. (*b*)	90. (*d*)	91. (*a*)	92. (*a*)	93. (*a*)	94. (*a*)	95. (*a*)
96. (*b*)	97. (*b*)	98. (*b*)	99. (*a*)	100. (*a*)	101. (*b*)	102. (*a*)
103. (*b*)	104. (*b*)	105. (*d*)	106. (*b*)	107. (*a*)	108. (*c*)	109. (*b*)
110. (*c*)	111. (*a*)	112. (*a*)	113. (*c*)	114. (*b*)	115. (*a*)	116. (*a*)

117. (*d*)	118. (*b*)	119. (*d*)	120. (*b*)	121. (*a*)	122. (*c*)	123. (*d*)
124. (*d*)	125. (*a*)	126. (*c*)	127. (*c*)	128. (*a*)	129. (*c*)	130. (*b*)
131. (*d*)	132. (*a*)	133. (*c*)	134. (*c*)	135. (*b*)	136. (*a*)	137. (*a*)
138. (*b*)	139. (*c*)	140. (*d*)	141. (*d*)	142. (*c*)	143. (*d*)	144. (*d*)
145. (*a*)	146. (*a*)	147. (*a*)	148. (*b*)	149. (*d*)	150. (*d*)	151. (*b*)
152. (*d*)	153. (*b*)	154. (*b*)	155. (*c*)	156. (*a*)	157. (*d*)	158. (*d*)
159. (*a*)	160. (*b*)	161. (*d*)	162. (*d*)	163. (*b*)	164. (*a*)	165. (*b*)
166. (*a*)	167. (*b*)	168. (*c*)	169. (*d*)	170. (*a*)	171. (*b*)	172. (*d*)
173. (*b*)	174. (*b*)	175. (*d*)	176. (*d*)	177. (*b*)	178. (*b*)	179. (*b*)
180. (*a*)	181. (*b*)	182. (*a*)	183. (*c*)	184. (*c*)	185. (*d*)	186. (*a*)
187. (*c*)	188. (*b*)	189. (*a*)	190. (*a*)	191. (*a*)	192. (*a*)	193. (*b*)
194. (*a*)	195. (*a*)	196. (*b*)	197. (*a*)	198. (*c*)	199. (*c*)	200. (*d*)
201. (*d*)	202. (*c*)	203. (*a*)	204. (*c*)	205. (*c*)	206. (*c*)	207. (*a*)
208. (*a*)	209. (*a*)	210. (*c*)	211. (*c*)	212. (*c*)	213. (*a*)	214. (*c*)
215. (*a*)	216. (*c*)	217. (*a*)	218. (*c*)	219. (*a*)	220. (*b*)	221. (*b*)
222. (*d*)	223. (*d*)	224. (*d*)	225. (*b*)	226. (*a*)	227. (*a*)	228. (*b*)
229. (*d*)	230. (*c*)	231. (*b*)	232. (*c*)	233. (*a*)	234. (*a*)	235. (*c*)
236. (*a*)	237. (*b*)	238. (*b*)	239. (*a*)	240. (*b*)	241. (*a*)	242. (*c*)
243. (*a*)	244. (*a*)	245. (*b*)	246. (*a*)	247. (*b*)	248. (*d*)	249. (*b*)
250. (*a*)	251. (*a*)	252. (*e*)	253. (*a*)	254. (*c*)	255. (*b*)	256. (*b*)
257. (*b*)	258. (*b*)	259. (*c*)	260. (*b*)	261. (*a*)	262. (*d*)	263. (*a*)
264. (*a*)	265. (*a*)	266. (*a*)	267. (*c*)	268. (*a*)	269. (*c*)	270. (*a*)
271. (*a*)	272. (*b*)	273. (*b*)	274. (*a*)	275. (*d*)	276. (*b*)	277. (*d*)
278. (*c*)	279. (*a*)	280. (*d*)	281. (*c*)			

2

Digital Electronics and Microprocessors

1. In memory mapped I/O system which of the following instruction will not be there.
   (*a*) LDA
   (*b*) STA
   (*c*) ADD
   (*d*) OUT

2. Consider a 8085 based system operated with the following specification, operating frequency = 6 MHz.
   ROM add-0000 through 07FF
   RAM add-1000 through 17FF
   ROM require-1 wait state
   RAM require no wait state
   If content of PC is 0200 instruction cycle time needed for instruction ORIA, 22 is.
   (*a*) 8
   (*b*) 9
   (*c*) 10
   (*d*) 16

3. Choose the correct statement for a microprocessor system using I/O mapped I/o.
   (*a*) Memory space available is greater
   (*b*) Not all data transfer instruction are available
   (*c*) I/O and memory address space are distinct
   (*d*) I/O address space is greater

4. RLC instruction is equivalent to.
   (*a*) STC
   (*b*) DAD H
   (*c*) CMC
   (*d*) ADC C

5. After executing CMP A instruction.
   (*a*) ZF is set, CY is reset
   (*b*) ZF is set, CY is unchanged
   (*c*) ZF is reset and CY is set
   (*d*) ZF is reset and CY is unchanged

6. 8085 up will enter into INA cycle after recognition of.
   (*a*) Any interrupt
   (*b*) TRAP only
   (*c*) INTR only
   (*d*) RST 7.5, 6.5 and 5.5 only

7. Interrupt vector address for TRAP is.
   (*a*) 0000 h
   (*b*) 0024 h
   (*c*) 0018 h
   (*d*) 0020 h

8. 8085 μp enters into a wait state after the recognition of.
   (*a*) HOLD
   (*b*) REAY
   (*c*) RESET-IN
   (*d*) INTR

9. During instruction execution in 8085, first operation is.
   (*a*) Instruction fetch from location 0000 h

(*b*) Memory read from location 0000 h
(*c*) Instruction fetch from location 8000 h
(*d*) Stack initialization

10. Which of the following is correct decreasing order of interrupts.
(*a*) TRAP, RST 7.5, RST 6.5, RST 5.5, INTR
(*b*) TRAP, RST 5.5, RST 6.5, RST 7.5, INTR
(*c*) INTR, TRAP, RST 7.5, RST 6.5, RST 5.5
(*d*) None of the above

11. On TRAP interrupt, the service routine jumps to location.
(*a*) 0000 h
(*b*) 0024 h
(*c*) 0018 h
(*d*) 002 h

12. In the program segment.
LXI H, 0106 H
DCR L
Loop: DCX H
NZ loop
HLT
Loop will be executed
(*a*) 115 times
(*b*) 261 times
(*c*) 0 times
(*d*) Infinite times

13. Consider following 4 instructions
(*a*) PUSH PSW
(*b*) CALL ADDR
(*c*) XTHL
(*d*) RST n
The stack pointer will be affected by instructions
(*a*) 1 only
(*b*) 1 and 2
(*c*) 1, 2, 4
(*d*) 1, 2, 3

14. Consider following program segment.
MVI B,00
MVI A, 1C
DCR B
DAA
STA TEMP
HLT
Contents of TEMP after execution of above program is
(*a*) 10 H
(*b*) 22 H
(*c*) 82 H
(*d*) 12 H

15. Which of the following instructions require more number of T states.
(*a*) MOV A, B
(*b*) MOV A, M
(*c*) LDAXB
(*d*) DAD D

16. The 8085 Up inters into wait state after recognition of.
(*a*) HOLD
(*b*) READY
(*c*) RESETN
(*d*) INTR

17. Maximum number of I/O devices that can be addressed by Intel 8085 is.
(*a*) 65,536
(*b*) 255
(*c*) 512
(*d*) 256

18. The μp may be made to exit from HALT state by asserting.
(*a*) RESET
(*b*) Any of the five interrupt lines
(*c*) READY line
(*d*) (*a*) and (*b*) above

19. How many RAM chips of size

(256Kx1) will be required to build memory of 1K byte.
(*a*) 8
(*b*) 32
(*c*) 10
(*d*) 24

20. The 8085 up enters into bus idle machine, whenever.
(*a*) INTR interrupt is recognized
(*b*) RST 6.5 is recognized
(*c*) DAD rp instruction is executed
(*d*) None of the above

21. If clock frequencies of 8085 μp is 4 MHz and 8085 μp2 is 4 MHz, this means that.
(*a*) μp_1 is faster than μp_2
(*b*) μp_2 is faster than μp_1
(*c*) Both will work at same speed
(*d*) None of the above

22. In order to complement the lower order nibble of the accumulator, one can use.
(*a*) ANI OF H
(*b*) XRI OF H
(*c*) ORI OF
(*d*) CMA

23. 8085 μp is a.
(*a*) 8 bit microprocessor
(*b*) 4 bit microprocessor
(*c*) 16 bit microprocessor
(*d*) 32 bit microprocessor

24. The data bus of 8085 processor is multiplexed with.
(*a*) Higher order address lines
(*b*) Lower order address lines
(*c*) Status lines
(*d*) None of the above

25. RST 3 instruction will cause the processor to branch to the location.
(*a*) 0000H
(*b*) 0018H
(*c*) 0024H
(*d*) 8018H

26. Which of the following interrupt is nonmaskable.
(*a*) TRAP
(*b*) RST 7.5
(*c*) INTR
(*d*) RST 6.5

27. Which of the following instruction will never affect flag.
(*a*) DCR reg
(*b*) ORA reg
(*c*) DCX rp
(*d*) XRA reg

28. The content of $A_{15} - A_8$, lines while executing "IN-addr' instruction are.
(*a*) 0000H
(*b*) FFFF H
(*c*) Same as contents of $A_7 - A_0$
(*d*) Cannot be determined

29. Which of the following peripheral ICs is used to interface keyboard and display.
(*a*) 8251
(*b*) 8279
(*c*) 8259
(*d*) 8253

30. Which of the following is edge triggered flip flop.
(*a*) INTR
(*b*) TRAP
(*c*) RST 7.5
(*d*) RST 5.5

31. Which one of the following instruction may be used to clear the accumulator content.
(*a*) CLRA
(*b*) ORA A
(*c*) SUBA
(*d*) MOVA,00H

32. Execution of RST n instruction causes the stack pointer to.
    (*a*) Increment by two
    (*b*) Decrement by two
    (*c*) Remain unaffected
    (*d*) None of the above

33. The stack is.
    (*a*) Reserved ROM address space
    (*b*) Reserved RAM address space
    (*c*) Reserved I/O address space
    (*d*) None of the above

34. Which instruction shift right the accumulator content by 1 bit through carry flag bit.
    (*a*) RLC
    (*b*) RAL
    (*c*) RRC
    (*d*) RAR

35. Maximum number of bits required to represent any character from ASCII code set is.
    (*a*) 10
    (*b*) 8
    (*c*) 7
    (*d*) 3

36. In the following program segment.

```
DEALY: LXI H, 0010H
LOOP:  DCXH
MOV A,L
ORA H
XRA A
JNZ LOOP
RET
```

Number of times LOOP will be executed is
    (*a*) 16
    (*b*) 10
    (*c*) 1
    (*d*) Infinite

37. Consider following program segment.

```
8000: START: LX1 H, 0001 H
             LX1 D, 8010H
             XCHG
             DCXD
             JZ 800 C
             PCHL
800C; JMP8000
      NOP
      HLT
```

Referring to above program which statement is true.
    (*a*) The program will loop infinitely
    (*b*) The program will reach halt state after first pass
    (*c*) Program will reach halt state after 8010 H
    (*d*) None of the above

38. In order to save accumulator value onto stack which of the following instruction may be used.
    (*a*) PUSH PSW
    (*b*) PUSH A
    (*c*) PUSH SP
    (*d*) POP PSW

39. A single instruction to clear lower 4 bits of accumulator.
    (*a*) XRI OF
    (*b*) ANI F0
    (*c*) XRI F0H
    (*d*) ANI OF H

40. Which of the following statements is true.
    (*a*) ROM is read/write memory
    (*b*) PC points to the last instruction that was executed
    (*c*) Stack works on the principle of LIFO
    (*d*) None of the above

41. In a vectored interrupt.
    (*a*) The branch address is assigned to a fixed location in memory

(*b*) The interrupting source supplies the branch information to the processor through an interrupt vector
(*c*) Branch address is obtained from a register in the processor
(*d*) None of the above

42. Number of address and data lines needed for memory of 4K x 16 is.
(*a*) 10, 16
(*b*) 11, 8
(*c*) 12,16
(*d*) 12, 12

43. The value of X, Y, Z, W that satisfies following booleam equation.
X' + XY = 0, XY = XZ, and
XY + XZ + ZW = ZW is
(*a*) X = 1, Y = 0, Z = 0, W = 1
(*b*) X = 1, Y = 1, Z = 0, W = 0
(*c*) X = 1, Y = 0, Z = 1, W = 1
(*d*) X = 1, Y = 0, Z = 0, W = 0

44. In virtual memory system the address space specified by address lines of CPU must be ___ than physical memory size and ___ and secondary storage size.
(*a*) Smaller, larger
(*b*) Smaller, smaller
(*c*) Large, smaller
(*d*) Larger, larger

45. Floating point number in a computer are represented by 10 bit mantissa and 6 bit exponent. The approximate value of maximum number than can be represented is.
(*a*) 2^{64}
(*b*) 2^{63}
(*c*) 2^{32}
(*d*) 2^{31}

46. Bit slice processor.
(*a*) Can be cascaded to get any desired word length processor
(*b*) Speed of operation is independent of word length configured
(*c*) Do not contain anything equivalent of a program counter in a normal μP
(*d*) Contain only a data path of a normal CPU

47. If the total number of states in the fetching and execution phases of an 8085 instruction is known to be 7, the number of machine cycle in that instruction is
(*a*) 0
(*b*) 1
(*c*) 2
(*d*) 3

48. Which of the following is true w.r.t micro programmed control unit.
(*a*) It is faster than hardwired unit
(*b*) Facilitates easy implementation of a new instruction
(*c*) Is useful when small programs are run
(*d*) All of the above

49. Consider a computer with 11 bit instruction format, the size of address field is 4 bits. The computer uses expanding opcode technique and has 5, two address instructions and 32 one address instruction. The number of zero address instruction it can support is.
(*a*) 256
(*b*) 2048
(*c*) 16
(*d*) 272

50. To change upper case to lowercase letter in ASCII, the correct mask and operation should be.
(*a*) 0100000 and NOR

(*b*) 1011111 and AND
(*c*) 0100000 and OR
(*d*) 0100000 and NAND

51. The number of flip flops needed to construct a binary modul N counter is.
(*a*) N
(*b*) 2^N
(*c*) N^2
(*d*) Log_2N

52. Which gate offers good resistance to radiation.
(*a*) ECL
(*b*) GaAs
(*c*) TTL
(*d*) CMOS

53. A Boolean operation α is defined as A α B = AB + A'B' then AαA is.
(*a*) A
(*b*) B
(*c*) 0
(*d*) 01

54. If a particular idea can be implemented in hardware/software, the factor that favor hardware implementation is/are.
(*a*) Cost effectiveness
(*b*) Speed of operation
(*c*) Reliability
(*d*) Frequent change expected

55. Tera is 2 to the power.
(*a*) 32
(*b*) 30
(*c*) 12
(*d*) 25

56. SIMD can be used for.
(*a*) Railway reservation
(*b*) Weather forecasting
(*c*) Matrix multiplication
(*d*) All of the above

57. Power PC, Cray T3E are example of.
(*a*) RISC m/c
(*b*) CISC m/c
(*c*) Parallel m/c
(*d*) None of the above

58. ADD # 5 is an example of.
(*a*) Base index addressing
(*b*) Indirect addressing
(*c*) Immediate addressing
(*d*) None of the above

59. Consider following memory configuration.

Address	Value	Register (R)
1	5	5
5	7	
6	5	

What is the result of following statement?
ADD 6 (immediate) to R (indirect)
(*a*) 10
(*b*) 6
(*c*) 5
(*d*) 13

60. Consider following memory configuration.

Address	Value	Register
4	9	6
5	7	
6	2	

The result of statement SUB R(direct) will be
(*a*) 4
(*b*) 3
(*c*) 5
(*d*) 9

61. The difference between LDA # 3 and LDA 3 is.
(*a*) First uses immediate addressing and second uses memory reference addressing
(*b*) First uses memory reference

instruction and second uses immediate addressing
(*c*) First uses immediate addressing and second uses register addressing
(*d*) None of the above

62. The address calculation in register indirect addressing mode is.
(*a*) (Register) + displacement
(*b*) Register + (displacement)
(*c*) (Register) + (displacement)
(*d*) Register + displacement

63. "Test Device" instruction in SIC architecture:
(*a*) Is used for testing O/S
(*b*) It tests whether the address device is ready to send and receive the data
(*c*) It tests the working of peripheral device
(*d*) None of the above

64. "External Reference" in an assembler stands for.
(*a*) Instruction in one control section refers to instruction or data in other control section
(*b*) The reference which are outside the program
(*c*) The reference made to peripheral device
(*d*) None of the above

65. The meaning of assembler directive START is.
(*a*) START the execution of instruction
(*b*) START the memory data transfer
(*c*) Indicate the starting address of assembled program
(*d*) None of the above

66. Which of the following is not a operation performd on data of 8085.
(*a*) Store 8 bit data
(*b*) Perform arithmetic and logical operation
(*c*) Sequence the execution of instructions
(*d*) None of the above

67. Instruction cycle is defined as.
(*a*) Time required to complete the execution of an instruction
(*b*) Time required to complete data transfer from memory
(*c*) Time taken to complete a CPU reference
(*d*) None of the above

68. Machine cycle is defined as.
(*a*) The machine used in making a cycle
(*b*) Time required to complete one operation of accessing a memory
(*c*) Cycle used to prepare a machine
(*d*) None of the above

69. Which of the following is not an example of 8085 instruction category.
(*a*) Data transfers
(*b*) Arithmetic and logic
(*c*) Branching
(*d*) Cache memory transfer

70. MVI A, 39H is an example of
(*a*) One byte instruction
(*b*) Two byte instruction
(*c*) Three byte instruction
(*d*) Four byte instruction

71. JMP 2345H is an example of
(*a*) One byte instruction
(*b*) Two byte instruction
(*c*) Three byte instruction
(*d*) None of the above

72. Bidirectional buffers are used.
    (*a*) To transmit double amount of data
    (*b*) To increase driving capacity of data bus
    (*c*) To transmit address and data both
    (*d*) None of the above

73. Microcontroller is a.
    (*a*) Miniature version of computer
    (*b*) Device which includes micro processor I/O signal link fabricated using VLSI
    (*c*) Extension of micro processor
    (*d*) None of the above

74. Which is not a characteristic of POP instruction.
    (*a*) It transfers the contents of top two location of start to specified register pair
    (*b*) It increments stack pointer by two
    (*c*) It stores data on to stack
    (*d*) None of the above

75. Which of the following are two classes of collision resolution techniques.
    (*a*) Division method
    (*b*) Open addressing
    (*c*) Chaining
    (*d*) b & c

76. Critical node in a graph can be defined as.
    (*a*) Node at the leaf end
    (*b*) Node in a height balanced tree, which makes tree unbalanced while performing addition and deletion
    (*c*) Node at the root level
    (*d*) None of the above

77. Program execution time containing instruction X can be defined as (if average number of basic steps needed to execute one machine instruction is S, clock rate is R cycles/sec.
    (*a*) T = XS/R
    (*b*) T = X/SR
    (*c*) T = RX/S
    (*d*) T = RS/X

78. System performance evaluation operation is defined as.
    (*a*) Ratio of running time on reference computer and running time of computer under test
    (*b*) Ratio of running time of computer under test and ratio of running time of reference.
    (*c*) Ratio of running time of two computers under test
    (*d*) None of the above

79. Condition code register.
    (*a*) The statue flags used to record results of various operation
    (*b*) Registers used to store program code
    (*c*) Registers used to store data code
    (*d*) None of the above

80. Binary equivalent of hexadecimal number (F4B7C) is.
    (*a*) 1111 0100 1011 0111 1100
    (*b*) 1001 0100 1111 0101 0000
    (*c*) 1011 1100 1100 1010 0000
    (*d*) None of the above

81. Link register can be defined as.
    (*a*) Register used to store return address of subroutine
    (*b*) Register in which linker is stored
    (*c*) Register which acts as a link between main memory and cache memory
    (*d*) None of the above

82. Stack frame is defined as.
(*a*) Memory frame used to store prefix expression
(*b*) Six top location of stack used to contain entries needed by subroutine
(*c*) Software which is used to implement stack
(*d*) None of the above

83. 8070 is a.
(*a*) Programmable peripheral interface
(*b*) Bus controller
(*c*) Programmable keyboard/ display interface
(*d*) Programmable timer

84. The number of segment registers existing in intel 80386 micro-processor is.
(*a*) 6
(*b*) 4
(*c*) 2
(*d*) 5

85. 80486 is a ———— bit processor.
(*a*) 8
(*b*) 16
(*c*) 32
(*d*) 64

86. Which signal is used to access odd addressed memory bank in 8086 when it is active low.
(*a*) AEN
(*b*) BHE
(*c*) AIOWC
(*d*) AMWC

87. Which interrupt has highest priority.
(*a*) Divide error
(*b*) NMI
(*c*) INTR
(*d*) Single step

88. 80286 has__________ address bus.
(*a*) 16 bit
(*b*) 24 bit
(*c*) 32 bit
(*d*) 64 bit

89. How many channels does 8257 has.
(*a*) 2
(*b*) 3
(*c*) 4
(*d*) 8

90. The latest A/D converter is.
(*a*) Ramp type
(*b*) Successive approximation type
(*c*) Integrating type
(*d*) Flash type

91. The memory size of 80486 is.
(*a*) 10M bytes
(*b*) 40M bytes
(*c*) 1 G bytes
(*d*) 4 G bytes

92. The function of 02H of DOS function call is.
(*a*) Terminate a program
(*b*) Read the keyboard
(*c*) Write to standard output device
(*d*) Read character from COM

93. Term 'Digital' can be defined as.
(*a*) Any process that can be accomplished using discreet units
(*b*) It can be defined as system which can perform accurate task
(*c*) It is a non deterministic term
(*d*) None of the above

94. EBCDIC code is an abbreviation of:
(*a*) Example Binary Computer Decimal Information Code
(*b*) Extended Binary Coded Decimal Information Code

(*c*) Ex-OR, Bits Coded Information Code
(*d*) None of the above

95. Propagation delay is defined as.
(*a*) Average transition delay time for signal to propagate from input to output
(*b*) Time gap between input & output
(*c*) Delay in implementation of a project
(*d*) None of the above

96. In signed magnitude representation system +ve and –ve numbers are represented as.
(*a*) +ve by 0 and –ve by value of sign bit
(*b*) +ve by 1 and –ve by value of sign bit
(*c*) Depends on the magnitude of a number
(*d*) None of the above

97. Which gate is inverted OR Gate.
(*a*) NAND
(*b*) NOR
(*c*) AND
(*d*) EX-OR

98. The function f(x, y, z) = 1 can be represented as sum of min terms.
(*a*) Minterms = {(0, 1, 2, 3, 4, 5, 6, 7)
(*b*) Minterms = {(x, y, z)}
(*c*) Minterms = {(1, 0, 1, 0, 1, 0, 1)
(*d*) None of the above

99. The algebraic function correspon-ding to EX-NOR gate is.
(*a*) F = x' y + xy'
(*b*) F = xy + x'y'
(*c*) F = xx' + yy'
(*d*) None of the above

100. Negative logic is defined as.
(*a*) When high level is associated with binary '0' and low level is associated with binary '1'
(*b*) When high level is associated with binary '1' and low level is '0'
(*c*) When the logics are decided according to problem
(*d*) None of the above

101. Which of the following is not a characteristic of digital IC.
(*a*) Propagation delay
(*b*) Power dissipation
(*c*) Noise margin
(*d*) None of the above

102. Parity bit is.
(*a*) It is an extra bit included with a binary message to make the number of '1' either even or odd
(*b*) It is bit named parity
(*c*) It is a bit having a level other than 0 or 1
(*d*) None of the above

103. Which of the following is not a method adopted to reduce Boolean function.
(*a*) Karnaugh map
(*b*) Quine mcc luskey method
(*c*) Variable entered map technique
(*d*) None of the above

104. Which is limitation of 'K' map.
(*a*) The size is generally limited to 6 variables
(*b*) It can only used for simplifying Boolean express-ion
(*c*) Both (*a*) and (*b*)
(*d*) None of the above

129. The threshold voltage of an 'n' channel MOSFET can be increased by.
(*a*) Increasing the channel length
(*b*) Reducing the channel length
(*c*) Increasing channel width
(*d*) Reducing channel width

130. A differential amplifier provide.
(*a*) Very high CMRR
(*b*) Very low CMRR
(*c*) Very low power
(*d*) Very high power

131. As compared to MOS memories, bipolar memories have.
(*a*) Faster access time and are costly
(*b*) Slower access time and are costly
(*c*) Faster access time and are cheap
(*d*) Slower access time and are cheap

132. Positive logic in logic circuit is one in which.
(*a*) Logic 0 voltage level is lower than logic 1 voltage level
(*b*) Logic 1 voltage level is lower than logic 0 voltage level
(*c*) Logic 0 voltage level is same than logic 1 voltage level
(*d*) None of the above

133. The highest conversion time of ADC is.
(*a*) Weighted register
(*b*) Successive approximation
(*c*) R_2R
(*d*) None of the above

134. Voltage gain of source follower amplifier using FET (Field Effect Transistor) is.
(*a*) > 100
(*b*) > 0
(*c*) > 1000
(*d*) > 106

135. The MOSFET in its on state is equivalent to.
(*a*) Inductor
(*b*) Capacitor
(*c*) Register
(*d*) None of the above

136. A switch mode power supply operating at 20 KHz to 100 KHz uses.
(*a*) CMOS
(*b*) MOSFET
(*c*) JFET
(*d*) None of the above

137. The output of time period to transistorized monostable multi vibrator using bypass register R_b and coupling capacitor C_b is.
(*a*) 0.69 R_bC_b
(*b*) 0.011 R_bC_b
(*c*) 1.69 R_bC_b
(*d*) None of the above

138. An amplifier with –ve resistive feedback has two half planes poles in its open loop transfer function. The amplifier.
(*a*) Will be stable for all frequency
(*b*) Will be unstable for all frequency
(*c*) Will be stable for band of frequency
(*d*) None of the above

139. Thermal runaway is not possible in FET because as temperature of FET increases.
(*a*) The mobility decreases
(*b*) The transconductance increases
(*c*) The drain current increases
(*d*) None of the above

140. The early effect in bipolar function transistor is caused by.
(*a*) Fast turn on
(*b*) Fast trun off
(*c*) Large collector base reverse bias
(*d*) Large emitter base forward bias

141. To obtain very high input and output impedances in feedback amplifier the topology must be.
(*a*) Voltage series
(*b*) Current shunt
(*c*) Current series
(*d*) Voltage shunt

142. The change in value of emitter resistance R_C in a differential amplifier.
(*a*) Effects the difference mode gain Ad
(*b*) Effects the common mode gain Ac
(*c*) Effects both Ad and Ac
(*d*) Does not effect either Ad and Ac

143. The use of preset input is done.
(*a*) To initially put the flip flop at specified value
(*b*) To give additional input to register
(*c*) To reset the register
(*d*) None of the above

144. The bridge rectifier has advantage of.
(*a*) Lower peak inverse voltage
(*b*) Higher peak inverse voltage
(*c*) Lower peak forward voltage
(*d*) Lower peak forward voltage

145. A class A transformer coupled transistor power amplifier is required to deliver a power output of 10 watts. The maximum power rating of transistor should not be less than.
(*a*) 30 W
(*b*) 20 W
(*c*) 10 W
(*d*) None of the above

146. The threshold voltage of an 'n' channel MOSFET can be increased by.
(*a*) Reducing channel length
(*b*) Increasing channel length
(*c*) Reducing channel width
(*d*) Increasing channel width

147. By placing an inverter between both input of SR flip flop, it becomes.
(*a*) D flip flop
(*b*) Inverted S-R flip flop
(*c*) J-K flip flop
(*d*) None of the above

148. The breakdown voltage of a transistor with its base open is βV_{CBO} and with emitter open is βV_{CBO} then.
(*a*) $\beta V_{CBO} < \beta V_{CBO}$
(*b*) $\beta V_{CBO} = \beta V_{CBO}$
(*c*) $\beta V_{CBO} > \beta V_{CBO}$
(*d*) Both voltage are unrelated

149. A high Q quartz exploits series resources at frequency W_S and parallel resources at W_P then.
(*a*) W_S is very close but less than Wp
(*b*) W_S << Wp
(*c*) W_S is very close, but greater than Wp
(*d*) W_S>>Wp

150. A differential amplifier is invariably used in input stage of all-opamps. This is done basically to provide OP-AMP's with a very high.

(*a*) CMRR
(*b*) Bandwidth
(*c*) Slew rate
(*d*) Open loop gain

151. At cut off, Q point is at one of the following location.
(*a*) Upper end of the load line
(*b*) Middle of load line
(*c*) Lower end of load line
(*d*) None of above

152. The saturatation point is same as
(*a*) Cut off point.
(*b*) Lower end of the load line
(*c*) Upper end of the load line
(*d*) Infinity
(*e*) None of above

153. When transistor operates at middle of load line, an increase in current gain will give the Q point.
(*a*) Down
(*b*) Up
(*c*) Nowhere
(*d*) Off the load line

154. With increase in temperature, current gain.
(*a*) Decreases
(*b*) Remains the same
(*c*) Increases
(*d*) None of above

155. When we draw a graph of current gain versus collector current then it shows that current gain is.
(*a*) Constant
(*b*) Varies slightly
(*c*) Varies enormously
(*d*) Equals collector current divided by base current

156. With dc alpha of 0.994, current gain of transitor is.
(*a*) 166
(*b*) 273
(*c*) 173
(*d*) 37
(*e*) None of above

157. If current gain of transitor is 125 and base current is 30 μA. Then collector current is
(*a*) 3.75 mA
(*b*) 1.75 mA
(*c*) 0.75 mA
(*d*) 1 mA
(*e*) None of above

158. If source voltage of an unloaded zener regulator is 20V, a series raistance of 330 and a zener voltage of 12V, what is zener current?
(*a*) 12.1 mA
(*b*) 24.2 mA
(*c*) 13.2 mA
(*d*) 48.8 mA
(*e*) None of above

159. Primary voltage of transformer is 120V rms and a secondary voltage of 25V rms. If secondary current is 1A rms. What is primary current?
(*a*) 208 mA
(*b*) 108 mA
(*c*) 64 mA
(*d*) 12 mA
(*e*) None of above

160. Peak value of a voltage is 50v. What is rms value?
(*a*) 32.3 V
(*b*) 28.9 V
(*c*) 35.4 V
(*d*) 11 V
(*e*) None of above

161. In a circuit Voltage across resistor is 4V and diode is in series with 220 Ω, what is current through the diode?

(*a*) 18.2 mA
(*b*) 12.3 mA
(*c*) 17.2 mA
(*d*) 11.2 mA
(*e*) None of above

162. What kind of a device is a diode?
(*a*) Bilateral
(*b*) Linear
(*c*) Non linear
(*d*) None of above

163. What kind of device is there, when the graph of current versus voltage is a straight line
(*a*) Active
(*b*) Linear
(*c*) Non linear
(*d*) None of above

164. What is barrier potential of a silicon diode at room temperature?
(*a*) 0.3V
(*b*) 0.7V
(*c*) 1V
(*d*) None of above

165. Positive ions are atoms that have
(*a*) Gained a proton
(*b*) Lost a proton
(*c*) Gained an electron
(*d*) Lost an electron

166. How many valence electrons are there in trivalent atoms?
(*a*) 1
(*b*) 3
(*c*) 4
(*d*) 5

167. How many types of flow are there in a conductor?
(*a*) 0
(*b*) 1
(*c*) 2
(*d*) 3

168. What is effect of temperature on number of free electrons and holes in an intrinsic semi conductor.
(*a*) Decreases with temperature rise
(*b*) Increases with temperature rise
(*c*) Stays same with temperature rise
(*d*) None of above

169. Absolute zero temperature equals.
(*a*) – 273°C
(*b*) 0°C
(*c*) 25°C
(*d*) 50°C

170. How many holes are there in a conductor at room temperature?
(*a*) Many
(*b*) None
(*c*) Only those produced by thermol energy
(*d*) Same number as free electorns

171. An intrinsic silicon crystal acts approximately like at room temperature
(*a*) A battery
(*b*) A conductor
(*c*) An insulator
(*d*) A piece of copper wire

172. An intrinsic semi conductor has some holes in it at room temperature. What is the cause of holes there?
(*a*) Doping
(*b*) Free electrons
(*c*) Thermal energy
(*d*) None of above

173. How many protons are there in a silicon atom?
(*a*) 4
(*b*) 14
(*c*) 29
(*d*) 32

174. How many valence electrons are there in a silicon atom?
(*a*) 0
(*b*) 1
(*c*) 2
(*d*) 4

175. The net charge of a neutral copper atom is.
(*a*) 0
(*b*) + 1
(*c*) – 1
(*d*) + 4

176. If ideal voltage is 6V and the shorted-load current is 150A and voltage source is temporarily shorted. What is internal resistance of source?
(*a*) 2.1 Ω
(*b*) 2.4 Ω
(*c*) 0.04 Ω
(*d*) 11 Ω

177. The internal resistance of a voltage source is 0.05 Ω. How much voltage is dropped across this internal resistance when current through it is 2A?
(*a*) 0.1 V
(*b*) 2.1 V
(*c*) 3.2 V
(*d*) 11 V

178. According to Thevenin's theorem, a complicated circuit facing a load is replaced by an
(*a*) Ideal voltage source and load is replaced by a series resistor
(*b*) Ideal voltage current source and parallel resistor
(*c*) Ideal voltage source and series resistor
(*d*) Ideal current source and series resistor

179. To achieve Norton circuit, we have to
(*a*) Short the load resistor
(*b*) Open the load resistor
(*c*) Short the voltage source
(*d*) Open the voltage source

180. The thevenin resistance is equal in value to the
(*a*) Load resistance
(*b*) Half the load resistance
(*c*) Internal resistance of a Norton circuit
(*d*) Open load resistance

181. Stiff voltage source has a resistance of Ω
(*a*) At least 10 Ω
(*b*) Less than 10 Ω
(*c*) More than 100 kΩ
(*d*) Less than 100 kΩ

182. An ideal voltage source has
(*a*) Zero internal resistance
(*b*) Infinite internal resistance
(*c*) A load dependent voltage
(*d*) A load dependent current

183. What is the highest address in a 48 K memory? Give it decimal form
(*a*) 1024
(*b*) 49152
(*c*) 49151
(*d*) 36,357

184. How many combinations are possible with only 20 bits?
(*a*) 10,48,576
(*b*) 59,833
(*c*) 1,048
(*d*) 1,096

185. What is understood by micro processors
(*a*) Instructions
(*b*) Fortran language

(*c*) Binary language
(*d*) Pascal language

186. What is op code for Nop instruction?
(*a*) 00
(*b*) 01
(*c*) 16
(*d*) 10

187. What is op code for Break instruction?
(*a*) 00
(*b*) BR
(*c*) BK
(*d*) 07

188. Calculate clock cycle time for a system that uses a clock with frequency of 150 KHz.
(*a*) 100 μ sec
(*b*) 167 μ sec
(*c*) 6.66 μ sec
(*d*) 13.3 μ sec

189. What is clock cycle time for a system that uses a clock that has a frequency of 10 MHz.
(*a*) 100 ns
(*b*) 167 ns
(*c*) 1.33 ns
(*d*) 13.3 ns

190. In following circuit LED voltage is 2 V and TTL output voltage is 0.4 V. What is sink current when LED is lighted?

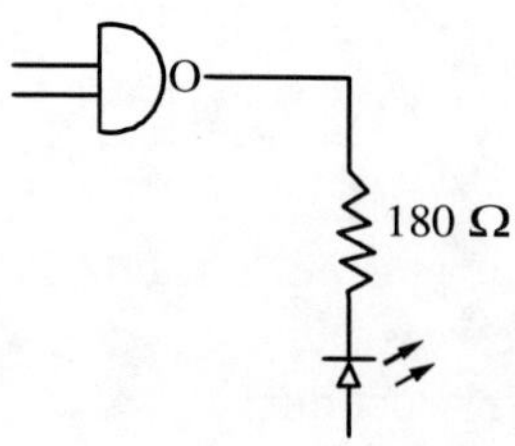

(*a*) 4.4 mA
(*b*) 11.4 mA
(*c*) 14.4 mA
(*d*) 3.7 mA
(*e*) None

191. What is fanout in case of a 74,500 device when it drives low-power TTL loads?
(*a*) 10
(*b*) 20
(*c*) 30
(*d*) 100

192. The 8 gate device is of type
(*a*) LSI
(*b*) MSI
(*c*) SSI
(*d*) None of above

193. The 108 gate device is of type
(*a*) LSI
(*b*) MSI
(*c*) SSI
(*d*) None of above

194. 1's complement of 9H in hexadecimal motation is
(*a*) DCH
(*b*) BAH
(*c*) 36H
(*d*) 02H

195. 8 bit signed magnitude representation of – 107 is
(*a*) 1011 1000
(*b*) 0111 1011
(*c*) 0001 0111
(*d*) 1110 1011

196. 8 bit signed-magnitude representation of + 23 is
(*a*) 1011 1000
(*b*) 0111 1011
(*c*) 0001 0111
(*d*) 1110 1010

197. Sum of $8_{16} + F_{16}$ = ?
(*a*) 10_{16}
(*b*) 12_{16}
(*c*) 11_{16}
(*d*) 17_{16}

298. $5_8 + 6_8$ = ?
(*a*) 11_8
(*b*) 13_8
(*c*) 17_8
(*d*) 11

299. $47_8 \times 52_8$ = ?
(*a*) $(3144)_8$
(*b*) $(3146)_8$
(*c*) $(4147)_8$
(*d*) $(3154)_8$

200. Addition of 110101101_2, 111011101_2, 000111111_2, 100101101_2, 111110111_2 is
(*a*) 1011010111010_2
(*b*) 1111011000010_2
(*c*) 1000101000101_2
(*d*) 01001000000010_2

201. 136_8 = ?
(*a*) $7E_{16}$
(*b*) $5E_{16}$
(*c*) $5A_{16}$
(*d*) $5D_{16}$

202. 31_{16} = ?
(*a*) 101010_2
(*b*) 110101_2
(*c*) 110001_2
(*d*) 100101_2

203. 63_{16} = ?
(*a*) 1100111_2
(*b*) 1100011_2
(*c*) 111011_2
(*d*) 1100111_2

204. 60_8 = ?
(*a*) 110000_2
(*b*) 10011_2
(*c*) 1100111_2
(*d*) 1100110_2

205. 1001010_2 = ?
(*a*) 74_{10}
(*b*) 97_{10}
(*c*) 72_{10}
(*d*) 63_{10}

206. $7B_{10}$ = ?
(*a*) $4a_{16}$
(*b*) $5A_{16}$
(*c*) $4A_{16}$
(*d*) $2D_{16}$

207. 101101_2 = ?
(*a*) 37_{16}
(*b*) $2D_{16}$
(*c*) $2E_{16}$
(*d*) 27_{16}

208. 1100011_2 = ?
(*a*) 63_{16}
(*b*) 57_{16}
(*c*) 46_{16}
(*d*) 40_{16}

209. 1100011_2 = ?
(*a*) 140_8
(*b*) 143_8
(*c*) 147_8
(*d*) 149_8

210. 1101100111111000_2 = ?
(*a*) $D8F8_{16}$
(*b*) $A8B9_{16}$
(*c*) 789_{16}
(*d*) $D9F8_{16}$

211. 7432_8 = ?
(*a*) 1111000110111_2
(*b*) 111100011010_2
(*c*) 1100110101111_2
(*d*) 111111111000_2

212. 67_{10} = ?
(*a*) 100_8
(*b*) 103_8

(*c*) 109_8
(*d*) 99_8

213. 99_{10} = ?
(*a*) 1100011_2
(*b*) 100011_2
(*c*) 1110001_2
(*d*) 1111000_2

214. Convert 01100111 BCD number into decimal
(*a*) 813
(*b*) 207
(*c*) 2729
(*d*) 67

215. How many nibbles are in 1111000011001001?
(*a*) 256
(*b*) 14×2
(*c*) 16,384
(*d*) None of above

216. What is fanout of a low power schottky device driving standard TTL devices?
(*a*) 10
(*b*) 20
(*c*) 12
(*d*) None

217. A real voltage source has
(*a*) Zero internal resistance
(*b*) Infinite internal resistance
(*c*) A small internal resistance
(*d*) A large internal resistance

218. If load resistance is 1 kΩ, a stiff current source has a resistance of
(*a*) At least 10 Ω
(*b*) Less than 10 Ω
(*c*) More than 100 kΩ
(*d*) Less than 100 kΩ

219. To get thevenin voltage, we have to
(*a*) Short the load resister
(*b*) Open the load resistor
(*c*) Short the voltage source
(*d*) Open the voltage source

220. Another name for Norton current is
(*a*) Shorted load current
(*b*) Open load current
(*c*) Thevenin current
(*d*) Thevenin voltage

221. Norton's theorem replaces a complicated circuit facing a load by an
(*a*) Ideal voltage source and parallel resistor
(*b*) Ideal current source and parallel resister
(*c*) Ideal voltage source and series resister
(*d*) Ideal current source and series resister

222. A current source has an internal resistance of 100 kΩ. What is the largest load resistance if current source must appear stiff?
(*a*) 3 kΩ
(*b*) 1 kΩ
(*c*) 4 kΩ
(*d*) 5 kΩ
(*e*) None

223. What kind of attraction is experienced by valence electron in copper atom
(*a*) None
(*b*) Weak
(*c*) Strong
(*d*) Impossible to say
(*e*) None of above

224. Which of the following is most widely used semiconductor?
(*a*) Copper
(*b*) Germanium
(*c*) Silicon
(*d*) All of above

225. Silicon atoms combine into an orderly pattern called a
   (*a*) Covalent bond
   (*b*) Crystal
   (*c*) Semiconductor
   (*d*) Valence orbit

226. What is the term used for merging of a free electron and a hole?
   (*a*) Covalent bonding
   (*b*) Life time
   (*c*) Recombination
   (*d*) Thermal energy

227. Time elapsed between creation of a hole and its disapperance is called
   (*a*) Doping
   (*b*) Lift time
   (*c*) Recombination
   (*d*) Valence

228. Number of free electrons in an intrinsic semi conductor,
   (*a*) equals the number of holes
   (*b*) is greater then number of holes
   (*c*) is less than number of holes
   (*d*) None of above

229. At room temperature, an intrinsic semi-conductor has
   (*a*) a few free electrons and holes
   (*b*) Many holes
   (*c*) Many free electron
   (*d*) No holes

230. Holes are
   (*a*) atoms
   (*b*) crystals
   (*c*) Negative charges
   (*d*) Positive charges

231. How many types of flow are there in a semiconductor?
   (*a*) 0
   (*b*) 1
   (*c*) 2
   (*d*) 3

232. Holes are the minority carriers in which type of semiconductor?
   (*a*) Extrinsic
   (*b*) Intrinstic
   (*c*) n-type
   (*d*) P-type

233. What is cause of depletion layer?
   (*a*) Doping
   (*b*) Recombination
   (*c*) Barrier potential
   (*d*) Ions

234. What is the net charge of a copper atom if it gains 3 electron?
   (*a*) 2
   (*b*) – 3
   (*c*) 4
   (*d*) 2

235. What kind of device is a resistor?
   (*a*) Unilateral
   (*b*) Linear
   (*c*) Non-linear
   (*d*) Bipolar

236. The knee voltage of a diode is approximately equal to the
   (*a*) Applied voltage
   (*b*) Barrier potential
   (*c*) Breakdown
   (*d*) Forw amd voltage

237. Two diodes are in series. The Ist diode has voltage of 0.75 V and the second has a voltage of 0.8 V. If current through first diode is 500 mA, what is current through the second diode?
   (*a*) 500 mA
   (*b*) 200 mA
   (*c*) 100 mA
   (*d*) 300 mA
   (*e*) None of above

238. A step up transformer has a turns ratio of 1 : 4. If line voltage is 115 V rms, what is the peak secondary voltage?
(*a*) 115 V
(*b*) 112 V
(*c*) 615 V
(*d*) 321 V

239. A bridge rectifier has a dc load current of 20 mA and a filter capacitance of 680 μF. What is peak to peak ripple out of a capacitor input filter?
(*a*) 0.245 V
(*b*) 0.347 V
(*c*) 1 V
(*d*) 12 V

240. A transistor has an emitter current of 10 mA and a collector current of 9.95 mA. What is the base current?
(*a*) 0.05 mA
(*b*) 2 mA
(*c*) 3 mA
(*d*) 14 mA

241. If transistor has a collector current of 100 mA and a collector emitter voltage of 3.5 V, what is its power dissipation?
(*a*) 0.35 W
(*b*) 3.9 W
(*c*) 100
(*d*) 3 W

242. Current gain of a transistor is defined as ratio of collector current to
(*a*) Base current
(*b*) Emitter current
(*c*) Supply current
(*d*) Collector current

243. When the collector current increases, the current gain
(*a*) Decreases
(*b*) Remains same
(*c*) Increases
(*d*) Can be any of above

244. If a transistor operates at middle of load line, an increase in base resistance will move Q point
(*a*) Down
(*b*) Up
(*c*) Nowhere
(*d*) Off the load line

245. When base supply voltage is increased, the point moves
(*a*) Down
(*b*) Up
(*c*) Nowhere
(*d*) Off the load line

246. When Q point moves along the load line, the voltage increases when current
(*a*) Decreases
(*b*) Stays the same
(*c*) Increases
(*d*) Does none of above

247. 28_{10} = ?
(*a*) 32_8
(*b*) 40_8
(*c*) 34_8
(*d*) 36_8

248. 1011011_2 = ?
(*a*) 81_{10}
(*b*) 91_{10}
(*c*) 100_{10}
(*d*) 200_{10}

249. Binary means base
(*a*) Eight
(*b*) Sixteen
(*c*) Two
(*d*) None of above

250. The digits used in a binary number system are .... and ....

(*a*) 3 and 4
(*b*) 0 and 1
(*c*) 1 and 2
(*d*) 9 and 0

251. A .... is a group of devices that store digital data
(*a*) Circuits
(*b*) Bit
(*c*) Register
(*d*) Variations

252. Solve the following equation for X : $X_{10} = 11001001_2$
(*a*) 201
(*b*) 132
(*c*) 214
(*d*) 64
(*e*) None of above

253. Express 8192 in K units
(*a*) 8×10^3 K
(*b*) 8.192 K
(*c*) 8 K
(*d*) All of the above

254. What does 4K represent?
(*a*) 4000
(*b*) 400
(*c*) 40
(*d*) 4096

255. What is the decimal equvalent of 2^{10}?
(*a*) 1024
(*b*) 4096
(*c*) 2048
(*d*) 512

256. What is the base of $F4C2_{16}$ number?
(*a*) 2
(*b*) 4
(*c*) 16
(*d*) 8

257. How many bytes are there in 1011 1001 0110 1110 numbers?
(*a*) 2
(*b*) 1
(*c*) 4
(*d*) 8

258. The binary number 1100 0101 has .... bytes
(*a*) 8
(*b*) 4
(*c*) 2
(*d*) 1

259. The ASCII code is a 7-bit code for
(*a*) Letters
(*b*) Numbers
(*c*) Other symbol
(*d*) All

260. Binary coded decimal number express each digit as a ....
(*a*) byte
(*b*) nibble
(*c*) bit
(*d*) None of above

261. The hexadecimal digits are 0 to 9 and A to ....
(*a*) E
(*b*) F
(*c*) G
(*d*) D

262. A micro computer is a computer that uses a .... for its CPU.
(*a*) Chips
(*b*) Registers
(*c*) Microprocessor
(*d*) Vacuum tube

263. A byte is a string of .... bits
(*a*) Two
(*b*) Ten
(*c*) Four
(*d*) Eight

264. How many nibbles are there in 1001 0000 0100 0011 number

(*a*) Two
(*b*) Four
(*c*) One
(*d*) Eight

265. What is the ASCII code for T?
(*a*) 1010100
(*b*) 1011010
(*c*) 1011100
(*d*) 1011111

266. An inverter is also called a .... gate
(*a*) NOT
(*b*) OR
(*c*) AND
(*d*) NANO

267. In boolean algebra, the 'addition' sign stands for the .... operation
(*a*) AND
(*b*) OR
(*c*) NAND
(*d*) NOR

268. How many inputs signals can a gate have?
(*a*) One
(*b*) More than one
(*c*) Two only
(*d*) Both a and b

269. How many output signals can a gate have?
(*a*) One
(*b*) Two only
(*c*) More than one
(*d*) Both a and b

270. An OR gate has 6 inputs. How many input words will be there in truth table?
(*a*) 64
(*b*) 32
(*c*) 16
(*d*) 128

271. An OR gate has 4 inputs. What is only input that produce 0 input?
(*a*) 0000
(*b*) 0011
(*c*) 1100
(*d*) 1111

272. An AND gate has 7 inputs. How many words are there in truth table?
(*a*) 64
(*b*) 32
(*c*) 128
(*d*) 16

273. A NOR gate recognizes only the input word whose bits are
(*a*) 0's and 1's
(*b*) 1's
(*c*) 0's
(*d*) 0'5 or 1's

274. An XOR gate recognizes only words with an .... no. of 1's
(*a*) Even
(*b*) Odd
(*c*) Different
(*d*) All of the above

275. The 2-inputs XOR gate has a high output only when the input bits are ....
(*a*) Even
(*b*) Different
(*c*) Low
(*d*) High

276. De morgon'a first theorem says that a NOR gate is equivatent to a bubbled .... gate.
(*a*) AND
(*b*) XAND
(*c*) XOR
(*d*) NOR
(*e*) None of above

277. The exclusive-NOR gate is equivalent to an .... gate followed by an invertor.
   (*a*) OR
   (*b*) AND
   (*c*) NAND
   (*d*) XOR

278. .... has become the most widely used bipolar family.
   (*a*) DTL
   (*b*) TTL
   (*c*) ECL
   (*d*) MOS

279. .... is used in high speed applications.
   (*a*) DTL
   (*b*) TTL
   (*c*) ECL
   (*d*) MOS

280. Standard TTL has a multiple emitter input transistor and a .... output.
   (*a*) Tolem-pole
   (*b*) High power
   (*c*) Standard
   (*d*) Schottky

281. A .... TTL device can sink up to 16 mA and can source 400 mA
   (*a*) Low power
   (*b*) High power
   (*c*) Standard
   (*d*) Schottky

282. Digital design often starts by constructions a .... table.
   (*a*) Standard
   (*b*) Two-stage
   (*c*) Truth
   (*d*) Two-dimensional

283. A bus is a group of .... carrying digital signals
   (*a*) Wires
   (*b*) Gates
   (*c*) Transistors
   (*d*) Registors

284. A half-adder adds .... bits
   (*a*) 16
   (*b*) 8
   (*c*) 10
   (*d*) 2
   (*e*) None of above

285. How many memory locations can 14 address bits access?
   (*a*) 16,384
   (*b*) 8,192
   (*c*) 4,096
   (*d*) 14

286. The 2,732 is a 4,096 × 8 EPROM. How many address lines does it have?
   (*a*) 12
   (*b*) 14
   (*c*) 13
   (*d*) 8

287. Address 200 H contains 3FH. What is its decimal equivalent
   (*a*) 63
   (*b*) 32
   (*c*) 16
   (*d*) 38

288. Flip-flop outputs are always
   (*a*) Complimenting
   (*b*) the same
   (*c*) independent of each other
   (*d*) Same as inputs

289. A positive AND gate is also a negative.
   (*a*) NAND
   (*b*) NOR
   (*c*) AND
   (*d*) OR

290. Which gates is known as universal gate?

(*a*) NOT
(*b*) AND
(*c*) NAND
(*d*) XOR

291. What logic function is produced by adding an inverter to the output of an AND gate?
(*a*) NAND
(*b*) NOR
(*c*) XOR
(*d*) OR

292. For what logic gate the output is complement of input?
(*a*) NOT
(*b*) AND
(*c*) OR
(*d*) XOR

293. The gray code for decimal 7 is
(*a*) 0111
(*b*) 1011
(*c*) 0100
(*d*) 0101

294. The octal equivalent of decimal 324.987 is
(*a*) 504.771
(*b*) 640.781
(*c*) 815.234
(*d*) 90.987

295. Which of following logic families use bipolar transistors?
(*a*) TTL
(*b*) GaAs
(*c*) NMOS
(*d*) CMOS

296. Which of the following TTL sub family is the fastest
(*a*) Standard TTL
(*b*) High-speed TTL
(*c*) Schottky TTL
(*d*) Low-speed TTL

297. The output 0 and 1 levels for TTL logic family is approx
(*a*) 0.1 and 5 V
(*b*) 0.6 and 3.5 V
(*c*) 0.9 and 1.75 V

298. The functional capacity of SSI devices is
(*a*) 1 to 11 gates
(*b*) 12 to 99 gates
(*c*) 100 to 10,000 gates
(*d*) More than 10,000

299. The functional capacity for LSI devices is
(*a*) 1 to 11 gates
(*b*) 12 to 99 gates
(*c*) 100 to 10,000 gates
(*d*) More than 10,000 gates

300. Which logic family dissipates the minimum power?
(*a*) DTL
(*b*) TTL
(*c*) ECL
(*d*) CMOS

301. Which of following is the first integrated logic family?
(*a*) RTL
(*b*) DTL
(*c*) TTL
(*d*) MOS

302. Which TTL sub-family has maximum speed
(*a*) Standard TTL
(*b*) Schottky-clomped TTL
(*c*) High speed TTL
(*d*) 100 power TTL

303. Which of the following electronic component is not found in IC's?
(*a*) Diodes
(*b*) Registors
(*c*) Transistors
(*d*) Inductors

304. The radix of the binary number is:
(*a*) 3
(*b*) 1
(*c*) 2
(*d*) 10

305. The number of binary bits required to represent hexadecimal number is
(*a*) 3
(*b*) 4
(*c*) 6
(*d*) 8

306. $\bar{A}+\bar{B}+\bar{C}+\bar{D}$ represents a:
(*a*) NAND gate
(*b*) OR gate
(*c*) AND gate
(*d*) EX-OR gate

307. The 1's complement of binary number 11010 is:
(*a*) 00101
(*b*) 00010
(*c*) 10101
(*d*) 00110

308. The 2's complement of binary number 001011 is:
(*a*) 110101
(*b*) 010101
(*c*) 110100
(*d*) 010100

309. A half adder is also known as .... circuit
(*a*) AND
(*b*) NAND
(*c*) NOR
(*d*) EX-OR gate

310. The output of following gate is 1 only if at least one of the input is 1.
(*a*) AND
(*b*) OR
(*c*) EX-OR
(*d*) NOR

311. Which of the following boolean algebra rules is wrong?
(*a*) 0 + A = A
(*b*) 0 + A = 1
(*c*) A + A = A
(*d*) 1.x = 1
(*e*) None

312. The simplification of AB + BC + $\bar{B}C$ gives:
(*a*) AB + BC
(*b*) $AB+\bar{B}C$
(*c*) $BC+\bar{B}C$
(*d*) $A\bar{B}C+C$

313. Which of the following is not functionally a complete set?
(*a*) AND, OR
(*b*) NAND
(*c*) NOR
(*d*) AND, OR, NOT

314. Which of the following is not true?
(*a*) 0 × 0 = 0
(*b*) 0 × 1 = 1
(*c*) 1 × 0 = 0
(*d*) 1 × 1 = 1

315. The reduced form of Boolean expression (A + B) (A + C) is:
(*a*) A + B + C
(*b*) AC + B
(*c*) A + BC
(*d*) None of the above

316. Which of the following is a universal gate?
(*a*) AND
(*b*) OR
(*c*) EX-OR
(*d*) NAND

317. Which of the following logic expression is wrong?
(*a*) 1 + 0 = 1
(*b*) 1 + 1 = 0

(*c*) 1 + 0 + 1 = 1
(*d*) 1 + 1 + 1 = 1

318. Which function in positive logic is equivalent to OR function in negative logic?
(*a*) NOT
(*b*) AND
(*c*) OR
(*d*) NOR

319. The m bit parallel adder consists of .... full adders
(*a*) (m + 1)
(*b*) (m/2)
(*c*) (m – 1)
(*d*) m

320. A flip-flop can store .... bits of data:
(*a*) 1
(*b*) 2
(*c*) 3
(*d*) 4

321. Parallel adders are .... logic circuits
(*a*) Combinational
(*b*) Sequential
(*c*) Both sequential and parallel
(*d*) None of the above

322. A demultiplexer is also known as
(*a*) Data selector
(*b*) Data distributor
(*c*) Multiplexer
(*d*) Encoder

323. A multiplexer is also known as
(*a*) Encoder
(*b*) Decoder
(*c*) Data selector
(*d*) None of above

324. The maximum count which a 6-bit binary word can represent
(*a*) 36
(*b*) 64
(*c*) 63
(*d*) 65

325. What is hexadecimal equivalent of binary no. 10101111
(*a*) AF
(*b*) AE
(*c*) 8C
(*d*) None of the above

326. Which of the following logic families has highest noise immunity?
(*a*) RTL
(*b*) DTL
(*c*) TTL
(*d*) HTL

327. How many valence electrons does a silicon atom have?
(*a*) 0
(*b*) 1
(*c*) 2
(*d*) 4

328. How much power is being dissipated by a 1000 resistance that has 25 V applied to it?
(*a*) 0.24 W
(*b*) 0.625 W
(*c*) 325 KW
(*d*) 80 W

329. The equivalent of 1 micro ampere is:
(*a*) 10,000 ampere
(*b*) 1,000 ampere
(*c*) one millionth ampere
(*d*) ten millionth of an ampere
(*e*) None of the above

330. The equivalent of 1 KV is:
(*a*) 1,000 mV
(*b*) 1,000 V
(*c*) 1.00 V
(*d*) 100 mV

331. The basic unit of measurement for resistance is the
   (*a*) Volt
   (*b*) Ampere
   (*c*) Watt
   (*d*) Ohm

332. A battery is a device composed of one or more:
   (*a*) Chemical cells
   (*b*) Voltage squrces
   (*c*) Solar cells
   (*d*) None of the above

333. A device that converts magnetic/chemical energy to electrical energy is called a:
   (*a*) Solar cell
   (*b*) Thermocouple
   (*c*) Chemical cell
   (*d*) None of the above

334. Current is
   (*a*) The flow of charged particles through a material
   (*b*) An imbalance of electrical charges
   (*c*) The force of free electrons in an atom
   (*d*) The number of free electrons in an atom

335. What is the power dissipation of a resistance that has 24V dropped across it and 0.25 A flowing through it?
   (*a*) 3 W
   (*b*) 6 W
   (*c*) 64 W
   (*d*) 122 W

336. How much current flows through a 60 W bulb that is operating at 120 V?
   (*a*) 0.5 A
   (*b*) 180 A
   (*c*) 2 A
   (*d*) 7200 A

337. A 100 μW resistors has 0.05 Amp current fowing through it. How much voltage is dropped across this resistors?
   (*a*) 20 mV
   (*b*) 15 mV
   (*c*) 2 V
   (*d*) 5 V
   (*e*) None of above

338. The equivalent of 1 mega Ohm is:
   (*a*) 1 K ohm
   (*b*) 10,000 ohm
   (*c*) one million ohm
   (*d*) one-millionth of ohm

339. A device that converts thermal energy to electrical energy is
   (*a*) Thermo couple
   (*b*) Chemical cell
   (*c*) Piezo electric devices
   (*d*) None of the above

340. A device that converts chemical energy to electrical energy
   (*a*) Solar cell
   (*b*) Thermo couple
   (*c*) Chemical cell
   (*d*) Electric device

341. Which one is used for measuring the rate of electron flow?
   (*a*) Voltmeter
   (*b*) Ammeter
   (*c*) Ohmmeter
   (*d*) Wattmeter

342. Suppose the voltage from power outlet is 120 V rms. What is peak voltage?
   (*a*) 100 V
   (*b*) 120 V
   (*c*) 170 V
   (*d*) 180 V

343. In a transformer if $N_1/N_2 = 2$, and primary voltage is 120 V. What is secondary voltage?
(*a*) 0 V
(*b*) 36 V
(*c*) 40 V
(*d*) 60 V

344. In a step-down transformer, which is lesser?
(*a*) Primary voltage
(*b*) Secondary voltage
(*c*) Both voltages are same
(*d*) Impossible to say

345. Suppose peak value of a sinusoidal voltage is 50 V. What is rms value?
(*a*) 37.4 V
(*b*) 35.4 V
(*c*) 38.74 V
(*d*) None of the above

346. What is the current through LED of figure

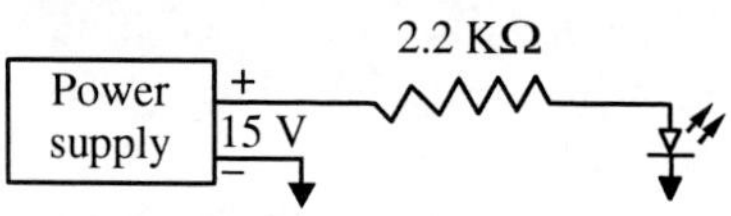

(*a*) 3 mA
(*b*) 5 mA
(*c*) 3.91 mA
(*d*) 6.81 mA

347. In above Fig. if the resistors is decreased to 1 KΩ, what is LED current
(*a*) 11 mA
(*b*) 9 mA
(*c*) 15 mA
(*d*) 13 mA

348. A transistor has a collector current of 2 mA. If the current gain is 135, what is the base current?
(*a*) 14.8 μA
(*b*) 10.3 μA
(*c*) 7.8 μA
(*d*) 7.75 μA

349. A transistor has a current gain of 175. If the base current is 0.1 mA. What is the collector current?
(*a*) 1750 mA
(*b*) 17.5 mA
(*c*) 175 mA
(*d*) 1.75 ma

350. What is one important thing transistors do?
(*a*) Emit eight
(*b*) Amplify weak signals
(*c*) Regulate voltage
(*d*) Rectify line voltage

351. An advantage of a transistor is
(*a*) Its small size
(*b*) Loss of heating
(*c*) Its losses infinitely
(*d*) All of the above

352. Who invented the first, functional transistor?
(*a*) Smith
(*b*) Gomes
(*c*) Shottkey
(*d*) Fisher

353. The light emitting diode is usually used in
(*a*) Forward bias
(*b*) Reverse-bias
(*c*) Non-conducting node
(*d*) Operates in the breakdown region

354. The barrier potenital across each depletion layer is
(*a*) 0
(*b*) 2.8 V
(*c*) 0.7 V
(*d*) 20 V

355. If the current gain is 200 and the collector current is 100 mA the base current is

(*a*) 2 mA
(*b*) 0.5 mA
(*c*) 2 A
(*d*) 200 A

356. What is capacitive reactance of an 0.01 micro F capacitor that is operating in a 1000 Hz circuit?
(*a*) 18.9
(*b*) 15.9 Ω
(*c*) 16.8 Ω
(*d*) 1.59 Ω

357. A dielectric material is:
(*a*) Good conductor
(*b*) Good insulator
(*c*) A poor conductor of electrostatic fields
(*d*) A poor conductor of magnetic fields

358. The energy absorbed by an inductor in a circuit is stored as:
(*a*) Counter emf
(*b*) Heat
(*c*) Magnetic lines of force
(*d*) Static electricity

359. A typical light switch in your home is a
(*a*) Knife switch
(*b*) Toggle swith
(*c*) Momentary p button switch
(*d*) Rotary switch

360. If the base supply voltage increase the Q point moves
(*a*) up
(*b*) down
(*c*) nowhere
(*d*) off the loadline

361. The saturation point is approximately the same
(*a*) Cut off point
(*b*) Lower end of the load line
(*c*) Upper end of the load line
(*d*) Infinity

362. What form of energy is used for creating static electricity
(*a*) Solar energy
(*b*) Mechanical energy
(*c*) Light energy
(*d*) Chemical energy

363. What are the main parts of a atom?
(*a*) Protons only
(*b*) Electrons, protons and neutrons
(*c*) Electrons, protons and ions
(*d*) Electrons, ions and neutrons

364. As the temperature increases the current gain
(*a*) Increases
(*b*) Decreases
(*c*) Constant
(*d*) Can be any of the above

ANSWERS

1. (*d*)	2. (*d*)	3. (*c*)	4. (*c*)	5. (*a*)	6. (*a*)	7. (*b*)
8. (*a*)	9. (*a*)	10. (*a*)	11. (*a*)	12. (*d*)	13. (*c*)	14. (*b*)
15. (*c*)	16. (*a*)	17. (*a*)	18. (*c*)	19. (*b*)	20. (*a*)	21. (*c*)
22. (*b*)	23. (*a*)	24. (*b*)	25. (*a*)	26. (*b*)	27. (*c*)	28. (*b*)
29. (*b*)	30. (*a*)	31. (*a*)	32. (*c*)	33. (*b*)	34. (*c*)	35. (*c*)
36. (*c*)	37. (*a*)	38. (*b*)	39. (*b*)	40. (*a*)	41. (*a*)	42. (*c*)
43. (*c*)	44. (*c*)	45. (*b*)	46. (*d*)	47. (*d*)	48. (*c*)	49. (*b*)

50. (*b*)	51. (*d*)	52. (*d*)	53. (*a*)	54. (*b*)	55. (*d*)	56. (*b*)
57. (*c*)	58. (*d*)	59. (*b*)	60. (*b*)	61. (*a*)	62. (*a*)	63. (*b*)
64. (*a*)	65. (*c*)	66. (*a*)	67. (*b*)	68. (*d*)	69. (*d*)	70. (*b*)
71. (*c*)	72. (*b*)	73. (*b*)	74. (*a*)	75. (*d*)	76. (*b*)	77. (*a*)
78. (*b*)	79. (*b*)	80. (*a*)	81. (*a*)	82. (*b*)	83. (*b*)	84. (*b*)
85. (*c*)	86. (*d*)	87. (*a*)	88. (*d*)	89. (*b*)	90. (*c*)	91. (*b*)
92. (*a*)	93. (*a*)	94. (*b*)	95. (*a*)	96. (*a*)	97. (*b*)	98. (*a*)
99. (*b*)	100. (*a*)	101. (*d*)	102. (*a*)	103. (*c*)	104. (*c*)	105. (*a*)
106. (*a*)	107. (*a*)	108. (*a*)	109. (*a*)	110. (*a*)	111. (*a*)	112. (*b*)
113. (*a*)	114. (*a*)	115. (*a*)	116. (*a*)	117. (*d*)	118. (*a*)	119. (*d*)
120. (*a*)	121. (*b*)	122. (*c*)	123. (*a*)	124. (*a*)	125. (*a*)	126. (*a*)
127. (*a*)	128. (*a*)	129. (*b*)	130. (*a*)	131. (*a*)	132. (*a*)	133. (*b*)
134. (*a*)	135. (*b*)	136. (*b*)	137. (*a*)	138. (*a*)	139. (*a*)	140. (*c*)
141. (*d*)	142. (*b*)	143. (*a*)	144. (*a*)	145. (*b*)	146. (*a*)	147. (*a*)
148. (*a*)	149. (*a*)	150. (*a*)	151. (*c*)	152. (*c*)	153. (*b*)	154. (*b*)
155. (*d*)	156. (*a*)	157. (*d*)	158. (*d*)	159. (*a*)	160. (*b*)	161. (*d*)
162. (*c*)	163. (*b*)	164. (*a*)	165. (*d*)	166. (*b*)	167. (*b*)	168. (*c*)
169. (*a*)	170. (*d*)	171. (*c*)	172. (*b*)	173. (*b*)	174. (*d*)	175. (*a*)
176. (*d*)	177. (*b*)	178. (*a*)	179. (*a*)	180. (*d*)	181. (*b*)	182. (*a*)
183. (*b*)	184. (*a*)	185. (*c*)	186. (*a*)	187. (*c*)	188. (*c*)	189. (*a*)
190. (*a*)	191. (*a*)	192. (*a*)	193. (*b*)	194. (*c*)	195. (*d*)	196. (*c*)
197. (*d*)	198. (*b*)	199. (*b*)	200. (*d*)	201. (*b*)	202. (*c*)	203. (*b*)
204. (*a*)	205. (*c*)	206. (*c*)	207. (*b*)	208. (*a*)	209. (*b*)	210. (*c*)
211. (*c*)	212. (*b*)	213. (*a*)	214. (*d*)	215. (*d*)	216. (*c*)	217. (*c*)
218. (*a*)	219. (*b*)	220. (*a*)	221. (*b*)	222. (*b*)	223. (*b*)	224. (*c*)
225. (*b*)	226. (*c*)	227. (*b*)	228. (*a*)	229. (*a*)	230. (*d*)	231. (*b*)
232. (*c*)	233. (*c*)	234. (*b*)	235. (*b*)	236. (*c*)	237. (*a*)	238. (*c*)
239. (*a*)	240. (*b*)	241. (*a*)	242. (*a*)	243. (*c*)	244. (*a*)	245. (*b*)
246. (*a*)	247. (*c*)	248. (*b*)	249. (*c*)	250. (*b*)	251. (*c*)	252. (*a*)
253. (*c*)	254. (*d*)	255. (*a*)	256. (*c*)	257. (*a*)	258. (*d*)	259. (*a*)
260. (*b*)	261. (*b*)	262. (*c*)	263. (*d*)	264. (*b*)	265. (*a*)	266. (*a*)
267. (*b*)	268. (*b*)	269. (*c*)	270. (*a*)	271. (*a*)	272. (*c*)	273. (*b*)
274. (*a*)	275. (*b*)	276. (*a*)	277. (*d*)	278. (*b*)	279. (*a*)	280. (*a*)
281. (*a*)	282. (*c*)	283. (*a*)	284. (*d*)	285. (*a*)	286. (*a*)	287. (*a*)
288. (*a*)	289. (*a*)	290. (*c*)	291. (*a*)	292. (*a*)	293. (*c*)	294. (*a*)
295. (*a*)	296. (*b*)	297. (*b*)	298. (*b*)	299. (*d*)	300. (*d*)	301. (*a*)

302. (*c*)	303. (*d*)	304. (*c*)	305. (*b*)	306. (*c*)	307. (*a*)	308. (*a*)
309. (*d*)	310. (*b*)	311. (*b*)	312. (*c*)	313. (*a*)	314. (*b*)	315. (*d*)
316. (*d*)	317. (*b*)	318. (*d*)	319. (*b*)	320. (*a*)	321. (*a*)	322. (*b*)
323. (*d*)	324. (*c*)	325. (*a*)	326. (*d*)	327. (*d*)	328. (*b*)	329. (*d*)
330. (*b*)	331. (*d*)	332. (*a*)	333. (*b*)	334. (*a*)	335. (*b*)	336. (*a*)
337. (*a*)	338. (*c*)	339. (*a*)	340. (*c*)	341. (*b*)	342. (*c*)	343. (*d*)
344. (*b*)	345. (*b*)	346. (*c*)	347. (*c*)	348. (*a*)	349. (*b*)	350. (*b*)
351. (*a*)	352. (*c*)	353. (*a*)	354. (*c*)	355. (*b*)	356. (*c*)	357. (*b*)
358. (*c*)	359. (*c*)	360. (*b*)	361. (*c*)	362. (*a*)	363. (*b*)	364. (*a*)

3

"C-Programming"

1. The conditional compilation:
   (*a*) It is taken care of by the compiler
   (*b*) It is setting the compiler option conditionally
   (*c*) It is compiling a program based on a condition
   (*d*) None of the above

2. Originally 'C' was developed as:
   (*a*) System programming language
   (*b*) General-purpose language
   (*c*) Data processing language
   (*d*) None of the above

3. Minimum number of temporary variable needed to swap the contents of 2 variable is
   (*a*) 1
   (*b*) 2
   (*c*) 3
   (*d*) 0

4. A direct access file is:
   (*a*) A file in which records are arranged in a way they are inserted in a file
   (*b*) A file in which records are arranged in a particular order
   (*c*) Files which are stored on a direct access storage medium
   (*d*) None of the above

5. Which of the following is not an advantage of secondary memory:
   (*a*) It is cost-effective
   (*b*) It has large storage capacity
   (*c*) It has highest speed
   (*d*) It is easily portable

6. An inverted file:
   (*a*) Locates information about data in small files that are maintained apart from actual data record
   (*b*) A file which stores opposite records
   (*c*) A file which stores information about records of a system
   (*d*) None of the above

7. Which of the following is not a file operation:
   (*a*) Repositioning
   (*b*) Truncating
   (*c*) Appending
   (*d*) None of the above

8. Which of the following is not a component of file system:
   (*a*) Access method
   (*b*) Auxiliary storage management
   (*c*) File integrity mechanism
   (*d*) None of the above

9. Seek time is:
   (*a*) Time taken to retrieve a data
   (*b*) Time taken by read/write head mechanism to position itself over appropriate cylinder
   (*c*) Time taken by appropriate sector to come under read/write
   (*d*) none of the above

10. Latency time is:
    (*a*) Time taken by read/write head mechanism to position itself over appropriate cylinder
    (*b*) Time taken to transfer a data from memory
    (*c*) Time taken by appropriate sector to come under read/ write head
    (*d*) None of the above

11. 'Prime area' in context of file system is defined as:
    (*a*) It is memory area created by operating system
    (*b*) it is an area into which data records are written
    (*c*) It is the main area of a web page
    (*d*) None of the above

12. The two types of file structures existing in VSAM file are:
    (*a*) Key sequenced structure, entry sequenced structure
    (*b*) Key sequence structure, exit sequenced structure
    (*c*) Entry sequence structure, exit sequenced structure
    (*d*) None of the above

13. In multi list organization:
    (*a*) Records that have equivalent value for a given secondary index item are linked together to form a list
    (*b*) Records are loaded in ordered sequence defined by collating sequence by content of the key
    (*c*) Records are directly accessed by record key field
    (*d*) none of the above

14. Which of the following is/are advantages of cellular partitioned structure:
    (*a*) Simultaneous read operations can be overlapped
    (*b*) Search time is reduced
    (*c*) Both (*a*) and (*b*)
    (*d*) None of the above

15. *ptr++ is equivalent to:
    (*a*) ptr++
    (*b*) *ptr
    (*c*) ++*ptr
    (*d*) None of the above

16. Statement scanf ("%d", 80):
    (*a*) Assign an integer to variable i
    (*b*) Give an error message
    (*c*) Print the value of i
    (*d*) Assign an float to variable i

17. Value of ix + j, if i, j are integer type and ix long type would be:
    (*a*) Integer
    (*b*) Float
    (*c*) Long integer
    (*d*) Double precision

18. In a C language '3' represents
    (*a*) A digit
    (*b*) An integer
    (*c*) A character
    (*d*) A word

19. In C language, a hexadecimal number is represented by writing:
    (*a*) x
    (*b*) xo
    (*c*) ox
    (*d*) h

20. Expression C = i++ causes:
    (*a*) Value of i assigned to C and then i incremented by 1
    (*b*) i to be incremented by 1, and then value of i assigned to C
    (*c*) Value of i assigned to C
    (*d*) i to be incremented by 1

21. Declaration int *(*p) int (*a) (i) is
    (*a*) A pointer to function that

accept an integer arguments and return an integer
(*b*) A pointer to a, which returns an integer
(*c*) A pointer to a sub-routine which returns result of evaluation
(*d*) None of the above

22. Null pointer and un-initialized pointers are same:
(*a*) True
(*b*) False
(*c*) Varies from program to program
(*d*) None of the above

23. In which header file NULL macro is defined:
(*a*) Stdio.h and stddeth
(*b*) IO stream.h
(*c*) String h
(*d*) Preprocessor

24. Null pointer is:
(*a*) A pointer which does not point anywhere
(*b*) Pointer defined with name null
(*c*) A pointer that returns 0 value
(*d*) None of the above

25. Null macro is:
(*a*) A macro with name null
(*b*) A macro which represents null pointer
(*c*) A macro defined with no name
(*d*) None of the above

26. Null string is:
(*a*) An empty string
(*b*) A string named null
(*c*) A string having null character
(*d*) None of the above

27. The size of pointer in small memory model is:
(*a*) 2 bytes
(*b*) 1 byte
(*c*) 3 bytes
(*d*) None of the above.

28. In large memory model size of pointer is:
(*a*) 2 bytes
(*b*) 4 bytes
(*c*) 1 byte
(*d*) None of the above

29. Bytes occupied by near, far and huge pointer is:
(*a*) 2,4,4 bytes
(*b*) 1,2,4 bytes
(*c*) 4,4,4 bytes
(*d*) 1,2,2 bytes

30. Are the declarations char. *apple, char.*orange [], char cherry [][] same
(*a*) Yes
(*b*) No
(*c*) Depends upon the values of variable
(*d*) None of the above

31. In a 'C' function maximum number of return statement is:
(*a*) 0
(*b*) 1
(*c*) 3
(*d*) None of the above

32. It is necessary that header files should have. h extension:
(*a*) Yes
(*b*) No
(*c*) Varies from compiler to compiler
(*d*) None of the above

33. Header file normally contain:
(*a*) Preprocessor directive
(*b*) Structure, enum declaration
(*c*) Global variable declaration
(*d*) All of the above

34. When are char a[] and char *a treated same by compiler:
    (*a*) If they are used as formal parameter while defining a function
    (*b*) They are never same
    (*c*) If they are used as constants
    (*d*) None of the above

35. Which bitewise operator is suitable for putting on a particular bit in a number:
    (*a*) I operator
    (*b*) X operator
    (*c*) AND operator
    (*d*) None of the above

36. To which number system can binary number 101101011111 000101 be easily converted to:
    (*a*) Decimal
    (*b*) Hexadecimal
    (*c*) Base 3
    (*d*) Base 30

37. In the following code p2 is of type:
    int * ptr; ptr p1, p2
    (*a*) Integer pointer
    (*b*) Float pointer
    (*c*) Pointer to pointer
    (*d*) Function pointer

38. The difference between following declaration is:
    Const char *const s;
    Char const *const s;
    (*a*) First returns a constant value and second returns a character value
    (*b*) Second returns a char value and first returns a const value
    (*c*) There is no difference
    (*d*) The second is not a valid declaration

39. How much memory can be allocated in a single call to malloc
    (*a*) 16 KB
    (*b*) 32 KB
    (*c*) 64 KB
    (*d*) None of the above

40. Which function should be used to free the memory allocated by calloc ( )
    (*a*) To free
    (*b*) Mem Free
    (*c*) Call free
    (*d*) The memory is automatically released

41. Can we dynamically allocate arrays in expanded memory:
    (*a*) Yes
    (*b*) No
    (*c*) Can't be said
    (*d*) None of the above

42. The proto type declaration syntax of variable argument list function is:
    (*a*) Print_f [const char * format, ...]
    (*b*) Print_f [char format ....]
    (*c*) Print_f (const * format ....]
    (*d*) None of the above

43. To allocate 100 KB of memory the function is:
    (*a*) Malloc
    (*b*) Farmalloc
    (*c*) Calloc
    (*d*) None of the above

44. Can we dynamically allocate arrays in expanded memory:
    (*a*) Yes
    (*b*) No
    (*c*) Varies from compiler to compiler
    (*d*) None of the above

45. Can we use switch statement to switch on strings:
    (*a*) Yes
    (*b*) No
    (*c*) Under special conditions
    (*d*) None of the above

46. To test whether a value lies in the range 2 to 4, or 5 to 7 the best statement used should be:
    (*a*) Switch
    (*b*) While
    (*c*) For
    (*d*) Printing

47. The different types of linkage are:
    (*a*) External
    (*b*) Internal
    (*c*) Local
    (*d*) All of the above

48. Scope of a variable is:
    (*a*) The region over which the variable declaration has effect
    (*b*) The region where function has effect
    (*c*) The return type of a variable
    (*d*) None of the above

49. In 'C' int I; is:
    (*a*) Declaration
    (*b*) Definition
    (*c*) Function
    (*d*) Recursion

50. The declaration *p++ = C is:
    (*a*) Valid expression
    (*b*) Invalid expression
    (*c*) Valid if the variables declared previously
    (*d*) None of the above

51. The output of following code
    main ( )
    {int I = –3, j = 2, k = 0, m;
    m = ++i&& ++j|| ++k;
    printf ("d%d%d%d", j,i,k,m)} is
    (*a*) –2301
    (*b*) 3205
    (*c*) 1234
    (*d*) None of the above

52. The output of following code
    main ( )
    {print$_f$ ("%f", sqrt (36.0), is
    (*a*) 36
    (*b*) 6.0
    (*c*) Absurd result
    (*d*) None of the above

53. The O/P of following code
    main ( )
    {printf ("%f", log(36.0);}
    (*a*) 6.0
    (*b*) 3.6
    (*c*) Absurd value
    (*d*) None of the above

54. To round of variable, x, float, to an integer the correct way to do so is:
    (*a*) y = (int)(x + 0.5);
    (*b*) y = (float) (x + 0.5);
    (*c*) int y = (int)(x + 0.5);
    (*d*) None of the above

55. By default a real number is treated as:
    (*a*) Double
    (*b*) Single
    (*c*) double precision
    (*d*) depends upon the declaration

56. The output of following code
    main ( )
    {Print$_f$ ("%d%d%d,"size of (3.14 f) size of (3.14), size of (3.141);} is
    (*a*) 4,8,10
    (*b*) 8,4,10
    (*c*) 10,8,4
    (*d*) None of the above

57. The output of following program would be

main ( )
{Printf ("%c," abcdefgh" [Y]);}
(*a*) a
(*b*) b
(*c*) c
(*d*) d

58. A self referential structure
(*a*) Contain pointer to itself
(*b*) Contain no pointer
(*c*) Contain pointer referring to a variable of that type
(*d*) None of the above

59. The output of following program
main ( )
{int a = 250;
Print$_f$ ("%d",a);}
(*a*) a
(*b*) 250;
(*c*) 0000
(*d*) garbage value

60. Output of following code
{printf ("\n%%%%");}
(*a*) error message
(*b*) %%
(*c*) 00
(*d*) None of the above

61. Binary equivalent of 5.375 is :
(*a*) 101.011
(*b*) 111.000
(*c*) 101.111
(*d*) None of the above

62. The code which combines following two statements into one
(i) char *p;
(ii) P = malloc (100);
(*a*) Char *p = malloc (100);
(*b*) *p = calloc (100);
(*c*) *p = Char malloc (100)
(*d*) None of the above

63. Write following statements in a split code
Char far *Scr = [(char far*) 0 x B8000000L;]
(*a*) Char far ;
Scr = (Char far *)
(*b*) Char far * Scr
Scr = (Char far *) 0 x B8000000L
(*c*) Char far *Scr
Scr = (char far *) 0 x B8000000L
(*d*) None of the above

64. Are the expressions
*ptr++ and ++*ptr same
(*a*) Yes
(*b*) No
(*c*) Depends upon the value of ptr
(*d*) None of the above

65. The correct declaration of array of three function pointers where each function receives two int and returns a float is:
(*a*) float (*arr[3])(int,int);
(*b*) int (*arr[3])(int, int);
(*c*) float (*arr[3])(float, float);
(*d*) int (*arr[3])(float, float);

66. For the array of 10 integers expressions arr and &arr are
(*a*) Same
(*b*) Different
(*c*) Depends upon the context
(*d*) None of the above

67. What does following declaration mean
Int (*ptr)[10];
(*a*) ptr is pointer to integer
(*b*) ptr is pointer to array of 10 integers
(*c*) ptr is an array of 10 elements
(*d*) None of the above

68. How would you display n on the screen

(*a*) printf ("\\n")
(*b*) printf ("\\\n")
(*c*) printf ("\n")
(*d*) None of the above

69. Output of following program will be:
main ( )
{printf ("\n%d%d%d", size of ('3')
size of ("3"), size of (3))
(*a*) 2,2,2
(*b*) 2,4,8
(*c*) 4,4,4
(*d*) 8,4,2

70. The output of following program would be
main ( )
{char *str[]={"Frogs", "Do",
"Not", "Die", "They", "Croak"};
printf ("%d%d, size of (str),
size of (str[0]));}
(*a*) 2,2
(*b*) 12,2
(*c*) 2,12
(*d*) 12,12

71. The command to read a salary variable from an input file named managers.dat
(*a*) infile >>salary
(*b*) salary>>infile
(*c*) infile<<salary
(*d*) salary<<infile

72. A function that change the state of count object is called:
(*a*) Descriptor
(*b*) Manipulator
(*c*) Definition
(*d*) None of the above

73. Statement get ( ); is
(*a*) Valid
(*b*) Invalid
(*c*) Does not exist
(*d*) None of the above

74. Bitwise OR operator is:
(*a*) Logical operator
(*b*) Binary operator
(*c*) Arithmetic operator
(*d*) None of the above

75. When accessing a structure member, the identifier to the left of dot operator is name of:
(*a*) Structure variable
(*b*) Member variable
(*c*) Member value
(*d*) Structure value

76. Equivalent expression of P>val is
(*a*) (*P) Val
(*b*) *(P) Val
(*c*) *(*P) Val
(*d*) None of the above

77. Contents of two pointers pointing to adjacent float variable differ by
(*a*) 2 bytes
(*b*) 4 bytes
(*c*) 1 byte
(*d*) None of the above

78. An address is ______ while pointer is a ______
(*a*) location, variable
(*b*) variable, location
(*c*) variable, constant
(*d*) constant, variable

79. One way pointers are useful to refer to memory address that has no _____
(*a*) Name
(*b*) Value
(*c*) Constant
(*d*) None of the above

80. Which C++ class is used to write to file rather than screen
(*a*) f stream
(*b*) io stream
(*c*) i stream

(d) int stream

81. Software that can be used in applications other than one for which it was originally written is called:
(a) Re-entrant software
(b) Re-usable code
(c) Cross code
(d) Migrant code

82. The range of int type of constants is
(a) 00000 to +65535
(b) -32768 to 32767
(c) -65535 to +65535
(d) -32768 to 0

83. What will be the output of following code segment
```
main ( )
{char s[10];
strcpy (s, "abc");
printf ("%d%d", strlen (s),
size of (s)) }
```
(a) 310
(b) 3^3
(c) 1010
(d) 103

84. Which of the following statements is the odd one out:
(a) i = j + 1;
(b) j++
(c) j + = 1
(d) j = +1;

85. The default return type of main ( ) is
(a) int
(b) void
(c) char
(d) float

86. Scope of a variable of automatic storage class is limited to the:
(a) Program in which it is defined
(b) Block in which it is defined
(c) Loop in which it is defined
(d) Function in which it is defined

87. ASCII stand for
(a) American Standard Code for Information Interchange
(b) American Statistical Code for Information Interchange
(c) Alphabetic Series Code for Information Interchange
(d) Alphabetic Standard Code for Information Interchange

88. CD-ROM device uses:
(a) Magnetic Storage Technique
(b) Optical Storage Technique
(c) Solid-state Storage Technique
(d) Electronic Storage Technique

89. Clip Board:
(a) Special file or memory area where data is stored temporarily before being copied to another location
(b) A temporary location on hard disk where data is stored temporarily before being copied to another location
(c) A temporary location on floppy disk where data is stored temporarily before being copied to another location
(d) A temporary location on compact disk where data is stored temporarily before being copied to another location.

90. "Booting of the system" means:
(a) Loading the operating system
(b) Running an application program called booting
(c) Physically kicking the computer

(*d*) Dismissing the computer

91. FORMAT command in DOS is used to establish:
   (*a*) The data storage characteristics of a diskette
   (*b*) The number of tracks and the number of sectors per track
   (*c*) The number of bytes/sector
   (*d*) All of the above

92. An example of volatile memory is:
   (*a*) CD-ROM
   (*b*) RAM
   (*c*) ROM
   (*d*) Hard Disk

93. LINUX is an example of:
   (*a*) Proprietary software
   (*b*) Free ware
   (*c*) Shareware
   (*d*) Open source software

94. Extension of power point file is:
   (*a*) .PPT
   (*b*) .PPS
   (*c*) .PPP
   (*d*) .TMT

95. Normally a high level language is:
   (*a*) Procedure oriented
   (*b*) Non-procedure oriented
   (*c*) Object oriented
   (*d*) None of the above

ANSWERS

1. (*c*)	2. (*b*)	3. (*d*)	4. (*c*)	5. (*c*)	6. (*a*)	7. (*d*)
8. (*d*)	9. (*b*)	10. (*c*)	11. (*b*)	12. (*c*)	13. (*a*)	14. (*c*)
15. (*d*)	16. (*a*)	17. (*c*)	18. (*c*)	19. (*d*)	20. (*a*)	21. (*a*)
22. (*b*)	23. (*a*)	24. (*a*)	25. (*b*)	26. (*a*)	27. (*a*)	28. (*a*)
29. (*a*)	30. (*b*)	31. (*b*)	32. (*b*)	33. (*d*)	34. (*a*)	35. (*a*)
36. (*b*)	37. (*a*)	38. (*a*)	39. (*c*)	40. (*a*)	41. (*a*)	42. (*a*)
43. (*b*)	44. (*a*)	45. (*a*)	46. (*a*)	47. (*d*)	48. (*a*)	49. (*a*)
50. (*a*)	51. (*a*)	52. (*b*)	53. (*b*)	54. (*a*)	55. (*b*)	56. (*a*)
57. (*c*)	58. (*a*)	59. (*b*)	60. (*a*)	61. (*a*)	62. (*a*)	63. (*b*)
64. (*b*)	65. (*a*)	66. (*b*)	67. (*b*)	68. (*a*)	69. (*a*)	70. (*b*)
71. (*a*)	72. (*b*)	73. (*c*)	74. (*b*)	75. (*a*)	76. (*a*)	77. (*b*)
78. (*b*)	79. (*a*)	80. (*a*)	81. (*b*)	82. (*b*)	83. (*a*)	84. (*b*)
85. (*b*)	86. (*a*)	87. (*a*)	88. (*b*)	89. (*b*)	90. (*a*)	91. (*d*)
92. (*b*)	93. (*d*)	94. (*a*)	95. (*a*)			

4

Data Structure and Algorithms

1. In linked lists there are no NULL links in:
   (*a*) Single linked list
   (*b*) Linear doubly linked list
   (*c*) Circular linked list
   (*d*) None of the above

2. In a stack the command to access nth element from the top of the stack s will be
   (*a*) S [Top-n]
   (*b*) S [Top+n]
   (*c*) S [top-n-1]
   (*d*) None of the above

3. If yyy, xxx and zzz are the elements of a lexically ordered binary tree, then in preorder traversal which node will be traverse first
   (*a*) xxx
   (*b*) yyy
   (*c*) zzz
   (*d*) cannot be determined

4. In a balance binary tree the height of two sub trees of every node can not differ by more than
   (*a*) 2
   (*b*) 1
   (*c*) 0
   (*d*) 3

5. The result of evaluating prefix expression */b+-dacd, where a = 3, b = 6, c = 1, d = 5 is
   (*a*) 0
   (*b*) 5
   (*c*) 10
   (*d*) 15

6. In array representation of binary tree the right child of root will be at location of
   (*a*) 2
   (*b*) 5
   (*c*) 3
   (*d*) 0

7. The total number of comparisons in a bubble sort is
   (*a*) 0(nlogn)
   (*b*) 0(2n)
   (*c*) 0(n2)
   (*d*) None of the above

8. The dummy header in linked list contain
   (*a*) First record of the actual data
   (*b*) Last record of the actual data
   (*c*) Pointer to the last record of the actual data
   (*d*) None of the above

9. Write the output of the following program: int a[ ] = {1,2,3}*P;
   (*a*) 3
   (*b*) Junk value
   (*c*) Run time error
   (*d*) Address of the third element

10. If the out degree of every node is exactly equal to M or 0 and

the numbers of nodes at level K is Mk – 1 [consider root at level 1], then tree is called as
(*i*) Full m-ary tree
(*ii*) Complete m-ary tree
(*iii*) Positional m-ary tree
(*a*) Only (*i*)
(*b*) Only (*iii*)
(*c*) Both (*i*) & (*ii*)
(*d*) Both (*ii*) & (*iii*)

11. In the following tree.

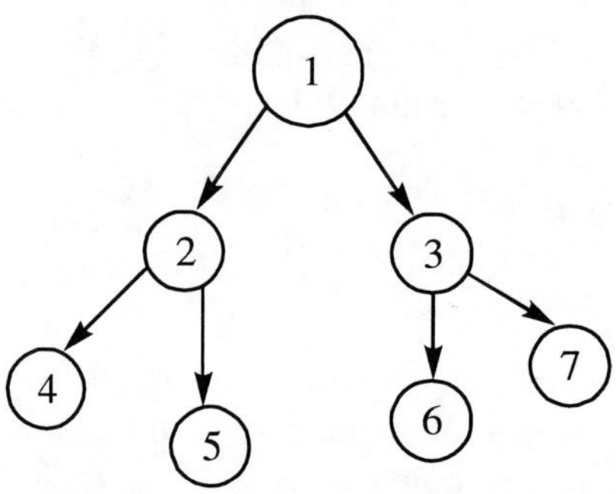

If post order traversal generates sequence xy-zw*+, then label of nodes 1,2,3,4,5,6,7 will be
(*a*) +, –, *, x, y, z, w
(*b*) x, –, y, +, z, *, w
(*c*) x, y, z, w, –, *, +
(*d*) –, x, y, +, *, z, w

12. If the following tree, is used for sorting, then a new number 10 should be placed at

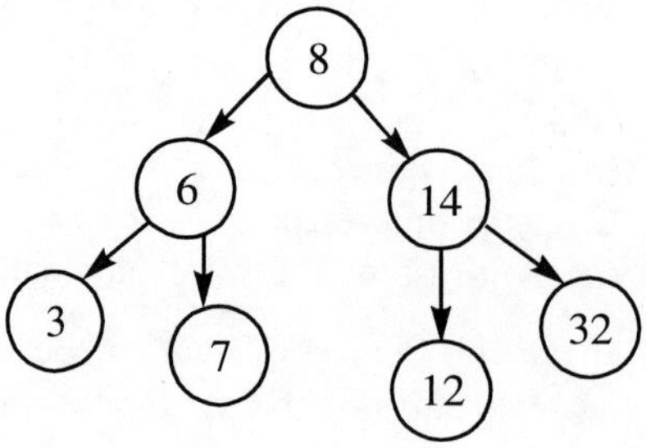

(*a*) Right child of node labeled 7
(*b*) Left child of node labeled 7
(*c*) Left child of node labeled 14
(*d*) Right child of node labeled 8

13. A queue has configuration a,b,c,d. To get configuration d, c, b, a. One needs a minimum of
(*a*) 2 deletions and 3 additions
(*b*) 3 deletions and 2 additions
(*c*) 3 deletions and 3 additions
(*d*) 3 deletions and 4 additions

14. Number of possible ordered trees with 3 nodes A,B,C is
(*a*) 16
(*b*) 12
(*c*) 6
(*d*) 10

15. Number of swapping, operations need to sort numbers 8, 22, 7, 9, 31, 19, 5, 13 in ascending order using bubble sort
(*a*) 11
(*b*) 12
(*c*) 13
(*d*) 14

16. Consider two sorted lists of size L1, L2. Number of comparisons needed in worst case by merge sort algorithm will be
(*a*) L1,L2
(*b*) Max(L1,L2)
(*c*) Min(L1,L2)
(*d*) L1+L2-1

17. A hash table with 10 buckets with one slot per bucket is depicted in following diagram. Symbols S1 to S7 are initially entered using a hashing function with linear probing. Maximum number of comparisons needed in searching an item that is not present is

0	S7
1	S1
2	
3	S4
4	S2
5	
6	S5
7	S6
8	S3
9	

(*a*) 4
(*b*) 5
(*c*) 6
(*d*) 3

18. Following sequence of operation is performed on a stack. Push (1), Push (2), Pop, Push (1), Push (2), Pop, Pop, Pop, Push (2), Pop. The sequences of popped out values are
(*a*) 2, 2, 1, 2, 2
(*b*) 2, 2, 1, 1, 2
(*c*) 2, 1, 2, 2, 1
(*d*) 2, 1, 2, 2, 2,

19. A binary tree in which every non-leaf node has non-empty left and right sub trees is called a strictly binary tree. Such a tree with 10 leaves
(*a*) Has 19 nodes
(*b*) Has 16 nodes
(*c*) Has 15 nodes
(*d*) None of the above

20. Depth of a binary tree with n nodes is
(*a*) log(n + 1) –1
(*b*) log(n)
(*c*) log(n – 1)n – 1
(*d*) log(n) + 1

21. To arrange a binary tree in ascending order we need
(*a*) Post order transversal
(*b*) In order transversal
(*c*) Pre order transversal
(*d*) None of the above

22. Average successful search time taken by binary search on sorted array of 10 items is
(*a*) 2.6
(*b*) 2.7
(*c*) 2.8
(*d*) 2.9

23. Hash function f is defined as f(key) = key mod 7. If linear probing is used to insert the key 37, 38, 72, 48, 98, 11, 56 into a table indexed from 0 to 6. 11 will be stored at the location
(*a*) 3
(*b*) 4
(*c*) 5
(*d*) 6

24. Average successful search time for sequential search on 'n' item is
(*a*) n/2
(*b*) (n – 1)/2
(*c*) (n + 1)/2
(*d*) log(n) +1

25. Running time of an algorithm T(n), where n is input size is given by T(n) = 8T(n/2) + qn, if n > 1 T(n) = p, if, n = 1, where p and q are constants. The order of algorithm is
(*a*) n^2
(*b*) n^n
(*c*) n^3
(*d*) n

26. 6 files X1, X2, X3, X4, X5, X6 have 150, 250, 55, 85, 125, 175

number of records, res-pectively. The order of storage to optimize access time is

(*a*) X1, X2, X3, X4, X5, X6
(*b*) X3, X4, X1, X5, X6, X2
(*c*) X1, X3, X2, X4, X5, X6
(*d*) None of the above

27. In above question average access time will be
(*a*) 150
(*b*) 140
(*c*) 55
(*d*) None of the above

28. An algorithm consists of two modules x1, x2. Their order is f(n) and g(n), respectively.
The order of algorithm is
(*a*) Max (f(n), g(n))
(*b*) Min (f(n), g(n))
(*c*) f(n)+g(n)
(*d*) f(n)*g(n)

29. Big (O) notation w.r.t algorithm signifies
(*a*) It decides the best algorithm to solve a problem
(*b*) It determines maximum size of a problem, that can be solved in given system in given time
(*c*) It is the lower bound of growth rate of algorithm
(*d*) None of the above

30. Runing time T(n), where 'n' is input size of recursive algorithm is given as follows
T(n) = c + T(n – 1), if n > 1,
T(n) = d if n < 1. The order of algorithm is
(*a*) n^2
(*b*) n
(*c*) n^3
(*d*) n^n

31. Four algorithm A1, A2, A3, A4 solves a problem with order log(n), log log(n), nlog(n), n. Which is best algorithm
(*a*) A1
(*b*) A2
(*c*) A3
(*d*) A4

32. Time complexity of an algorithm T (n), where n is the input size is given by T (n) = T (n – 1) + 1/n, if n > 1 otherwise T(n) = 1. The order of algorithm is
(*a*) Log n
(*b*) n
(*c*) n^2
(*d*) n^n

33. Which of the following is correct
(*a*) Internal sorting is used, if number of items to be sorted is very large
(*b*) External sorting is used, if number of items to be sorted is very large
(*c*) External sorting needs auxiliary storage
(*d*) Internal sorting needs auxiliary storage

34. A sorting technique which guarantees that records with same primary key occurs in the sorted list as in the original unsorted list is said to be
(*a*) Stable
(*b*) Consistent
(*c*) External
(*d*) Linear

35. A text is made up of five characters. T1, T2, T3, T4, T5. The probability of occurance of each character is .12, .4, .15, .88 and .25, respectively. The optimal

coding technique will have average length of
(*a*) 2.15
(*b*) 3.01
(*c*) 2.3
(*d*) 1.78

36. If running time of an algorithm is given by T (n) = T (n – 1) + T (n – 2) + T (n – 3), if n > 3 otherwise T(n) = n, what should be relation between T(1), T(2), T(3) where algorithm order becomes constant
(*a*) T (1) = T (2) = T (3)
(*b*) T (1) + T (2) = 2T2
(*c*) T (1) – T (3) = T (2)
(*d*) T (1) + T (2) = T (3)

37. Arranging a pack of cards by picking one by one is an example of
(*a*) Bubble sort
(*b*) Selection sort
(*c*) Insertion sort
(*d*) Merge sort

38. In evaluating arithmatic expression 2*3 – (4 + 5) using postfix stack form. Which of the following stack configuration is not possible

(*a*)

4
6

(*b*)

5
4
6

(*c*)

9
6

(*d*)

9
3
2

39. The order of an algorithm that finds whether a given Boolean function of 'n' variable produces a '1' is
(*a*) Constant
(*b*) Linear
(*c*) Logarithmic
(*d*) Exponential

40. The average number of comparisons performed by merge sort algorithm in merging two-sorted list of length 2 is
(*a*) 8/3
(*b*) 8/5
(*c*) 11/7
(*d*) 11/6

41. To arrange the books of library the best method is
(*a*) Bubble sort
(*b*) Quick sort
(*c*) Merge sort
(*d*) Heap sort

42. Which of the following algorithm has n log (n) time complexity
(*a*) Heap sort
(*b*) Quick sort
(*c*) Insertion sort
(*d*) Selection sort

43. Which algorithm solves all pair shortest path problem
(*a*) Dijkstra's algorithm
(*b*) Floyd's algorithm
(*c*) Prim's algorithm
(*d*) Worshal's algorithm

44. The eccentricity of node labeled 5 is
(*a*) 6
(*b*) 7
(*c*) 2
(*d*) 5

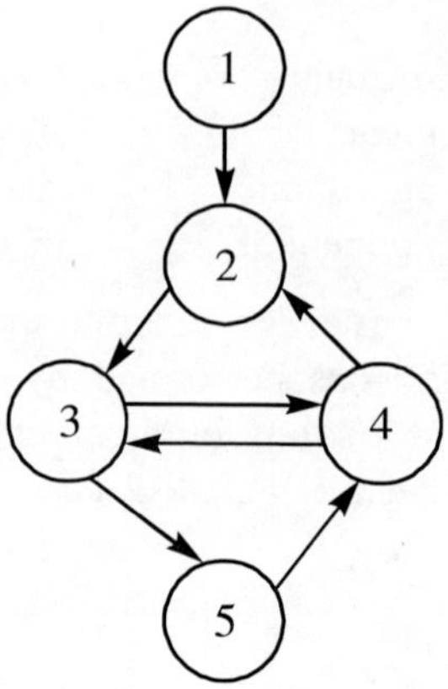

45. The information about an array used in a program will be stored in
    (*a*) Symbol table
    (*b*) Dope vector
    (*c*) Register vector
    (*d*) Activation table

46. In which of the following cases linked list implementations of sparse matrices consumes same memory as normal array
    (*a*) 5 × 6 matrix with 9 non-zero entries
    (*b*) 5 × 6 matrix with 8 non-zero entries
    (*c*) 6 × 5 matrix with 8 non-zero entries
    (*d*) 6 × 5 matrix with 9 non-zero entries

47. The advantage of sparse matrix linked list representation over dope vector method is, that the former is
    (*a*) Conceptually easier
    (*b*) Completely dynamic
    (*c*) Efficient in accessing an entry
    (*d*) Efficient if the sparse matrix is a band matrix

48. If the address of (I, J)th entry, in dope vector representation, where it stores the position of first and last non-zero entries of each row is given by C, assume l(n) and f(n) represent the last and first non-zero entries in row x
    (*a*) Σ(l(k) – f(k) + 1) + (i – f(j))
    K = 1
    (*b*) Σ(l(k) – f(k) + 1 + (i – f(i))
    K = 1
    (*c*) Σ(l(k) – f(k) + 1) + (i – f(i) + 1)
    K = 1
    (*d*) Σ(l(k) – f(k) + 1) + (i – f(i) + 1)
    K = 1

49. The post fix equivalent of the prefix *+ ab – cd is
    (*a*) ab + cd–*
    (*b*) abcd + –*
    (*c*) ab + cd* –
    (*d*) ab + –cd*

50. The order of binary search algorithm is
    (*a*) n
    (*b*) n^2
    (*c*) n log n
    (*d*) log n

51. The value of load factor, which reduces average search time of hashing with linear probing should be
    (*a*) Equal to one
    (*b*) Far less than one
    (*c*) Far greater than one
    (*d*) None of the above

52. A hash table can store a maximum of 10 records. Currently there are records in locations 1, 3, 4, 7, 8, 9, 10. The probability of new records going into location 2, with a hash function resolving collisions by linear probing is
    (*a*) 0.6

(*b*) 0.1
(*c*) 0.2
(*d*) 0.5

53. A hash table has a space for 100 records. What is the probability of collision before the table is 10% full
(*a*) 0.45
(*b*) 0.5
(*c*) 0.3
(*d*) 0.34 (approximately)

54. Which of the following remarks about this indexing are true
(*a*) It is an m-ary tree
(*b*) It is search tree of order m
(*c*) Successful searches may terminate in leaf nodes
(*d*) Successful searches may terminate at any level of tree structure

55. Pick the correct statement
(*a*) Sequential file organization is suitable for batch processing
(*b*) Sequential file organization is suitable for interactive processing
(*c*) Indexed sequential file organization is suitable for batch processing
(*d*) None of the above

56. In which of the following application stack cannot be used
(*a*) Evaluate arithmetic expression in postfix form
(*b*) Implement recursion
(*c*) Convert a given arithmetic expression in infix form to its equivalent postfix form
(*d*) Allocate resources by operating system

57. In the following graph, what should be labels of nodes marked 1 and 2 if the breadth first traversal yields the list a b c d e.

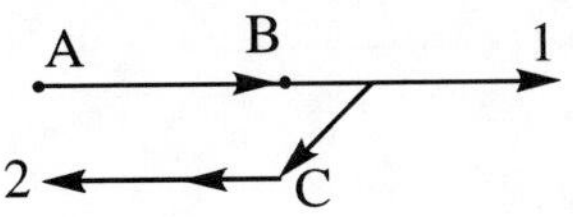

(*a*) D and E
(*b*) E and D
(*c*) A and C
(*d*) Unpredictable

58. In above graph if depth first transversal fields the list A B C D E then the label of nodes marked 1 and 2 will be
(*a*) E and D
(*b*) D and E
(*c*) A and C
(*d*) Unpredictable

59. Which of the following abstract data types can be used to represent a many to many relation
(*a*) Tree
(*b*) Stack
(*c*) Graph
(*d*) Queue

60. Consider following graph. Which is valid topological string

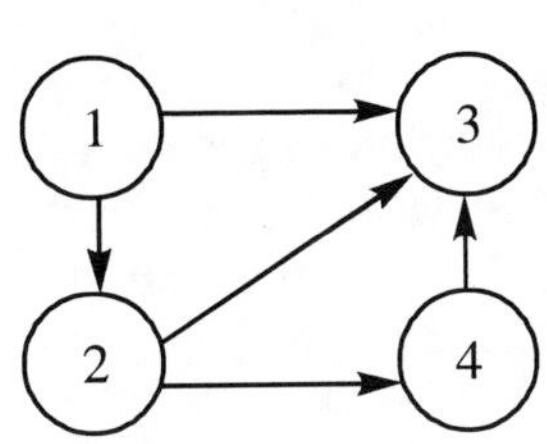

(*a*) 1 2 3 4
(*b*) 2 1 3 4
(*c*) 2 1 4 3
(*d*) 1 2 4 3

61. In the following graph which is valid strong component

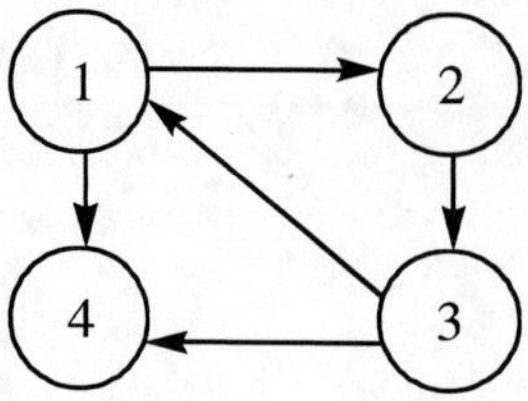

(*a*) 1, 3, 4
(*b*) 1, 2, 4
(*c*) 2, 3, 4
(*d*) 1, 2, 3

62. In following graph, minimum cost spanning tree has the cost

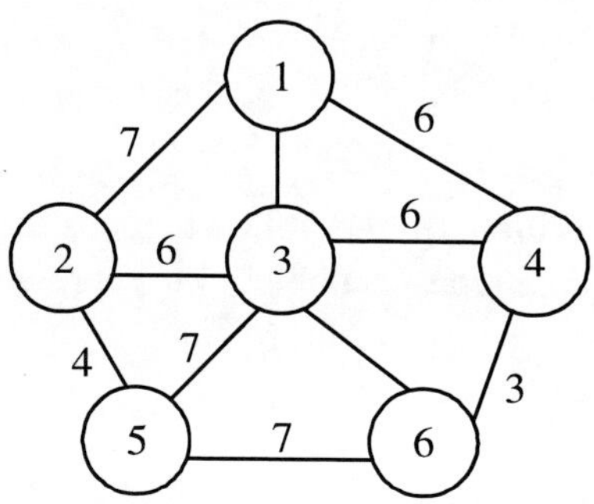

(*a*) 18
(*b*) 20
(*c*) 24
(*d*) 22

63. Merge sort uses
(*a*) Back tracking approach
(*b*) Divide and conquer strategy
(*c*) Heuristic approach
(*d*) Greedy approach

64. Locality of reference gives rise to use of
(*a*) Interrupts
(*b*) DMA
(*c*) Polling
(*d*) Cache memory

65. For merging two sorted lists of sizes m and n into a sorted list of size m + n, the numbers of comparisons required are
(*a*) O(m)
(*b*) O(n)
(*c*) O (m + n)
(*d*) O (logm + logn)

66. Minimum number of edges in a connected cycle graph on n vertices is
(*a*) n – 1
(*b*) n
(*c*) n + 1
(*d*) None of the above

67. A binary tree T has n leaf nodes. Number of nodes of degree 2 in T is
(*a*) $\log_2 n$
(*b*) n – 1
(*c*) n
(*d*) 2^n

68. Consider following expression: x + y*(z + w)/*p + w – q. Its postfix expression is
(*a*) xy + zw/*pw + q-
(*b*) xyzw + *p/ + wq*+
(*c*) x*y + zw/p*zw++
(*d*) x + *yzw/p*wq++

69. Which of the following statements are true
(*i*) Number of collisions increases with the number of entries
(*ii*) Program efficiency increases with the fuse of recursion
(*iii*) Worst time complexity of quick sort is O(n2)
(*iv*) Binary search using linked list is efficient
(*a*) i and ii
(*b*) ii and iii
(*c*) i and iv
(*d*) i and iii

70. Minimum number of colors needed to color a graph of n>3 vertices and 2 edges is
(*a*) 4
(*b*) 3
(*c*) 2
(*d*) 1

71. Expressions 1*2^3*4^5*6 will be evaluated as
(*a*) 32^{30}
(*b*) 162^{30}
(*c*) 49152
(*d*) 173458

72. In a circularly linked list organization insertion of a record involved the modification of
(*a*) No pointer
(*b*) 1 pointer
(*c*) 2 pointer
(*d*) 3 pointer

73. Stack is useful for implementing
(*a*) Radix sort
(*b*) Breadth first search
(*c*) Recursion
(*d*) Depth first search

74. A record has size 100 character. A magnetic tape having storage density of 1000 character per inch is used. The blocking factor of storage so that wastage does not exceed 1/3rd of the tape will be
(*a*) 0.05
(*b*) 20
(*c*) 10
(*d*) 0.1

75. A m/c needs minimum of 100 sec to sort 1000 names by quick sort. Minimum time needed to sort 100 names will be approximately
(*a*) 50.2 sec
(*b*) 6.7 sec
(*c*) 72.7 sec
(*d*) 11.2 sec

76. Which of the following is useful in traversing a given graph by breadth first search
(*a*) List
(*b*) Set
(*c*) Stack
(*d*) Queue

77. Which of the following is useful in implementing quick sort
(*a*) Stack
(*b*) Set
(*c*) List
(*d*) Depth first search

78. The following tree gives 1 after evaluation, values of variables are

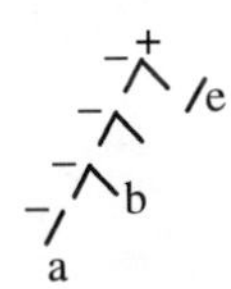

(*a*) a = –b and e = 0
(*b*) a = –b and e = 1
(*c*) a = b and e = 0
(*d*) a = b and e = 1

79. Hash function randomly distributes records one by one in space that can hold x number of records. Probability that mth record is first record to result in collision is
(*a*) (x – 1)(x – 2)......(x – (m –2))(m – 1)/xm – 1
(*b*) (x – 1)(x – 2)......(x – (m – 1))(m – 1)/xm – 1
(*c*) (x – 1) (x – 2)……(x – (m – 2))(m – 1)/xm
(*d*) (x – 1) (x – 2)……(x – (m – 1))(m – 1)/xm

80. If the hashing function is remainder of division, then

clustering is more likely to occur if the storage space is divided into 40 sectors rather than 41. This conclusion is
(*a*) False
(*b*) True
(*c*) Cannot be determined
(*d*) None of the above

81. In programming the program should not use GO TO because
(*a*) It makes debugging difficult
(*b*) It increases running time of program
(*c*) It increases memory required for the program
(*d*) None of the above

82. Maximum degree in any vector in a graph with n vertices is
(*a*) n
(*b*) n – 1
(*c*) n + 1
(*d*) 2n – 1

83. Recurence relation that arises in relation with complexity of binary search is
(*a*) T (n) = T (n/2) + k
(*b*) T (n) = 2T (n/2) + k
(*c*) T (n) = 2T (n/2) + log(n)
(*d*) T (n) = 2T (n/2) + n

84. In a sequence of 1, 2, 3, 4, 5, which of the following can be obtained as output in a stack
(*a*) 3, 4, 5, 1, 2
(*b*) 3, 4, 5, 2, 1
(*c*) 1, 5, 2, 3, 4
(*d*) 5, 4, 3, 1, 2

85. Quick sort algorithm uses which technique
(*a*) Dynamic programming
(*b*) Backtracking
(*c*) Divide and conquer
(*d*) Greedy method

86. For which application linked list are not suitable
(*a*) Insertion sort
(*b*) Binary search
(*c*) Radix sort
(*d*) Polynomial manipulation

87. Which of the following statement is false
(*a*) Optimal binary search tree construction can be performed efficiently using dynamic programming
(*b*) Breadth first search cannot be used to find connected components of a graph
(*c*) Given prefix and postfix values of a binary tree, the binary tree cannot be uniquely constructed
(*d*) Depth first search can be used to find the connected components

88. Number of edges in a regular graph of tree d and n vertices is
(*a*) Maximum of n, d
(*b*) n + d
(*c*) nd
(*d*) nd/2

89. A 3-ary tree is the tree in which every internal node has exactly 3 children. Number of leaf nodes in such a tree with 6 internal nodes will be
(*a*) 10
(*b*) 23
(*c*) 17
(*d*) 13

90. Which of the following is not a characteristic of an algorithm
(*a*) Definiteness

(*b*) Finiteness
(*c*) Dividing into multiple tasks
(*d*) Efficiency

91. Space complexity refers to
(*a*) Memory required by an algorithm needs to run to completion
(*b*) Complexities involved in space mission transmission
(*c*) Complexities of a 3D graphics creation
(*d*) None of the above

92. Time complexity refers to
(*a*) Complexities involved in calculation of execution time of a program
(*b*) Amount of time a program needs to run to completion
(*c*) Complexities involved with input time of a program
(*d*) None of the above

93. Which among the following is not an asymptotic notation used to define efficiency of an algorithm
(*a*) Big(O)
(*b*) Omega
(*c*) Small O
(*d*) None of the above

94. Which of the following defines most appropriate Markov algorithm
(*a*) It is used to find efficiency of an algorithm
(*b*) It takes input string x and through a number of steps transforms x string to an output string y
(*c*) It calculates space complexity of an algorithm
(*d*) None of the above

95. Pointer is a
(*a*) It is a reference to a data structure
(*b*) It is used in multimedia devices
(*c*) It is a input device
(*d*) None of the above

96. Data structure can be defined as
(*a*) The collection of data used in a program
(*b*) It is the way of representing data that contains both data item and their relationship
(*c*) It is collection of data and program
(*d*) None of the above

97. Which among the following is not a valid operation on a queue
(*a*) INSERT
(*b*) REMOVE
(*c*) PUSH
(*d*) Both a & b

98. Valid application of stack is
(*a*) Implementing subroutine calls in a computer
(*b*) Recursion
(*c*) Evaluation of arithmetic expression
(*d*) All of the above

99. A dummy header is
(*a*) A head node in the linked list before actual data nodes
(*b*) Header used for dummy operations
(*c*) Header used to indicate starting of stack
(*d*) None of the stack

100. Valid notation for empty Q, full Q are
(*a*) Rear < front, Rear = Array size (N)
(*b*) Rear = front, Rear < Array size (N)
(*c*) Rear > front, Rear = Array size (N)

(*d*) Rear < front, Rear > Array size (N)

101. Postfix expression of (a + b)* (b + d)/f is
(*a*) /* + ab + cdf
(*b*) ab + cd + *f/
(*c*) a + b/c*df
(*d*) None of the above

102. Simulation is a
(*a*) Imitation of the operation of real world process or system over time
(*b*) A software package for real-time applications
(*c*) A hardware designed for performing calculation
(*d*) None of the above

103. The prefix equivalent of (a + b)* (c + d) is
(*a*) ab + cd + *f/
(*b*) /* + ab + cdf
(*c*) + ab + cd + *f/
(*d*) None of the above

104. Priority queue is a
(*a*) Special purpose queue where insertion and deletion is made at both ends
(*b*) A queue in which, items are inserted or removed from any position based on some priority
(*c*) A queue used to stores priority data
(*d*) None of the above

105. Which of the following is not a technique of tree traversal
(*a*) Pre order
(*b*) In order
(*c*) Post order
(*d*) Order

106. A-spanning tree is
(*a*) Undirected tree consisting of only those edges necessary to connect all nodes in original graph
(*b*) Tree containing more than 2 leaves at every node
(*c*) Tree of depth more than n + 1
(*d*) None of the above

107. PERT graph is
(*a*) A graph used to perform PERT calculation
(*b*) Has exactly one source node and one sink node
(*c*) A cycle graph where nodes have essentially multiple edges
(*d*) None of the above

108. A dope vector is
(*a*) A vector that contains the information that will help us to interpret arrays containing actual data item
(*b*) A vector which is used for dope operation
(*c*) A vector that contains the value of elements
(*d*) None of the above

109. The first fit strategy
(*a*) Uses linked list for implementation
(*b*) It finds first block in the free list of size greater than desired size
(*c*) Both a & b
(*d*) None of the above

110. Best-fit strategy
(*a*) Uses doubly linked list for representation
(*b*) Finds block in the free list of size equal to or at least equal to the desired size
(*c*) Both a & b
(*d*) None of the above

111. Searching can be defined as
   (*a*) It is the process of finding a record in a table according to a given key value
   (*b*) It is the operation of arranging the records of table into some sequential order
   (*c*) It is movement of data from secondary to primary storage in large blocks
   (*d*) None of the above
112. A null graph is defined as
   (*a*) A graph having only isolated node
   (*b*) A graph having no node
   (*c*) Graph having no edge
   (*d*) None of the above
113. Forest is
   (*a*) Set of n ≥ 0 joint trees which are connected with a root
   (*b*) Set of n ≥ 0 disjoint trees which are obtained when root is removed
   (*c*) Set of n ≥ 0 disjoint nodes
   (*d*) None of the above
114. In context of tree, a cross arc is defined as
   (*a*) The set of edges that are not included in depth first spanning forest
   (*b*) Natural descent from one adjacent node to its next adjacent node
   (*c*) A cycle in the graph
   (*d*) None of the above
115. An AVL tree is
   (*a*) Binary search tree with property that each node has equal difference between left and right sub tree
   (*b*) A tree having finite member of nodes
   (*c*) A tree having single node
   (*d*) None of the above
116. A symmetric digraph is
   (*a*) A directed graph such that for every edge VW there is a reverse edge WV
   (*b*) A graph with symmetrical node
   (*c*) A graph whose reflection is a similar graph
   (*d*) None of the above
117. A heap is
   (*a*) Collection of waste material
   (*b*) A complete binary tree with property that the value at each node should be as large as the value of its children
   (*c*) A spanning tree of order n
   (*d*) None of the above
118. Which of the following is not a criterion of algorithm analysis
   (*a*) Amount of work done
   (*b*) Amount of space used
   (*c*) Optimality
   (*d*) None of the above
119. The worst-case complexity of algorithm to find max element in array is
   (*a*) W (n)=n-1
   (*b*) W (n)=o
   (*c*) W (n)=n
   (*d*) W (n)=n/2
120. Conditional probability for event s given event t is
   (*a*) Pr (s/t)=Pr (s and t)/Pr (t)
   (*b*) Pr (s/t)=Pr (s)*Pr (t)/Pr (s)
   (*c*) Pr (s/t)=Pr (s)*Pr (t)/Pr (t)
   (*d*) Pr (s/t)=Pr (s or t)/Pr (t)
121. Given $A \Rightarrow B$ and $B \Rightarrow C$ then we can conclude

(*a*) $\dashv A \Rightarrow C$
(*b*) $A \Rightarrow C$
(*c*) $C \Rightarrow B$
(*d*) $C \Rightarrow A$

122. If $B \Rightarrow C$ and $\dashv B \Rightarrow C$ then we can conclude that
(*a*) C
(*b*) ⊣ C
(*c*) B
(*d*) ⊣ B

123. The best case and the worst case time for searching an element using linear search is
(*a*) n, 1
(*b*) 1, n
(*c*) n, n
(*d*) n logn

124. Big O notation is defined for
(*a*) Time and Space complexity
(*b*) Optimality
(*c*) Searching
(*d*) None of the above

125. If s and t are stochastically independent, then
(*a*) Pr (s and t) = Pr (s)*Pr (t)
(*b*) Pr (s and t) = Pr (s)/Pr (t)
(*c*) Pr (s and t) = Pr (s or t)
(*d*) Pr (s and t) = Pr (s)+Pr (t)

126. Some software tools used in developing computer programs are
(*a*) Text editors
(*b*) Compilers and assemblers
(*c*) Operating system and debugging programs
(*d*) None of the above

127. What is the first step in developing any software program
(*a*) System design
(*b*) System study
(*c*) Coding
(*d*) None of the above

128. Examples of O (1) algorithms is case of
(*a*) Printing a character to screen
(*b*) Incrementing a variable
(*c*) Adding two numbers together
(*d*) All of the above

129. What should never be found in top level of top down design?
(*a*) Details
(*b*) Coding
(*c*) Decisions
(*d*) None of the above

130. The structured data types that are built in Pascal are
(*a*) Arrays and records
(*b*) Variant records
(*c*) Sets and files
(*d*) All of the above

131. Evaluate the following Pretix expression + * 2 + / 14251
(*a*) 23
(*b*) 37
(*c*) 24
(*d*) 25

132. Evaluate the following Prefix expression ++ 26 + – 1324
(*a*) 25
(*b*) 12
(*c*) 15
(*d*) 23

133. Which of following can be described as a pointer?
(*a*) Stack
(*b*) List^
(*c*) List^.Info
(*d*) Stack^.Info

134. Which of the following can be described as integer?
(*a*) Stack

(*b*) List^
(*c*) List^.Info
(*d*) Stack^.Info

135. Which of the following can be described as a pointer?
(*a*) Queue
(*b*) Queue.Real
(*c*) Queue.Real^
(*d*) Queue.Font^.Info

136. Which of the following can be described as an array?
(*a*) Stack
(*b*) List^
(*c*) List^.Info
(*d*) Stack^.Info

137. Evaluate the following Prefix expression – * 63 – 41
(*a*) 25
(*b*) 15
(*c*) 12
(*d*) 23

138. Convert the expression in postfix notation ((c * 2) + 1)/(A + 0)
(*a*) (2 * 1 + AB + /)
(*b*) (21 + * AB + /)
(*c*) (21 AB * + + /)
(*d*) None of the above

139. Which of the following can be described as a record?
(*a*) Stack
(*b*) List^
(*c*) List^.Info
(*d*) Stack^.Info

140. Which of the following can be described as a integer?
(*a*) Queue
(*b*) Queue.Real
(*c*) Queue.Real^
(*d*) Queue.Font^.Info

141. Which of following can be described as a record?
(*a*) Queue.Front^.Next^
(*b*) Queue.Front
(*c*) List^
(*d*) Stack

142. Which of the following can be identified as a character?
(*a*) List^.Next
(*b*) List^.Next^
(*c*) Ptr^.Back
(*d*) Ptr^.Info.Name[1]

143. Which of the following can be identified as a character strings.
(*a*) List^.Next
(*b*) List^.Info.Name
(*c*) Ptr^.Info.Name [1]
(*d*) None

144. What data structures would you most likely see in nonrecursive implementation of a recursive algorithm?
(*a*) Link list
(*b*) Queue
(*c*) Stack
(*d*) Trees

145. What is maximum number of nodes in a tree that has N levels? Note that the root is level (zero).
(*a*) 2^{2N}
(*b*) $2^{N+1} - 1$
(*c*) $2^{N} - 1$
(*d*) $2^{N} - 2N$

146. How many binary search tree can be made from three nodes that contain the key values 1, 2 and 3?
(*a*) 30
(*b*) 20
(*c*) 10
(*d*) 15

147. How many ancestors does a node in the nth level of a binary search tree have? (root level = 0)

(*a*) N
(*b*) 2^N
(*c*) $2^N + 1$
(*d*) N + 1

148. The best average behaviour is shown by
(*a*) Quick sort
(*b*) Merge sort
(*c*) Heap sort
(*d*) Insertion sort

149. The average number of comparisons in sequential search is
(*a*) n^2
(*b*) $\frac{n(n-1)}{2}$
(*c*) $\frac{n(n+1)}{2}$
(*d*) $\frac{n+1}{2}$

150. Which data structure is needed to convert infix notations to prefix notations?
(*a*) Stack
(*b*) Queue
(*c*) Tree
(*d*) Graph

151. A link list in which elements can be added or removed at either end but not in the middle, is known as
(*a*) Queue
(*b*) Stack
(*c*) Dequeue
(*d*) Tree

152. A list is ordered from smallest to biggest when a sort is called. Which sort would take shortest time to execute?
(*a*) Heap sort
(*b*) Short bubble
(*c*) Quick sort
(*d*) Selection sort

153. Tell whether the following tree is

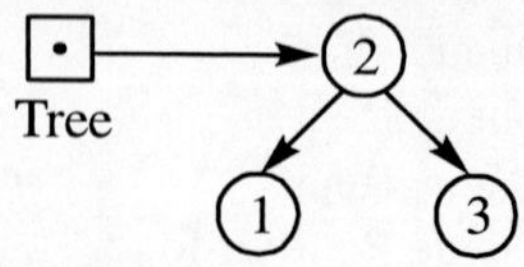

(*a*) Heap
(*b*) Full and complete
(*c*) Heap complete
(*d*) None

154. On a PC, how much memory is available to application software?
(*a*) 1024 KB
(*b*) 760 KB
(*c*) 640 KB
(*d*) 2048 KB

155. In a relational schema, each tuplet is divided into fields called
(*a*) Relations
(*b*) Domains
(*c*) Queries
(*d*) All of the above

156. A command that lets you change one or more fields in record
(*a*) Insert
(*b*) Modify
(*c*) Look-up
(*d*) all of the above

157. Which of the following is not a relational database?
(*a*) dBASE IV
(*b*) 4th dimension
(*c*) Foxpro
(*d*) Reflex

158. One data dictionary software package is called
(*a*) DB/DC dictionary
(*b*) TOTAL

(c) ACCESS
(d) None of the above

159. A scheme describes
(a) Data elements
(b) Records and files
(c) Record relationship
(d) All of the above

160. Data item characteristics that are important in data management include
(a) Punctuation
(b) Language
(c) Spellings
(d) Width

161. The modify operation is likely to be done after.
(a) Delete
(b) Look-up
(c) Insert
(d) All of above

162. A command that lets you change one or more fields in a record is
(a) Insert
(b) Modify
(c) Look-up
(d) All of above

163. Data security threats include
(a) Hardware failure
(b) Privacy invasion
(c) Fradulant manipulation of data
(d) All of the above

164. The index consists of
(a) A list of keys
(b) Pointers to the master list
(c) Both (a) and (b)
(d) All of the above

165. Periodically adding, changing and deleting file records is called file
(a) Updating
(b) Upgrading
(c) Restructuring
(d) Renewing

166. Data items grouped together for storage purposes are called a
(a) Record
(b) Title
(c) List
(d) String

167. Large collections of files are called
(a) Fields
(b) Records
(c) Databases
(d) File system

168. The distinguishable parts of a record are called.
(a) Files
(b) Data
(c) Fields
(d) Database

169. Large collections of files are called
(a) Fields
(b) Records
(c) Databases
(d) File system

170. A number of related records that are treated as a single unit is
(a) File
(b) Field
(c) Data
(d) Batch

171. The designator of a form includes
(a) Field designators
(b) Prompts
(c) Data
(d) both a and b

172. A form can be used to
(a) Modify records
(b) Delete records
(c) Format printed output
(d) All of the above

173. Embedded pointer provide
(*a*) A secondary access part
(*b*) A physical record key
(*c*) An inverted index
(*d*) All of the above

174. A list in alphabetical order
(*a*) Is in desending order
(*b*) Is in Ascending order
(*c*) Is the result of sort operation
(*d*) Both (b) and (c)

175. Versatile report generators can provide
(*a*) Columnar operation
(*b*) Subtotals
(*c*) Calculation
(*d*) All of above

176. The highest level in the hierarchy of data organization is called
(*a*) Data bank
(*b*) Database
(*c*) Data file
(*d*) Data record

177. Internal auditors should review data system design before they are
(*a*) Developed
(*b*) Implemented
(*c*) Modified
(*d*) All of the above

178. An operation that will increase the length of a list is
(*a*) Insert
(*b*) Look-up
(*c*) Modify
(*d*) All of the above

179. If a numeric field has a width of 5.2, then the value of field could be
(*a*) 23.10
(*b*) 121.8
(*c*) 143.87
(*d*) Both (a) and b)

180. The key to a cost-effective data input operation is
(*a*) OCR equipment
(*b*) Validity checks
(*c*) Validation
(*d*) Employee motivation

181. The logical data structure with one to many relationship is a
(*a*) Network
(*b*) Tree
(*c*) Chain
(*d*) Relational

182. Which of the following is not a logical data-base structure?
(*a*) Tree
(*b*) Relational
(*c*) Network
(*d*) Chain

183. In the SQL, which of the following is not a data definition language commands?
(*a*) RENAME
(*b*) REVOKE
(*c*) GRANT
(*d*) UPDATE

184. In SQL, which of the following is not a data manipuation language commands?
(*a*) DELETE
(*b*) SELECT
(*c*) UPDATE
(*d*) CREATE

185. In SQL, which command is used to change data in table?
(*a*) UPDATE
(*b*) INSERT
(*c*) BROWSE
(*d*) APPEND

186. In SQL, which command is used to add new rows to a table?
(*a*) ADD ROW

(*b*) INSERT
(*c*) APPEND
(*d*) ALTER TABLE

187. In SQL, which command is used to remove rows from table
(*a*) DELETE
(*b*) REMOVE
(*c*) TRUNCATE
(*d*) Both (a) and (c)

188. Which command is used to remove a table from database in SQL?
(*a*) DELETE
(*b*) DROP
(*c*) ERASE
(*d*) UNATTACH

189. In SQL, the .... command is used to recompile a view
(*a*) COMPILE
(*b*) DEFINE
(*c*) CREATE
(*d*) AITER

190. In SQL, which command is used to recompile a stored function?
(*a*) SET
(*b*) ALTER
(*c*) SET STORED
(*d*) All

191. The data dictionary tells the DBMS
(*a*) What files are in database
(*b*) What attribute are possessed by data
(*c*) What these file contain
(*d*) All of the above

192. Which of the following is a type of DBMS software?
(*a*) DML
(*b*) Query language
(*c*) Utilities
(*d*) Report writer

193. A form can be used to
(*a*) Modify records
(*b*) Delete records
(*c*) Format printed output
(*d*) All of the above

194. A feasibility study should focus on
(*a*) Technical feasibility
(*b*) Economic feasibility
(*c*) Operational feasibility
(*d*) All of the above

195. An example of a hierarchial data structure is
(*a*) Array
(*b*) Link list
(*c*) Tree
(*d*) Ring

196. The system study project included
(*a*) System analysis
(*b*) System design
(*c*) Implementation
(*d*) Both (a) and (b)

197. Data dictionary contains detail of
(*a*) Data structure
(*b*) Data flows
(*c*) Data stores
(*d*) All of the above

198. What type of software is most useful in financial planning and calculation?
(*a*) Graphics
(*b*) Communication
(*c*) Database
(*d*) Spread sheet

199. A feasibility documents should contain all of the following except
(*a*) Project name
(*b*) Problem descriptions
(*c*) Feasible alternative
(*d*) data flow diagrams

200. The consert method of conversion is
    (*a*) Direct
    (*b*) Parallel
    (*c*) Phased
    (*d*) Pilot

201. Structured design produces computer programs that are
    (*a*) easily maintained
    (*b*) easily understood
    (*c*) both (a) and (b)
    (*d*) None of the above

202. The primary tool used in structured design is a
    (*a*) Structure chart
    (*b*) Data flow diagram
    (*c*) Program flow chart
    (*d*) Module

203. The conditions immediately outside a system is called
    (*a*) Boundary
    (*b*) Interface
    (*c*) Environment
    (*d*) Protocols

204. A turnkey package includes
    (*a*) Software
    (*b*) Hardware
    (*c*) Firm ware
    (*d*) All of the above

205. A word processor designed for programmers is called
    (*a*) Formatter
    (*b*) Compiler
    (*c*) Editor
    (*d*) Debugger

206. A graphic representation of information system is called
    (*a*) Flow chart
    (*b*) Pietogram
    (*c*) Histogram
    (*d*) DFD

207. The DFD shows
    (*a*) The flow of data
    (*b*) The areas where they are stored
    (*c*) The processes
    (*d*) All of the above

208. Which of the following is not a symbol of DFD:
    (*a*) Square
    (*b*) Circle
    (*c*) Bubble
    (*d*) Triangle

209. A group of related fields, is known as
    (*a*) Tuple
    (*b*) Schema
    (*c*) Records
    (*d*) File

210. An example of hier archical data structure is
    (*a*) Array
    (*b*) Link list
    (*c*) Tree
    (*d*) All of above

211. Coding and testing are done in which manner.
    (*a*) Adhoc
    (*b*) Bottom up
    (*c*) Top down
    (*d*) Cross sectional

212. Which of the following is a function of the 'process step' of data processing?
    (*a*) Protect
    (*b*) Index
    (*c*) Retrieval
    (*d*) Update

213. Which of the following file types has the least file
    (*a*) Master
    (*b*) Program

(*c*) Transaction
(*d*) Work

214. Which of the following is the characterstics of a system?
(*a*) Organisation
(*b*) Interaction
(*c*) Inter dependence
(*d*) All of the above

215. Which of the following is not a characteristics of a system
(*a*) Operates for some purpose
(*b*) Has homogeneous components
(*c*) Has interacting components
(*d*) Operates within boundary

216. Which of the following is not a part of DFD?
(*a*) Disk storage
(*b*) Arrow
(*c*) Data store
(*d*) Process represented by a bubble circle

217. Which of the following decides which system development process work on the project first?
(*a*) Data diagram
(*b*) Developing Project dictionary
(*c*) Systems flow chart
(*d*) Meeting of screening committee

218. A decision table facilitates conditions related to
(*a*) Actions
(*b*) Programs
(*c*) Tables
(*d*) Operation

219. Mistakes made in the system analysis stage show up in
(*a*) Implementation
(*b*) System design
(*c*) System development
(*d*) All of the above

220. A common reason for changing a information system is
(*a*) New requirements
(*b*) New technology
(*c*) Problems in the existing system
(*d*) All of the above

221. Procedure development occurs within the
(*a*) Structured design phase
(*b*) Conversion phase
(*c*) Maintenance phase
(*d*) System building phase

ANSWERS

1. (*c*)	2. (*a*)	3. (*a*)	4. (*b*)	5. (*c*)	6. (*c*)	7. (*a*)
8. (*a*)	9. (*b*)	10. (*c*)	11. (*a*)	12. (*c*)	13. (*c*)	14. (*c*)
15. (*c*)	16. (*d*)	17. (*b*)	18. (*d*)	19. (*a*)	20. (*a*)	21. (*b*)
22. (*d*)	23. (*c*)	24. (*c*)	25. (*c*)	26. (*a*)	27. (*b*)	28. (*a*)
29. (*d*)	30. (*b*)	31. (*a*)	32. (*c*)	33. (*b*)	34. (*a*)	35. (*a*)
36. (*c*)	37. (*c*)	38. (*d*)	39. (*d*)	40. (*a*)	41. (*d*)	42. (*c*)
43. (*a*)	44. (*c*)	45. (*b*)	46. (*c*)	47. (*b*)	48. (*c*)	49. (*a*)
50. (*c*)	51. (*b*)	52. (*c*)	53. (*d*)	54. (*b*)	55. (*c*)	56. (*d*)
57. (*a*)	58. (*a*)	59. (*c*)	60. (*d*)	61. (*d*)	62. (*c*)	63. (*b*)
64. (*d*)	65. (*c*)	66. (*a*)	67. (*a*)	68. (*b*)	69. (*c*)	70. (*b*)

71. (*c*) 72. (*c*) 73. (*c*) 74. (*b*) 75. (*d*) 76. (*d*) 77. (*a*)
78. (*b*) 79. (*a*) 80. (*a*) 81. (*b*) 82. (*b*) 83. (*a*) 84. (*d*)
85. (*c*) 86. (*b*) 87. (*c*) 88. (*a*) 89. (*d*) 90. (*c*) 91. (*c*)
92. (*b*) 93. (*d*) 94. (*b*) 95. (*a*) 96. (*b*) 97. (*c*) 98. (*d*)
99. (*a*) 100. (*a*) 101. (*b*) 102. (*a*) 103. (*b*) 104. (*b*) 105. (*d*)
106. (*a*) 107. (*b*) 108. (*a*) 109. (*c*) 110. (*c*) 111. (*a*) 112. (*a*)
113. (*b*) 114. (*a*) 115. (*a*) 116. (*a*) 117. (*b*) 118. (*d*) 119. (*a*)
120. (*a*) 121. (*b*) 122. (*c*) 123. (*b*) 124. (*a*) 125. (*d*) 126. (*a*)
127. (*a*) 128. (*a*) 129. (*b*) 130. (*a*) 131. (*a*) 132. (*a*) 133. (*b*)
134. (*a*) 135. (*b*) 136. (*b*) 137. (*a*) 138. (*a*) 139. (*a*) 140. (*c*)
141. (*d*) 142. (*b*) 143. (*a*) 144. (*a*) 145. (*b*) 146. (*a*) 147. (*a*)
148. (*a*) 149. (*a*) 150. (*a*) 151. (*c*) 152. (*c*) 153. (*b*) 154. (*b*)
155. (*d*) 156. (*a*) 157. (*d*) 158. (*d*) 159. (*a*) 160. (*b*) 161. (*d*)
162. (*c*) 163. (*b*) 164. (*a*) 165. (*d*) 166. (*b*) 167. (*b*) 168. (*c*)
169. (*a*) 170. (*d*) 171. (*c*) 172. (*b*) 173. (*b*) 174. (*d*) 175. (*a*)
176. (*d*) 177. (*b*) 178. (*a*) 179. (*a*) 180. (*d*) 181. (*b*) 182. (*a*)
183. (*b*) 184. (*a*) 185. (*c*) 186. (*a*) 187. (*c*) 188. (*c*) 189. (*a*)
190. (*a*) 191. (*a*) 192. (*a*) 193. (*b*) 194. (*c*) 195. (*d*) 196. (*c*)
197. (*d*) 198. (*b*) 199. (*b*) 200. (*d*) 201. (*b*) 202. (*c*) 203. (*b*)
204. (*a*) 205. (*c*) 206. (*c*) 207. (*b*) 208. (*a*) 209. (*b*) 210. (*c*)
211. (*c*) 212. (*b*) 213. (*a*) 214. (*d*) 215. (*d*) 216. (*c*) 217. (*c*)
218. (*b*) 219. (*a*) 220. (*b*) 221. (*b*)

5

Computer Organisation

1. A magnetic disk storage device in which data is stored on a cylindrical drum is called.
(*a*) Punch card
(*b*) Magnetic disk
(*c*) Magnetic tape
(*d*) Drum

2. The tracks on a disk which can be accessed without repositioning of read write head is.
(*a*) Surface
(*b*) Cylinder
(*c*) Cluster
(*d*) All of the above

3. Which of the following technique is used for planning and controlling the time schedule for projects.
(*a*) CPA
(*b*) CPM
(*c*) PERT
(*d*) CP/M

4. A path joining two devices in which the data and control signal can flow is called
(*a*) Channel
(*b*) Signaling
(*c*) Modulation
(*d*) De modulation

5. Temporary storage used to compensate for a difference in the speed of data flow is.
(*a*) Main memory
(*b*) Buffer
(*c*) Protocol
(*d*) RAM

6. A prescribed set of well defined rules or processes for the solution of a problem in a series of steps is.
(*a*) Flow chart
(*b*) Program
(*c*) Algorithm
(*d*) System analysis

7. The least –ve value that a 16 bit 2's complement number can take is.
(*a*) -2^{14}
(*b*) -2^{15}
(*c*) -2^{16}
(*d*) None of the above

8. A toggle flip flop can be constructed using JK flip flop by connecting.
(*a*) Toggle input to J and K
(*b*) Toggle input to J and inverted form of toggle input to K
(*c*) Inverted form of toggle input to K
(*d*) None of the above

9. Minimum hardware required to construct a 3 × 8 decoder is using.
(*a*) Two 2 × 4 decoders
(*b*) Two 2 × 4 decoder and one 1 × 2 decoder
(*c*) One 2 × 4 decoder
(*d*) Depends upon the style of manufacturing

10. Simplified form of expression AB + ABC is.
    (*a*) AB
    (*b*) A(B + C)
    (*c*) A(B+A)
    (*d*) None of the above

11. The sum of two hexadecimal numbers '23D' and '9AA' gives the hexadecimal number.
    (*a*) AF7
    (*b*) BF6
    (*c*) BE7
    (*d*) BE5

12. How many memory locations are required to store instruction LXI H, 0800H in an assembly language.
    (*a*) 1
    (*b*) 2
    (*c*) 3
    (*d*) 4

13. If we want to derive another tautology then following replacements need to be applied.
    (*a*) 0 and 1
    (*b*) AND and OR
    (*c*) 0 and 1 and AND and OR
    (*d*) It is not possible to derive

14. If X is a Boolean variable then which of the following is true.
    (*a*) 0*X = X
    (*b*) 1 + X = X
    (*c*) X + X = X
    (*d*) $X + X^1 = 0$

15. If X,Y,Z are Boolean variable then.
    (*a*) X* X = 1
    (*b*) X(Y + Z) = (X + Y)(X + Z)
    (*c*) X + XZ = X
    (*d*) X + Y = Y + X

16. Which of the following code uses 7 bits to represent a character.
    (*a*) EBCDIC
    (*b*) BCD
    (*c*) GRAY
    (*d*) ASCII

17. Which of the following are not weighted code.
    (*a*) Roman number system
    (*b*) Decimal number system
    (*c*) Binary number system
    (*d*) Excess 3 code

18. Minimum time delay between initiation of two independent memory is called.
    (*a*) Acess time
    (*b*) Cycle time
    (*c*) Transfer time
    (*d*) Latency time

19. If X, Y, Z are three Boolean varibles then X (Y + Z) equals (X + Y) (Y + Z) if X, Y, Z take the values
    (*a*) 1, 0, 0
    (*b*) 0, 1, 0
    (*c*) 1, 1, 0
    (*d*) 0, 1, 1

20. Program counter is a.
    (*a*) Cell in ROM
    (*b*) Register
    (*c*) Buffer
    (*d*) None of the above

21. If $(123)_5 = (X3)_7$ the number of possible value of X is.
    (*a*) 4
    (*b*) 1
    (*c*) 3
    (*d*) 5

22. Speed mismatch between CPU and memory access is reduced by.
    (*a*) Reducing size of memory
    (*b*) Memory interleaving
    (*c*) Cache memory

(*d*) None of the above

23. Which of the following does not need extra hardware for DRAM refreshing.
(*a*) 8085
(*b*) Motorola 6800
(*c*) Z-80
(*d*) None of the above

24. Which of the following is not an advantage of MOS devices over bipolar devices.
(*a*) Easy to fabricate
(*b*) It allows higher bit densities
(*c*) Its higher impedance
(*d*) Its operational speed

25. Boolean expression X + X'Y equals.
(*a*) X + Y
(*b*) X + XY
(*c*) Y + YX
(*d*) X'Y + Y'

26. (X + Y) + Z = X + (Y + Z) means.
(*a*) Operator OR is distributive
(*b*) Operator OR is associative
(*c*) Operator AND is associative
(*d*) None of the above

27. Which of the following is not a normal register.
(*a*) Accumulator
(*b*) Stack pointer
(*c*) Program counter
(*d*) Buffer

28. Registers are used for.
(*a*) Temporary storage
(*b*) Storing the instruction
(*c*) Permanent storage
(*d*) None of the above

29. Any truth table.
(*a*) Can be represented by K map
(*b*) Can be represented by sum of product of Boolean expression
(*c*) Can be represented by product of sum of Boolean function
(*d*) All of the above

30. Choose correct statement.
(*a*) Bus is a group of information carrying wires
(*b*) Bus can carry data or address
(*c*) A bus can be shared by more than one device
(*d*) All of the above

31. Bipolar devices are desirable in the fabrication of which of the following components.
(*a*) Main memory
(*b*) Cache memory
(*c*) All of the above
(*d*) None of the above

32. The programmable interval timer is.
(*a*) 8251
(*b*) 8250
(*c*) 8253
(*d*) 8275

33. Sequence of operation in fetch operation is.
(*a*) PC → MAR→ Memory → MDR → IR
(*b*) PC → Memory → MDR → IR
(*c*) PC → Memory → IR
(*d*) PC → MAR → Memory → IR

34. Which of the following is universal gate.
(*a*) OR gate
(*b*) NAND and NOR
(*c*) AND gate
(*d*) AND and OR

35. The Boolean expression AB + AB' + A'C + AC is independent of Boolean variable.

(*a*) A
(*b*) B
(*c*) C
(*d*) None of the above

36. Minimum number of gate required to implement the Boolean expression.
AB + AB' + A'C is
(*a*) 1 AND gate and 1 OR gate
(*b*) 2 NAND gate
(*c*) 3 AND gate 2 OR gate
(*d*) None of the above

37. Locality of reference concept will fail in which of the following cases.
(*a*) Many conditional jumps
(*b*) Many unconditional jumps
(*c*) Many operands
(*d*) None of the above

38. Binary equivalent of decimal number 2.35 is.
(*a*) 11.0110
(*b*) 10.0101
(*c*) 00.0101
(*d*) None of the above

39. Boolean expression (A + C) (AB' + AC) (A'C' + B") can be simplified to.
(*a*) AB
(*b*) AB + A'C
(*c*) A'B + BC
(*d*) AB + BC

40. A byte addressable computer has a memory capacity of m bytes and can perform 2^n operations. An instruction involving 3 operands and one operator needs a maximum of.
(*a*) 3 m bits
(*b*) 3m + n bits
(*c*) m + n bits
(*d*) None of the above

41. A computer having m byte memory, which can perform 2^n operation. It is word accessible, then an instruction involving 3 operands and 1 operator needs a maximum of.
(*a*) 3m bits
(*b*) 3m + n bits
(*c*) m + n bits
(*d*) None of the above

42. Number of columns in a state table for a sequential circuit with m flip flop and 'n' input is.
(*a*) m + n
(*b*) m + 2n
(*c*) 2m + n
(*d*) 2m + 2n

43. The length of a binary n bit string, in ternary number system will be.
(*a*) 3 + n
(*b*) 2n/3
(*c*) n $\log_3 3$
(*d*) n $\log_2 2$

44. If simplification of expression A'BE + BCDE + BC'D'E' + A'B'DE' + B'C'DE' is BE + B'DE' then don't care conditions are.
(*a*) ABCDE + AB'CDE'
(*b*) ABCD + AB'CDE' + ABCD'E
(*c*) ABC'DE + AB'CDE' + ABCD'E
(*d*) None of the above

45. Decimal equivalent of binary number 1101.011 is.
(*a*) 13.375
(*b*) 15.25
(*c*) 5.5
(*d*) None of the above

46. Which of the following does not have 8 data line.

(*a*) 8086
(*b*) 8085
(*c*) 8088
(*d*) 8080

47. Which of the following logic families supports high-speed operation.
(*a*) TTL
(*b*) ECL
(*c*) MOS
(*d*) CMOS

48. Following is a circuit of.

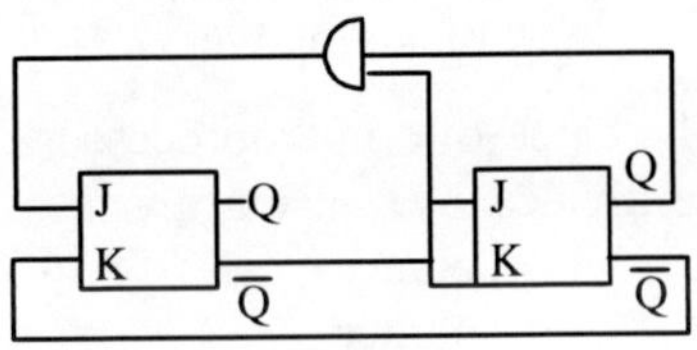

(*a*) Mod 3 counter
(*b*) Mod 2 counter
(*c*) Mod 5 counter
(*d*) None of the above

49. Which of the following format can not represent –ve number.
(*a*) Signed magnitude form
(*b*) 1's complement form
(*c*) 2's complement form
(*d*) None of the above

50. In instruction ADD X, Y the addressing mode is.
(*a*) Absolute
(*b*) Immediate
(*c*) Indirect
(*d*) Index

51. One possible replacement of the following circuit is.

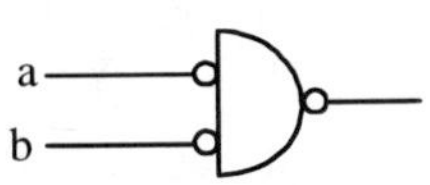

(*a*) OR gate
(*b*) XOR gate
(*c*) NOR gate
(*d*) AND gate

52. $(1100\ 01100101)_2$ in Hexadecimal number system will be.
(*a*) $(C65)_{16}$
(*b*) $(ABC)_{16}$
(*c*) $(201)_{16}$
(*d*) None of the above

53. The XOR operator is.
(*a*) Only commutative
(*b*) Only associative
(*c*) Only distributive
(*d*) Commutative and distributive

54. Use of Bubble memories are preferred over floppy disks.
(*a*) Because of high transfer rate
(*b*) Less cost/bit storage
(*c*) Power consumption is less
(*d*) None of the above

55. Addressing capacity of 8086/88 is.
(*a*) 64 KB
(*b*) 512 KB
(*c*) 2 MB
(*d*) 1 MB

56. Speed of computer is measured in.
(*a*) FLOPS
(*b*) BAUD
(*c*) SYPS FLOPS
(*d*) None of the above

57. If A + B = C is true, then.
(*a*) A + B = C
(*b*) B + C = A
(*c*) A + B + C = 0
(*d*) None of the above

58. If $(11\ X\ 1Y)_8 = (12C\ 9)_{16}$, Then value X and Y is.
(*a*) 5, 1
(*b*) 5, 7
(*c*) 7, 5
(*d*) None of the above

59. The total number of possible Boolean function involving n Boolean variable is.
    (*a*) n^2
    (*b*) n^n
    (*c*) 2^n
    (*d*) None of the above

60. Which of the following architecture is not suitable for realizing SIMD.
    (*a*) Vector processor
    (*b*) Array processor
    (*c*) Von Neumann
    (*d*) All of the above

61. How many input multiplexers are required to construct a 2^{10} input multiplexes.
    (*a*) 1023
    (*b*) 31
    (*c*) 10
    (*d*) 127

62. In the equation $(X567)_8 + (2YX5)_8 = (71YX)_8$, the value of X and Y are.
    (*a*) 4,3
    (*b*) 3,3
    (*c*) 4,4
    (*d*) 4,5

63. In BCD representation each digit is represented by.
    (*a*) 2 bits
    (*b*) 4 bits
    (*c*) Number of bits depends upon the number
    (*d*) None of the above

64. The number of instructions required for adding n number and storing the result in memory using only one address instruction is.
    (*a*) n
    (*b*) n-1
    (*c*) n+1
    (*d*) Independent of n

65. Output of corresponding circuit will be.

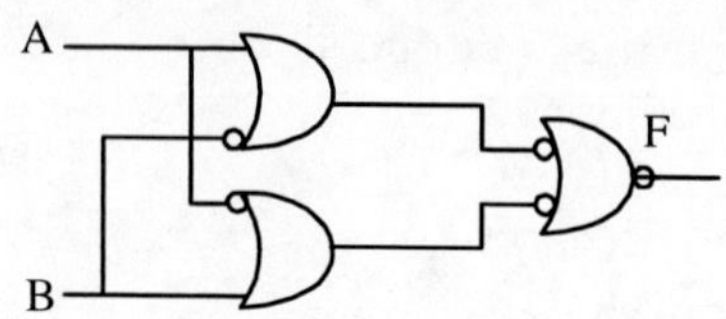

    (*a*) Independent of a
    (*b*) Is a tautology
    (*c*) Is an inconsistency
    (*d*) None of the above

66. The clock of a microprocessor can be divided by 5 using a.
    (*a*) 3 bit counter
    (*b*) 5 bit counter
    (*c*) Mod 5 counter
    (*d*) Mod 3 counter

67. The minimal cover for maximal compatibility classes {ae, acd, ad, bd} is.
    (*a*) ae, acd, bd
    (*b*) ae, ad, bd
    (*c*) ae, acd, ad
    (*d*) acd, ad, bd

68. Values of a,x,y if 47 × 80 is the 10's complement of Ya Yx 0 are.
    (*a*) 4, 3, 2
    (*b*) 5, 4, 4
    (*c*) 3, 4, 5
    (*d*) 2, 4, 5

69. ALE pin is used in 8085 because.
    (*a*) It has I/O mapped I/O
    (*b*) It has interrupt line
    (*c*) It has multiplexed bus
    (*d*) None of the above

70. If a memory access takes 20 n sec with cache and 110 n sec without it, then the hit ratio (cache access time is 10 n sec) is.

(*a*) 93%
(*b*) 90%
(*c*) 87%
(*d*) None of the above

71. In which of the following instruction, bus idle situation occurs.
(*a*) EI
(*b*) DADrp
(*c*) ADD
(*d*) None of the above

72. Minimum number of operands in any instruction is.
(*a*) 2 operands
(*b*) 1 operand
(*c*) 3 operands
(*d*) None of the above

73. Given the fact that the following logic circuit is a tautology. The logic gate in A would be.

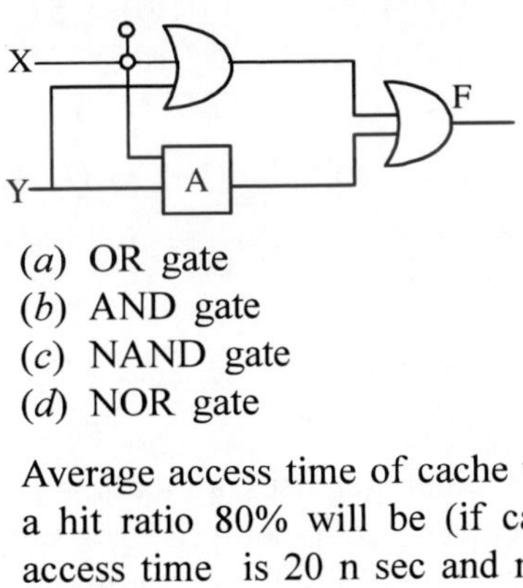

(*a*) OR gate
(*b*) AND gate
(*c*) NAND gate
(*d*) NOR gate

74. Average access time of cache with a hit ratio 80% will be (if cache access time is 20 n sec and main memory access time is 120 n sec).
(*a*) 20 ns
(*b*) 120 ns
(*c*) 40 ns
(*d*) 50 ns

75. In case the code is position dependent which addressing mode is most suitable.
(*a*) Direct mode
(*b*) Indirect mode
(*c*) Relative mode
(*d*) Indexed mode

76. In 2's complement representation form, which addition rule is correct.
(*a*) Add sign bit and discard carry, if any
(*b*) Add sign bit and add carry, if any
(*c*) Don't add sign bit and discard carry, if any
(*d*) Don't add sign bit and add carry, if any

77. The jump address corresponding to INTR is.
(*a*) 0024 H
(*b*) Call address instruction issued by I/O device
(*c*) 0000H
(*d*) None of the above

78. Advantage of a single bus over the multi bus is the.
(*a*) Low cost
(*b*) Flexible in attaching peripheral device
(*c*) High operating speed
(*d*) All of the above

79. Character equivalent of ASCII character 56 is.
(*a*) V
(*b*) 8
(*c*) 9
(*d*) None of the above

80. Parallel printer uses.
(*a*) RS 232
(*b*) Modem
(*c*) Hand shake mode
(*d*) Synchronous data transfer mode

81. A micro programmed control unit.
(*a*) Is faster than hard wired control unit
(*b*) Facilitaties easy implementation of new instructions
(*c*) Is useful when very small programs are to be run
(*d*) Usually refers to the control unit of a microprocessor

82. A peculiar feature of RISC machine is.
(*a*) Instruction taking multiple cycles
(*b*) Highly pipelined
(*c*) Instruction interpreted by micro program
(*d*) Multiple register sets

83. Which of the following logical operation can be used in staircase switch.
(*a*) OR
(*b*) NOR
(*c*) EX-OR
(*d*) EX-NOR

84. Component of a floating point number is represented in excess-N code so that
(*a*) The dynamic range is large
(*b*) The preset is high
(*c*) The smallest number is represented by all zeros
(*d*) Overflow is avoided

85. What action does CPU takes when interrupt comes.
(*a*) It halts for a predetermined time
(*b*) Hands over control over address bus and data bus to the interrupting devices
(*c*) Branches off to the interrupt service routine
(*d*) None of the above

86. In serial communication an extra clock is needed.
(*a*) To synchronize the devices
(*b*) For programmed baud rate control
(*c*) To make efficient use of RS-232
(*d*) None of the above

87. One disadvantage of 2's complement notation is.
(*a*) More number of bits in code
(*b*) Different representation for +0 and –0
(*c*) Hardware implementation is difficult
(*d*) None of the above

88. Meaning of SUB 5(R0),*6(R1) is.
(*a*) (((R1) + 6)) – 5*(R0))
(*b*) (((R1) + 6)) – ((R0) + 5)
(*c*) ((R1) + 6) – (5*(R0))
(*d*) ((R1) + 4) – (R0 + 4))

89. Binary equivalent of gray code 11100 is.
(*a*) 10111
(*b*) 00111
(*c*) 01011
(*d*) 10101

90. A computer uses a floating point representation comprising a signed magnitude fractional mantissa and an excess 16 base 8 compound. What decimal number is represented by a floating point number whose exponent is 10011 and mantissa 101000 and sign bit set.
(*a*) + 62500
(*b*) – 20000
(*c*) – 320
(*d*) – 0.00122

91. Minimum number of 2 input NAND gate required to implements function F = (A' + B') (C + D) will be
(*a*) 3
(*b*) 4
(*c*) 5
(*d*) 6

92. Which of the following is the minimum error code.
(*a*) Octal code
(*b*) Binary code
(*c*) Gray code
(*d*) Excess three code

93. A certain machine uses expanding opcode. It has 16 bit instructions and 6 bit addresses. It supports one address and two address, instruction only. If there are two n address instructions, the maximum number of one address instruction is.
(*a*) $2^{16} - n$
(*b*) $2^{10} - n$
(*c*) $(2^4 - n)2^6$
(*d*) 2^{10}

94. In a 2400 bps line how many character per sec can be transmitted, if every character is represented by 8 bit code.
(*a*) 240
(*b*) 360
(*c*) 2400
(*d*) None of the above

95. The Boolean expression A + BC equals.
(*a*) (A' + B')(A' + C)
(*b*) (A + B)(A + C)
(*c*) (A + B)(A' + C)
(*d*) None of the above

96. In a ripple counter using edge triggered JK flip flop, the pulse input is applied to.
(*a*) Clock input of all flip flop
(*b*) Clock input of one flip flop
(*c*) J and K input of one flip flop
(*d*) J and K input of all flip flop

97. In the edge triggered flip flop a low J and low K produces.
(*a*) High state
(*b*) Low state
(*c*) Toggle state
(*d*) No change

98. A component level programming in computer can be called.
(*a*) Microprogramming
(*b*) System programming
(*c*) Assembly language programming
(*d*) Machine language programming

99. An assembler that runs on one m/c but produces m/c code for another m/c is called.
(*a*) Simulator
(*b*) Emulator
(*c*) Cross assembler
(*d*) Decoder

100. Which of the following is not typically found in the status register of a microprocessor.
(*a*) Overflow
(*b*) Zero result
(*c*) Negative result
(*d*) None of the above

101. The output of following circuit will be.

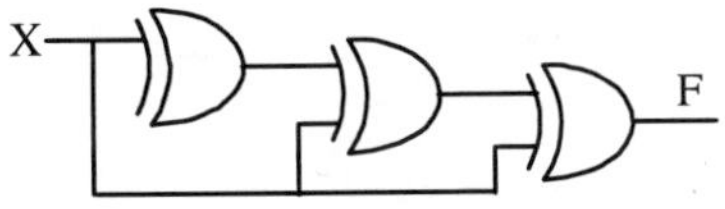

(*a*) 1

(*b*) 0
(*c*) X
(*d*) X[1]

102. Digital computer normally do not use floating point hardware because.
(*a*) It is costly
(*b*) It is slower than software
(*c*) Floating point addition can not be performed by hardware
(*d*) None of the above

103. n flip flops can divide the clock frequency by a factor of.
(*a*) n^2
(*b*) n
(*c*) 2^n
(*d*) log (n)

104. A toggle operation can not be performed using a single.
(*a*) NOR gate
(*b*) AND gate
(*c*) NAND gate
(*d*) XOR gate

105. Micro program is.
(*a*) Name of source program in micro computer
(*b*) The set of instructions indicating primitive operations in a system
(*c*) Primitive form of macros used in assembly language programming
(*d*) None of the above

106. If number X has binary representation $a_n a_{n-1} - a_1 a_0$ then X is divisible by 3 if.
(*a*) Number of 1's is divisible by 3
(*b*) Number of 1's is divisible by 3, but not by 9
(*c*) Number of zeros is divisible by 3
(*d*) The difference of alternate sum i.e. $(a_1 + a_0 \ldots)$, $(a_1 + a_2)$ ..... is divisible by 3

107. FFFF will be last memory location in the memory of size.
(*a*) 1 K
(*b*) 16 K
(*c*) 32 K
(*d*) 64 K

108. Suppose the largest n bit binary number requires 'd' digits in decimal representation, which of the following is correct.
(*a*) $d = 2^n$
(*b*) $n = 2^d$
(*c*) $d < n \log 10^2$
(*d*) $d > n \log 10^2$

109. A computer uses 8 digit mantissa and 2 digit exponent, if a = 0.052 and b = 28E + 11 then b + a – b will.
(*a*) Result in an overflow error
(*b*) Result in an underflow error
(*c*) be 0
(*d*) be 5.28E + 11

110. A computer with 32 bit wide data bus uses 4Kx8 static RAM memory chips. The smallest memory size of this computer is.
(*a*) 32kb
(*b*) 16kb
(*c*) 8kb
(*d*) 24kb

111. An index register in a digital computer is used for.
(*a*) Pointing to the stack address
(*b*) Indirect addressing
(*c*) Keeping track of number of time a loop is executed
(*d*) Address modification

112. A chip having 150 gates will be classified as.
(*a*) SSI
(*b*) MSI
(*c*) LSI
(*d*) VLSI

113. Following code.
a = a + b
b = a + b
c = b + a
(*a*) Swaps a and b
(*b*) Retains the values of a and b
(*c*) Complements the value of a and b
(*d*) None of the above

114. Which memory is volatile.
(*a*) Bubble memory
(*b*) RAM
(*c*) ROM
(*d*) Magnetic disk

115. Pseudo instructions are.
(*a*) Assembler directive
(*b*) Instructions in any program that have no corresponding m/c code instruction
(*c*) Instructions in any program whose presence or absence will not change the output for any input
(e) None of the above

116. Cost of storing a bit is minimum in.
(*a*) Cache
(*b*) RAM
(*c*) Magnetic tape
(*d*) None of the above

117. Introducing parity bit for error detecting does not imply.
(*a*) Increase in the length of the code
(*b*) Increase in the hardware of the system
(*c*) Automatic error detection
(*d*) Odd number of error detection

118. Flip flops can be used for.
(*a*) A counting
(*b*) Scaling
(*c*) Rectification
(*d*) Demodulation

119. How many flip flop circuits are needed to divide by 16.
(*a*) 2
(*b*) 4
(*c*) 8
(*d*) 16

120. Binary equivalent of 78_{10} is.
(*a*) 1100110
(*b*) 1001111
(*c*) 1001100
(*d*) 1110001

121. Binary equivalent of $(ABC)_{16}$ is.
(*a*) 111100001010
(*b*) 101010111100
(*c*) 110110111110
(*d*) None of the above

122. Binary equivalent of $(F9)_{16}$ is.
(*a*) 01001001
(*b*) 11111001
(*c*) 101010101
(*d*) None of the above

123. Binary equivalent of 89_{10} is.
(*a*) 1011011
(*b*) 1100111
(*c*) 10001001
(*d*) 10011000

124. Octal equivalent of 13_{10} is.
(*a*) 15_8
(*b*) 17_8
(*c*) 13_8
(*d*) 11_8

125. Conversion of decimal number 28_{10} to it's octal equivalent is.

(*a*) 32_8
(*b*) 40_8
(*c*) 34_8
(*d*) 36_8

126. The octal equivalent of 3137_{10} is.
(*a*) 6000
(*b*) 6001
(*c*) 6101
(*d*) 6600

127. The octal equivalent of binary number 1100011 is.
(*a*) 101
(*b*) 120
(*c*) 119
(*d*) None of the above

128. The hexadecimal equivalent of binary number 110011 is.
(*a*) 63
(*b*) 59
(*c*) c3
(*d*) None of the above

129. The hexadecimal equivalent of 11001 is.
(*a*) 25
(*b*) 35
(*c*) 49
(*d*) 50

130. The hexadacimal equivalent of 15 is.
(*a*) 23
(*b*) 0F
(*c*) 49
(*d*) 50

131. The decimal equivalent of 1100011 is.
(*a*) 99
(*b*) 93
(*c*) 97
(*d*) None of the above

132. The decimal equivalent of 1001010 is.
(*a*) 74
(*b*) 97
(*c*) 72
(*d*) None of the above

133. The decimal equivalent of binary number 101101 is.
(*a*) 45
(*b*) 50
(*c*) 70
(*d*) None of the above

134. The binary equivalent of octal number 47 is.
(*a*) 110011
(*b*) 100111
(*c*) 110011
(*d*) 1111011

135. The binary equivalent of octal number 60 is.
(*a*) 110000
(*b*) 100111
(*c*) 1111011
(*d*) None of the above

136. The binary equivalent of octal number 73_8 is.
(*a*) 110111
(*b*) 111100
(*c*) 110010
(*d*) 111011

137. The binary equivalent of hexadecimal number $3D_{16}$ is.
(*a*) 111101
(*b*) 101101
(*c*) 111111
(*d*) None of the above

138. The binary equivalent of hexadecimal number $3A_{16}$ would be.
(*a*) 111110
(*b*) 111010
(*c*) 110011
(*d*) None of the above

139. The binary equivalent of hexadecimal number 31_{16} is.
   (*a*) 101010
   (*b*) 110101
   (*c*) 110001
   (*d*) 100101

140. The decimal equivalent of octal number 143_8 is.
   (*a*) 90
   (*b*) 971
   (*c*) 99
   (*d*) 107

141. The decimal equivalent of octal number 125_8 is.
   (*a*) 90
   (*b*) 85
   (*c*) 87
   (*d*) 99

142. The decimal equivalent of octal number 110_8 is.
   (*a*) 70
   (*b*) 72
   (*c*) 73
   (*d*) 110

143. The hexadecimal equivalent of octal number 143_8 is.
   (*a*) 63
   (*b*) 60
   (*c*) 50
   (*d*) 57

144. The hexadecimal equivalent of octal number 112_8 is.
   (*a*) 4A
   (*b*) 5A
   (*c*) 15
   (*d*) 62

145. The hexadecimal equivalent of octal number 56_8 is.
   (*a*) 2A
   (*b*) 3A
   (*c*) 2E
   (*d*) None of the above

146. The binary equivalent of octal number 7432_8 is.
   (*a*) 1111000110111
   (*b*) 111100011010
   (*c*) 110011010111
   (*d*) 111111111000

147. The decimal equivalent of hexadecimal number $1D7F_{16}$ is.
   (*a*) 7551
   (*b*) 8771
   (*c*) 5557
   (*d*) 7781

148. The binary equivalent of hexa-decimal number $6B2_{16}$ is.
   (*a*) 1111000110111
   (*b*) 1010111010111
   (*c*) 111100001100
   (*d*) None of the above

149. The hexadecimal equivalent of binary number 1101100111111000_2 is.
   (*a*) $D9F8_F$
   (*b*) 789
   (*c*) BBBB
   (*d*) None of the above

150. The decimal equivalent of binary number 1000000000000_2 is.
   (*a*) 1024
   (*b*) 512
   (*c*) 1036
   (*d*) 4096

151. The octal equivalent of binary number 10011_2 is.
   (*a*) 23
   (*b*) 52
   (*c*) 47
   (*d*) None of the above

152. The result of binary addition of 110101 and 101111 is.

(*a*) 1100100
(*b*) 1101000
(*c*) 1110111
(*d*) 110011

153. Subtraction of 100101100 from 1110101010 is.
(*a*) 1001011110
(*b*) 0110100001
(*c*) 1111000001
(*d*) 1111011111

154. Multiplication of 111 by 101 is.
(*a*) 110011
(*b*) 100011
(*c*) 111100
(*d*) None of the above

155. Multiplication of 101 by 011 is.
(*a*) 1111
(*b*) 1001
(*c*) 1110
(*d*) None of the above

156. Division of 100011 by 101 is.
(*a*) 100
(*b*) 111
(*c*) 101
(*d*) None of the above

157. Multiplication of octal numbers 47 and 52 is.
(*a*) 3144_8
(*b*) 4147_8
(*c*) 3146_8
(*d*) 3184_8

158. Addition of binary numbers 10 and 11 is.
(*a*) 100
(*b*) 101
(*c*) 001
(*d*) 111

159. Addition of binary numbers 1101 and 1010 is.
(*a*) 10111
(*b*) 11000
(*c*) 11011
(*d*) 10111

160. The diagrammatic representation illustrating the order of functions in a program is called a
(*a*) Flow chart
(*b*) Data flow diagram
(*c*) Entity relationship diagram
(*d*) None of the above

161. The removal of error in the language of computer is called as.
(*a*) Debugging
(*b*) Assembling
(*c*) Interpreting
(*d*) None of the above

162. How many addresses are required for 25 × 40 video RAM?
(*a*) 1,800
(*b*) 1,940
(*c*) 1,000
(*d*) 2,000

163. Terminals can accomodate
(*a*) Inputs only
(*b*) Outputs only
(*c*) Both input and output
(*d*) Turn around document only

164. The binary equivalent of the decimal no. 13.75 is
(*a*) 1101.1
(*b*) 101.011
(*c*) 3785.73
(*d*) 1110.110

165. Who invented the microprocessor?
(*a*) Marcian E Huff
(*b*) Joseph Iucquard
(*c*) Hesmon H gold stein
(*d*) All of the above

166. What hardware was used by first generation computers?
(*a*) Transistors

(*b*) ICs
(*c*) Valves
(*d*) SSI

167. A computer has no more sense than a light
(*a*) Bulb
(*b*) Pen
(*c*) Switch
(*d*) Pad

168. The digital computer was developed primarily in
(*a*) UK
(*b*) USA
(*c*) Japan
(*d*) China

169. When was the X window system born?
(*a*) 1984
(*b*) 1986
(*c*) 1989
(*d*) 1990

170. The first IBM PC did not have any
(*a*) RAM
(*b*) Disk Drive
(*c*) ROM
(*d*) Port

171. In computer Jargon, wetware means
(*a*) Human intelligence
(*b*) High intelligence
(*c*) Any organic intelligence
(*d*) Artificial intelligence

172. The subject of cybernetics deals with science of
(*a*) Genetics
(*b*) Molecular bilogy
(*c*) Bio chemistry
(*d*) Control and communications

173. Who launched IBM's first PC in 1981?
(*a*) Jan Timmer
(*b*) Jack Smith
(*c*) C.B. Rogers Jr.
(*d*) Buckminster Fuller

174. How many address lines are needed to address each memory location in a 2048 × 4 memory chip?
(*a*) 10
(*b*) 11
(*c*) 12
(*d*) 8

175. The octal equivalent of 111010 is
(*a*) 82
(*b*) 72
(*c*) 71
(*d*) 81

176. Which of the following is a secondary memory device
(*a*) Keyboard
(*b*) Disk
(*c*) ALU
(*d*) Mouse

177. A name or number used to identify a storage location is called
(*a*) Byte
(*b*) Nibble
(*c*) Bit
(*d*) Address

178. The computer device primarily used to provide hardcopy is the
(*a*) CRT
(*b*) Line printer
(*c*) Card reader
(*d*) Mouse

179. How many users in a single bus structure communicate at a time?
(*a*) One
(*b*) Two
(*c*) Three
(*d*) Four

180. A collection of wire that connects several devices is called
(*a*) Link
(*b*) Bus
(*c*) Bidirectional wire
(*d*) Cable

181. The octal equivalent of hexadecimal number 3DE is
(*a*) 1376
(*b*) 1736
(*c*) 3176
(*d*) 1037

182. The binary equivalent of octal no. 13.54 is
(*a*) 1011.1011
(*b*) 1101.111
(*c*) 1110.0100
(*d*) 1001.1100

183. A winchester disk is a
(*a*) Disk storage
(*b*) Removable disk
(*c*) Flexible disk
(*d*) All of the above

184. Which of the following is a product of data processing.
(*a*) Data
(*b*) Information
(*c*) Software
(*d*) Computer

185. The heart of any computer is the
(*a*) CPU
(*b*) Memory
(*c*) I/O
(*d*) Disks

186. An error in computer data is called
(*a*) Chip
(*b*) Bus
(*c*) Bit
(*d*) None of above

187. Everything computer does is controlled by its
(*a*) Keyboard
(*b*) Mouse
(*c*) CPU
(*d*) RAM

188. The monitor of a computer is connected to it by a
(*a*) Wire
(*b*) Cable
(*c*) Bus
(*d*) Line driver

189. Which computer memory is essentially empty?
(*a*) RAM
(*b*) ROM
(*c*) EPROM
(*d*) PROM

190. Which memory does not forget?
(*a*) ROM
(*b*) RAM
(*c*) PROM
(*d*) EPROM

191. Which of the following is not an O/P device of computer?
(*a*) Printer
(*b*) Keyboard
(*c*) VDU
(*d*) CRT

192. The CPU chip used in computer is partially made out of:
(*a*) Copper
(*b*) Iron
(*c*) Silver
(*d*) Silica

193. The hardware in which data may be stored for computer
(*a*) Registers
(*b*) Bus
(*c*) Memory
(*d*) Control unit

194. RAM is used as a short memory because it

(*a*) Is volatile
(*b*) Has small capacity
(*c*) Is very expensive
(*d*) Is programmable

195. A character is represented in EBCDIC code by:
(*a*) 1 bit
(*b*) 4 bit
(*c*) 6 bit
(*d*) 8 bit

196. Which is a unit of measurement of memory size used with computer systems?
(*a*) Kilo byte
(*b*) Mega byte
(*c*) Giga byte
(*d*) All of the above

197. Which of the following is used for manufacturing chips
(*a*) Bus
(*b*) Control unit
(*c*) semiconductors
(*d*) (a) and (b) only

198. The computer code for interchange of information between terminals is
(*a*) ASCII
(*b*) BCD
(*c*) EBCDIC
(*d*) All of above

199. Which of the following is considered a direct entry input device?
(*a*) Mouse
(*b*) Light pen
(*c*) Optical scanner
(*d*) All of above

200. EBCDIC can code up to how many different characters
(*a*) 8
(*b*) 16
(*c*) 32
(*d*) 64

201. Which of the following is a nonvolatile memory?
(*a*) ROM
(*b*) RAM
(*c*) VLSI
(*d*) LSI

202. Which is widely used in academic testing?
(*a*) MICR
(*b*) POS
(*c*) OCR
(*d*) OMR

203. Magnetic tape can serve as a
(*a*) Input media
(*b*) Output media
(*c*) Secondary storage media
(*d*) All of the above

204. The third generation of computers cover period:
(*a*) 1971-82
(*b*) 1982-94
(*c*) 1965-71
(*d*) 1959-64

205. Who was the father of punched card processing
(*a*) J. Presper Eckert
(*b*) Charles Babbage
(*c*) Dr. Hermon Hollerith
(*d*) Blaise Pascal

206. A typical modern computer uses
(*a*) LSI chips
(*b*) Vacuum tube
(*c*) Valves
(*d*) All of the above

207. Where was the India's first computer installed and when?
(*a*) Institute of Social Science, Agra, 1955

(*b*) Indian Institute of Statistics, Delhi, 1957
(*c*) Indian Statistical Institute, Calcutta, 1955
(*d*) Indian Institute of Science, Banglore, 1971

208. Computer can not do anything wothout a
(*a*) CPU chip
(*b*) Memory
(*c*) O/P device
(*d*) Problem

209. How many input lines are needed to construct 1024 bit coincident core plane?
(*a*) 8
(*b*) 10
(*c*) 32
(*d*) 64

210. How many types of storage loops exist in magnetic bubble memory?
(*a*) 8
(*b*) 4
(*c*) 16
(*d*) 2

211. Which memory is volatile?
(*a*) RAM
(*b*) ROM
(*c*) EPROM
(*d*) PROM

212. When was the first mini computer built?
(*a*) 1965
(*b*) 1966
(*c*) 1962
(*d*) 1971

213. Which one of the following is the first-2nd generation computer?
(*a*) IBM 7090
(*b*) IBM 7070
(*c*) IBM 801
(*d*) IBM 650

214. Which one of the following computers was the first to use stored problem?
(*a*) ENIAC
(*b*) EOVAC
(*c*) EDSAC
(*d*) ACE

215. The magnetic tape consists of a plastic tape with a surface coating of magnetic material. When was it invented?
(*a*) 1946
(*b*) 1952
(*c*) 1956
(*d*) 1965

216. First integrated circuit chip was developed by
(*a*) C.V. Raman
(*b*) W.H. Britain
(*c*) J.S. Kilbey
(*d*) Robert Noyce

217. Which of the following is used for manufacturing chips?
(*a*) Control bus
(*b*) Control unit
(*c*) Parity unit
(*d*) Semiconductor

218. The parity bit is added for .... purposes
(*a*) Coding
(*b*) Indexing
(*c*) Controlling
(*d*) Error control detection

219. Which of the following is true?
(*a*) Field are composed of character
(*b*) Files are compose of records
(*c*) Records are compose of field
(*d*) All of above

220. Which of following can be output produced by computer?

(*a*) Graphics
(*b*) Voice
(*c*) Text
(*d*) All of the above

221. The personal computer industry was started by:
(*a*) IBM
(*b*) Apple
(*c*) Compaq
(*d*) HCL

222. Personal computer for business purpose have RAM of
(*a*) 4 K
(*b*) 64 K
(*c*) 16 K
(*d*) 256 K

223. The arranging of data in a logical sequence is known as
(*a*) Sorting
(*b*) Classifying
(*c*) Reproducing
(*d*) Summarizing
(*e*) None

224. When was the IBM XI microcomputer appeared in market?
(*a*) 1970
(*b*) 1971
(*c*) 1986
(*d*) 1987

225. When was apple mocintosh II microcomputer introduced in the market?
(*a*) 1964
(*b*) 1970
(*c*) 1983
(*d*) 1986

226. Example of non numerical data is
(*a*) Employee address
(*b*) Examination score
(*c*) Bank balance
(*d*) None of the above

227. The 2's complement of the binary number 11001 is
(*a*) 00111
(*b*) 00110
(*c*) 0111
(*d*) None of the above

228. Which of the following memories does not need refreshing?
(*a*) SRAM
(*b*) DRAM
(*c*) ROM
(*d*) All of above

229. Which of the following device can be used to directly input printed text?
(*a*) OCR
(*b*) OMR
(*c*) MICR
(*d*) All of above

230. Which of the following printers cannot print graphics?
(*a*) Ink-jet
(*b*) Daisy wheel
(*c*) Laser
(*d*) Dot matrix

231. Which Indian company designed and manufactured super-computer?
(*a*) C-DAC
(*b*) CMC
(*c*) C-DOT
(*d*) All of the above

232. Who is creator of PASCAL language?
(*a*) Niklaus Writh
(*b*) Diskstra
(*c*) Donald Knuth
(*d*) Blazie Pascal

233. Where are silicon chips

manufactured in India?
(*a*) Chandigarh
(*b*) Punjab
(*c*) U.P
(*d*) Tamil Nadu

234. No computer can do anything without a
(*a*) Program
(*b*) Memory
(*c*) Chip
(*d*) O/P device

235. Modern computers are very reliable but they are not
(*a*) Fast
(*b*) Powerful
(*c*) Infallible
(*d*) Cheap

236. The word length of computer is measured in
(*a*) Byte
(*b*) Bits
(*c*) Nibble
(*d*) Metres

237. The only things moving inside a computer are
(*a*) 1's and 0's
(*b*) Electrons
(*c*) Bytes
(*d*) Proton

238. Preparing a magnetic disk for data storage is called
(*a*) Booting
(*b*) formatting
(*c*) Debuffing
(*d*) Purchasing disk

239. Computer stores its programs and data in its
(*a*) ALU
(*b*) Control unit
(*c*) Memory
(*d*) Cache memory

240. The act of retrieving existing data from memory is called
(*a*) read-out operation
(*b*) read from operation
(*c*) read in operation
(*d*) All of the above

241. All modern computers operate on
(*a*) Information
(*b*) Floppies
(*c*) Data
(*d*) Words

242. What is the number of bit patterns provided by 7-bit code?
(*a*) 256
(*b*) 128
(*c*) 64
(*d*) 512

243. What is the number of binary digits which can be added by full-adder?
(*a*) 12
(*b*) 3
(*c*) 4
(*d*) 16

244. Instructions and memory addresses are represented by
(*a*) Character codes
(*b*) Binary codes
(*c*) Binary word
(*d*) Parity bit

245. A common example of data storage medium is
(*a*) Cartidge
(*b*) Floppies
(*c*) Mouse
(*d*) Disk

246. What is the number of bits needed for an address in 4K memory?
(*a*) 16
(*b*) 8
(*c*) 12
(*d*) 4

247. The number of tracks on a ½ inch wide magnetic tape
(*a*) 7
(*b*) 9
(*c*) 18
(*d*) 20

248. What are the concentric circles on floppy disk known as?
(*a*) Tracks
(*b*) Cylinder
(*c*) Sectors
(*d*) Segments

249. Which part of diskette should never be touched?
(*a*) Hub
(*b*) Centre
(*c*) Oval slot
(*d*) Corner

250. Dot matrix is a type of
(*a*) Tape
(*b*) Printer
(*c*) Disk
(*d*) Bus

251. A track ball is manipulated by
(*a*) Palm
(*b*) Foot
(*c*) Fingers
(*d*) Sound

252. Point out the odd item amongst the following
(*a*) Mouse
(*b*) Touchpad
(*c*) Light pen
(*d*) Printer

253. How many bits can be stored in 8K RAM?
(*a*) 8000
(*b*) 8192
(*c*) 4000
(*d*) 4096

254. A computer has a 1024K memory. What does letter K stand
(*a*) Kilometre
(*b*) Thousand
(*c*) 1024
(*d*) 10,000 bits

255. The storage locations in the internal storage of CPU is
(*a*) Contents
(*b*) Addresses
(*c*) Locations
(*d*) Mask

256. Which computer company invented the RAM chip?
(*a*) Motorola
(*b*) Intel
(*c*) Toshiba
(*d*) IBM

257. The computer memory holds data and
(*a*) Bytes
(*b*) Program
(*c*) Registers
(*d*) Bits

258. The usual expected basic life of any processor is
(*a*) 5 years
(*b*) 7 years
(*c*) 9 years
(*d*) 16 years

259. The Intel come out with its RISC 1860 chip in
(*a*) 1983
(*b*) 1984
(*c*) 1985
(*d*) 1989

260. When did intel announce its 16-bit 80286 chip?
(*a*) 1982
(*b*) 1894

(*c*) 1985
(*d*) 1986

261. When did intel announce its 80386 processor?
(*a*) 1983
(*b*) 1985
(*c*) 1986
(*d*) 1988

262. The CPU chip used in computer is partially made out of
(*a*) Silica
(*b*) Carbon
(*c*) Copper
(*d*) Sold

263. The binary number 1000 is equivalent to decimal number
(*a*) One thousand
(*b*) Eight
(*c*) One
(*d*) Sisteen

264. Which of the following is not an octal number?
(*a*) 32
(*b*) 750
(*c*) 1642
(*d*) 902

265. Main memory contains
(*a*) Data
(*b*) Instruction
(*c*) Both (a) and (b)
(*d*) Operating System
(*e*) None

266. In mark sensing data is read
(*a*) Optically
(*b*) Electrically
(*c*) Magnetically
(*d*) Mechanically

267. The central computer in a distributed processing system is
(*a*) Main frame
(*b*) CPU
(*c*) Host
(*d*) Multiplexes

268. The amount of cheque is recorded in magnetic ink, using an
(*a*) Encodes
(*b*) Embosses
(*c*) Inscribes
(*d*) Imprinter

269. A billionth of a second is defined as a:
(*a*) Milli second
(*b*) Micro second
(*c*) Nano second
(*d*) Pico second

270. The ASCII code for the character J is:
(*a*) 1001 0001
(*b*) 1001 1010
(*c*) 1010 1010
(*d*) 1010 0001

271. Thick-film ICs use .... technique
(*a*) Screen printing
(*b*) Cathode suffering
(*c*) Mono alithic
(*d*) Hybrid

272. dBASE-III was developed by
(*a*) DEC
(*b*) IBM
(*c*) Ashton-tate
(*d*) All of the above

273. The 68000 series of micro-processor are from
(*a*) DEC
(*b*) INTEL
(*c*) HP
(*d*) Motorola

274. WAN hardware includes
(*a*) Multiplexers and routers
(*b*) EDI
(*c*) Bridge and modems
(*d*) All of the above

275. The collection of command is called
(*a*) Information
(*b*) Program
(*c*) File
(*d*) Data Processing

276. A NOR gate is ON only when all its inputs are
(*a*) On
(*b*) Positive
(*c*) High
(*d*) Off

277. How many alphanumeric character are in BLT 1987?
(*a*) 10
(*b*) 63
(*c*) 14
(*d*) 7

278. What is the name given to a 8-bit unit used for coding data
(*a*) Block of characters
(*b*) Byte
(*c*) Word
(*d*) K

279. The RAMAC address 12345 identifies
(*a*) Disk 12
(*b*) Disk 32
(*c*) Disk 34
(*d*) Disk 16

280. First computer in India was manufactured by
(*a*) CMC
(*b*) ECIL
(*c*) BEL
(*d*) HCL

281. Ethernet uses the topology
(*a*) Tree
(*b*) Ring
(*c*) Star
(*d*) Bus

282. What type of magnetic material is normally used in bubble memories?
(*a*) Magnetic core
(*b*) Cobalt
(*c*) Garnet
(*d*) Metallic

283. A 32 bit microprocessor has the word length equal to
(*a*) 2 bytes
(*b*) 8 bytes
(*c*) 4 bytes
(*d*) 32 bytes

284. Which of the following topologies is not broadcast type?
(*a*) Star
(*b*) Bus
(*c*) Ring
(*d*) Tree

285. Conversion of decimal number $(61)_{10}$ to binary gives
(*a*) 111101_2
(*b*) 001101_2
(*c*) 110011_2
(*d*) 111111_2

286. Conversion of decimal number 99_{10} to binary
(*a*) 1100011_2
(*b*) 100011_2
(*c*) 1100001_2
(*d*) 1010111_2

287. Conversion of decimal number 13_{10} to octal gives
(*a*) 17_8
(*b*) 11_8
(*c*) 13_8
(*d*) 15_8

288. Conversion of 1011011_2 to its decimal number is
(*a*) 81_{10}
(*b*) 91_{10}

(*c*) 100_{10}
(*d*) 200_{10}

289. Conversion of octal number 3137_8 to decimal number
(*a*) 1931_{10}
(*b*) 1632_{10}
(*c*) 1531_{10}
(*d*) 1631_{10}

290. Conversion of octal number 134_8 to binary number
(*a*) 001011011_2
(*b*) 110011_2
(*c*) 001101100_2
(*d*) 001011100_2

291. Conversion of hexadecimal number $207F_{16}$ to decimal is
(*a*) 7551_{10}
(*b*) 7561_{10}
(*c*) 8551_{10}
(*d*) 8319_{10}

292. Conversion of decimal number 8_{10} to hexadecimal is
(*a*) 20_{16}
(*b*) 50_{16}
(*c*) 31_{16}
(*d*) None of the above

293. Conversion of decimal number 125_8 to hexadecimal is
(*a*) 14_{16}
(*b*) 13_{16}
(*c*) OF_{16}
(*d*) $7D_{16}$

294. Conversion of octal number 125_8, to decimal is
(*a*) 90_{10}
(*b*) 85_{10}
(*c*) 87_{10}
(*d*) 99_{10}

295. Multiplication of 111_2 by 101_2 is
(*a*) 110011_2
(*b*) 100011_2
(*c*) 111100_2
(*d*) 000101_2

296. Division of 100011_2 by 101_2 is
(*a*) 100_2
(*b*) 111_2
(*c*) 101_2
(*d*) 1010_2

297. Addition of 10_2 and 11_2 is
(*a*) 100_2
(*b*) 101_2
(*c*) 111_2
(*d*) 110_2

298. Subtraction of 100101100_2 from 1110101010_2 is
(*a*) 110000010
(*b*) 0110100001_2
(*c*) 1111000001
(*d*) 1111011111

299. To set a resister or counter the all-zero-stage is
(*a*) Return
(*b*) Reset
(*c*) Remote
(*d*) Release

300. A code that is written into serially accessed memory is
(*a*) Gray code
(*b*) EOP
(*c*) Bar code
(*d*) Ary

301. The number of logical records in physical record is
(*a*) Group
(*b*) Sector
(*c*) Field
(*d*) Blocking factor

302. The control of jobs running within a system is
(*a*) Job monitoring
(*b*) Job stream
(*c*) Job performance

(*d*) Job step

303. The most widely used logic programming language
(*a*) BASIC
(*b*) COBOL
(*c*) PROLOG
(*d*) LOGO

304. In which of the following, each data item contains at most 2 pointers
(*a*) List structure
(*b*) LISP
(*c*) List sorting
(*d*) List head

305. A device that both transmits and receive data
(*a*) Transture
(*b*) Transponder
(*c*) Translator
(*d*) Transceiver

306. Allocator and manager of memory in operating system is
(*a*) Keyboard
(*b*) Kludge
(*c*) Kernel
(*d*) Key punch

307. The smallest logical data entry is called data item or data
(*a*) Base
(*b*) Field
(*c*) Bank
(*d*) Collection

308. Which of the following are used to bring fields to a standard size
(*a*) Flags
(*b*) Files
(*c*) Fillers
(*d*) Flow charts

309. A device or system not directly connected to CPU is
(*a*) On-line
(*b*) Keyboard
(*c*) Memory
(*d*) Off line

310. The number of characters that can be stored in a given physical space is
(*a*) Word length
(*b*) Bytes
(*c*) Data density
(*d*) Field

311. Which of the following is a part of a operator console
(*a*) Keyboard
(*b*) CPU
(*c*) Control panel
(*d*) Printer

312. Condensing output data to exhibit specific information is
(*a*) Calculations
(*b*) Recording
(*c*) Merging
(*d*) Summarising

313. The earliest calculating device still in use is the
(*a*) Differential engine
(*b*) Calculator
(*c*) Abacus
(*d*) Mini computer

314. Which of the following is also known as SOROBAN
(*a*) ENIAC
(*b*) Abacus
(*c*) EDSAC
(*d*) UNIVAC

315. Which is used to store firmware
(*a*) RAM
(*b*) ROM
(*c*) PROM
(*d*) EPROM

316. A computer that works with descrete quantities is

(*a*) Analog
(*b*) Digital
(*c*) Hybrid
(*d*) Optical

317. The arrangement of input data, stored data or output information is
(*a*) Format
(*b*) Instruction
(*c*) Processing
(*d*) File

318. The imitation of one device or system by another is
(*a*) Simulation
(*b*) Emulation
(*c*) Regilience
(*d*) Compaction

319. Which is called main storage or memory
(*a*) EDP
(*b*) IAS
(*c*) CCITT
(*d*) CAI

320. One Picosecond have how many seconds
(*a*) 100
(*b*) 10
(*c*) 1000
(*d*) None of the above

321. Which is American data communication network
(*a*) LAN
(*b*) TELE net
(*c*) ARC net
(*d*) BBS

322. The begining of first generation computers
(*a*) Abacus
(*b*) EDVAC
(*c*) EDSAL
(*d*) ENIAC

323. How many bit microprocessor is used in personal computer
(*a*) 8
(*b*) 6
(*c*) 16
(*d*) 32

324. A 32 bit computer word consists of
(*a*) 8 bytes
(*b*) 4 bytes
(*c*) 32 bytes
(*d*) 16 bytes

325. Which is computer's output on micro film
(*a*) CAD
(*b*) COM
(*c*) CAM
(*d*) CAI

326. Which is physical feature of a magnetic tape
(*a*) Panel
(*b*) Bot maker
(*c*) Surface
(*d*) Cluster

327. Which memory is actual working memory
(*a*) SAM
(*b*) ROM
(*c*) RAM
(*d*) TAB MEMORY

328. Any memory system that allows only serial access
(*a*) ROM
(*b*) SAM
(*c*) RAM
(*d*) PROM

329. The system that is used for serial transmission of data
(*a*) Rs 232C
(*b*) MS-DOS

(*c*) PC-DOS
(*d*) CP/M

330. PL/M is reduced version of
(*a*) LOGO
(*b*) ADA
(*c*) PL/I
(*d*) CP/M

331. One pico is
(*a*) 1/6"
(*b*) 10^{-14}
(*c*) 10^{-12}
(*d*) 10×18

332. A set of related programs are
(*a*) File
(*b*) Arrays
(*c*) Package
(*d*) Subscripts

333. The central part of a disk is known as
(*a*) Surface
(*b*) Hub
(*c*) Cylinder
(*d*) None of the above

334. A group of terminals that operate together is
(*a*) Cylinder
(*b*) Cluster
(*c*) Combines
(*d*) Compiler

335. Burner is a circuit that allows .... to be loaded with data
(*a*) EEPROM
(*b*) RAM
(*c*) PROMS
(*d*) EPROM

336. PILOT language is meant for
(*a*) Tailors
(*b*) School gains children
(*c*) Mother, teachers and trainers
(*d*) Use in process control

337. A VDU is used for
(*a*) Input device
(*b*) Output device
(*c*) Voice data entry device
(*d*) Both a and b
(*e*) None of above

338. A single dimensional array is called
(*a*) List
(*b*) Subscripts
(*c*) Matrix
(*d*) File

339. A break in the normal flow of processing is called
(*a*) Huns
(*b*) Crash
(*c*) Interrupt
(*d*) Hit

340. A subset of characters within a data field is konwn as
(*a*) Record
(*b*) Files
(*c*) Bytes
(*d*) Data string

341. Which is a sequence of micro instructions
(*a*) Micro instruction
(*b*) Macro code
(*c*) Micro output
(*d*) Micro program

342. The process of combining strings are known as
(*a*) Compiler
(*b*) Concatenation
(*c*) Interpreter
(*d*) All of the above

343. Which is a basic technique, using activity networking
(*a*) CPA
(*b*) VLSI

(*c*) GIGO
(*d*) MSI

344. An input device with a joystick is
(*a*) Punched card
(*b*) Paddle
(*c*) Magnetic tape
(*d*) None of the above

345. A device used to measure the circuit density of a chip is
(*a*) Light pen
(*b*) Mouse
(*c*) LSI
(*d*) All of the above

346. ISOT is a .... bit code
(*a*) 8
(*b*) 7
(*c*) 16
(*d*) 32

347. Micro computer meant for a signal user is
(*a*) CP/M
(*b*) PC
(*c*) UNIX
(*d*) PC-AT

348. The mechanical, magnetic, electronic and electrical devices from which a computer is fabricated is called
(*a*) Magnetic core
(*b*) Firm ware
(*c*) Hardware
(*d*) Software

349. The display size of the typical visual display screen is
(*a*) 80 columns wide by 24
(*b*) 40 columns wide by 20
(*c*) 60 cloumns wide by 30
(*d*) 15 columns wide by 10

350. Which is a single intergated circuit
(*a*) Gate
(*b*) Mother board
(*c*) Chip
(*d*) CPU

351. A 4 bit synchronous counter uses flip flop with propagation delay time 25 n seconds of each flip flop stage. Max possible time required for change of state will be.
(*a*) 25 n sec
(*b*) 0 n sec
(*c*) 50 n sec
(*d*) None of the above

352. A 12 bit ADCs operating with a 1 μ sec clock period and total conversion time is seen to be 14 μ sec. the ADC must be of type.
(*a*) Successive approximation type
(*b*) Weighted register
(*c*) Any type
(*d*) None of the above

353. Which memory is volatile
(*a*) RAM
(*b*) ROM
(*c*) EPROM
(*d*) PROM

354. The advantages of ROM are its .... and ....
(*a*) Compact size; readability
(*b*) Compact size; speed
(*c*) Readability; speed
(*c*) Low cost; readability

355. The personal computer industry was started by
(*a*) IBM
(*b*) APPLE
(*c*) COMPAQ
(*d*) HCL

356. The language that computer can understand and execute is called
(*a*) Machine language
(*b*) Application language
(*c*) System program

(*d*) All of the above

357. The ALU of a computer responds to the commands coming from
(*a*) Primary memory
(*b*) Control selection
(*c*) External memory
(*d*) Cache memory

358. A peripheral device in which a large number of cartridges or reels of magnetic tape are stored in cells in a storage matrix is
(*a*) Keyboard
(*b*) Monitor
(*c*) Printer
(*d*) Automated Tape Library

359. A software package to implement a database is
(*a*) System Analysis
(*b*) DBMS
(*c*) Database handler
(*d*) DASD

360. The place where the data or information is stored for a short time is
(*a*) Buffer
(*b*) Memory
(*c*) Control Unit
(*d*) ALU

361. Accessing a computer from a distant station using communication facilities is
(*a*) RAM
(*b*) Remote access
(*c*) ROM
(*d*) PROM

362. A pen-shaped device which can sense light, and is used to point at spots on a video screen
(*a*) Mouse
(*b*) Light pen
(*c*) Joystick
(*d*) Plotter

363. Which can be used to control the movement of a cursor on a video screen
(*a*) Mouse
(*b*) Joystick
(*c*) Touch panel
(*d*) Light pen

364. Keyboard is an
(*a*) Input device
(*b*) Memory device
(*c*) Output device
(*d*) All of the above

365. To change the dimension of a window
(*a*) Arrange icons
(*b*) Arrange window
(*c*) Scroll through a window
(*d*) Size window

366. To change the location of a window
(*a*) Move a window
(*b*) Size a window
(*c*) Arrange window
(*d*) Arrange icons

367. To use one of Windows two methods (cascade or tile) to position the open group windows on the screen so that they can all be seen
(*a*) Move a window
(*b*) Size a window
(*c*) Arrange window
(*d*) Arrange icons

368. Use the Windows command to distribute group icons in a row at the bottom of the program Manager's window or to distribute program-item icons evenly within the selected group window

(*a*) Move a window
(*b*) Size a window
(*c*) Arrange window
(*d*) Arrange icons

369. To use Windows to run the Write program
(*a*) Start Write
(*b*) Start Editor
(*c*) Start Word Perfect
(*d*) Start Paintbrush

370. The most popular interactive delivery medium for PCs and video games is
(*a*) CD-ROM
(*b*) Floppy Disks
(*c*) DVDs
(*d*) None of the above

371. Business use interactive multimedia for video conferencing, reaching customers with catalogs and customer support and...
(*a*) Attraction
(*b*) Training
(*c*) All of the above
(*d*) None of the above

372. What is the widest application of multimedia in a home today
(*a*) Entertainment
(*b*) Training
(*c*) Home Security
(*d*) All of the above

373. In education, interactive multimedia can enrich the learning experience by engaging students in the content, connecting students in different locations and simulating real-world actions and their consequences. The above statement is true or false
(*a*) True
(*b*) False
(*c*) Cannot say
(*d*) None of the above

374. Most time-consuming part of creating a multimedia program or presentation is ...
(*a*) Planning
(*b*) Understanding Audience
(*c*) Selecting Tools
(*d*) None of these

ANSWERS

1. (*d*)	2. (*c*)	3. (*c*)	4. (*a*)	5. (*b*)	6. (*c*)	7. (*b*)
8. (*a*)	9. (*b*)	10. (*d*)	11. (*c*)	12. (*c*)	13. (*c*)	14. (*c*)
15. (*d*)	16. (*d*)	17. (*a*)	18. (*d*)	19. (*c*)	20. (*b*)	21. (*d*)
22. (*c*)	23. (*c*)	24. (*a*)	25. (*a*)	26. (*b*)	27. (*a*)	28. (*a*)
29. (*d*)	30. (*d*)	31. (*a*)	32. (*c*)	33. (*a*)	34. (*b*)	35. (*b*)
36. (*a*)	37. (*a*)	38. (*b*)	39. (*a*)	40. (*c*)	41. (*b*)	42. (*a*)
43. (*d*)	44. (*c*)	45. (*a*)	46. (*a*)	47. (*b*)	48. (*a*)	49. (*d*)
50. (*a*)	51. (*a*)	52. (*a*)	53. (*a*)	54. (*b*)	55. (*d*)	56. (*a*)
57. (*d*)	58. (*a*)	59. (*c*)	60. (*c*)	61. (*b*)	62. (*a*)	63. (*b*)
64. (*a*)	65. (*b*)	66. (*c*)	67. (*a*)	68. (*d*)	69. (*c*)	70. (*b*)
71. (*b*)	72. (*d*)	73. (*c*)	74. (*c*)	75. (*c*)	76. (*a*)	77. (*b*)
78. (*b*)	79. (*b*)	80. (*c*)	81. (*b*)	82. (*b*)	83. (*c*)	84. (*c*)

85. (*b*)	86. (*b*)	87. (*b*)	88. (*b*)	89. (*a*)	90. (*c*)	91. (*a*)
92. (*c*)	93. (*c*)	94. (*c*)	95. (*b*)	96. (*b*)	97. (*d*)	98. (*d*)
99. (*c*)	100. (*d*)	101. (*c*)	102. (*a*)	103. (*c*)	104. (*b*)	105. (*b*)
106. (*d*)	107. (*d*)	108. (*a*)	109. (*c*)	110. (*a*)	111. (*b*)	112. (*a*)
113. (*d*)	114. (*b*)	115. (*b*)	116. (*c*)	117. (*d*)	118. (*a*)	119. (*b*)
120. (*c*)	121. (*b*)	122. (*b*)	123. (*c*)	124. (*a*)	125. (*c*)	126. (*c*)
127. (*d*)	128. (*d*)	129. (*a*)	130. (*b*)	131. (*a*)	132. (*a*)	133. (*a*)
134. (*b*)	135. (*a*)	136. (*d*)	137. (*a*)	138. (*b*)	139. (*c*)	140. (*c*)
141. (*b*)	142. (*b*)	143. (*a*)	144. (*d*)	145. (*c*)	146. (*b*)	147. (*a*)
148. (*d*)	149. (*a*)	150. (*d*)	151. (*a*)	152. (*a*)	153. (*a*)	154. (*b*)
155. (*a*)	156. (*b*)	157. (*a*)	158. (*b*)	159. (*a*)	160. (*a*)	161. (*a*)
162. (*b*)	163. (*c*)	164. (*a*)	165. (*a*)	166. (*c*)	167. (*c*)	168. (*b*)
169. (*d*)	170. (*b*)	171. (*c*)	172. (*d*)	173. (*c*)	174. (*c*)	175. (*b*)
176. (*b*)	177. (*d*)	178. (*b*)	179. (*b*)	180. (*b*)	181. (*c*)	182. (*b*)
183. (*b*)	184. (*b*)	185. (*a*)	186. (*d*)	187. (*c*)	188. (*a*)	189. (*d*)
190. (*a*)	191. (*b*)	192. (*a*)	193. (*c*)	194. (*a*)	195. (*b*)	196. (*d*)
197. (*c*)	198. (*a*)	199. (*d*)	200. (*b*)	201. (*a*)	202. (*d*)	203. (*d*)
204. (*b*)	205. (*c*)	206. (*a*)	207. (*b*)	208. (*a*)	209. (*b*)	210. (*d*)
211. (*a*)	212. (*d*)	213. (*b*)	214. (*a*)	215. (*c*)	216. (*c*)	217. (*d*)
218. (*d*)	219. (*d*)	220. (*d*)	221. (*b*)	222. (*d*)	223. (*a*)	224. (*b*)
225. (*c*)	226. (*d*)	227. (*b*)	228. (*c*)	229. (*a*)	230. (*d*)	231. (*a*)
232. (*d*)	233. (*a*)	234. (*a*)	235. (*d*)	236. (*a*)	237. (*a*)	238. (*b*)
239. (*c*)	240. (*a*)	241. (*d*)	242. (*b*)	243. (*b*)	244. (*c*)	245. (*b*)
246. (*c*)	247. (*a*)	248. (*a*)	249. (*c*)	250. (*b*)	251. (*a*)	252. (*d*)
253. (*b*)	254. (*c*)	255. (*c*)	256. (*a*)	257. (*b*)	258. (*a*)	259. (*a*)
260. (*d*)	261. (*d*)	262. (*d*)	263. (*b*)	264. (*d*)	265. (*c*)	266. (*a*)
267. (*a*)	268. (*a*)	269. (*b*)	270. (*c*)	271. (*c*)	272. (*c*)	273. (*d*)
274. (*c*)	275. (*b*)	276. (*d*)	277. (*c*)	278. (*b*)	279. (*a*)	280. (*c*)
281. (*d*)	282. (*c*)	283. (*c*)	284. (*c*)	285. (*a*)	286. (*a*)	287. (*d*)
288. (*d*)	289. (*b*)	290. (*a*)	291. (*d*)	292. (*d*)	293. (*d*)	294. (*b*)
295. (*b*)	296. (*b*)	297. (*b*)	298. (*a*)	299. (*b*)	300. (*a*)	301. (*d*)
302. (*a*)	303. (*c*)	304. (*a*)	305. (*d*)	306. (*c*)	307. (*b*)	308. (*c*)
309. (*d*)	310. (*c*)	311. (*c*)	312. (*d*)	313. (*c*)	314. (*b*)	315. (*b*)
316. (*b*)	317. (*a*)	318. (*a*)	319. (*a*)	320. (*a*)	321. (*b*)	322. (*d*)
323. (*d*)	324. (*b*)	325. (*d*)	326. (*b*)	327. (*c*)	328. (*b*)	329. (*a*)
330. (*c*)	331. (*c*)	332. (*c*)	333. (*d*)	334. (*b*)	335. (*d*)	336. (*d*)

337. (*b*)	338. (*a*)	339. (*c*)	340. (*d*)	341. (*d*)	342. (*b*)	343. (*a*)
344. (*d*)	345. (*c*)	346. (*c*)	347. (*b*)	348. (*c*)	349. (*a*)	350. (*c*)
351. (*a*)	352. (*b*)	353. (*a*)	354. (*c*)	355. (*b*)	356. (*c*)	357. (*b*)
358. (*c*)	359. (*c*)	360. (*b*)	361. (*c*)	362. (*a*)	363. (*b*)	364. (*a*)
365. (*b*)	366. (*c*)	367. (*a*)	368. (*b*)	369. (*a*)	370. (*b*)	371. (*c*)
372. (*a*)	373. (*b*)	374. (*a*)				

6

Parallel Processing

1. The two best known approaches to update the protocols are?
   (*a*) Firefly
   (*b*) Dragon
   (*c*) Both (*a*) and (*b*)
   (*d*) None of the above

2. If a 10-MIPS processor has 9.75 misses per 100 instructions and each miss creates a 300 nsec bus transaction. Then what would be the offered instruction rate?
   (*a*) 7.70 MIPS
   (*b*) 8.75 MIPS
   (*c*) 7.00 MIPS
   (*d*) 7.75 MIPS

3. The performance of a processer is given by 10 MIPS. References per instruction is 1.3 and cache miss rate is given as 0.05. If the dirty line ratio is 0.5 and bus transaction time is 300 nsec. Then what would be processor execution time per 100 instruction?
   (*a*) 10 us
   (*b*) 100 us
   (*c*) 0.1 sec
   (*d*) 10 us

4. What is shared bas multi processor considered as?
   (*a*) Multiprocessor
   (*b*) Uniprocessor
   (*c*) Processor cluster
   (*d*) All of the above

5. A single instruction replacing multiple (Scalar) instructions is a characteristic of which processor?
   (*a*) Multiprocessor
   (*b*) Uniprocessor
   (*c*) Concurrent processor
   (*d*) Vector processor

6. Which of the following is not a characteristic of Vector instruction?
   (*a*) They improve code density
   (*b*) Organize the data argument in sequence
   (*c*) Both (*a*) and (*b*)
   (*d*) None of the above

7. Vector Register may typically consist of how many registers set?
   (*a*) 2
   (*b*) 8
   (*c*) 10
   (*d*) Both (*b*) and (*c*)

8. Vector load instruction is also known as?
   (*a*) Scatter
   (*b*) Gather
   (*c*) Both (*a*) and (*b*)
   (*d*) None of the above

9. Generic vector operation include.
   (*a*) Arithmetic operation
   (*b*) Logical operation
   (*c*) Both (*a*) & (*b*)
   (*d*) None of the above

10. The concept of Using the results of one vector arithmetic operation as operand in another instruction without first passing it into vector register is called?
    (*a*) Expand
    (*b*) Compress
    (*c*) Chained
    (*d*) None of the above

11. The most significant bits of address of memory that are used for comparison are called?
    (*a*) Index
    (*b*) Offset
    (*c*) Tag
    (*d*) Word

12. What is the advantage of the write-through cache?
    (*a*) Memory bandwidth is high
    (*b*) Retains consistent image of program activity in memory
    (*c*) Dirty bit is set
    (*d*) None of the above

13. A wafer of diameter 21 cm had cost $ 5000 for a particular production. Compute the cost per die. For a die are of 2.3cm^2. If defect density is 1cm^2?
    (*a*) 405 $
    (*b*) 735 $
    (*c*) 360 $
    (*d*) 385 $

14. In which process the original program is decomposed into basic sub-program units or tasks.
    (*a*) Scheduling of tasks
    (*b*) Partitioning
    (*c*) Synchronization
    (*d*) None of the above

15. Which property of the memory ensures that the value returned after read is same as value stored by the latest write?
    (*a*) Clustering
    (*b*) Synchronization
    (*c*) Value conherence
    (*d*) Coherency

16. A process is a sequence of commands and an initial state. Which process is applied to an initial state and generates a final state?
    (*a*) Instruction set
    (*b*) Macro command
    (*c*) Micro instruction
    (*d*) Memory cycle

17. What is the range and domain of the commands called?
    (*a*) Storage
    (*b*) Registers
    (*c*) ALU
    (*d*) Cycle

18. Image instructions and the commands comprising the host are called?
    (*a*) Instructions
    (*b*) Decoder
    (*c*) Microinstruction
    (*d*) Instruction counter

19. The address register for the memory operation is called?
    (*a*) Memory address register
    (*b*) Storage register
    (*c*) Instruction Register
    (*d*) Microinstruction register

20. Which register holds the instruction being interpreted or executed?
    (*a*) Instruction Register
    (*b*) Memory Address Register
    (*c*) Stack Register
    (*d*) Memory Instruction Register

21. Micro programmed decoders are designed using which of the following?
    (*a*) Random Access Memory
    (*b*) Memory Address Register
    (*c*) Registers
    (*d*) Read Only Memory

22. The protocol that maintains the consistency of data in all level cache is called?
    (*a*) Cache coherency protocol
    (*b*) Broadcast protocol
    (*c*) Directory based protocol
    (*d*) Snoopy bus protocol

23. In which protocol a write transaction is forwarded to only those processors that are known to posses a copy of newly altered cache line?
    (*a*) Snoopy bus protocol
    (*b*) Cache coherency protocol
    (*c*) Directory based protocol
    (*d*) Broadcast protocol

24. In which type of protocol the information about the use of line is contained in a directory?
    (*a*) Snoopy protocol
    (*b*) Directory base protocol
    (*c*) Cache coherency protocol
    (*d*) None of the above

25. Which type of the directory can be placed or associated with the memory system in which each line in memory has an entry defining the users of the line?
    (*a*) Central directory
    (*b*) Distribute directory
    (*c*) Local directory
    (*d*) None of the above

26. In which order does processor sees sequence of loads followed by store to be performed?
    (*a*) Program order
    (*b*) Register order
    (*c*) Processor consistency
    (*d*) None of the above

27. Which operation precedes a synchronization operation and ensures that the outstanding memory operations are performed?
    (*a*) Fence
    (*b*) Weak consistency
    (*c*) Release
    (*d*) None of the above

28. The process of looping on a shared variable with test and set type of instruction is called?
    (*a*) Spinlock
    (*b*) Semaphore
    (*c*) Granularity
    (*d*) None of the above

29. Robust processor memory configurations offer adequate resources for communication among various processors in memory some of these configuration are limited by few things what are these limitation?
    (*a*) Shared data cache shared memory
    (*b*) Separate data cache with separate buses
    (*c*) Delay through the communication network
    (*d*) None of the above

30. Which multimedia documents are managed by computer?
    (*a*) Graphics
    (*b*) Video
    (*c*) Voice
    (*d*) All of the above

31. Assume we have four processor and each processor makes a disk request at 100 ms. There is one

disk with Ts = 10 ms, and $C^2 = 1$. Find λ_a, the achieved number of I/o transaction per second and relative performance (λ_a/λ) due to disk contention.
(*a*) 35.33, .0.58
(*b*) 35.33, 0.97
(*c*) 35, 1.97
(*d*) 35.68, 1.58

32. What is disk latency time?
(*a*) Seek time
(*b*) Rotational delay
(*c*) Sum of seek time and rotational delay
(*d*) None of the above

33. In a multiprocessor system for m = 2 and Ts = 20 ms. For M ≠ 1, it is inappropriate to use the low population model. There is more contention is a system with n = 4, M = 2 than in a system with n = 2 and equivalent server occupancy. Find relative performance?
(*a*) 0.58
(*b*) 0.37
(*c*) 1.51
(*d*) 0.97

34. If M ratio is defined as the ratio of data movement in instructions to functional instruction. The formula of M-ratio is :

(*a*) $\dfrac{\text{Number of M-type instruction}}{\text{Number of F-type instruction}}$

(*b*) $\dfrac{\text{Number of F-type instruction}}{\text{Number of M-type instruction}}$

(*c*) $\dfrac{\text{Number of P-type instruction}}{\text{Number of F-type instruction}}$

(*d*) $\dfrac{\text{Number of F-type instruction}}{\text{Number of P-type instruction}}$

35. Which is not a pipeline action of a 3 cycle access to a cache?
(*a*) Access to cache directory
(*b*) Access to data array
(*c*) Transmission of result to processor ALU
(*d*) Decoding of instruction

36. Which of the following is not a model of multiple single processor and memory?
(*a*) Hellerman's model
(*b*) Rossmann model
(*c*) Flynn model
(*d*) Both (*b*) and (*c*)

37. By which way Multiprocessor can not share memory by:
(*a*) sharing a common data cache
(*b*) sharing a common instruction cache
(*c*) sharing a common bus to RAM
(*d*) Sharing a network

38. Which of the following time can be reduced by ensuring that the minimum pipeline segment delay is close to maximum?
(*a*) Cycle organisation
(*b*) Cycle time
(*c*) Both (*a*) and (*b*)
(*d*) None of the above

39. Assume a wafer has diameter of 21 cm and cost Rs. 5000 for a particular production nine Compute the cost per die area = 2.3 cm^2 and for 1 cm^2 if P_D = 1 defect / cm^2.
(*a*) Rs. 635
(*b*) Rs. 485
(*c*) Rs. 385
(*d*) Rs. 400

40. In how many ways the die cost can be determined?

(*a*) 1
(*b*) 2
(*c*) 3
(*d*) 4

41. The unit of processor sub-units area proposed by Mead and Conway is
(*a*) Distance^2
(*b*) Mils^2
(*c*) λ
(*d*) None of the above

42. Which of the following registers consist of one dedicated read port and a time multiplexed read and write port?
(*a*) Dual register
(*b*) Single-ported register
(*c*) both (*a*) and (*b*)
(*d*) None of the above

43. The area of the three ported register is given by?
(*a*) (number of regs) (bits per reg + 6) rbe
(*b*) (number of regs + 6) (bits per reg) rbe
(*c*) (number of regs + 6) (bits per reg + 6) rbe
(*d*) None of the above

44. The area of the cache is given by which of the following?
(*a*) 195 + 0.6 k_1 (data bits) + 0.6 k_2 (tag bits) rbe
(*b*) 0.6 k_1 (data bits) + 0.6 k_2 (tag bits) rbe
(*c*) 195 + (data bits) + 0.6 k_2 (tag bits) rbe
(*d*) 195 + 0.6 k_1 (tag bits) rbe

45. Which of the following is not a issue to determine overall program execution time?
(*a*) Cycle time
(*b*) Cache and memory size
(*c*) Data stream
(*d*) No. of instructions required to execute a program

46. Which of the following is not an important constituent of performance of the program execution?
(*a*) Data stream
(*b*) Instruction stream
(*c*) Processor cycle
(*d*) Cycle time

47. UMA is acronym for which of the following?
(*a*) Uniform Memory Access
(*b*) Universal Memory Access
(*c*) Uniform Mapping of Address
(*d*) Uniform Mapping to Adder

48. Which of the following is a way for comparing the networks?
(*a*) By nodes
(*b*) By links of channel connecting
(*c*) Both (*a*) and (*b*)
(*d*) None of the above

49. How many separate access time for the processor to access an item in memory are there?
(*a*) 1
(*b*) 2
(*c*) 3
(*d*) 4

50. Which of the following in not a way of characterizing the links?
(*a*) Cycle time of link
(*b*) Width of channel
(*c*) Both (*a*) and (*b*)
(*d*) None of the above

51. Which of the following snoopy protocols has a feature that they can supply data from any cache with a clean copy?

(*a*) Illinois
(*b*) Berkeley
(*c*) Firefly
(*d*) Dragon

52. A Pipelined processors is assumed to operate under full capacity. Which of the following is not one of the constraint?
(*a*) One instruction is decoded in each cycle
(*b*) Instruction are decoded in the sequence they are stored in memory
(*c*) Instruction are decoded in the sequence they appear in program representation
(*d*) None of the above

53. Which of the following allows the by passing of one or more of the stages of the pipeline, depending upon the requirement of instruction with specification of the instruction.
(*a*) Dynamic pipeline
(*b*) Shallow pipeline
(*c*) Deep pipeline
(*d*) None of the above

54. Which of the following can issue multiple instructions in a single cycle?
(*a*) MIPS R 2000
(*b*) IBM RS 6000
(*c*) HP PA – RISC
(*d*) All of these

55. Which of the following concurrent processors are further divided into very long instruction word and superscalar processors?
(*a*) Vector processor
(*b*) Multiple issue processor
(*c*) Uniprocessor
(*d*) None of the above

56. The basic I/O request rate is dominated by which of the following request?
(*a*) Data request
(*b*) Operand fetch
(*c*) Instruction request
(*d*) None of the above

57. The technique of placing successful blocks on differed disks up to some minute is known as?
(*a*) File striping
(*b*) Distributed disk operation
(*c*) Both a & b
(*d*) None of the above

58. Which model is frequently used to describe disk behavior?
(*a*) Open stack model
(*b*) Closed stack model
(*c*) Open queue model
(*d*) Closed queue model

59. Rotational delay for the disk to move to correct sector is also known as?
(*a*) Seek time
(*b*) Latency time
(*c*) Transfer time
(*d*) Total disc access time

60. Which of the following is not the type of data presentation devices?
(*a*) Sensors
(*b*) CRT display
(*c*) Line printer
(*d*) None of the these

61. Which among the following has least access time?
(*a*) Hitachi DK 516
(*b*) IBM 3380
(*c*) DEC RK 81
(*d*) All have same access time

62. Seek time can be calcuted using which expression?

(*a*) $0.5\times(A+B\sqrt{n})$
(*b*) $0.5\times(a+b+\sqrt{n})$
(*c*) $a+b\times\sqrt{\text{seek distance in track}}$
(*d*) None of the above

63. The sum of seek time and rotational delay is known as?
(*a*) Disk latency time
(*b*) Access time
(*c*) Seek time
(*d*) Expected seek time

64. Virtual memory is implemented through.
(*a*) Segmentation
(*b*) Paging
(*c*) Demand paging
(*d*) None of the above

65. The increasing performance of processors in the phase of relatively static improvement of disk access time is called?
(*a*) Crisis in I/O
(*b*) I/O traffic
(*c*) I/o management
(*d*) "Wolf"

66. What is the size of data block in the typical current system?
(*a*) 16 kb
(*b*) 8 kb
(*c*) 2 kb
(*d*) 4 kb

67. Which of the following have the shortest access time?
(*a*) Cache
(*b*) RAM
(*c*) ROM
(*d*) Hardisk

68. The processor references that are found in the cache are called?
(*a*) Cache mises
(*b*) Cache hits
(*c*) Cache more cohereney
(*d*) Cache lateney

69. The processor-cache interface can be characterized by number of parameters. Which of the following do not affect the processor performance?
(*a*) access time(hit)
(*b*) Time to initially compute read add
(*c*) Time to access the memory
(*d*) None of the above

70. Which type of the cache is usually restricted to certain instruction cache application?
(*a*) Demand fetch code
(*b*) Prefetch cache code
(*c*) Fetch code
(*d*) None of the above

71. Which one of the following is the disadvantage of simultaneously access to TLB, directory and array?
(*a*) Fewer higher-order bits involved in directory access
(*b*) Additional multiplexing increases cycle time
(*c*) Translate VPN to RPN
(*d*) None of the above

72. The tables performing address translation are in memory and a mechanism for the translation are called?
(*a*) TLB
(*b*) Instruction fetch
(*c*) Both (*a*) and (*b*)
(*d*) None of the above

73. The cycles required to generate the effective memory address of the data operand are called?
(*a*) IF

(*b*) RF
(*c*) AG
(*d*) Translate

74. In which system the cycle time is usually determined by assuming the worst-case time for each step?
(*a*) Synchronous system
(*b*) Asynchronous system
(*c*) Both (*a*) and (*b*)
(*d*) None of the above

75. The maximum deviation from the expected time of clock arrival is called?
(*a*) Clock skew
(*b*) Clock latency
(*c*) Clock inversion
(*d*) None of the above

76. Which register consists of two latches-an input latch and an output latch?
(*a*) Single rank register
(*b*) Dual rank register
(*c*) Both (*a*) and (*b*)
(*d*) None of the above

77. If the arrival of clock is not carefully controlled, then the time ambiguity is called?
(*a*) Controlled clock skew
(*b*) Uncontrolled clock skew
(*c*) Both (*a*) and (*b*)
(*d*) None of the above

78. R/M architecture is used in which of the following processors?
(*a*) DEC – 10
(*b*) POP – 11
(*c*) S/370
(*d*) All of the above

79. What is the measure of the instruction traffic called?
(*a*) Density
(*b*) Code density
(*c*) Data density
(*d*) None of the above

80. How registers may be organized?
(*a*) SRS
(*b*) MRS
(*c*) Both (*a*) and (*b*)
(*d*) None of the above

81. Eight register processor may be defined as?
(*a*) Data processor
(*b*) Processor cluster
(*c*) Base line processor
(*d*) Multi processor

82. What is a technology independent measure of area?
(*a*) RBE
(*b*) SRS
(*c*) MRS
(*d*) Contour buffer

83. Compute the cost of $1m \times 1b$ die using assumptions that diameter of wafer is 21 cm and wafer costs $ 5000:
(*a*) 35000 $
(*b*) 10000 $
(*c*) 7530 $
(*d*) None of the above

84. How many types of peripheral device are there?
(*a*) 1
(*b*) 2
(*c*) 3
(*d*) 4

85. Devises that are used to transport data between processor and user are known as?
(*a*) Data presentation deviser
(*b*) Storage devises
(*c*) Both (*a*) and (*b*)

(*d*) None of the above

86. Devises that are used to communicate data between processors are known as?
(*a*) Networking devises
(*b*) Storage devises
(*c*) data presentation devises
(*d*) All of the above

87. Processor speed is measured in terms of?
(*a*) MIPS
(*b*) MBPS
(*c*) Mhz
(*d*) Ghz

88. Bits per unit area is a measure of?
(*a*) Processor speed
(*b*) Disc transfer
(*c*) Disk density
(*d*) All of the above

89. Disk access time decreases at the 2x per— year?
(*a*) 1 year
(*b*) 5 year
(*c*) 8 yr
(*d*) 10 yr

90. What are the functions for floating point operations?
(*a*) Add/subtract
(*b*) Multiplication/division
(*c*) Logical operation
(*d*) None of the above

91. What factors affect the cost-area of a program?
(*a*) Compatibility
(*b*) Upgradability
(*c*) Both (*a*) and (*b*)
(*d*) None

92. Suppose a die with square aspect ratio has area A and a diameter d then what would be N given as?
(*a*) $\frac{\pi}{4A}\left(d-\sqrt{A}\right)^2$
(*b*) $\frac{\pi}{A}\left(d-\sqrt{A}\right)^2$
(*c*) $\frac{1}{4A}\left(d-\sqrt{A}\right)^2$
(*d*) $\frac{\pi}{4A}\left(d-\sqrt{A}\right)$

93. How can instruction like A: = B + (C*D) can be implemented in computer?
(*a*) Stack
(*b*) Queue
(*c*) List
(*d*) Tree

94. Which is not regarded as the ideal policy for line replacement?
(*a*) LRU
(*b*) FIFO
(*c*) LIFO
(*d*) RAND

95. A disk has an access time of 17.5 ms and a read time of 2.5 ms. Find the effective performance and total response time for each disk access assume $C^2 = 1$.
(*a*) 15.9
(*b*) 18.5
(*c*) 18.9
(*d*) 19.9

96. What is the formula for execution time of CPU performance?
(*a*) Instruction count/program * cycle time
(*b*) Instruction count/program * CPI * cycle time
(*c*) Instruction count/program * CPI
(*d*) None

97. The in line refrence traffic is calculated as?
    (*a*) (1/m) * IF access time * instr/IF
    (*b*) (1/m) * IF access time
    (*c*) (1/m) * instr/IF
    (*d*) None of the above

98. What is the formula of cache size given by?
    (*a*) Line size * no. of sets
    (*b*) (line size * assoc) * no. of sets
    (*c*) Line size * assoc
    (*d*) None of the above

99. Instructions create three types of cache traffic. Which of the following is a type of cache traffic?
    (*a*) Instruction traffic
    (*b*) Data read traffic
    (*c*) Data write traffic
    (*d*) All of the above

100. The normal clock frequency of supercomputers is in the range of
    (*a*) Microsecond
    (*b*) Nanosecond
    (*c*) 10^{-12} second
    (*d*) None of the above

101. A machine running at a clock of 1n sec. requires everything to be packaged in sphere of
    (*a*) 30 cm
    (*b*) 300 cm
    (*c*) 3 cm
    (*d*) None of the above

102. The approximate operating frequency of CRAY 2 is
    (*a*) 200 MHz
    (*b*) 250 MHz
    (*c*) 1000 MHz
    (*d*) None of the above

103. Which is not the application area of high-speed computers
    (*a*) Design of VLSI circuits
    (*b*) Nuclear research
    (*c*) Weather forecasting
    (*d*) None of the above

104. Granularity of parallelism refers to
    (*a*) Amount of work (computation) constituting the unit of allocation to the processing element
    (*b*) It refers to dependencies involved in data
    (*c*) It refers to redundancy in memory storage
    (*d*) None of the above

105. Which of the following is not valid type parallelism
    (*a*) Instructions level parallelism
    (*b*) Task level parallelism
    (*c*) Logic and circuit level parallelism
    (*d*) None of the above

106. Which of the following is most coarse level parallelism
    (*a*) Logic and circuit level parallelism
    (*b*) Instruction level parallelism
    (*c*) Statement level parellelism
    (*d*) Task level parallelism

107. Which of the following is a design Criteria for general purpose high-speed computers
    (*a*) Pipeline architecture
    (*b*) Systolic arrays
    (*c*) Neural network
    (*d*) Array processors

108. Which among the following is special purpose architecture
    (*a*) Neural networks
    (*b*) Data flow computers
    (*c*) Pipeline processor
    (*d*) None of the above

109. Which architecture is based on a concept of industrial assembly line
  (*a*) Array processor
  (*b*) Pipeline processor
  (*c*) Systolic processor
  (*d*) None of the above

110. Ideally a pipeline with n stages provides the speedup of
  (*a*) n
  (*b*) 2^n
  (*c*) log n
  (*d*) None of the above

111. Array processor is a
  (*a*) SIMD m/c
  (*b*) MIMD m/c
  (*c*) MISD m/c
  (*d*) SISD m/c

112. Most popular array processor is
  (*a*) ILLIAC
  (*b*) CRAY
  (*c*) IBM
  (*d*) None of the above

113. In a synchronous multiprocessor
  (*a*) Multiple CPUs and memory banks are connected via interconnection network
  (*b*) Multiple CPUs are connected with common clock
  (*c*) Multiple CPUs work independently
  (*d*) None of the above

114. Following diagram depicts

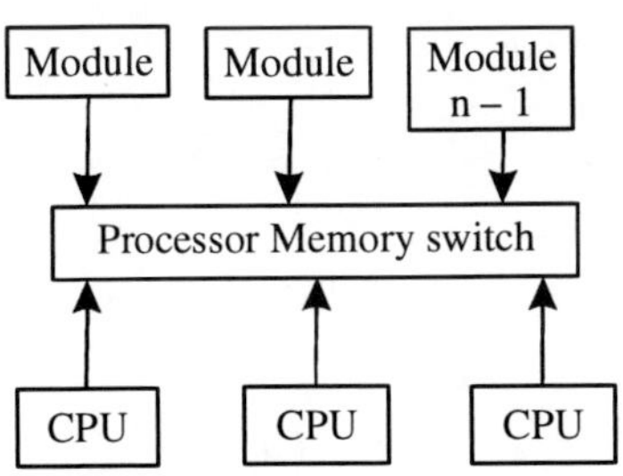

  (*a*) Common bus architecture
  (*b*) Switched bus multiprocessor
  (*c*) Message based architecture
  (*d*) None of the above

115. Following diagram is
  (*a*) Switch based multiprocessor
  (*b*) Message based architecture
  (*c*) Multiprocessor architecture
  (*d*) None of the above

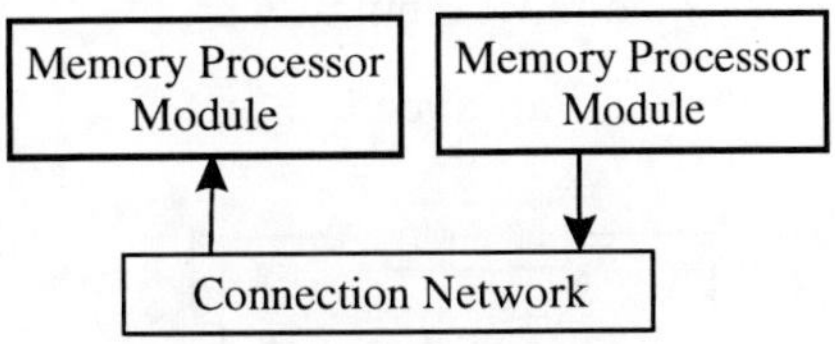

116. Which of the following is not a basic multiprocessor architecture
  (*a*) Shared memory multiprocessor
  (*b*) Message based multiprocessor
  (*c*) Hybrid architecture using both shared memory and massage based multiprocessor
  (*d*) None of the above

117. The number of processors in common bus system is usually
  (*a*) 3
  (*b*) 10
  (*c*) 1000
  (*d*) 10000

118. The following diagram is
  (*a*) Data flow diagram
  (*b*) Flow diagram
  (*c*) Data flow graph
  (*d*) Transition network

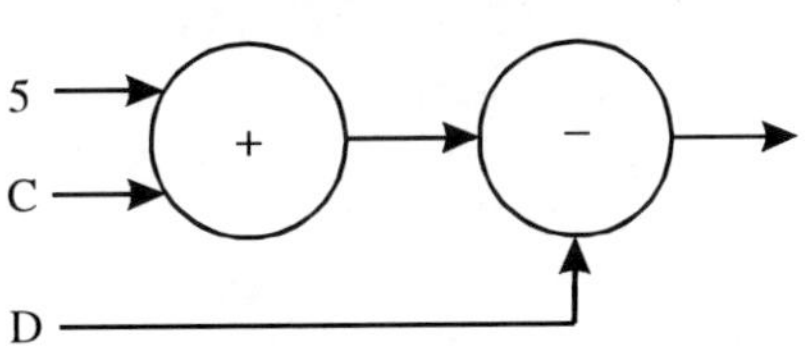

119. Manchester machine is an example of
   (*a*) Array architecture
   (*b*) Data flow architecture
   (*c*) Systolic architecture
   (*d*) Pipeline architecture

120. The data flow computer provides
   (*a*) Coarse granularity
   (*b*) Fine granularity
   (*c*) No granularity
   (*d*) Medium granularity

121. Following architecture is

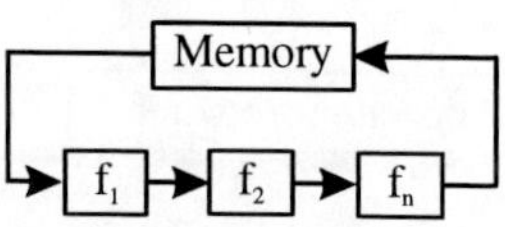

   (*a*) Systolic architecture
   (*b*) Pipeline architecture
   (*c*) Data flow architecture
   (*d*) None of the above

122. The systolic architecture:
   (*a*) Give very high computing throughput
   (*b*) Useful in designing special processors in graphic
   (*c*) is implemented using VLSI
   (*d*) All of the above

123. An architecture based on basic working of human brain is
   (*a*) Pipeline architecture
   (*b*) Systolic array
   (*c*) Neural network
   (*d*) Biomedical architecture

124. Which is true for Neural network
   (*a*) It has set of nodes and connections
   (*b*) Each node computes its weighted input
   (*c*) Node could be in excited state or non-excited state
   (*d*) All of the above

125. Shore had classified computers on the basis of
   (*a*) Organization of constituent elements
   (*b*) Number of processing elements
   (*c*) Based on memory configuration
   (*d*) None of the above

126. A-computing environment in Handler's classification is defined as
   (*a*) Tc = <k × k', d × d', w × w'>
   (*b*) Tc = <k, D, w>
   (*c*) Tc = <k', D′, w' >
   (*d*) None of the above

127. CRAY-1 system according to Handler's classification is characterized as
   (*a*) T < CRAY 1> = (1 × 1, 2 × 2, 64 × S)
   (*b*) T < CRAY a > = (1 × 1, 12 × 8, 64 × (1 – 14)
   (*c*) T< CRAY 1 > = (1 × 1, 4 × 1, 64 × 8)
   (*d*) None of the above

128. Speedup is defined as (Ts = single processor execution, Tn = N processor execution time)
   (*a*) Speedup = Ts/Tn
   (*b*) Speedup = Tn/Ts
   (*c*) Speedup = Tn*Ts
   (*d*) None of the above

129. Amdahl's law is

   (*a*) $S \leq \dfrac{1}{f + \dfrac{(1-f)}{n}}$

   (*b*) $S > \dfrac{1}{f + \dfrac{(1-f)}{n}}$

(*c*) $S \leq f + \frac{(1-f)}{n}$

(*d*) $S \leq {}^{f}\!\big/_{(1-f)/n}$

Where f is sequential fraction of given program.

130. A few elephants approach says
   (*a*) Connect one processor
   (*b*) Connect few extremally powerful processor
   (*c*) Connect very large number of inexpensive processor
   (*d*) None of the above

131. Folk theorem says speedup of n processor parallel system is limited by
   (*a*) $S \leq n/\log_2 n$
   (*b*) $S = n*\log_2 n$
   (*c*) $S = 1/n*\log_2 n$
   (*d*) None of the above

132. Distributed computing deals with
   (*a*) Physical distribution of sub jobs
   (*b*) Logical distribution of sub jobs
   (*c*) Task is handled at one level
   (*d*) None of the above

133. A RAW hazard between two instructions I and J occurs when
   (*a*) Instruction J attempts to read some object that is being modified by instruction I
   (*b*) Instructions I and J read the same data
   (*c*) Instruction I and J writes in the same memory.
   (*d*) None of the above

134. Floating point multiplication does not involve following
   (*a*) Multiplication of fraction
   (*b*) Addition of exponent
   (*c*) Normalization of result
   (*d*) None of the above

135. Dynamic pipeline is
   (*a*) A pipeline which can be reconfigured
   (*b*) A pipeline operating upon dynamic data
   (*c*) A pipeline whose stages are dynamic
   (*d*) None of the above

136. Reservation Table indicates
   (*a*) Occupancy of pipelined stages in various clock cycles
   (*b*) A table reserved for dinner in a restaurant
   (*c*) The table displaying railway reservation
   (*d*) None of the above

137. For two instructions I and J where J logically follows I $> R_i * D_j <> \{\}$ indicates
   (*a*) RAW hazard
   (*b*) WAR hazard
   (*c*) WAW hazard
   (*d*) None of the above

138. For two instructions I and J (where J logically follows I), $D_i * R_j <>$ indicates
   (*a*) RAW hazard
   (*b*) RAR hazard
   (*c*) WAR hazard
   (*d*) WAW hazard

139. For two instructions I and J (where j logically follows i)
   $Ri*Rj <>$ indicates
   (*a*) WAW hazard
   (*b*) RAW hazard
   (*c*) RAR hazard
   (*d*) None of the above

140. To resolve the hazard, the pipeline processor

(*a*) Should suspend the pipeline initiation at point of hazards
(*b*) Pipeline should be redesigned
(c) The execution should be stopped
(*d*) None of the above

141. The performance gain or speedup of memory, if it is divided into modules, is defined as
(*a*) Speedup = Throughput of interleaved system/Throughput of single bank system
(*b*) Speedup = Throughputs of interleaved system/Throughput of reference system
(*c*) Speedup = Throughput of single bank system/Throughputs of interleaved system
(*d*) None of the above

142. In 'C' access memory organization, the
(*a*) Higher order bits are used to access the module
(*b*) Lower order bits are used to access the module
(*c*) All the bits are used to access the module
(*d*) None of the above

143. In 'S' access memory organization
(*a*) Higher order address bits are used to access the module
(*b*) Lower order address bits are used to access the module
(*c*) All the bits are used to access the module
(*d*) All of the above

144. For addresses spaced at a distance of m, the average data access time per word access in synchronous organization is
(*a*) $t = \begin{cases} m \cdot \frac{T}{n} \text{ for } m << n \\ T \text{ for } m >> n \end{cases}$
where T = Bank cycle time and n number of banks
(*b*) $t = \begin{cases} T/n \text{ for } m << n \\ T \text{ for } m >> n \end{cases}$
where T = Bank cycle time and n number of banks
(*c*) $\begin{cases} m \cdot T \text{ for } m << n \\ T \text{ for } m >> n \end{cases}$
where T = bank cycle time and n number of banks
(*d*) None of the above

145. Synchronous memory organization works well for systems where
(*a*) Requests have consecutive addresses
(*b*) Requests have interleaved addresses
(*c*) Few memory references are made
(*d*) None of the above

146. Average access time per element with requests spaced m addresses apart for asynchronous organization is
(*a*) t = gcd (m, n).T/n where T = Memory cycle
(*b*) t = Lm (m, n).T/n where T = Memory cycle
(*c*) t = m.n.T where T = Memory cycle
(*d*) None of the above

147. The data out rate for asynchronous memory organization is
(*a*) T/n

(*b*) T*n
(*c*) n/T
(*d*) None of the above

148. If m is a reservation table for some pipeline, then element $m_{i,j}$ of m is given by

(*a*) $m_{i,j} = \begin{cases} 1, \text{ if stage i is used at time j} \\ 0 \text{ otherwise} \end{cases}$

(*b*) $m_{i,j} = \begin{cases} 1, \text{ if stage j is used at time i} \\ 0 \text{ otherwise} \end{cases}$

(*c*) $m_{i,j} = \begin{cases} 1, \text{ if stage i is used at time j} \\ 0 \text{ otherwise} \end{cases}$

(*d*) None of the above

149. In reservation table if the marks are continuous in a row it represents
(*a*) Pipeline has only single stage
(*b*) A slower stage node needing more time
(*c*) Pipeline will not work properly
(*d*) None of the above

150. A dynamic pipeline
(*a*) Accepts initiation from same reservation table
(*b*) Accepts initiation from different reservation table
(*c*) Does not require initiation
(*d*) None of the above

151. Basic tasks of pipeline scheduler is to
(*a*) Determine the time instances at which initiations can be made without conflict
(*b*) To find out number of stages in pipeline
(*c*) To provide input data to pipeline
(*d*) None of the above

152. Latency is
(*a*) Number of time units between successive initiation
(*b*) Number of clock cycles required to complete a job
(*c*) Number of unused stages of pipeline
(*d*) None of the above

153. Average latency is
(*a*) Inverse of initiation time
(*b*) Proportional to initiation time
(*c*) Inverse of completion time
(*d*) None of the above

154. Forbidden latency is
(*a*) The set consisting of all latencies
(*b*) Latency that will cause a collision
(*c*) A non-existent latency
(*d*) None of the above

155. Minimum achievable latency is
(*a*) Smallest average latency achievable by any control algorithm implementing the scheduler
(*b*) The latency below which nothing can be achieved
(*c*) The latency achieved by single stage pipeline
(*d*) None of the above

156. Consider following reservation table. Its collision vector is
(*a*) 111011
(*b*) 111111
(*c*) 0000000
(*d*) None of the above

X				X	X
X			X		
		X			X

157. Consider following reservation table. Its collision vector is
(*a*) 11111111
(*b*) 1001001
(*c*) 1010101
(*d*) None of the above

S1	X		X				X
S2				X		X	
S3			X		X		

158. Consider following reservation table. Its distance set is
(*a*) 0, 1, 2, 3, 4, 5, 6, 7
(*b*) 0, 1, 5, 6, 7
(*c*) (S1, S2, S3)
(*d*) None of the above

S_1	X	X					X	X
S_2		X	X					
S_3					X	X		

159. For a statically configured pipeline, MAL is always greater than or equal to the maximum number of marks in any row of reservation table
(*a*) True
(*b*) False
(*c*) Partially true
(*d*) Varies from situation to situation

160. Consider the following graph, which of the following latency cycle is invalid
(*a*) <3, 8>
(*b*) <4, 8>
(*c*) <4>
(*d*) None of the above

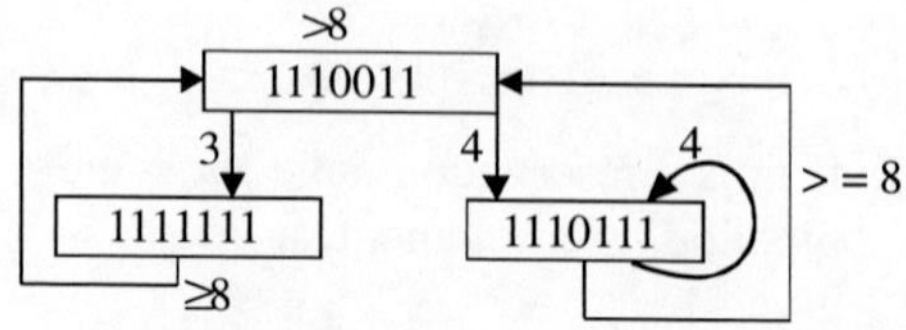

161. Average latency of any greedy cycle is less than or equal to the number of ones in collision vector of reservation table
(*a*) False
(*b*) True
(*c*) Latency and collision vector has no relevance
(*d*) None of the above

162. MAL is always equal to or greater than the maximum number of marks in any row of reservation table
(*a*) True
(*b*) False
(*c*) Cannot be determined
(*d*) None of the above

163. If latency cycle is C = < 258 >, the initiation time sequence is
(*a*) T = 0 2 7 15 17 22 30
(*b*) T = 2 5 0 2 5 0
(*c*) T = 1011011
(*d*) None of the above

164. Which of the following is a memory address register
(*a*) Tore address register
(*b*) Read address register
(*c*) Current operation address register
(*d*) None of the above

165. The exchange permutation is defined as

(*a*) Ek (*a*) = $a_{n-1}a_k....a_0$
where prime denotes Boolean components
(*b*) Ek (*a*) =$a_k.a_k......a_k$
where a_k is the transposed bit
(*c*) It can be defined in multiple ways
(*d*) None of the above

166. The perfect shuffle operation can be expressed as
(*a*) $S(a_{n-1}.........a_1a_0) = a_{n-2}a_1a_0a_{n-1}$
(*b*) $S(a_{n-1}.........a_1a_0) = a_{n-1}\ a_1\ a_0$
(*c*) $S(a_{n-1}.........a_1a_0) = a_{n-1}\ a_{n-1}....a_{n-1}$
(*d*) $S(a_{n-1}.........a_1a_0) = a_0\ a_0.........a_0$

167. In perfect shuffle S(010) is mapped to
(*a*) 100
(*b*) 000
(*c*) 111
(*d*) None of the above

168. The product cycle of perfect shuffle can be represented as
(*a*) S = (0) (7)
(*b*) S = (0) (124) (365) (7)
(*c*) S = (0) (124) (0)
(*d*) None of the above

169. The butterfly permutation can be expressed as
(*a*) B(*a*) = $a_0\ a_{n-2}......a_1\ a_{n-1}$
(*b*) B(*a*) = $a_0\ a_1......a_{n-1}\ a_n$
(*c*) B(*a*) = $a_n\ a_{n-1}....a_0$
(*d*) B(*a*) = $a_0\ a_{n-1}.....a_1\ a_n$

170. For 8 node system in cyclic notation the butterfly network is
(*a*) B = (0) (1, 2) (3, 4) (5, 6) (7)
(*b*) B = (0) (1, 4) (2) (36) (5 × 7)
(*c*) B = (0) (1, 2, 3, 4, 5, 6) (7)
(*d*) None of the above

171. Bit reversal permutation is defined as
(*a*) R(a)= $a_0\ a_1.........a_{n-1}$
(*b*) R(a)= $a_{n-1}\ a_{n-2}.....a_1\ a_0$
(*c*) R(a)= $a_0\ a_n\ a_1\ a_{n-1}.......$
(*d*) None of the above

172. In cyclic notation, bit reversal permutation can be represented as
(*a*) R_1 = (0) (12) (3) (4) (56) (7)
(*b*) R_1 = (0 12 34) (5 6 7 8)
(*c*) R_1 = (0 7) (16) (25) (34)
(*d*) None of the above

173. Shift permutation is defined as
(*a*) L = (a + 1) mod 2^K
(*b*) L = (a + 1) mod N
(*c*) L = (a + 2^{n-1}) mod N
(*d*) None of the above

174. Which of the following is not a network criteria
(*a*) Connectivity
(*b*) Circuit switching
(*c*) Packet switching
(*d*) None of the above

175. A non-blocking network
(*a*) Allows n nodes to connect to all other nodes simultaneously
(*b*) Allows n nodes to talk to n/2 nodes
(*c*) Gives a irregular connectivity
(*d*) None of the above

176. A network employing more than one stage to implement the permutation is called
(*a*) Single stage network
(*b*) Multiple stage network
(*c*) Single node network
(*d*) Multi node network

177. Cross bar is a
(*a*) Non-blocking network

(*b*) Blocking network
(*c*) Varies from connection to connection
(*d*) Multistage network

178. The hardware cost for a N switch crossbar network is proportional to
(*a*) 2N
(*b*) N^2
(*c*) $log2^N$
(*d*) log_2^{N2}

179. Clos network is a
(*a*) Blocking network
(*b*) Non-blocking network
(*c*) Has n^2 switches
(*d*) None of the above

180. For a N input/output clos network, the number of switches is
(*a*) $3N^{1.5}$
(*b*) $3N^2$
(*c*) N^2
(*d*) $N^{1.5}$

181. The middle stage of n input Benz network uses
(*a*) 2 × 2 switches
(*b*) N/2 Crossbar switches of order N/2
(*c*) Crossbar switch of order N
(*d*) None of the above

182. Hardware complexity of Benz's network is
(*a*) N^2
(*b*) $3N^{1.5}$
(*c*) $N\ log_2^{N-N/2}$
(*d*) None of the above

183. For large inputs number of switches will be least in
(*a*) Crossbar network
(*b*) Clos network
(*c*) Benz network
(*d*) None of the above

184. PM 2_i (plus minus 2_i) network is defined as
(*a*) B_{+i} (a) = (a + 2_i) mod N,
B_{-i} (*a*) = (a – 2_i) mod N
(*b*) B (*a*) = (a*2i) mod N
(*c*) B + I (a) = (a – 2i) mod N,
B – I (a) = (a – 2i) mod N
(*d*) None of the above

185. For 8 node $PM2_i$ the product of cycles is given by
(*a*) B_{+0} = (01) (12) (23) (34) (45) (56) (67) (70)
B_{-0} = (07) (10) (2,1) (32) (43) (54) (65) (76)
(*b*) B_{+0} = (0123) (4567)
B_{-0} = (0716) (2534)
(*c*) Varies from connection to connection
(*d*) None of the above

186. Number of switches in N input/output interconnection network is
(*a*) log_2N
(*b*) (N/2) log_2N
(*c*) N^2
(*d*) 4N.log_2 N – 2N

187. Which of the following is not a field of micro instruction
(*a*) Operand field
(*b*) Control field
(*c*) Next address field
(*d*) None of the above

188. Which of the following is not a type of stack
(*a*) Register stack
(*b*) Memory stack
(*c*) Auxiliary stack
(*d*) None of the above

189. The effective address is defined as
(*a*) The address of the operand in any computation instruction or the target address in branch instruction

(*b*) The address which is very effective
(*c*) The address of instruction which is computed
(*d*) None of the above

190. Reverse polish notation is
(*a*) Prefix notation
(*b*) Postfix notation
(*c*) Infix notation
(*d*) None of the above

191. Which of the following is not a valid CPU organization
(*a*) Single accumulator organization
(*b*) General register organization
(*c*) Stack organization
(*d*) None of the above

192. Addressing mode is
(*a*) Method of specifying data
(*b*) Method of specifying the instruction
(*c*) Method of specifying the program
(*d*) None of the above

193. Which of the following is an approach of control unit design
(*a*) Micro programming
(*b*) Java Programming
(*c*) Parallel programming
(*d*) None of the above

194. Which is a valid ALU expansion
(*a*) Spatial expansion
(*b*) Temporal expansion
(*c*) Both (*a*) and (*b*)
(*d*) None of the above

195. A valid method of hardwired control is
(*a*) Classical method
(*b*) One hot method
(*c*) Both (*a*) and (*b*)
(*d*) None of the above

196. Which of the following is not a characteristic of vertical micro-instruction
(*a*) Short format
(*b*) Limited ability to express parallel micro operation
(*c*) Considerable encoding of control information
(*d*) None of the above

197. Rotational latency is defined as
(*a*) Time taken to move read write head to a particular sector
(*b*) Average time to move a head from one track to another
(*c*) Average time to read a fixed amount of information from memory
(*d*) None of the above

198. Multiprogramming is used for
(*a*) Program interleaving to promote better resource utilization
(*b*) Use of multiple processing units for program execution
(*c*) It is a method to implement control unit
(*d*) None of the above

199. In Control flow computer
(*a*) Data is executed sequentially
(*b*) Data is executed parallely
(c) Instructions are executed sequentially
(*d*) None of the above

200. RISC stands for
(*a*) Removed Instruction Set Computer
(*b*) Reduced Instruction Set Computer
(*c*) Reduced Instruction Sequence Command
(*d*) Removed Instruction Sequence Command

201. Machine cycle is
   (*a*) Time taken to fetch two operands from register performing an ALU operation and storing results in a register
   (*b*) Time taken to boot the machine
   (*c*) Time taken to fetch two operands
   (*d*) None of the above

202. SPARC is
   (*a*) Scalable Processor Architecture
   (*b*) Scalable Processor Alu Register Computer
   (*c*) Small Processor Architecture
   (*d*) None of the above

203. Which of the following is not a characteristic of CISC architecture
   (*a*) Large number of instructions
   (*b*) Some instructions perform specialised tasks
   (*c*) A large variety of addressing modes
   (*d*) None of the above

204. RISC is a
   (*a*) Vector processor
   (*b*) Scalar processor
   (*c*) Coprocessor
   (*d*) None of the above

205. Fault tolerance is
   (*a*) Ability of system to execute specified algorithm correctly regardless of hardware failure and program errors
   (*b*) Motherboard in which the probability of fault occurrence is minimum
   (*c*) A program that checks the fault of motherboard and fixes it
   (*d*) None of the above

206. Data flow graph is
   (*a*) Directed graph where nodes correspond to operators and arc are pointers to forwarding tokens
   (*b*) A flow chart indicating the operands or data
   (*c*) It shows the data storage of operands
   (*d*) None of the above

207. Data flow language is
   (*a*) Language used to store data
   (*b*) High-level language for data flow computers, which should be able to express parallelism
   (*c*) A language which stores data corresponding to instructions
   (*d*) None of the above

208. Which is CISC machine
   (*a*) Intel i 486
   (*b*) Intel i 860
   (*c*) Motorola 88100
   (*d*) AMD 29000

209. Which is RISC machine
   (*a*) Motorola PIC 68040
   (*b*) Motorola 88100
   (*c*) NS32532
   (*d*) None of the above

210. Which of the following is not a register window
   (*a*) INS
   (*b*) OUTS
   (*c*) LOCALS
   (*d*) None of the above

211. Systolic array differ from conventional system in which of the following aspect
   (*a*) A single processing element is replaced with array of PE's
   (*b*) It has a single unified memory
   (*c*) It has distributed memory
   (*d*) Both (*a*) and (*b*)

212. Wave front array processor
    (*a*) Has localized connection
    (*b*) Performs asynchronous communication
    (*c*) Multiple processing elements
    (*d*) All of the above

213. Efficiency of a 'n' stage pipeline is given by
    (*a*) $E(n) = \frac{\text{Actual speedup}}{\text{Maximum speedup}}$
    (*b*) $E(n) = \frac{\text{Maximum speedup}}{\text{Actual speedup}}$
    (*c*) $E(n) = \frac{\text{Minimum speedup}}{\text{Maximum speedup}}$
    (*d*) $E(n) = \frac{\text{Maximum speedup}}{\text{Minimum speedup}}$

214. Memory interleaving can be used for
    (*a*) To reduce memory conflict
    (*b*) To remove memory conflict
    (*c*) To reduce memory size
    (*d*) To remove memory size

215. Concept of delayed branch is used in
    (*a*) CISC
    (*b*) RISC
    (*c*) MISC
    (*d*) PISC

216. In a 8 module memory interleaved memory system maximum words which can be accessed concurrently
    (*a*) 4
    (*b*) 8
    (*c*) 16
    (*d*) Depends upon memory size

217. Which is not an advantage of single bus organization
    (*a*) Overall system capacity is limited by transfer rate
    (*b*) Poor fault tolerant ability
    (*c*) In case of expansion system throughput is reduced
    (*d*) None of the above

218. In multi port memory organization
    (*a*) Control, switching and priority arbitration logic is distributed throughout cross switch matrix
    (*b*) It is used for multi peripheral I/O channels
    (*c*) Well-suited to uni and multiprocessor system
    (*d*) Both (*a*) and (*c*)

219. The content addressable memory is also called
    (*a*) Secondary memory
    (*b*) Associative memory
    (*c*) Working memory
    (*d*) Cache memory

220. Which of the following is not an advantage of tagged memory
    (*a*) More protection to items against misuse
    (*b*) Elegant error detection mechanism
    (*c*) Minimum programming effort
    (*d*) None of the above

221. Ferrite core memory is a
    (*a*) Destructive read out memory
    (*b*) Non-destructive read out memory
    (*c*) Destructive write memory
    (*d*) Non-destructive write memory

222. To create a RAM of size of M × N with a chip of capacity of M × N, the number of chips required are
    (*a*) MN/M*N
    (*b*) M*N/MN

(*c*) M*N/N*M
(*d*) N*M/M*N

223. Bank switching is a technique
(*a*) It involves turning on between memory banks under software control
(*b*) Keeping the memory in safe custody
(*c*) Using the memory for banking application
(*d*) None of the above

224. Probability to occur hit at level i and miss at level i – 1 is
(*a*) hi = $H(S_i - 1) - H(s_i)$
(*b*) hi = $H(S_i) - H(S_i - 1)$
(*c*) hi = H(n) – H(o)
(*d*) None of the above

ANSWERS

1. (*c*)	2. (*d*)	3. (*d*)	4. (*c*)	5. (*d*)	6. (*d*)	7. (*d*)
8. (*a*)	9. (*c*)	10. (*c*)	11. (*c*)	12. (*b*)	13. (*c*)	14. (*b*)
15. (*c*)	16. (*b*)	17. (*a*)	18. (*c*)	19. (*a*)	20. (*a*)	21. (*d*)
22. (*a*)	23. (*c*)	24. (*b*)	25. (*a*)	26. (*a*)	27. (*a*)	28. (*a*)
29. (*c*)	30. (*b*)	31. (*c*)	32. (*a*)	33. (*d*)	34. (*a*)	35. (*d*)
36. (*d*)	37. (*c*)	38. (*b*)	39. (*a*)	40. (*b*)	41. (*c*)	42. (*a*)
43. (*c*)	44. (*a*)	45. (*a*)	46. (*d*)	47. (*b*)	48. (*a*)	49. (*c*)
50. (*a*)	51. (*a*)	52. (*b*)	53. (*a*)	54. (*b*)	55. (*b*)	56. (*a*)
57. (*c*)	58. (*c*)	59. (*b*)	60. (*d*)	61. (*a*)	62. (*c*)	63. (*a*)
64. (*c*)	65. (*a*)	66. (*d*)	67. (*a*)	68. (*b*)	69. (*c*)	70. (*b*)
71. (*b*)	72. (*a*)	73. (*c*)	74. (*a*)	75. (*a*)	76. (*b*)	77. (*c*)
78. (*d*)	79. (*b*)	80. (*c*)	81. (*c*)	82. (*a*)	83. (*d*)	84. (*c*)
85. (*b*)	86. (*a*)	87. (*a*)	88. (*c*)	89. (*d*)	90. (*c*)	91. (*c*)
92. (*a*)	93. (*a*)	94. (*c*)	95. (*c*)	96. (*b*)	97. (*a*)	98. (*b*)
99. (*d*)	100. (*b*)	101. (*a*)	102. (*c*)	103. (*d*)	104. (*a*)	105. (*d*)
106. (*d*)	107. (*a*)	108. (*a*)	109. (*b*)	110. (*a*)	111. (*a*)	112. (*a*)
113. (*a*)	114. (*a*)	115. (*b*)	116. (*c*)	117. (*b*)	118. (*c*)	119. (*b*)
120. (*b*)	121. (*a*)	122. (*d*)	123. (*c*)	124. (*d*)	125. (*c*)	126. (*a*)
127. (*a*)	128. (*a*)	129. (*a*)	130. (*b*)	131. (*a*)	132. (*a*)	133. (*a*)
134. (*d*)	135. (*a*)	136. (*a*)	137. (*b*)	138. (*c*)	139. (*a*)	140. (*a*)
141. (*a*)	142. (*a*)	143. (*b*)	144. (*a*)	145. (*a*)	146. (*a*)	147. (*a*)
148. (*a*)	149. (*b*)	150. (*a*)	151. (*a*)	152. (*a*)	153. (*a*)	154. (*b*)
155. (*a*)	156. (*a*)	157. (*b*)	158. (*b*)	159. (*a*)	160. (*d*)	161. (*b*)
162. (*a*)	163. (*a*)	164. (*d*)	165. (*a*)	166. (*c*)	167. (*c*)	168. (*b*)
169. (*a*)	170. (*b*)	171. (*a*)	172. (*a*)	173. (*b*)	174. (*d*)	175. (*a*)
176. (*b*)	177. (*a*)	178. (*b*)	179. (*b*)	180. (*a*)	181. (*b*)	182. (*c*)
183. (*c*)	184. (*a*)	185. (*a*)	186. (*b*)	187. (*a*)	188. (*c*)	189. (*a*)

190. (*b*)	191. (*d*)	192. (*a*)	193. (*a*)	194. (*c*)	195. (*c*)	196. (*d*)
197. (*a*)	198. (*a*)	199. (*d*)	200. (*b*)	201. (*a*)	202. (*a*)	203. (*d*)
204. (*b*)	205. (*a*)	206. (*a*)	207. (*b*)	208. (*a*)	209. (*b*)	210. (*d*)
211. (*d*)	212. (*d*)	213. (*a*)	214. (*a*)	215. (*b*)	216. (*b*)	217. (*d*)
218. (*d*)	219. (*b*)	220. (*d*)	221. (*a*)	222. (*b*)	223. (*a*)	224. (*b*)

7

Theory of Computation

1. Which of the following sentence is not a proposition.
   (*a*) Dr. Manmohan Singh is prime minister of India
   (*b*) Square of –1 is a real number.
   (*c*) Psychology is a difficult subject.
   (*d*) I wish you all the best.

2. The following is a well-formed formula.
   (*a*) $(P \land Q) \Rightarrow (P \lor Q)$
   (*b*) $(P \land Q) \Rightarrow (P \lor Q) \land R)$
   (*c*) $(P \land (Q \land R)) \Rightarrow (P \land Q)$
   (*d*) $\neg(Q \land \neg (P \lor \neg Q)$

3. P + Q is called
   (*a*) Addition
   (*b*) Conjunction
   (*c*) Simplification
   (*d*) Modus ponens

4. $\neg A \land \neg B \land C$ can be a minterm of
   (*a*) $A \lor B$
   (*b*) $\neg A \land \neg B \land C$
   (*c*) $A \land B \land C \land D$
   (*d*) $A \land B$

5. $(A \cup A) \cap (B \cap B)$ is
   (*a*) A
   (*b*) $A \cap B$
   (*c*) B
   (*d*) None of the above

6. The reflexive-transitive closure of the relation {(1, 2), (2, 3)} is
   (*a*) {(1, 2), (2, 3), (1, 3)}
   (*b*) {(1, 2), (2, 3), (1, 3), (3, 1)}
   (*c*) {(1, 1), (2, 2), (3, 3), (1, 3), (1, 2), (2, 3)}
   (*d*) {(1, 1), (2, 2), (3, 3), (1, 3)}

7. There exists a function f : {1, 2 ...., 10} $\xrightarrow[j]{}$ {2, 3, 4, 5, 6, 7, 9, 10, 11, 12} which is
   (*a*) One-to-one and onto
   (*b*) One-to-one but not onto
   (*c*) Onto but not one-to-one
   (*d*) None of the above

8. A tree with 10 vertices has
   (*a*) 10 edges
   (*b*) 9 edges
   (*c*) 8 edges
   (*d*) 7 edges.

9. The number of binary trees with 7 vertices is
   (*a*) 7
   (*b*) 6
   (*c*) 2
   (*d*) 1

10. Let N = {1, 2, 3, ...). Then f : $N \to N$ defined by f(n) = n + 1 is
    (*a*) Onto but not one-to-one
    (*b*) One-to-one but not onto
    (*c*) Both one-to-one and onto
    (*d*) Neither one-to-one nor onto

11. QST is a substring of
    (*a*) PQRST
    (*b*) QRSTU
    (*c*) QSPQSTUT
    (*d*) QQSSTT

12. If x = 01, y = 101 and z = 011, then xyzy is
   (*a*) 01011011
   (*b*) 01101101011
   (*c*) 01011101101
   (*d*) 01101011101

13. A binary tree with seven vertices has
   (*a*) One leaf
   (*b*) Two leaves
   (*c*) Three leaves
   (*d*) Four leaves

14. A binary operation 'O' on N = {1, 2, 3, ...) is defined by a O b = a + 2b. Then
   (*a*) O is commutative
   (*b*) O is associative
   (*c*) N has an identity element with respect to O
   (*d*) None of these

Answer following 5 questions based on following automata

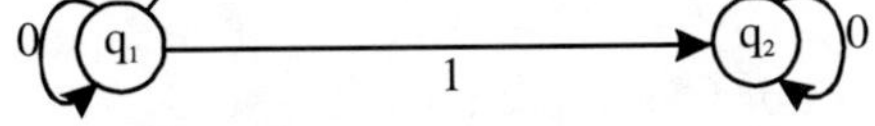

15. M is a
   (*a*) Nondeterministic automaton
   (*b*) Deterministic automaton accepting {0, 1}*
   (*c*) Deterministic automaton accepting all strings over {0, 1} having 3m 0's and 3n 1's, m, n ≥ 1
   (*d*) Deterministic automaton

16. M accepts
   (*a*) 01110
   (*b*) 10001
   (*c*) 01010
   (*d*) 11111

17. T (M) is equal to
   (*a*) $\{0^{3m}\ 1^{3n}|m, n \geq 1\}$
   (*b*) $\{0^{3m}\ |1^{3n}|\ m, n \geq 0\}$
   (*c*) {w | w has 111 as a substring}
   (*d*) {w | w has 3n 1's, n ≥ 1}

18. If q2 is also made a final state, then M accepts
   (*a*) 01110 and 01100
   (*b*) 10001 and 10000
   (*c*) 0110 but not 0111101
   (*d*) 0^{3m} n ≥ 1 but not 1^{3n}, n ≥ 1

19. If q2 is also made a final state, then T (M) is equal to
   (*a*) $\{0^{3m}\ 1^{3n}\,|\ m, n \geq 0\} \cup \{0^{2m}\ 1^{n}\ |\ m, n \geq 0\}$
   (*b*) $\{0^{3m}\ 1^{3n}\ |\ m, n \geq 1\} \cup \{0^{2m}\ 1^{n}\ |\ m, n \geq 1\}$
   (*c*) {w | w has 111 as a substring or 11 as a substring}
   (*d*) {w| the number of 1's in w is divisible by 2 or 3}

Answer questions 21-30 from following automatam

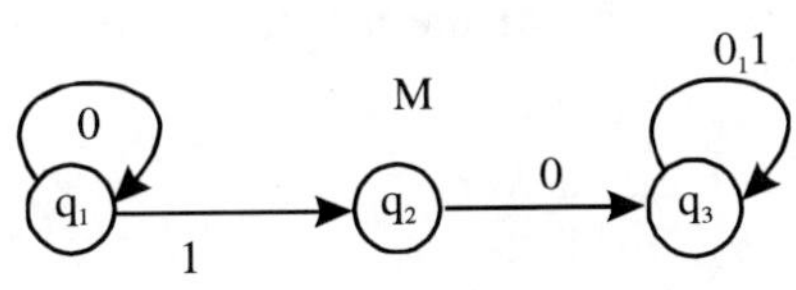

20. M is a
   (*a*) Deterministic automaton
   (*b*) Non deterministic automata
   (*c*) Can be converted to deterministic automata
   (*d*) None of the above

21. δ (q_1, 1) is
   (*a*) Defined
   (*b*) Undefined
   (*c*) Can't be said
   (*d*) None of the above

22. String 0100111 is
(*a*) Accepted by M
(*b*) Not accepted by M
(*c*) Can't be said
(*d*) None of the above

23. String 010101010 is
(*a*) Not accepted by M
(*b*) Accepted by M
(*c*) Can't be said
(*d*) None of the above

24. Transition $\delta(q_0, 01001)$ is not equal to
(*a*) $\{q_1q_2\}$
(*b*) $\{q_1\}$
(*c*) $\{q_1q_2q_3\}$
(*d*) $\{\phi\}$

25. $\delta(q_0, 011000)$ is equivalent to
(*a*) $\{q_1\}$
(*b*) $\{q_1q_2\}$
(*c*) $\{q_0, q_1, q_2\}$
(*d*) None of the above

26. $\delta(q_2, w) = q_2$ for any string
(*a*) $w \in \{0, 1\}^*$
(*b*) $w \in \{0, 0\}^*$
(*c*) $w \in \{1, 1\}^*$
(*d*) None of the above

27. $\delta(q_1, 11001)$ is
(*a*) Equal to ϕ
(*b*) Not Equal ϕ
(*c*) Can't be said
(*d*) None of the above

28. T(M) = (w/w = x00y, where x, y $\in \{0, 1\}^*$
(*a*) True
(*b*) False
(*c*) Can't be said
(*d*) None of the above

29. A string accepted by M is
(*a*) having even number of 0's
(*b*) having odd number of 0's
(*c*) having alternate number 0's and 1's
(*d*) None of the above.

30. If $\alpha \overset{*}{\Rightarrow} \beta$ in a grammar G, then
(*a*) $\alpha \overset{*}{\Rightarrow} \beta$
(*b*) $\beta \overset{*}{\Rightarrow} \alpha$
(*c*) $\beta \overset{*}{\Rightarrow} \alpha$
(*d*) none of these

31. If $\alpha \rightarrow \beta$ is a production in a grammar G. then
(*a*) $\alpha\alpha \overset{*}{\Rightarrow} \beta\beta$
(*b*) $\alpha\alpha\beta \overset{*}{\Rightarrow} \beta\beta\alpha$
(*c*) $\alpha\alpha \overset{*}{\Rightarrow} \beta\alpha$
(*d*) $\alpha\alpha\alpha \overset{*}{\Rightarrow} \beta\beta\beta$

32. If a grammar G has three productions S → aSa | bsb | c, then
(*a*) abcba and bacab ∈ L(G)
(*b*) abcba and abcab ∈ L(G)
(*c*) accca and bcccb ∈ L(G)
(*d*) acccb and bcca ∈ L(G)

33. The minimum number of productions for a grammar G = ({S}, {0, 1, 2, ..., 9}, P, S) for generating {0, 1, 2, ..., 9} is
(*a*) 9
(*b*) 10
(*c*) 1
(*d*) 2

34. If G_1 = N, T, P_1, S) and G_2 = (N, T, P_2, S) and $P_1 \subseteq P_2$, then
(*a*) $L(G_1) \subseteq L(G_2)$
(*b*) $L(G_2) \subseteq L(G_1)$
(*c*) $L(G_1) \subseteq (L(G_2)$
(*d*) none of the above.

35. The regular grammar generating $\{a^n : n \geq 1\}$ is
(*a*) $(\{S\}, \{a\}, \{S \rightarrow aS^2S, S\})$
(*b*) $(\{S\}, \{a\}, \{S \rightarrow SS, S \rightarrow a\})$
(*c*) $(\{S\}, \{a\}, \{S \rightarrow aS\}, S)$
(*d*) $(\{S\}, \{a\}, \{S \rightarrow aS, S \rightarrow a, S)$

36. L – {theory, of, computer, science} can be generated by
(*a*) A regular grammar
(*b*) A context-free grammar but not a regular grammar
(*c*) A context-sensitive grammar but not a context-free grammar
(*d*) Only by a type 0 grammar.

37. $\{a^n \mid n \geq 1\}$ is
(*a*) Regular
(*b*) Context-free but not regular
(*c*) Context-sensitive but not context-free
(*d*) None of the above

38. $\{a^n b^n \mid n \geq 1 \}$ is
(*a*) Regular
(*b*) Context-free but not regular
(*c*) Context-sensitive but not context-free
(*d*) None of these

39. $\{a^nb^nc^n \mid n \geq 1\}$ is
(*a*) Regular
(*b*) Context-free but not regular
(*c*) Context-sensitive but not context-free
(*d*) None of the above

40. $\{a^nb^nc^m \mid n, m \geq 1\}$ is
(*a*) Regular
(*b*) Context-free but not regular
(*c*) Context-sensitive but not context-free
(*d*) None of these.

41. In a grammar G = (VN, Σ P, S), VN and Σ are finite but P can be infinite.
(*a*) True
(*b*) False
(*c*) Can't be said
(*d*) None of the above

42. Statement "two grammars of different types can generate the same language."
(*a*) True
(*b*) False
(*c*) Can't be said
(*d*) None of the above

43. If G = 1/N, Σ, P, S) and $P \neq \Phi$, then $L(G) \neq \Phi$
(*a*) True
(*b*) False
(*c*) Can't be said
(*d*) None of the above

44. If a grammar G has three productions, i.e. $S \rightarrow AA$, $A \rightarrow aa$, $A \rightarrow bb$, then
(*a*) L(G) is finite
(*b*) L(G) is infinite
(*c*) L(G) is undecidable
(*d*) None of the above

45. If $L_1 = \{a^nb^m \mid m, n \geq 1\}$ and $L_2 = \{b^mc^p \mid m, p \geq 1\}$ then $L_1 \cap L_2 = \{a^nb^nc^n \mid n \geq 1\}$.
(*a*) True
(*b*) False
(*c*) Can't be said
(*d*) None of the above

46. If a grammar G has productions $S \rightarrow aS \mid bS \mid a$, then
(*a*) L(G) = the set of all strings over {a, b} ending in a.
(*b*) The set of all strings over (a,b) ending in b
(*c*) The set of all strings over (a,b)
(*d*) None of the above.

47. The language $\{a^nbc^n \mid n \geq 1\}$ is
(*a*) regular

(*b*) Context free
(*c*) irregular
(*d*) None of the above.

48. If the productions of G are S → aS | Sb | a | b, then abab ∈ L(G) is
(*a*) True
(*b*) False
(*c*) Can't be said
(*d*) None of the above

49. The set of all strings over {a, b} of even length is represented by the regular expression
(*a*) (ab + aa + bb + ba)*
(*b*) (a + b)* (a* + b)*
(*c*) (aa + bb)*
(*d*) (ab + ba)*

50. The set of all string over {a, b} of length 4, starting with a is represented by the regular expression
(*a*) a (a + b)*
(*b*) a(ab)*
(*c*) (ab + ba)(aa + bb)
(*d*) a(a + b) (a + b) (a + b)

51. (0*1*)* is same as
(*a*) (0 + 1)*
(*b*) (01)*
(*c*) (10)*
(*d*) none of the above

52. If L is the set of all strings over {a, b} containing at least one a, then it is not represented by the regular expression
(*a*) b*a(a + b)*
(*b*) (a + b)*a(b + a)*
(*c*) (a + b)* ab*
(*d*) (a + b)*a

53. $\{a^{2n} \mid n \geq 1\}$ is represented by the regular expression
(*a*) (aa)*
(*b*) a*
(*c*) aa*a
(*d*) a*a*

54. The set of strings over {a, b} having exactly 3b's is represented by the regular expression
(*a*) a*bbb
(*b*) a*ba*ba*b
(*c*) ba*ba*b
(*d*) a*ba*ba*ba*

55. The set of all strings over {a, b} having abab as a substring is represented by
(*a*) a*ababb*
(*b*) (a + b)*abab(a + b)*
(*c*) a*b*ababa*b*
(*d*) (a + b)*abab

56. (a + a)* is equivalent to
(*a*) a(a*)*
(*b*) a*
(*c*) aa*
(*d*) none of these

57. a*(a + b)* is equivalent to
(*a*) a* + b*
(*b*) (ab)*
(*c*) a*b*
(*d*) none of these

58. ab* + b* represents all strings w over {a, b}
(*a*) starting with an 'a' and having no other a's or having no a's but only b's
(*b*) starting with an a followed by b's
(*c*) having no a's but only b's
(*d*) none of these.

59. Every finite subset of Σ* is a regular language
(*a*) True
(*b*) False
(*c*) Can't be said

(*d*) None of the above

60. Every regular language over Σ is finite
(*a*) True
(*b*) False
(*c*) Can't be said
(*d*) None of the above

61. aa* + bb* is the same as
(*a*) (a + b)*
(*b*) (a + a)*
(*c*) (b + b)*
(*d*) None of the above

62. The set of all string starting with a and ending in ab is defined by the regular expression
(*a*) a(a + b)*b
(*b*) a*(a + b)*b
(*c*) a(b + b)b
(*d*) None of the above

63. A regular language is context-free.
(*a*) True
(*b*) False
(*c*) Can't be said
(*d*) None of the above

64. There exist context-free languages that are not regular.
(*a*) True
(*b*) False
(*c*) Can't be said
(*d*) None of the above

65. The class of context-free languages is closed under union.
(*a*) True
(*b*) False
(*c*) Can't be said
(*d*) None of the above

66. The statement "There exist a class of context free language that is closed under intersection" is
(*a*) True
(*b*) False
(*c*) Can't be said
(*d*) None of the above

67. The statement "There exist a class of context free language that is closed under complementation is
(*a*) True
(*b*) False
(*c*) Can't be said
(*d*) None of the above

68. Statement "any derivation tree for a regular grammar is a binary tree" is
(*a*) True
(*b*) False
(*c*) Can't be said
(*d*) None of the above

69. $\{a^m b^n c^n \mid n \geq 1\}$ is
(*a*) Context-free language
(*b*) Context-sensitinelanguage
(*c*) Not context free language
(*d*) None of the above

70. If $\delta(q, a_1, Z_1)$ contains (q', β), then
(*a*) $(q, a_1a_2, Z_1Z_2) - (q', a_2, \beta Z_2)$
(*b*) $(q, a_2a_2, Z_1Z_2) - (q', a_1a_2, \beta Z_2)$
(*c*) $(q, aa_2, Z_2) - (q', a_1, Z_1)$
(*d*) $(q, a_1a_2, Z_1Z_2) - (q', a_2, Z_1Z_2)$

71. In a deterministic pda, $|\delta(q, a, Z)|$ is
(*a*) equal to 1
(*b*) less than or equal to 1
(*c*) greater than 1
(*d*) greater than or equal to 1

72. In a deterministic pda:
(*a*) $\delta(q, a, Z) = \Phi \Rightarrow \delta(q\ \Lambda\ Z) \neq \Phi$
(*b*) $\delta(q, a, Z) \neq \Phi \Rightarrow \delta(q\ \Lambda\ Z) = \Phi$,
(*c*) $\delta(q\ \Lambda\ Z) \neq \Phi \Rightarrow \delta(q, a, Z) \neq \Phi$
(*d*) $\delta(q\ \Lambda\ Z) \neq \Phi \Rightarrow \delta(q, a, Z) \neq \Phi$

73. $\{a^nb^n \mid n \geq 1\}$ is accepted by
(*a*) A finite automaton
(*b*) A non-deterministic finite automaton
(*c*) A pda
(*d*) None of the above.

74. The intersection of a context-free language and a regular language is
(*a*) Context-free
(*b*) Regular but not context-free
(*c*) Neither context-free nor regular
(*d*) Both regular and context-free.

75. An LR (k) grammar has to be
(*a*) A type 0 grammar
(*b*) A type 1 grammar
(*c*) A type 2 grammar
(*d*) None of the above

76. An LR (k) grammar is
(*a*) Always unambiguous
(*b*) Always ambiguous
(*c*) Need not be unambiguous
(*d*) None of these

77. A handle is
(*a*) A string of variables and terminals
(*b*) A string of variables
(*c*) A string of terminals
(*d*) A production.

78. The automaton corresponding to an LR(k) grammar is
(*a*) A deterministic finite automaton
(*b*) A nondeterministic finite automaton
(*c*) A deterministic PDA
(*d*) A nondeterministic PDA.

79. $\mathcal{L}_{\text{dcfl}}$ is closed under
(*a*) Union
(*b*) Complementation
(*c*) Intersection
(*d*) None of the above

80. For the standard TM :
(*a*) $\Sigma = \Gamma$
(*b*) $\Gamma \subseteq \Sigma$
(*c*) $\Sigma \subseteq \Gamma$
(*d*) Σ is a proper subset of Γ.

81. In a standard TM, $\delta(q, a)$, $q \in Q$, $a \in \Gamma$ is
(*a*) Defined for all $(q, a) \in Q \times \Gamma$
(*b*) Defined for some, not necessarily for all $(q, a) \in Q \times \Gamma$
(*d*) A set of triples with more than one element.

82. If $\delta(q, xi) = (p, y, L)$, then
(*a*) $x_1x_2\ldots.\ x_{i-1}qx_i\ldots x_n \vdash x_1x_2 \ldots x_{i-2}\ px_{i-1}yx_{i+1}\ldots x_n$
(*b*) $x_1x_2\ldots.\ xi_{-1}qx_i\ldots x_n \vdash x_1x_2 \ldots x_{i-1}ypx_{i+1}\ldots x_n$
(*c*) $x_1x_2\ldots.\ xi_{-1}\ qx_i\ldots x_n \vdash x_1\ldots x_{i-3}\ px_{i-2}yx_{i-1}\ yxi_{+1}\ldots x_n$
(*d*) $x_1x_2\ldots.\ xi_{-1}qx_i\ldots x_n \vdash x_1x_2 \ldots x_{i-1}\ ypx_{i+2}\ldots x_n$

83. If $\delta(q, xi) = (p, y, R)$, then
(*a*) $x_1x_2\ldots.x_{i-1}\ qx_i\ldots x_n \vdash x_1x_2\ldots x_{i-1}ypx_{i+1}\ldots x_n$
(*b*) $x_1x_2\ldots.x_{i-1}qx_i\ldots x_n \vdash x_1x_2 \ldots x_ipx_{i+1}\ldots x_n$
(*c*) $x_1x_2\ldots.\ xi_{-1}qx_i\ldots x_n \vdash x_1x_2 \ldots x_{i-1}px_{i+1}\ldots x_n$
(*d*) $x_1x_2\ldots.\ xi_{-1}qx_i\ldots x_n \vdash x_1x_2 \ldots x_{i-1}ypx_{i+1}\ldots x_n$

84. If $\delta(q, x1) = (p, y, L)$, then
(*a*) $qx_2x_2\ldots x_n \vdash pyx_2\ldots x_n$
(*b*) $qx_1x_2\ldots x_n \vdash ypx_2\ldots x_n$
(*c*) $qx_1x_2\ldots x_n \vdash pbx_1\ldots x_n$
(*d*) $qx_1x_2\ldots x_n \vdash pbx_2\ldots x_n$

85. Which of the following is not a proposition.
(*a*) No thank you
(*b*) New Delhi is capital of India
(*c*) The square of 4 is 16
(*d*) The square of 5 is 27

86. Preposition is a.
   (*a*) Logical statement
   (*b*) Declarative sentence to which only one of the truth value can be assigned
   (*c*) Mathematical statement giving answer in a finite range
   (*d*) None of the above

87. Which of the following is not a valid propositional connective.
   (*a*) Implication
   (*b*) If and only if
   (*c*) Negation
   (*d*) None of the above

88. Consider the situation
   P : Represent dress is good,
   Q : Represent dress is cheap,
   The logical formula for the dress is not good but cheap is.
   (*a*) $\neg$ P Λ Q
   (*b*) P Λ Q
   (*d*) $\neg$ Q Λ P
   (*d*) $\neg$ P Λ $\neg$ Q

89. In above question formula for "the dress is neither good nor cheap is.
   (*a*) P $\vee$ Q
   (*b*) $\neg$ P $\vee$ $\neg$ Q
   (*c*) $\neg$ P Λ $\neg$ Q
   (*d*) P Λ Q

90. The correct truth table for implication is P $\rightarrow$ Q is.

(*a*) P Q P $\rightarrow$ Q
T T T
T F F
F T T
F F T

(*b*) T T T
T F F
F T F
F F T

(*c*) T T F
T F T
F T T
F F F

(*d*) T T F
T F T
F T T
F F F

91. Truth table for if and only if (i.e. P $\Leftrightarrow$ Q).

(*a*) P Q P
T T T
T F F
F T T
F F T

(*b*) T T T
T F F
F T F
F F T

(*c*) T T P
T F T
F T T
F F F

(*d*) T T F
T F T
F T T
F F F

92. The propositional forms of "If it is not raining and I have the time, then I will go a movie" will be, consider the propositions as
   A: It is raining
   B: I have the time
   C: I will go to a movie
   (*a*) ($\neg$ A Λ B) $\Rightarrow$ C
   (*b*) $\neg$ A Λ $\neg$ B $\Rightarrow$ $\neg$ C
   (*c*) (A Λ B) $\Rightarrow$ C
   (*d*) C $\Rightarrow$ $\neg$ P)

93. In question 8 the proposition form of "if it is raining I will not go to a movie will be.
   (*a*) A Λ $\neg$ C
   (*b*) $\neg$A
   (*c*) A Λ C
   (*d*) None of the above

94. The proposition for "I will go to a movie only if it is not raining is.
(*a*) R ⇒ ¬ P
(*b*) P Λ ¬ R
(*c*) ¬ P
(*d*) P Λ ¬ R

95. Preposition for I will not go to a movie.
(*a*) ¬ P
(*b*) ¬ R
(*c*) P Λ ¬ R
(*d*) R ⇒ ¬ P

96. With above proposition write sentences for the following
¬ P Λ Q ⇔ R
(*a*) I will go to movie if and only if I have time
(*b*) I will not go to movie if and only if I have time
(*c*) I will go to a movie if and only if it is not raining and I have time
(*d*) None of the above

97. A well defined formula is a.
(*a*) Recursive formula
(*b*) Non recursive formula
(*c*) Can be converted to a recursive formula
(*d*) None of the above

98. If α is wff then ¬α is wff".
(*a*) True
(*b*) false
(*c*) can't be said
(*d*) None of the above

99. If α and β are well formed formulas then α ⇒ β will be
(*a*) Well formed formula
(*b*) Will not be wff
(*c*) Can be converted to wff
(*d*) None of the above

100. If P & Q are two assertions then truth table for(P ∨ Q) Λ (P ⇒ Q) Λ (Q ⇒ P) will be
(*a*)

P	Q	α
T	T	T
T	F	F
F	T	F
F	F	F

(*b*)

P	Q	α
T	T	F
T	F	F
F	T	F
F	F	T

(*c*)

P	Q	α
T	T	T
T	F	T
F	T	T
F	F	F

(*d*) None of the above

101. Which of the following is true.
(*a*) P ⇒ (Q ∨ R) ≡ (P ⇒ Q) ∨ (P ⇒ R)
(*b*) P Λ Q ∨ R ≡ (P ⇒ Q) ∨ (P ⇒ R)
(*c*) P ⇒ (Q ∨ R) ≡ (P Λ Q) ∨ (P ⇒ R)
(*d*) P ⇒ (Q ∨ R) ≡ (P ⇒ Q) ∨ (P Λ R)

102. The disjunctive normal form of P ∨ (¬P ⇒ Q ∨ (Q ⇒ ¬ R)) will be
(*a*) P ∨ Q Λ ¬ Q ∨ ¬ R
(*b*) P ∨ Q ∨ ¬ Q ∨ ¬ R
(*c*) P Λ Q ∨ ¬ Q ∨ R
(*d*) None of the above

103. The disjunctive normal form of P Λ ¬ (Q Λ R)) ∨ (P ⇒ Q)
(*a*) (P ∨ ¬ Q) Λ (P ∨ ¬ R) Λ ¬ P ∨ Q
(*b*) (P Λ ¬ Q) ∨ (P Λ ¬ R) ∨ ¬ P ∨ Q
(*c*) P Λ Q ∨ ¬ R Λ ¬ P
(*d*) None of the above

104. Principal disjunctive form of $\alpha = P \vee (\neg P \wedge \neg Q \wedge R)$ is
(*a*) $(P \wedge Q \wedge R) \vee (P \wedge Q \wedge \neg R)$ $(P \wedge \neg Q \wedge \neg R) \vee (\neg P \wedge \neg Q \wedge R)$
(*b*) $(P \wedge Q \wedge R) \wedge (P \vee Q \vee \neg R) \wedge (P \vee \neg Q \vee R) \wedge (P \vee \neg Q \vee \neg R) \wedge (\neg P \vee \neg Q \wedge R)$
(*c*) $P \wedge Q \wedge R$
(*d*) $P \vee Q \vee R$

105. If C(*x*) denote '*x* is clever' and S(*x*) denote '*x* is successful, then predicate representation of all students are clever will be
(*a*) $\exists x (\neg S(x))$
(*b*) $\forall x ((x)$
(*c*) $\forall x\, S(x)$
(*d*) $\exists x\, C(x)$

106. Every clever student is successful is represented as.
(*a*) $\forall x (C(x) \Rightarrow S(x))$
(*b*) $\forall x\, C(x) \Leftrightarrow S(x)$
(*c*) $\exists x (C(x) \neg S(x))$
(*d*) None of the above

107. Some students are clever and successful is represented as.
(*a*) $\exists x (\neg S(x)$
(*b*) $\exists x (S(x) \wedge \neg C(x))$
(*c*) $\exists x (C(x) \neg S(x))$
(*d*) None of the above

108. In predicate calculus a well formed formula is.
(*a*) String of constants and connectives
(*b*) String of variables and connectives
(*c*) Connectives, parenthesis and quantifier
(*d*) None of the above

109. Which of the following is true.
(*a*) $\neg(\exists x\, P(x)) \equiv \forall x \neg (P(x))$
(*b*) $\forall x \neg p(x) \equiv \neg x p(x)$
(*c*) $\neg p(x) \equiv \forall x p(x)$
(*d*) None of the above

110. Which of the following inference rule is true for predicate calculus.
(*a*) $\neg (\forall x\, P(x)) \equiv x \neg (P(x))$
(*b*) $\neg (\forall x\, P(x)) \equiv \exists x \neg (P(x))$
(*c*) $\neg P(x) \equiv \exists x\, P(x)$
(*d*) None of the above

111. Which of the following inference rule is true for predicate calculus.
(*a*) $\forall x P \vee (x Q(x)) \equiv Q \vee \exists x P(x)$
(*b*) $\exists x(\neg P \wedge P) \equiv Q \vee \exists x P(x)$
(*c*) $\exists x\, (P \wedge Q(x) \equiv P \wedge (\exists x Q(x))$
(*d*) None of the above

112. Which of the following inference is true for predicate calculus.
(*a*) $\forall x(P \vee Q(x)) \equiv P \vee (P x Q(x))$
(*b*) $\forall x(P \wedge Q(x)) \equiv P \wedge (P(x) Q(x))$
(*c*) $\forall x(P \wedge Q(x)) \equiv P \wedge Q(x)$
(*d*) None of the above

113. The universal instantiation rule means.
(*a*) $\dfrac{\forall x P(x)}{\therefore P(c)}$
(*b*) $\dfrac{\forall x P(c)}{\therefore P(x)}$
(*c*) $\forall x\, P(x)\_ \Rightarrow P(c)$
(*d*) None of the above

114. The Existential instantiation rule means.
(*a*) $\dfrac{\exists x P(x)}{\therefore P(c)}$
(*b*) $\dfrac{\exists x P(c)}{\therefore P(x)}$

(*c*) $\exists\, x\, P(x) = P(c)$
(*d*) None of the above

115. The universal generalization rule means.
(*a*) $\dfrac{P(x)}{\forall x P(x)}$
(*b*) $\dfrac{\neg P(x)}{\forall x P(x)}$
(*c*) $\dfrac{\forall x P(x)}{P(x)}$
(*d*) $\dfrac{\exists x P(x)}{P(x)}$

116. The rule Existential generali-zation means.
(*a*) $\dfrac{P(x)}{\therefore \exists x P(x)}$
(*b*) $\dfrac{\exists x P(x)}{P(x)}$
(*c*) $\dfrac{xP(x)}{P(x)}$
(*d*) $\dfrac{P(x)}{\forall x P(x)}$

117. Which of the following is not a proposition.
(*a*) Milind is gentlemen
(*b*) $\sqrt{0}$ is a real number
(*c*) Computer science is difficult to understand
(*d*) I wish you all the best

118. Choose the WFF.
(*a*) $(P \wedge Q) \Rightarrow (P \vee Q)$
(*b*) $(P \wedge Q) \Rightarrow (P \vee Q) \wedge R)$
(c) $(P \wedge Q \wedge R)) \Rightarrow (P \wedge Q)$
(*d*) $\neg (Q \wedge \neg (P \vee \neg Q)$

119. Modus Ponens is.
(*a*) $\neg Q$
$\dfrac{P \Rightarrow Q}{\therefore \neg P}$
(*b*) $\neg P$
$\dfrac{P \vee Q}{\therefore Q}$
(*c*) P
$\dfrac{P \Rightarrow Q}{\therefore Q}$
(*d*) None of the above

120. $\neg P \wedge \neg Q \wedge R$ is a minterm of:
(*a*) $P \vee Q$
(*b*) $\neg P \wedge \neg Q \wedge R$
(*c*) $P \wedge Q \wedge R \wedge S$
(*d*) $P \wedge R$

121. Which of the following is not a proposition.
(*a*) A triangle has three sides
(*b*) Go home and take rest
(*c*) Advait ran home
(*d*) An even number is a prime number

122. The value of *xy* and *yx* where $x = 0\ 0$, and $y = 1$.
(*a*) 0101 and 1010
(*b*) 1010 and 0101
(*c*) 0000 and 1111
(*d*) 1111 and 0000

123. The value of *xy* and *yx* for $x =$ a Λ and $y =$ BASIC will be.
(*a*) *a* Λ BASIC and BASIC *a* Λ
(*b*) BASIC *a* Λ and *a* Λ BASIC
(*c*) BASIC
(*d*) *a* Λ

124. Concatenation operation on a set Σ^* is
(*a*) Distributive
(*b*) Associative

(c) Reflexive
(d) None of the above

125. Which of the following is true for the transpose operation.
(a) $(xa)^T = a(x)^T$
(b) $(ax)^T = x(a)^T$
(c) $(ax)^T = a^T x^T$
(d) $(ax)^T = ax$

126. Which of the following is not true for principle of Induction.
(a) 0 is a natural number
(b) No two natural number have same successors
(c) The successor of any natural number is also a natural number
(d) None of the above

127. If g = ({ S}, { 0, 1}, { S → 0S1, S → Λ} the language generated will be
(a) $0^n1^n \in$ L (G) for $n \geq 0$
(b) $1^n0^n \in$ L (G) for $n \geq 0$
(c) $1^n \in$ L (G) for $n \geq 0$
(d) $0^n \in$ L (G) for $n \geq 0$

128. The language generated by G = ({S}, {a}, {S → SS}, S) is.
(a) ϕ
(b) a
(c) a^n
(d) aa

129. The language generated by g = ({S,C}, {a, b}, P,S) where P is S → aCa, c → aCa/b will be.
(a) a^nb^n
(b) a^nba^n
(c) aba
(d) $a^nb^nc^n$

130. If G is S → aS/bS/a/b, then L(G) is
(a) $\{a, b\}^+$
(b) $\{a^n, b^n\}$
(c) $\{a^n, b^n\}^+$
(d) None of the above

131. If G is S → aS/a the L(G) is
(a) $\{a\ a\}^+$
(b) $\{a\}^+$
(c) $\{a^n\}$
(d) a^n

132. The productions to generate grammar L = $\{WCW^T\}/W \in \{a, b\}^*\}$ is.
(a) S → aSa/bSb/c
(b) S → aSa
(c) bSb
(d) None of the above

133. The production rules for grammar generating $\{a + b^nc^n_n > 1, j > 0\}$ are
(a) S → as/A/bΛc
(b) S → aa/S/abc
(c) S → ab^nc^n/a/s
(d) None of the above

134. Language generated by G = ({S,A,}, {0, 1, 2}, P, S} where P consists of S → 0SA2, S → 012, $2A_1 \to A_12$, 1A → 11 is.
(a) L(G) = $\{0^n1^n2^n/n \geq 1\}$
(b) LG = $\{012^n/n \geq 1\}$
(c) LG = $\{2^n/n \geq 1\}$
(d) None of the above

135. A grammar is called type 1 or context sensitive if.
(a) All its productions are type – 1
(b) All its productions are defined
(c) All its productions are deterministic
(d) None of the above

136. A grammar G = (V_N, Σ, P, S) is monotonic if every production P is of the form.
(a) $\alpha \to \beta$ with $|\alpha| \leq |\beta|$

(*b*) $\alpha \leftrightarrow \beta$ with $|\alpha| \le |\beta|$
(*c*) $\beta \to \alpha$ with $|\beta| \le |\alpha|$
(*d*) None of the above

137. The context free grammar generating $\{a^n b^{2n} / n \ge 1\}$ is
(*a*) G = ({S}, {a, b}, P, S} where P consists of S → aSbb, S → abb
(*b*) G = ({S}, {a, b}, P, S} where P consists of S → as, S → ab
(*c*) G = ({S}, {a, b}, P, S} where P consists of S → b, S → a
(*d*) G = ({S}, {a, b}, P, S} P, S → b, S → a

138. Statement, if R is a regular expression, then (R) is also a regular expression is.
(*a*) True
(*b*) False
(*c*) Cannot be said
(*d*) None of the above

139. Statement, if R1 and R2 is a regular expression then R1 + R2 is regular expression.
(*a*) True
(*b*) False
(*c*) Cannot be determined
(*d*) None of the above

140. Statement, if R1 and R2 are regular expression then (R1R2) is a regular set is
(*a*) True
(*b*) False
(*c*) Cannot be determined
(*d*) None of the above

141. The set of regular expression {101} is.
(*a*) 1,0
(*b*) 101
(*c*) {101}
(*d*) 10101.......

142. The regular expression corresponding to {abba} is.
(*a*) abba
(*b*) {abba}
(*c*) {a, b}
(*d*) None of the above

143. The set corresponding to regular expression {Λ, ab} is
(*a*) Λ
(*b*) ab
(*c*) Λ + ab
(*d*) None of the above

144. The set corresponding to regular expression {abb, a, b, bba} is.
(*a*) abb + a + b + bba
(*b*) abb
(*c*) a + b
(*d*) bba

145. The regular expression corresponding to {1, 11, 111, ...} is
(*a*) 1
(*b*) 1(1)*
(*c*) (1)
(*d*) None of the above

146. The regular expression corresponding to regular set {Λ, ab} is
(*a*) Λ + ab
(*b*) Λ
(*c*) ab
(*d*) (Λ, ab)

147. The regular set corresponding to regular expression "the set of all strings of 0's and 1's ending in 00" is.
(*a*) (0 + 1)*
(*b*) (0 + 1)*00
(*c*) 01*00
(*d*) (010)*

148. The regular expression corresponding to set all strings of 0's and

1's beginning with 0 ending with 1" is.
(*a*) 0 (0 + 1)*1
(*b*) (0011)*
(*c*) (01)*
(*d*) None of the above

149. Regular set corresponding to regular expression {Λ, 11, 1111, 111111 ...}
(*a*) (11)*
(*b*) 11*
(*c*) 1*
(*d*) Λ

150. Two regular expressions P and Q are said to be equivalent if.
(*a*) P & Q represent same set of strings
(*b*) P & Q represent same alphabet
(*c*) P & Q have same domain
(*d*) None of the above

151. Which of the following identity is correct.
(*a*) Λ + RR* = R* = Λ + R*R
(*b*) ΛR = ΛR*
(*c*) RΛ = R*Λ
(*d*) None of them is correct

152. Which of the following identity is correct
(*a*) (PQ)* P = P (QP)*
(*b*) (PQP)* = (PQP)
(*c*) PQP = P*Q*P*
(*d*) None of the above

153. (P + Q)* = (P*Q*)* is
(*a*) True
(*b*) False
(*c*) Cannot be determined
(*d*) None of the above

154. (P + Q)R = PR + QR is
(*a*) False
(*b*) True
(*c*) Can't be said
(*d*) None of the above

155. Arden's theorem says for two regular expressions P & Q.
(*a*) R = Q + RP
(*b*) R* = Q + RP
(*c*) R = Q* + R*P*
(*d*) None of the above

156. The regular expression for set L of strings in which every 0 is immediately followed by at least two 1's.
(*a*) (1 + 011)
(*b*) (1+011)*
(*c*) (011)
(*d*) (011)*

157. The expression equivalent to (1 + 00*1) + (1 + 00*1) (0 + 10*1$^+$)$^+$ (0 + 10*1).
(*a*) 0*1 (0) (0 + 10*1)*
(*b*) 010 (0 + 10)
(*c*) (010)* (0 + 10)*
(*d*) None of the above

158. The language accepted by following automata is

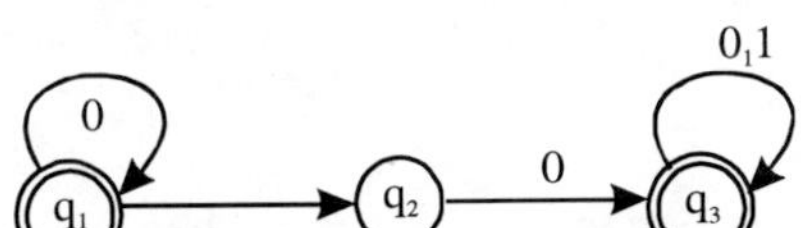

(*a*) 0* 1*
(*b*) 10
(*c*) .0101
(*d*) None of the above

159. Finite automata equivalent the (01)* (00 + 11) (01)* is

(*a*) 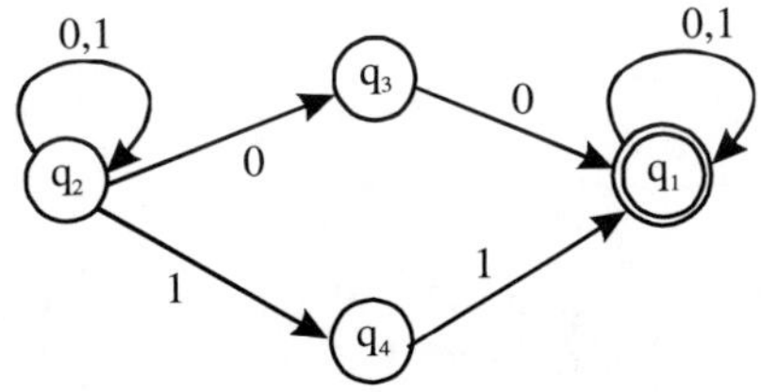

(*b*) 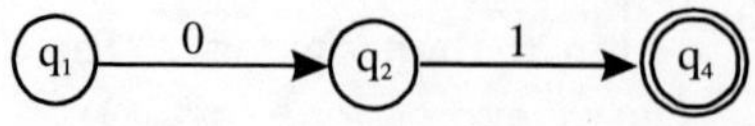

(*c*) 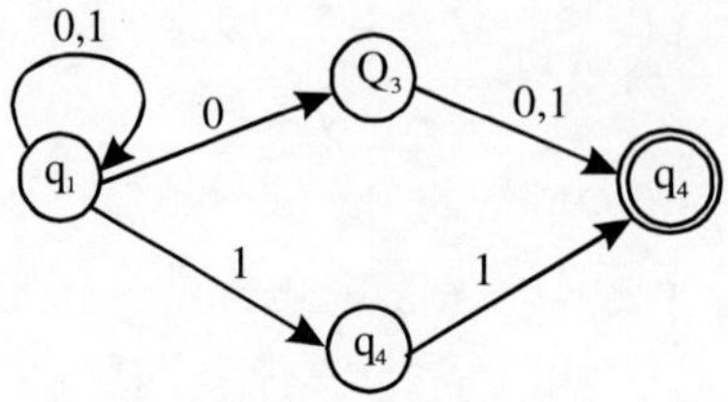

(*d*) None of the above

160. Set L = $\{a^{i^2} / i \geq 1\}$ is
(*a*) Regular
(*b*) Not regular
(*c*) Can't be decided
(*d*) None of the above

161. Set L = $\{a^p$ is prime$\}$
(*a*) Not regular
(*b*) Regular
(*c*) Can't be decided
(*d*) None of the above

162. The regular expression corresponding to {0, 1, 2} will be
(*a*) 0, 1, 2
(*b*) 01
(*c*) 2
(*d*) 0 + 1 + 2

163. Statement if Σ is finite then Σ* is finite is
(*a*) True
(*b*) False
(*c*) Σ and Σ* has no relationship
(*d*) None of the above

164. Represent $\{1^{2n+1} | n / \geq 0\}$ by regular expression
(*a*) 1*
(*b*) 1(1)*
(*c*) 1^n
(*d*) None of the above

165. W ∈ {a, b}* /W has only one a, is represented as
(*a*) bab
(*b*) a, b
(*c*) b*ab*
(*d*) None of the above

166. The set of all strings over {a,b} which has at most two a's
(*a*) b* + b*ab* + b*ab*ab*
(*b*) (baa)*
(*c*) baa
(*d*) None of the above

167. Regular set of $\{a^2, a^5, a^8 ....\}$ is
(*a*) aa (aaa)*
(*b*) a^{n+3}
(*c*) a^8
(*d*) None of the above

168. Regular set $\{a^n/n$, n is divisible by n = 2Or 3Or 5$\}$ is
(*a*) (aa)* + (aaa)* + aaaaa
(*b*) (a)* + (aa)* + (aaa)*
(*c*) (aaaaa)
(*d*) (a)* + a

169. The set of all strings over {a, b} beginning and ending with a.
(*a*) a (a + b)*a
(*b*) ab*a
(*c*) aba
(*d*) None of the above

170. All strings of length 3 in the regular set represented by expression (ab + a)* (aa + b)
(*a*) aab, aba
(*b*) aba
(*c*) aab
(*d*) None of the above

171. String of length 3 in set (a*b + b*a)*a is
(*a*) $(ab + a) + (ab + a)^2$
(*b*) (ab + a)
(*c*) $(ab + a)^2$
(*d*) None of the above

172. (a*ab + ba)*a* is equivalent to
   (*a*) (a + ab + ba)*
   (*b*) a + ab + ba
   (*c*) (a*ab, ba)* a*
   (*d*) None of the above

173. Set (a^nb^{2n}/n > o) is a
   (*a*) Regular set
   (*b*) Not regular
   (*c*) Cannot be determined
   (*d*) None of the above

174. {0^n1^n/gcd(m, n) = 1} is
   (*a*) Regular
   (*b*) Not regular
   (*c*) Can't be determined?
   (*d*) None of the above

175. Derivation tree is used to generate.
   (*a*) The derivations of CFG
   (*b*) The derivations of decisions
   (*c*) The derivations of regular set
   (*d*) None of the above

176. A derivation which allows production only to left most variable is.
   (*a*) Leftmost derivation
   (*b*) Rightmost derivation
   (*c*) Linear derivation
   (*d*) None of the above

177. Consider a grammar
   S → 0B/1A,
   A → 0/0S/1AA
   B → 1/1S/0BB
   For the string 00110101 the leftmost derivation will be.
   (*a*) 0^21^20101
   (*b*) 010101
   (*c*) 00110101
   (*d*) None of the above

178. In above question the rightmost derivation will be
   (*a*) $0110^21^20^21^2$
   (*b*) $0^2110101$
   (*c*) 0110101
   (*d*) None of the above

179. A terminal string W∈L(G) is ambiguous; if
   (*a*) If there exists two or more derivation trees
   (*b*) If there exist one leftmost derivation tree
   (*c*) If there exist one rightmost derivation tree
   (*d*) None of the above

180. Grammar S → sbs/a is
   (*a*) Ambiguous grammar
   (*b*) Unambiguous
   (*c*) Regular grammar
   (*d*) None of the above

181. Grammar supporting a + a*b is
   (*a*) Ambiguous
   (*b*) Unambiguous
   (*c*) Undecidable
   (*d*) None of the above

182. A Grammar having production rule S → sbs /a is
   (*a*) Unambiguous
   (*b*) Ambiguous
   (*c*) Undecidable
   (*d*) None of the above

183. Grammar L = {$a^nb^nc^n$/n ≥ 1} is
   (*a*) Context free
   (*b*) Context sensitive
   (*c*) Undecidable
   (*d*) None of the above

184. Language L = {a^p|p is prime} is.
   (*a*) Context sensitive language
   (*b*) Context free language
   (*c*) Undecidable language
   (*d*) None of the above

185. Grammar S → aAb, A → aAb/a is
   (*a*) LR (1)
   (*b*) LR (0)

(*c*) LR (n)
(*d*) LR

186. Grammar S → OA2, A → 1A1, A → 1 is not an
(*a*) LR (0)
(*b*) LR (1)
(*c*) LR (n)
(*d*) LR

187. Find whether S → AB, S → aA, A → aA, A → a, B → a an LR (K) for some K
(*a*) No
(*b*) Yes
(*c*) Undecidable
(*d*) None of the above

188. String $\{a^m b^m c^n / m, n \geq 1\} U \{a^m b^n c^n / m, n \geq 1\}$ cannot be generated by LR (K) grammar for any K
(*a*) True
(*b*) False
(*c*) Undecidable
(*d*) None of the above

189. A problem with two answers (Y/N) is decidable if corresponding language is
(*a*) Recursive
(*b*) Non-recursive
(*c*) Decidable
(*d*) None of the above

190. For $f(n) = 4n^3 + 5n^2 + 7n + 3$ the order of complexity is
(*a*) $0 (n^2)$
(*b*) $0 (n^3)$
(*c*) 0 (n)
(*d*) Constant

191. If a turing m/c M at input W of length n halts after making at most T(n) moves the time complexity of this is.
(*a*) T(n)
(*b*) T(m)
(*c*) T(ω)
(*d*) None of the above

192. A language L is said to be in class P if
(*a*) There exists some polynomial T(n) such that L = T(M) for some deterministic T(M)
(*b*) There exists some polynomial T(n) such that L = T(M) for some non-deterministic T(M)
(*c*) If it is undecidable
(*d*) None of the above

193. Which of the following is true for incremental compiler?
(*a*) That compiles only modified portion of compiler
(*b*) It is written in a language different from source language
(*c*) It generates object code for host m/c
(*d*) None of the above

194. An advantage of interpreter over compiler is.
(*a*) It is faster
(*b*) It is helpful in initial stage of program development
(*c*) In this debugging is easier
(*d*) None of the above

195. Optimizing compiler.
(*a*) Is written in minimum number of lines
(*b*) Optimizes the code
(*c*) Works fastest
(*d*) None of the above

196. A grammar will be meaning less.
(*a*) If terminal set and non-terminal set are disjoint
(*b*) If the left hand side of a production is single terminal
(*c*) If the left-hand side of a terminal has no non-terminal

(*d*) None of the above

197. Module of compiler responsible for grouping of characters into tokens is known as.
(*a*) Code generator
(*b*) Scanner
(*c*) Code optimizer
(*d*) None of the above

198. Context sensitive grammar is
(*a*) Phrase structured
(*b*) Non phrase structured
(*c*) Regular
(*d*) None of the above

199. In a context sensitive grammer.
(*a*) $\in$ can't be right-hand side of any production
(*b*) Number of grammar symbols on the left-hand side of a production can't be greater than the number of grammar symbols on right-hand side
(*c*) Number of grammar symbols on left-hand side can't be greater than number of terminals on right-hand side
(*d*) None of the above

200. If W is a string of terminals and A, B are two non-terminals, then which of the following are right linear grammar
(*a*) $A \rightarrow BW$
(*b*) $A \rightarrow BW/W$
(*c*) $A \rightarrow WB/W$
(*d*) None of the above

201. If G is a terminal and S, A, B are three non-terminals, then which of the following are regular grammars.
(*a*) $S \rightarrow \in$
(*b*) $A \rightarrow abB/Ab$ $A \rightarrow aS/b$
(*c*) $A \rightarrow Ba/Bab$
(*d*) $A \rightarrow aB/a$ $B \rightarrow bA/b$

202. Context free grammar can be recognized by a.
(*a*) Push down automata
(*b*) Push up automata
(*c*) Finite state automata
(*d*) None of the above

203. Which of the following is not an important design issue of lexical analyzer.
(*a*) Specification of the token of the language
(*b*) Designing a suitable recognizer for identifying tokens
(*c*) Both (*a*) and (*b*)
(*d*) None of the above

204. String is defined as.
(*a*) Infinite variable sequence of symbols
(*b*) Finite sequence of symbols
(*c*) Finite sequence of words
(*d*) None of the above

205. If W = abc is a string, then which of the following is not a prefix.
(*a*) E
(*b*) ab
(*c*) W
(*d*) abc

206. Finite automata is defined as.
(*a*) $M = (Q, \Sigma, \delta, q_0, F)$
(*b*) $M = (\Sigma, \delta, F)$
(*c*) $M = (q_0, F, \delta)$
(*d*) None of the above

207. If M is a finite automata, then language accepted by this L(M) is.
(*a*) $\{x/\delta, (q_0, x) = \text{member of } F\}$
(*b*) $\{x/\text{member of } F, \delta,\}$
(*c*) $\{x/\delta, (q_0, x)\}$
(*d*) None of the above

208. Non-deterministic automata is.
   (*a*) Finite state automata which does not determine anything
   (*b*) Modified finite state automata where from a state on a input symbol zero, one or more transitions are permitted
   (*c*) It does not have a final state
   (*d*) None of the above

209. Optimization of a deterministic finite automata means
   (*a*) Detecting those states of DFA whose presence or absence does not affect language accepted by auto-mata
   (*b*) It is infinite automata converted to finite automata
   (*c*) It is finite automata coverted to infinite automata
   (*d*) None of the above

210. Dead states are defined as.
   (*a*) No such state exist
   (*b*) A dead state is nonfinal state of a DFA whose transition on every input symbol terminates on itself
   (*c*) It is non-distinguishable state
   (*d*) None of the above

211. Following finite automata will accept.

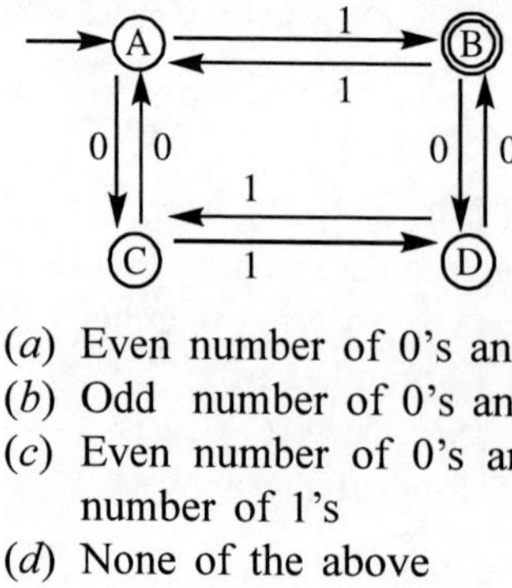

   (*a*) Even number of 0's and 1's
   (*b*) Odd number of 0's and 1's
   (*c*) Even number of 0's and odd number of 1's
   (*d*) None of the above

212. The following FA will accept

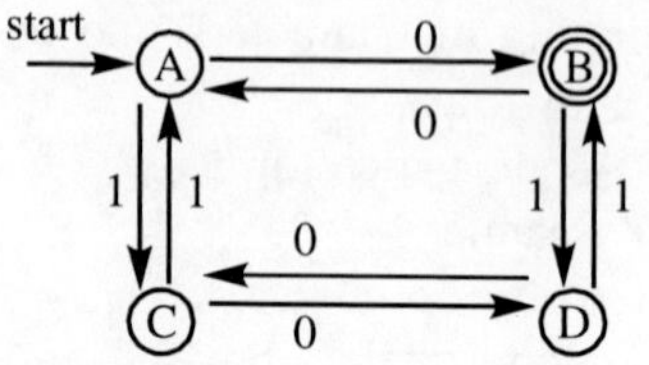

   (*a*) Even no of 0's and 1's
   (*b*) Odd no of 0's and 1's
   (*c*) Odd no of zeros and even number of 1's
   (*d*) None of the above

213. Regular set is
   (*a*) Set of strings for which there exist some finite automata accepting that set
   (*b*) Set of FA which accepts regular expression
   (*c*) Set of NFA which accepts regular expression
   (*d*) None of the above

214. Source file of lexical analyzer contains
   (*a*) Auxiliary definition like name = Regular expression & translation rule like pattern = action
   (*b*) Set of token
   (*c*) Data dictionary
   (*d*) None of the above

215. Context free grammar consists it of.
   (*a*) Set of nonterminal, terminal production rule, start symbol
   (*b*) Terminal, production rule, start symbol
   (*c*) Nonterminal, production rule, start symbol
   (*d*) None of the above

216. Which of the following is true for derivation tree.

(*a*) All the leaf nodes of the tree are labelled by terminals of grammar

(*b*) The interior nodes are labelled by non-terminals

(*c*) If interior node has label A, and has n descendent with labels X_1,X_2, X_n from left to right, then there must exist production rule A → $X_1X_2X_3X_n$

(*d*) None of the above

217. The Derivation tree for string id + id * id

(*a*) 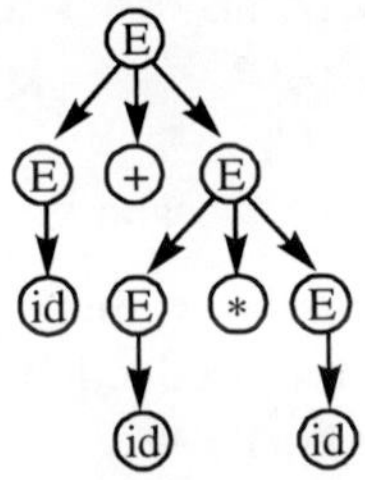

(*b*) 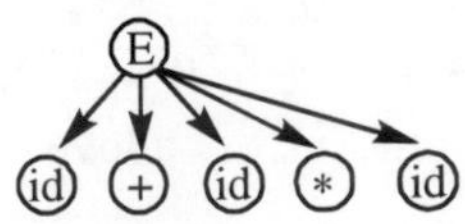

(*c*) 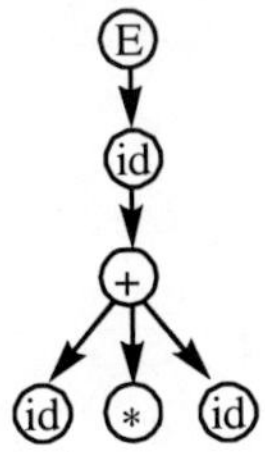

(*d*) None of the above

218. An ambiguous grammar is one in which.

(*a*) There is one parse tree for every string

(*b*) There are multiple parse tree for every string

(*c*) There is no parse tree for every string

(*d*) None of the above

219. Consider following grammar

S → aBDh

B → Bb/c

D → EF

E → g/∈

F → f/∈

It is an example of

(*a*) Right recursive grammar

(*b*) Left recursive grammar

(*c*) Bilinear grammar

(*d*) It cannot be defined

220. Consider following grammar

S → 0S / A/1

A → 0A/ A/0/1

The transition diagram of finite automata accepting the language generated by above grammar is.

(*a*) 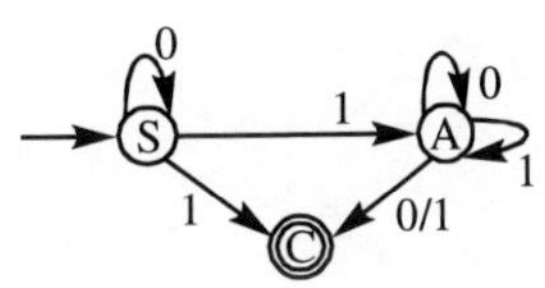

(*b*) 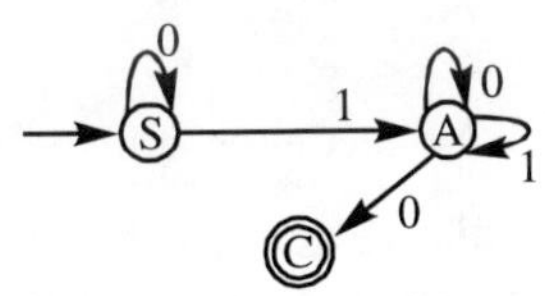

(*c*) 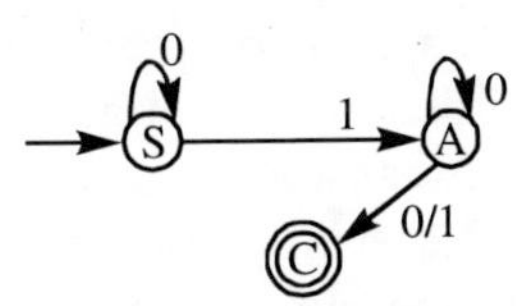

(*d*) None of the above

221. Which is not correct for right linear grammar?

(*a*) It is a context free grammar

(*b*) In it every production is of the form (*a*) A → WB (*b*) A → W

(*c*) It is a regular grammar

(*d*) None of the above

222. Consider following grammar
S → 0/B/0
B → /B/II
The regular expression of this grammar is.
(*a*) (0/111 * 10)
(*b*) (0111 * 10)
(*c*) (101 * 10)
(*d*) None of the above

223. Consider following grammar
S → gA
A → aA /gB/g
B → gA
Equivalent left linear grammar will be
(*a*) S → Ag
A → Aa/Bg/g
B → Ag
(*b*) S → gA
A → aA/gB/g
B → gA
(*c*) S → AB
A → aA/gB/g
B → gA
(*d*) None of the above

224. Predictive top down parser.
(*a*) Non-deterministic recognizer
(*b*) Capable of predicting which alternative is right choice for expansion
(*c*) No such parser exists
(*d*) None of the above

225. Consider the grammar
(*a*) S → AaAb/bbBa
A → ∈
B → ∈
This grammar is
(*a*) LL(1)
(*b*) LR 1
(*c*) Bidirectional grammar
(*d*) None of the above

226. Consider following grammar
S → AB/∈
A → AC/OC
B → OC
C → 1
This grammar is
(*a*) LR (1)
(*b*) LL (1)
(*c*) Not a grammar
(*d*) None of the above

227. The shift reduce conflict during Bottom up parsing contains term
(*a*) A → α, B → ν
(*b*) A → α, aβ, β → ν
(*c*) A → α.b
β → α.b
(*d*) None of the above

228. A reduce – reduce conflict indicates the production rules
(*a*) A → α, B → ν
(*b*) A → α, a β, β → ν
(*c*) A → α, b, β → ν.b
(*d*) None of the above

229. The following grammar
E → E+E
E → E*E
E → id
is an example of
(*a*) Ambiguous grammar
(*b*) LR grammar
(*c*) CFG grammar
(*d*) None of the above

230. The unambiguous grammar corresponding to grammar
E → E + E
E → E * E
E → id
is
(*a*) E → E + T/T
T → T * F/F
F → id

(*b*) E → T
T → F
F → id

(*c*) E → E + id + T
T → T*F
F → id

(*d*) None of the above

231. The best data structure for representing parsing table is.
(*a*) Structure
(*b*) Two dimensional array
(*c*) Stack
(*d*) Queue

232. Consider the expression id + id * id. It's parse tree will be.

(*a*) 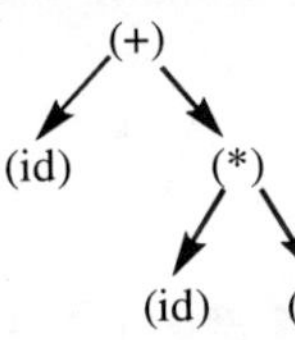

(*b*) 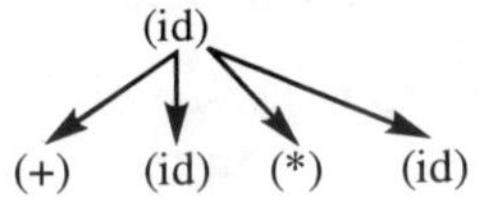

(*c*) 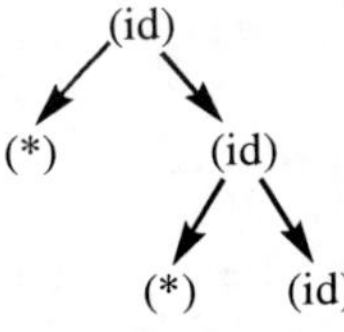

(*d*) None of the above

233. Symbol table is.
(*a*) Data structure to keep track of scope and binding information about names
(*b*) It is a name of a table
(*c*) It is adjacency list
(*d*) None of the above

234. The best implementation of hash table is.
(*a*) Linked list
(*b*) Adjacency list
(*c*) Two-dimensional matric
(*d*) None of the above

235. In static allocation of memory.
(*a*) Binding of names with specific storage allocation is done during compilation
(*b*) The memory is allocated in auxiliary storage
(*c*) Memory is allocated at the time of execution
(*d*) None of the above

236. The error is identified at
(*a*) Syntactic analysis phase
(*b*) Semantic analysis phase
(*c*) Data entry phase
(*d*) None of the above

237. YACC is used to.
(*a*) Generate a parser and automatic recovers from error
(*b*) Execute the program
(*c*) Enter the data
(*d*) None of the above

238. Code optimization is used to
(*a*) Increase execution efficiency
(*b*) Decrease run time
(*c*) Used to run code on a different system
(*d*) None of the above

239. Loop jamming.
(*a*) Merging of two loops if they have same number of iterations
(*b*) It is incomplete termination of loop
(*c*) It is using jam statement inside the loop
(*d*) None of the above

240. Consider following code
for (I = 0; I < 10; I++)
for (J = 0; J < io; J++)
X [I, J] = 0;

For (I = 0; I < 10; I++)
X [I, J] = 1;
After application of loop jamming it will be.
(*a*) For (I = 0; I < 10; I++)
{for (J = 0; J < 10 J++)
X [I, J] = O;
X {I, 1} = 1;}
(*b*) For (I = O;J = O; I < 10, J < 10 < I++, J++)
X [I, J] = 1;
(*c*) It cannot be determined before runtime
(*d*) None of the above

241. The last phase of compilation processes is.
(*a*) Lexical analysis
(*b*) Code generation
(*c*) Code optimization
(*d*) Error handling

242. The length of instruction MOV Ro, Ri is
(*a*) 1 memory word
(*b*) 2 memory word
(*c*) 3 memory word
(*d*) None of the above

243. Length of MOV Ro,M is
(*a*) 1 memory word
(*b*) 2 memory word
(*c*) 3 memory word
(*d*) None of the above

244. Length of MOV M1,M2 is.
(*a*) 1 memory word
(*b*) 2 memory word
(*c*) 3 memory word
(*d*) None of the above

245. Consider an expression X = (a + b) – ((c + d) – e)
The three address code for this is.
(*a*) t1 = a + b
t2 = c + d
t3 = t2 – e
x = t1 – t3
(*b*) t1 = (a + b)
t2 = ((c + d) – e)
t3 = (a + b – ((c + d)e)
(*c*) It cannot be determined
(*d*) None of the above

246. The demerit of statement by statement code generation is.
(*a*) Redundant instruction and suboptimal constructs
(*b*) Compilation time is more
(*c*) Compiled code size is more
(*d*) None of the above

247. Peep hole optimization is technique for.
(*a*) Locally improving target code
(*b*) Generate ready to execute code
(*c*) It does not generate code
(*d*) None of the above

248. During algebraic simplification the statement a+o can be replaced by.
(*a*) o
(*b*) a
(*c*) a + o
(*d*) None of the above

249. Code a*1 can be replaced by.
(*a*) 1
(*b*) o
(*c*) a
(*d*) None of the above

250. Consider the grammar
S → ABSC/Abc
BA → AB
Bb → bb
Ab → ab
Aa → aa
Which of the following sentences can be generated by this grammar?
(*a*) abc

(*b*) aab
(*c*) ab cc
(*d*) abbc

251. The difference between DFSA and NDFSA is.
(*a*) In DFSA, ∈ transitions may be present
(*b*) In NDFSA, ∈ transitions may be present
(*c*) In DFSA, from any given state, there can't be any alphabet leading to two different states
(*d*) None of the above

252. Two finite state machines are equivalent if.
(*a*) They have same number of states
(*b*) They have same number of edges
(*c*) They have same number of states and edges
(*d*) They recognize the same data token

253. If two finite state m/c M1 and M2 are isomorphic then.
(*a*) By relabelling edges M1 can be transformed to M2
(*b*) By relabelling states M1 can be transformed to M2
(*c*) They cannot be transformed into each other
(*d*) None of the above

254. The graph showing inter dependencies of the attributes of different nodes in parse tree is..
(*a*) Flow graph
(*b*) Data flow diagram
(*c*) Dependency graph
(*d*) None of the above

255. Which of the following is not an intermediate code form?
(*a*) Post fix notation
(*b*) Syntax trees
(*c*) Three address codes
(*d*) Quadruples

256. Number of codes in 'three address code' involves
(*a*) Maximum 3 addresses
(*b*) Minimum 3 addresses
(*c*) Number of addresses are identified at run time
(*d*) None of the above

257. The transcription error can be repaired by.
(*a*) Insertion alone
(*b*) Deletion alone
(*c*) Insertion and deletion alone
(*d*) Replacement alone

258. Graph showing basic block and their successor relationship is called.
(*a*) Control graph
(*b*) Flow graph
(*c*) DAG
(*d*) Hamiltonian graph

259. Running time of a program does not depend upon.
(*a*) The way the registers are used
(*b*) The order in which computations are performed
(*c*) The way the addressing modes are used
(*d*) None of the above

260. Recursive descent parsing is an example of
(*a*) Top down passing
(*b*) Bottom up passing
(*c*) Predictive passing
(*d*) None of the above

261. In operator precedance parsing, precedence relations are defined
(*a*) For all pair of non-terminals and terminals
(*b*) To delimit the handler
(*c*) Only for a certain pair of terminals
(*d*) None of the above

262. An example of most powerful parser is
(*a*) SLR
(*b*) LALR
(*c*) Canonical LR
(*d*) Operator precedance

263. LR(K) grammar
(*a*) Can only examine a maximum of K input symbols
(*b*) Can be used to identify handles
(*c*) Can be used to identify the production associated with a handle
(*d*) Covers the LL(K) class

264. Back patching is useful for handling
(*a*) Conditional jumps
(*b*) Unconditional jumps
(*c*) Backward references
(*d*) Forward references

265. 'C' is a
(*a*) Regular language
(*b*) Context free language
(*c*) Context sensitive language
(*d*) None of the above

266. Which of the following are (is) language processor (s)
(*a*) Assembler
(*b*) Compilers
(*c*) Interpreters
(*d*) All of the above

267. When a computer is first turned on or restarted, a special type of absolute loader is executed. It is called
(*a*) Compile and Go loader
(*b*) Boot loader
(*c*) Bootstrap loader
(*d*) Relating loader

268. In an absolute loading scheme, which loader function (s) is (are) accomplished by programmer.
(*a*) Allocation
(*b*) Linking
(*c*) Reallocation
(*d*) Both (a) and (b)

269. The action of parsing the source program into the proper syntactic layer is known as
(*a*) Syntax analysis
(*b*) Lexical analysis
(*c*) Interpretation analysis
(*d*) General syntax analysis

270. Which is a permanent database in the general model of computer?
(*a*) Literal table
(*b*) Identifier table
(*c*) Terminal table
(*d*) Source code

271. The function (s) of scheduler is (are)
(*a*) It selects which ready process is to be run next
(*b*) It specifies the time slice
(*c*) It is waiting for an event to occur before continuing execution
(*d*) Both (a) and (b)

272. A hardware device that is capable of executing a sequence of instructions, is known as
(*a*) CPU

(*b*) ALU
(*c*) CU
(*d*) Processor

273. Which of the following file name extension suggests that the file is a backup copy of another file?
(*a*) TXT
(*b*) COM
(*c*) BAS
(*d*) BAK

274. Name of the major operating system used in computer is?
(*a*) MS DOS
(*b*) OS/2
(*c*) UNIX
(*d*) All of the above

275. What is the name of the operating system that reads and reacts in terms of actual time
(*a*) Batch system
(*b*) Quick response system
(*c*) Real time system
(*d*) Time sharing system

276. The primary job of the operating system of a computer is to
(*a*) Manage resources
(*b*) Command resources
(*c*) Provide utilities
(*d*) Be user friendly

277. Which of the following is not applications software?
(*a*) Word processing
(*b*) Spreadsheet
(*c*) UNIX
(*d*) Desktop publishing

ANSWERS

1. (*d*)	2. (*a*)	3. (*a*)	4. (*b*)	5. (*b*)	6. (*c*)	7. (*d*)
8. (*b*)	9. (*c*)	10. (*b*)	11. (*c*)	12. (*d*)	13. (*d*)	14. (*d*)
15. (*d*)	16. (*a*)	17. (*d*)	18. (*a*)	19. (*d*)	20. (*b*)	21. (*b*)
22. (*a*)	23. (*a*)	24. (*b*)	25. (*c*)	26. (*a*)	27. (*b*)	28. (*a*)
29. (*c*)	30. (*d*)	31. (*c*)	32. (*a*)	33. (*b*)	34. (*a*)	35. (*d*)
36. (*a*)	37. (*a*)	38. (*b*)	39. (*c*)	40. (*b*)	41. (*b*)	42. (*a*)
43. (*b*)	44. (*a*)	45. (*b*)	46. (*a*)	47. (*d*)	48. (*b*)	49. (*a*)
50. (*d*)	51. (*a*)	52. (*d*)	53. (*a*)	54. (*d*)	55. (*b*)	56. (*b*)
57. (*d*)	58. (*a*)	59. (*b*)	60. (*b*)	61. (*d*)	62. (*a*)	63. (*a*)
64. (*a*)	65. (*a*)	66. (*b*)	67. (*b*)	68. (*a*)	69. (*c*)	70. (*a*)
71. (*b*)	72. (*d*)	73. (*a*)	74. (*a*)	75. (*c*)	76. (*a*)	77. (*c*)
78. (*c*)	79. (*b*)	80. (*d*)	81. (*b*)	82. (*a*)	83. (*d*)	84. (*d*)
85. (*a*)	86. (*b*)	87. (*d*)	88. (*a*)	89. (*c*)	90. (*a*)	91. (*b*)
92. (*a*)	93. (*a*)	94. (*a*)	95. (*b*)	96. (*a*)	97. (*a*)	98. (*b*)
99. (*d*)	100. (*a*)	101. (*a*)	102. (*b*)	103. (*b*)	104. (*a*)	105. (*b*)
106. (*a*)	107. (*c*)	108. (*b*)	109. (*a*)	110. (*a*)	111. (*a*)	112. (*a*)
113. (*a*)	114. (*a*)	115. (*a*)	116. (*c*)	117. (*d*)	118. (*a*)	119. (*c*)
120. (*b*)	121. (*b*)	122. (*a*)	123. (*a*)	124. (*b*)	125. (*a*)	126. (*d*)
127. (*a*)	128. (*a*)	129. (*b*)	130. (*a*)	131. (*b*)	132. (*a*)	133. (*a*)

134. (*a*)	135. (*a*)	136. (*a*)	137. (*a*)	138. (*a*)	139. (*a*)	140. (*b*)
141. (*b*)	142. (*a*)	143. (*b*)	144. (*a*)	145. (*b*)	146. (*a*)	147. (*b*)
148. (*a*)	149. (*b*)	150. (*a*)	151. (*a*)	152. (*a*)	153. (*a*)	154. (*b*)
155. (*a*)	156. (*b*)	157. (*a*)	158. (*a*)	159. (*a*)	160. (*a*)	161. (*a*)
162. (*a*)	163. (*b*)	164. (*d*)	165. (*a*)	166. (*a*)	167. (*a*)	168. (*a*)
169. (*a*)	170. (*a*)	171. (*a*)	172. (*a*)	173. (*b*)	174. (*b*)	175. (*a*)
176. (*a*)	177. (*a*)	178. (*b*)	179. (*a*)	180. (*a*)	181. (*a*)	182. (*b*)
183. (*b*)	184. (*a*)	185. (*a*)	186. (*a*)	187. (*a*)	188. (*a*)	189. (*a*)
190. (*b*)	191. (*a*)	192. (*a*)	193. (*a*)	194. (*a*)	195. (*b*)	196. (*b*)
197. (*b*)	198. (*b*)	199. (*b*)	200. (*c*)	201. (*d*)	202. (*a*)	203. (*c*)
204. (*b*)	205. (*c*)	206. (*a*)	207. (*a*)	208. (*b*)	209. (*b*)	210. (*b*)
211. (*c*)	212. (*c*)	213. (*a*)	214. (*a*)	215. (*a*)	216. (*c*)	217. (*a*)
218. (*b*)	219. (*b*)	220. (*a*)	221. (*b*)	222. (*a*)	223. (*a*)	224. (*b*)
225. (*a*)	226. (*b*)	227. (*b*)	228. (*a*)	229. (*a*)	230. (*a*)	231. (*b*)
232. (*a*)	233. (*a*)	234. (*c*)	235. (*a*)	236. (*a*)	237. (*a*)	238. (*a*)
239. (*a*)	240. (*a*)	241. (*b*)	242. (*a*)	243. (*b*)	244. (*c*)	245. (*a*)
246. (*a*)	247. (*a*)	248. (*b*)	249. (*c*)	250. (*a*)	251. (*c*)	252. (*d*)
253. (*a*)	254. (*a*)	255. (*d*)	256. (*a*)	257. (*c*)	258. (*b*)	259. (*d*)
260. (*a*)	261. (*a*)	262. (*c*)	263. (*d*)	264. (*d*)	265. (*b*)	266. (*d*)
267. (*b*)	268. (*d*)	269. (*b*)	270. (*d*)	271. (*a*)	272. (*b*)	273. (*d*)
274. (*d*)	275. (*c*)	276. (*a*)	277. (*c*)			

8

Operating System

1. Which of the following is not a characteristic of real time system:
   (*a*) It is well-defined fixed time constraints
   (*b*) It guarantees completion of tasks in minimum time
   (*c*) It consists of collection of processors
   (*d*) It is often used as control device in dedicated applications

2. Which of the following is not a feature of distributed system:
   (*a*) It consists of collection of processors
   (*b*) Processor communicate with one another through high-speed buses
   (*c*) Processing must be done within defined constraint or system will fail
   (*d*) Each processor has its own local memory

3. The dual mode operation of O/S is:
   (*a*) It provides the means for protecting the O/S from errant user from one another
   (*b*) It provide multiple memory bank
   (*c*) It provides multiple I/O features
   (*d*) None of the above

4. Which of the following is not a hardware protection of O/S:
   (*a*) Dual mode operation
   (*b*) CPU protection
   (*c*) I/O protection
   (*d*) None of the above

5. System call is defined as:
   (*a*) It provides interface between process and O/S
   (*b*) It provides interface between I/O and memory
   (*c*) It provides interface between peripheral and computer system
   (*d*) None of the above.

6. Which of the following is not a category of system call:
   (*a*) Information maintenance
   (*b*) Device management
   (*c*) File management
   (*d*) None of the above

7. The process states are:
   (*a*) Running
   (*b*) Waiting
   (*c*) Ready
   (*d*) All of the above

8. CPU scheduling algorithms are:
   (*a*) Multilevel feedback queue scheduling
   (*b*) Multilevel queue scheduling
   (*c*) Multiple processor scheduling
   (*d*) All of the above

9. Which of the following is not a distributed computing model:
   (*a*) Minicomputer model
   (*b*) Workstation model
   (*c*) Processor pool model
   (*d*) None of the above

10. Hybrid model is:
    (*a*) A combination of both workstation server and processor pool model
    (*b*) A simple extension of centralized time sharing system
    (*c*) It has several workstation interconnected by communication network
    (*d*) None of the above

11. "Transparency" refers to:
    (*a*) It makes existence of multiple computer invisible and provide a single system image to its users
    (*b*) It runs the program transparently
    (*c*) It is a technique to shift the program to other computer
    (*d*) None of the above

12. Which of the following is not a type of transparency:
    (*a*) Replication transparency
    (*b*) Application transparency
    (*c*) Migration transparency
    (*d*) Failure transparency

13. DCE stands for:
    (*a*) Disturbed Computing Environment
    (*b*) Distributed Computing Environment
    (*c*) Disk Computer Engineering
    (*d*) None of the above

14. Migration transparency is:
    (*a*) when object is migrated from one node to another in a distributed system
    (*b*) it is opposite of application transparency
    (*c*) masking of an object from being linked
    (*d*) none of the above

15. Which of the following is not a guideline to design better scalable distributed system:
    (*a*) Avoid centralized entities
    (*b*) Avoid centralized algorithm
    (*c*) Perform most operations on client workstation
    (*d*) None of the above

16. In monolithic model:
    (*a*) Most operating system services like process management, memory management, device management are provided by kernel
    (*b*) Each task is given to each service and kernel size is made smaller
    (*c*) Non-replicate non-migration blocks are created
    (*d*) None of the above

17. DCE contains:
    (*a*) DCE application, DCE software operating system and networking
    (*b*) Coprocessor computing
    (*c*) Multi processor computing environment
    (*d*) None of the above

18. Which of the following is not a component of DCE:
    (*a*) Remote procedure call
    (*b*) Distributed time service
    (*c*) Security services
    (*d*) None of the above

19. A message passing system is:
    (*a*) A mobile messaging scheme

(*b*) A subsystem that provides a set of messages based IPC protocols for communication
(*c*) A distributed time service
(*d*) None of the above

20. Which of the following are not content of IPC message structure:
(*a*) Actual data and number of byte
(*b*) Sequence number or message ID
(*c*) Sending process address
(*d*) None of the above

21. Multiple message buffer is a:
(*a*) Unbounded capacity buffer
(*b*) Finite bound buffer
(*c*) Single message buffer
(*d*) None of the above

22. Which of the following is a type of processing addressing:
(*a*) Explicit addressing
(*b*) Content addressing
(*c*) Flow controlled addressing
(*d*) None of the above

23. Which of the following are not components of RPC mechanism
(*a*) The client stub
(*b*) The RPC run time
(*c*) The server stub
(*d*) None of the above

24. What are complicated RPCs:
(*a*) RPC involving long duration calls
(*b*) RPC involving peer to peer paradigm
(*c*) RPC where binding agent returns server location
(*d*) None of the above

25. A batch mode RPC stands for:
(*a*) A peer to peer paradigm among participant processes
(*b*) Used to quick separate RPC request in transition buffer
(*c*) RPC involving long duration call
(*d*) None of the above.

26. Neuro software is:
(*a*) A software used to analyze the neurons
(*b*) It is powerful and easy neural network
(*c*) Designed to aid experts in real world
(*d*) It is software used by neuro surgeon
(v) None of the above

27. Which of the following is not the system development characteristics
(*a*) The transition from analysis to construction
(*b*) Requirement are input to system development
(*c*) A system is the output generated from system development
(*d*) None of the above

28. Encapsulation stands for:
(*a*) The behavior and information bundled together in the object
(*b*) The encasing of medicine capsule
(*c*) Existence in simultaneous multiple form
(*d*) None of the above

29. Abstract class is:
(*a*) Ancestors (classes) developed with the main purpose of being inherited by others
(*b*) A class within class
(*c*) A class developed with main purpose of creating instances
(*d*) None of the above

30. Descendents of a class is:
    (*a*) Class lying below a class in the inheritance hierarchy
    (*b*) A class lying above a class in inheritance hierarchy
    (*c*) A class using descendent elements of a class
    (*d*) None of the above

31. Ancestors of a class is:
    (*a*) Classes lying above a class in inheritance hierarchy
    (*b*) A class lying below a class in inheritance hierarchy
    (*c*) A class directly inherited from another class
    (*d*) None of the above.

32. The main purpose of using inheritance is:
    (*a*) Reuse
    (*b*) Specialization
    (*c*) Conceptual
    (*d*) All of the above

33. Which of the following is not an important concept of object oriented language:
    (*a*) Encapsulated objects
    (*b*) Class and instance objects
    (*c*) Polymorphism
    (*d*) None of the above

34. Static binding occurs at:
    (*a*) Compilation time
    (*b*) Run time
    (*c*) Program storage time
    (*d*) None of the above

35. Dynamic binding occurs at:
    (*a*) Compilation time
    (*b*) Data transfer time
    (*c*) Run time
    (*d*) None of the above

36. Directory can be defined as:
    (*a*) It is a file that contains directory entries
    (*b*) It is a location in buffer
    (*c*) It stores program
    (*d*) None of the above

37. File descriptor can be defined as:
    (*a*) It is non-negative integer that kernel used to identify the file being accessed by a particular process
    (*b*) It is the access mode of a file
    (*c*) It explains nature of program in a file
    (*d*) None of the above

38. Two different time values supported by UNIX is
    (*a*) Clock time, execution time
    (*b*) Calendar time, process time
    (*c*) Access time, execution time
    (*d*) It varies from program to program

39. System CPU time is defined as:
    (*a*) It is time attributed to kernel, when it executes on behalf of the process is called system time
    (*b*) Time attributed to user instructions
    (*c*) Time taken to feed a program in the system
    (*d*) None of the above

40. Which of the following is not a kernel data structure used to open files:
    (*a*) Process table entry
    (*b*) File table entry
    (*c*) V mode structure
    (*d*) None of the above

41. Which of the following is not a valid file type:
    (*a*) Character special file
    (*b*) Block special file

(c) Symbolic link
(d) None of the above

42. In UNIX bit S_ISUTX is known as:
(a) Dirty bit
(b) Sticky bit
(c) Parity bit
(d) None of the above

43. Symbolic link is defined as:
(a) It is an indirect pointer to file unlike hard link
(b) It is a link having special symbol
(c) It is link used in linked list
(d) None of the above

44. Which of the following is not different time fields maintained for each file are:
(a) Last access time for file data
(b) Last modification time of file data
(c) Last change time of I mode status
(d) None of the above

45. The different types of buffering supported by UNIX is:
(a) Fully buffered
(b) Line buffered
(c) Un-buffered
(d) All of the above

46. The functions for process termination are:
(a) Return from main
(b) Calling abort
(c) Terminated by signal
(d) None of the above

47. Zombie process is defined as:
(a) The process that has terminated but whose parent has not yet waited for it.
(b) A process executed in the starting of a UNIX system
(c) A process created temporarily during program execution
(d) None of the above

48. The difference between wait and waitpid functions is:
(a) Wait can block the caller until a child process terminates while waitpid has no option that prevent it from blocking
(b) Waitpid can block the caller until a child process terminates while wait has no option that prevent it from blocking
(c) There is no difference
(d) None of the above

49. Which of the following is not a rule for changing user ID:
(a) The process must have super user privileges
(b) If the process does not have super user privileges but uid equals either the real user ID or saved set user ID
(c) Both (a) and (b)
(d) None of the above

50. Which of the following is not a users of interpreter file:
(a) They hide the fact that certain programs are scripts in some other language
(b) Interpreter script provides an efficiency gain
(c) It allows us to write shell scripts using shells other than |bin| extensions
(d) None of the above

51. How register to register instructions are translated in assembler:

(*a*) The object code is created using OPTAB, then numeric equivalent is found using SYMTAB
(*b*) First numeric equivalent is found using SYMTAB, then object code is created using OPTAB
(*c*) It is created according to input program
(*d*) None of the above

52. Assembler directive "EXTDEF" means
(*a*) External symbols that are defined in a particular control section
(*b*) External symbols that are defined in a particular control section and also defined in another control section
(*c*) The symbols that are defined in data
(*d*) None of the above

53. What is the use of assembler directive "CSECT"
(*a*) It indicates starting of section control
(*b*) It divides program into many control sections
(*c*) Divides program into many blocks
(*d*) None of the above

54. The assembler directive "START" indicates:
(*a*) Name and starting address of memory where object program is stored
(*b*) Starting address of block
(*c*) Starting address of operand
(*d*) None of the above

55. What are the ways to share memory between unrelated processes:
(*a*) By using memory mapped files
(*b*) By using shared memory objects
(*c*) Both (*a*) and (*b*)
(*d*) None of the above

56. Socket is defined as:
(*a*) Communication path between computer provided by hiding underlying networking concepts
(*b*) It is a UNIX process terminator
(*c*) It is networking software
(*d*) None of the above

57. Little byte endian order is defined as:
(*a*) Is 16 bit integer number and the low order byte at starting address
(*b*) Is 16 bit integer number and the high order byte at starting address
(*c*) The middle 8 bits of 16 bit address
(*d*) None of the above

58. Which is not a byte manipulation function
(*a*) Bzero
(*b*) Memset
(*c*) Memopy
(*d*) None of the above

59. Concurrent server can be defined as:
(*a*) Server that handles one request at a time
(*b*) Server that can handle multiple client – simultaneously
(*c*) Server that runs special UNIX program

(*d*) None of the above

60. Iterative server is defined as:
    (*a*) Servers that can handle multiple clients serially are called interative server
    (*b*) Servers that can handle multiple clients simultaneously
    (*c*) Servers that run special UNIX program
    (*d*) None of the above

61. Which of the following is not a I/O model
    (*a*) Non-blocking I/O
    (*b*) Blocking I/O
    (*c*) I/O multiplexing
    (*d*) None of the above

62. UDP socket is:
    (*a*) Connectionless unreliable datagram protocol
    (*b*) Connection oriented unreliable datagram protocol
    (*c*) Connectionless reliable datagram protocol
    (*d*) Connection oriented reliable protocol.

63. What is the name given to all the programs inside the computer with makes it usuable?
    (*a*) Application software
    (*b*) System software
    (*c*) Firm ware
    (*d*) Share ware

64. A front-end processor is usually used in
    (*a*) Multi-programming
    (*b*) Virtual storage
    (*c*) Time sharing
    (*d*) Multi-processing

65. The problem of thrashing is affected significantly by:
    (*a*) Program structure
    (*b*) Program size
    (*c*) Primary storage size
    (*d*) None of the above

66. Which of the following is not a part of the operating system?
    (*a*) Supervisor
    (*b*) Performance monitor
    (*c*) I/O control program
    (*d*) None of the above

67. Which policy replace a page if it is not in the favoured subset of a process's pages?
    (*a*) Working set
    (*b*) FIFO
    (*c*) LIFO
    (*d*) None of the above

68. What problem is solved by Dijkstra's banker's algorithm?
    (*a*) Deadlock recovery
    (*b*) Deadlock avoidance
    (*c*) Deadlock prevention
    (*d*) None of the above

69. Moving process from main memory to disk is called
    (*a*) Swapping
    (*b*) Spooling
    (*c*) Scheduling
    (*d*) None of the above

70. Producer consumer problem can be solved using
    (*a*) Semaphores
    (*b*) Event counters
    (*c*) Monitors
    (*d*) All of the above

71. Non-modifiable procedures are called
    (*a*) Topdown procedures
    (*b*) Reentrant procedures
    (*c*) Concurrent procedures
    (*d*) Serially usable procedures

72. In order to allow only one process to enter its critical section binary semaphore are initialized to
(*a*) 2
(*b*) 1
(*c*) 0
(*d*) None of the above

73. In which addressing mode the operand is given explicitly in the instruction?
(*a*) Immediate mode
(*b*) Index mode
(*c*) Absolute mode
(*d*) Direct mode

74. Which of the following is not programmes utility?
(*a*) Debugger
(*b*) Editor
(*c*) Spooler
(*d*) None of the above

75. Operating system is a collection of
(*a*) Hardware components
(*b*) I/O devices
(*c*) Software routines
(*d*) All of the above

76. Which of the following checks, cannot be carried out on the input data to a system
(*a*) Consistency check
(*b*) Syntax check
(*c*) Range check
(*d*) None of the above

77. Indicate which is a pre-emptive scheduling algorithm:
(*a*) Round-robin
(*b*) Shortest-job-next
(*c*) Priority-based
(*d*) None of the above

78. A characteristic of an on-line real-time system is
(*a*) No delay in processing
(*b*) More than one CPU
(*c*) Off-time batch processing
(*d*) None of the above

79. If special forms are needed for printing the output, the programmer specifies these forms through?
(*a*) JCL
(*b*) IPL
(*c*) Load modules
(*d*) Utility programs

80. Which of the following is a type of systems software used on micro-computers?
(*a*) MS-DOS
(*b*) PC-DOS
(*c*) UNIX
(*d*) All of the above

81. What is the name of operating system for the laptop computer called Mac Life?
(*a*) DOS
(*b*) Window
(*c*) OZ
(*d*) MS-DOS

82. What is the operating system used by Macintosh computers?
(*a*) System 7.0
(*b*) AU/X
(*c*) UNIX
(*d*) Either (a) and (b)

83. When did IBM release the first version of disk operating system DOS version 1.0?
(*a*) 1981
(*b*) 1982
(*c*) 1983
(*d*) 1984

84. Information in a memory that is no longer valid or wanted is known as

(*a*) Non-voilatide
(*b*) Surplus
(*c*) Garbage
(*d*) All of the above

85. Special software to create a job queue is called
(*a*) Drive
(*b*) Spooler
(*c*) Interpreter
(*d*) Linkage editor

86. A process is another name for
(*a*) Job
(*b*) A task
(*c*) Paying
(*d*) All of the above

87. The computational technique used to compute the disk storage address of individual records is called:
(*a*) Hashing
(*b*) Bubble memory
(*c*) Key fielding
(*d*) None of the above

88. System programs such as compilers are designed so that they are
(*a*) Reenterable
(*b*) Non-reusable
(*c*) Serially usable
(*d*) Recursive

89. The operating system manages
(*a*) Memory
(*b*) Processor
(*c*) Disk and I/O devices
(*d*) All of the above

90. The register or main memory location which contains the effective address of the operand is known as
(*a*) Pointer
(*b*) Index register
(*c*) Scratch pad
(*d*) Special location

91. Round robin scheduling is essentially the preemptive version of
(*a*) FILO
(*b*) FIFO
(*c*) FCFS
(*d*) Congest time first

92. For how many processes which are sharing common data, the Dekker's algorithm implements mutual exclusion?
(*a*) 1
(*b*) 2
(*c*) 3
(*d*) 4

93. Which of the following is a block device
(*a*) Terminals
(*b*) Printer
(*c*) Mouse
(*d*) Disk

94. The principles of structured programming for b/d is the use of
(*a*) WHILE-DO
(*b*) GO-TO
(*c*) IF-THEN-EI-SE
(*d*) DO-WHILE

95. Which of the following, is necessary to work on a computer.
(*a*) Computer
(*b*) Operating system
(*c*) Assembly
(*d*) Interpreter of above

96. The error that can be pointed out by the compiler are
(*a*) Syntax error
(*b*) Semantic error
(*c*) Logical error
(*d*) Internal error

97. A translator is best described as
(*a*) Application software

(*b*) System software
(*c*) Microprogram
(*d*) None of the above

98. Which of the following instruction, would be written within the diamond-shaped box, of a flowchart?
(*a*) S = B – C
(*b*) 15 < A < 10
(*c*) PRINT A
(*d*) DATA S, 4, 2

99. The part of machine level instruction, which tells the central processor what has to be done, is
(*a*) Operation code
(*b*) Address
(*c*) Locator
(*d*) None of above

100. The memory allocation scheme subject to "external" fragmentation is
(*a*) Segmentation
(*b*) Swapping
(*c*) Pure demand paging
(*d*) None of the above

101. In which of the following page replacement policies, Balady's anomaly occurs
(*a*) FIFO
(*b*) LRU
(*c*) NRU
(*d*) LFU

102. The principal of locality of reference justifies the use of
(*a*) Reenterable memory
(*b*) Non-reusable memory
(*c*) Virtual memory
(*d*) Cache memory

103. A system program that sets up an executable program in main memory ready for execution is
(*a*) Linker
(*b*) Loader
(*c*) Compiler
(*d*) Assembler

104. A computer cannot "boot" if it does not have the
(*a*) Compiler
(*b*) Loader
(*c*) Assembler
(*d*) Operating system

105. Page-map table is
(*a*) A data file
(*b*) A directory
(*c*) Used for address translation
(*d*) None of above

106. To avoid the race condition, the number of process that simultaneously inside the critical section is
(*a*) 8
(*b*) 1
(*c*) 16
(*d*) 0

107. Which of the following rules out the use of GO TO?
(*a*) Flow chart
(*b*) HIPO-DIAGRAMS
(*c*) Naui-Shneiderman diagram
(*d*) All of the above

108. Which of the following is a phase of a compilation process
(*a*) Lexical analysis
(*b*) Code generation
(*c*) syntatic analysis
(*d*) All of the above

109. Which of the following is true about pseudo code
(*a*) Machine language
(*b*) Assembly language
(*c*) A high-level language
(*d*) All of above

110. Seek analysis is used for analyzing:
    (*a*) Paying problems
    (*b*) Device busy problems
    (*c*) Control-unit busy problems
    (*d*) None of the above

111. Access time is the highest in the case of
    (*a*) Floppy disk
    (*b*) Cache
    (*c*) Swapping device
    (*d*) Magnetic disk

112. Which of the following is characteristic of an operating system?
    (*a*) Resource management
    (*b*) Error recovery
    (*c*) Memory management
    (*d*) All of the above

113. Files can have
    (*a*) Read access
    (*b*) Copy access
    (*c*) Write access
    (*d*) All of the above

114. The most common systems security method is
    (*a*) Passwords
    (*b*) Encryption
    (*c*) Firewall
    (*d*) All of the above

115. Poor response times are caused by
    (*a*) Processor busy
    (*b*) High I/O rate
    (*c*) High paging rates
    (*d*) any of above

116. Resolution of externally defined symbols is performed by
    (*a*) Linker
    (*b*) Loader
    (*c*) Compiler
    (*d*) Assembler

117. The I.O processors execute I/O instructions that are stored in memory
    (*a*) True
    (*b*) False
    (*c*) Can't be said
    (*d*) None of the above

118. The input to an assembler program is called the object program
    (*a*) Object program
    (*b*) Source program
    (*c*) System program
    (*d*) None of the above

119. The size of the IBM 360 memory is upto 2 to the power 260 bytes
    (*a*) True
    (*b*) False
    (*c*) Can't be said
    (*d*) None of the above

120. Pass 2 assign address to all statement in the program
    (*a*) True
    (*b*) False
    (*c*) Depends upon the program
    (*d*) None of the above

121. A file is a collection of records of information
    (*a*) True
    (*b*) False
    (*c*) Depends upon the application
    (*d*) None of the above

122. In sequential file organisation, explicialy record addressing is used
    (*a*) True
    (*b*) False
    (*c*) Partially true
    (*d*) None of the above

123. Both the address and data bus should be unidirectional only
    (*a*) Unidirectional
    (*b*) Bididirectional only

(*c*) Varies acording to application
(*d*) None of the above

124. CX register is assumed to work like a counter
(*a*) True
(*b*) False
(*c*) Partially true
(*d*) None of the above

125. Trag flag is a conditional flag
(*a*) True
(*b*) False
(*c*) Can't be said
(*d*) None of the above

126. NEG instruction produces 1's complement of a number
(*a*) True
(*b*) False
(*c*) Can't be said
(*d*) None of the above

127. The instruction ADD AD, ARRAY [BP + SI] is incorrect
(*a*) True
(*b*) False
(*c*) No such instruction exist
(*d*) None of the above

128. Conditional jump instructions require one of the flags to be tested
(*a*) True
(*b*) False
(*c*) Partially true
(*d*) None of the above

129. Motorola 6800 operates in three states viz. use, supervisor, idle.
(*a*) True
(*b*) False
(*c*) Partially true
(*d*) None of the above

130. ASC-VAL DB 'TESTI' is a valid statement.
(*a*) True
(*b*) False
(*c*) No such instructors exist
(*d*) None of the above

131. The directive DT defines a quadword in the memory.
(*a*) True
(*b*) False
(*c*) No such directive exist
(*d*) None of the above

132. Wordstar is an editor package.
(*a*) True
(*b*) False
(*c*) It is operating system
(*d*) None of the above

133. A com program is longer than an EXE program.
(*a*) True
(*b*) False
(*c*) Partially true
(*d*) None of the above

134. A small page size causes
(*a*) Smaller tables.
(*b*) Larger tables
(*c*) True depends upon O/S
(*d*) None of the above

135. A computer is intelligent enough to understand an ambiguity in algorithm.
(*a*) True
(*b*) False
(*c*) Partially true
(*d*) None of the above

136. COBOL supports a hierarchical structure of data.
(*a*) True
(*b*) False
(*c*) Partially true
(*d*) None of the above

137. JCL (Job Control Language) is used only on IBM computers.

(*a*) True
(*b*) False
(*c*) Partially true
(*d*) None of the above

138. Dispatcher in another name for low-level schedulor.
(*a*) True
(*b*) False
(*c*) Partially true
(*d*) None of the above

139. Polling is more efficient than interrupts.
(*a*) True
(*b*) False
(*c*) Partially true
(*d*) None of the above

140. A file is sometimes called
(*a*) Collection of input data
(*b*) Data set
(*c*) Program
(*d*) None of above

141. File record length should always be
(*a*) Fixed
(*b*) Variable
(*c*) Depends upon size of file
(*d*) Chosen to match the data characteristics

142. The details of all external symbols and relocation formation (relocation list or map) is provided to linker by
(*a*) Macro processor
(*b*) Translator
(*c*) Loader
(*d*) Editor

143. Disk drive seek time should be
(*a*) Maximized
(*b*) Minimized
(*c*) Optimized
(*d*) None of the above

144. Boundry registers are used for memory protection.
(*a*) True
(*b*) False
(*c*) Partially true
(*d*) None of the above

145. Beginning of a new process is also known as a "fork"
(*a*) True
(*b*) False
(*c*) Partially true
(*d*) None of the above

146. Loader loads and executes object code.
(*a*) True
(*b*) False
(*c*) Partially true
(*d*) None of the above

147. Time sharing is an example of multi programming.
(*a*) True
(*b*) False
(*c*) Can't be said
(*d*) None of the above

148. A single instruction cannot swap two nibbles of a bytes register
(*a*) True
(*b*) False
(*c*) Partially true
(*d*) None of the above

149. Which is an impact printer
(*a*) Daisy wheel
(*b*) Inkjet printer
(*c*) Plotter
(*d*) Laser printer

150. A type of channel used to connect a central processor and peripherals which uses multiplesing is known as
(*a*) Modem

(*b*) Network
(*c*) Multiplexer
(*d*) All of the above

151. A stand alone system which produces one page of printed output at a time is
(*a*) Page printer
(*b*) Line printer
(*c*) Laser printer
(*d*) Dot matrix printer

152. The earliest medium for storing data was
(*a*) Magnetic tape
(*b*) Magnetic disk
(*c*) Punched card
(*d*) Plotter

153. An assembler is a
(*a*) Program
(*b*) Person who assemble the parts
(*c*) Symbol
(*d*) Language

154. Memory
(*a*) Is a device that performs a sequence of operations in memory
(*b*) Is a sevice where information is stored
(*c*) Is a sequence of instructions
(*d*) Is typically characterised by interactive processing and time-slicing of the CPU's time to allow quick response to each user

155. A program
(*a*) Is a device that performs a sequence of operations specified by instructions in memory.
(*b*) Is the device where information is stored
(*c*) Is a sequence of instructions
(*d*) Is typically characterised by interactive processing and time of the CPU's time to allow quick response to each user

156. A processor
(*a*) Is a device that performs a sequence of operations specified by instructions in memory.
(*b*) Is the device where information is stored
(*c*) Is a sequence of instructions
(*d*) Is typically characterised by interactive processing and time of the CPU's time to allow quick response to each user

157. Assembler is
(*a*) A program that places programs into memory and prepares them for execution.
(*b*) A program that automates the translation of assembly language into machine language.
(*c*) A program that accepts a program written in a high-level language and produces an object program.
(*d*) Is a program that appears to execute a source program as if it were in machine languages.

158. An interpreter is
(*a*) A program that places programs into memory and prepares them for execution.
(*b*) A program that automates the translation of assembly language into machine language.
(*c*) Program that accepts a program written in a high-level language and produces an object program
(*d*) Is a program that appears to

execute a source program as if it were in machine language

159. A compiler is
 (*a*) A program that places programs into memory and prepare them for execution.
 (*b*) A program that automates the translation of assembly language into machine language.
 (*c*) A program that accepts a program written in a high-level language and produces an object program
 (*d*) A program that appears to execute a source program as if it were machine language

160. A loader is
 (*a*) A program that places programs into memory and prepare them for execution.
 (*b*) A program that automates the translation of assembly language into machine language.
 (*c*) Program that accepts a program written in a high-level language and produces an object program
 (*d*) Is a program that appears to execute a source program as if it were machine language

161. Virtual memory
 (*a*) Is a method of memory allocation by which program is sub-divided into equal portions, or phases and core is subdivided into equal portions or blocks
 (*b*) Consists of those addresses that may be generated by a processor during executive on a computation.
 (*c*) Is a method of allocating processor time
 (*d*) Allows multiple programs to reside in separate areas of core at a time

162. A hardware device that is capable of executing a sequence of instructions is known as
 (*a*) CPU
 (*b*) ALU
 (*c*) CU
 (*d*) PROCESSOR

163. While working with MS-DOS, which command will you use to transfer a specific file from one disk to another
 (*a*) Disk copy
 (*b*) Copy
 (*c*) Rename
 (*d*) Format

164. What is the name of the operating system which was originally designed by scientists and engineers mainly for scientific purposes
 (*a*) XENIX
 (*b*) UNIX
 (*c*) OS/2
 (*d*) MS-DOS

165. An operating system of a computer serves as a sotware interface between the user and
 (*a*) Hardware
 (*b*) Peripherals
 (*c*) Memory
 (*d*) Screen

166. The term “Operating System” means
 (*a*) A set of programs which controls computer working
 (*b*) The way a computer operator works
 (*c*) Conversion of high-level languages into machine code

(*d*) The way a floppy disk drive operates

167. What is the name of system, which deals with the running of actual computer and not with the programming problem
(*a*) Operating system
(*b*) Systems program
(*c*) Object program
(*d*) Source program

168. Which of the following operating system used write through caches
(*a*) UNIX
(*b*) DOS
(*c*) ULTRIX
(*d*) XENIX

169. Assembley language is
(*a*) Usually the printer user interface
(*b*) Requires fixed format commands
(*c*) A mnemonic form of machine language
(*d*) Different from the SCL interpreter

170. The errors that can be pointed out by a compiler are
(*a*) Syntax errors
(*b*) Semanetic errors
(*c*) Logical errors
(*d*) Internal errors

171. Block or buffer caches are used to
(*a*) Improve disk performance
(*b*) Handle interrupts
(*c*) Increase the capacity of main memory
(*d*) Speed up main memory read operation

172. A program that convert a high-level language program to a set of instructions that can run on a computer is called a
(*a*) Compiler
(*b*) Debugger
(*c*) Editor
(*d*) All of the above

173. The functions of the storage assignment are
(*a*) To assign storage to all variables referenced in the source program
(*b*) To assign storage to all temporary locations that are necessary for intermediate results
(*c*) To assign storage to literals, and to ensure that the storage is allocated and appropriate locations are initialized
(*d*) All of the above

174. A hardware device that is capable of executing a sequence of instructions, is known as
(*a*) Pre-eptive scheduling
(*b*) Non-pre-eptive scheduling
(*c*) Shortest job first
(*d*) First come first served

175. Part of a program where the shared memory is assessed and which should be executed indivisualy is called
(*a*) Semaphores
(*b*) Directory
(*c*) Critical section
(*d*) Mutual exclusion

176. The techniques of sharing of time in a computer among several jobs which switches between jobs so rapidly such that each job appears to have the computer itself is called
(*a*) Time sharing
(*b*) Time out
(*c*) Time domain
(*d*) FIFO

177. The operating system manages
   (*a*) Memory
   (*b*) Processor
   (*c*) Disk and I/O devices
   (*d*) All of the above

178. Which of the following is a block device
   (*a*) Mouse
   (*b*) Printer
   (*c*) Terminals
   (*d*) Disk

179. Resolution of externally defined symbols is performed by
   (*a*) Linker
   (*b*) Loader
   (*c*) Compiler
   (*d*) Assembler

180. System generation;
   (*a*) Is always quite simple
   (*b*) Is very difficult
   (*c*) Varies in difficulty between systems
   (*d*) Requires extensive tools to be understandable

181. Object code
   (*a*) Is ready to execute
   (*b*) Is the output of compilers but not assembler
   (*c*) Must be "loaded" before execution
   (*d*) Must be rewritten before execution

182. Virtual memory is
   (*a*) Simple to implement
   (*b*) Used in all major commercial operating systems
   (*c*) Less efficient in utilization of memory
   (*d*) Useful when passed I/O devices are not available

183. System maintenance;
   (*a*) Usually not necessary
   (*b*) Is necessary on all sytems; regardless of how good
   (*c*) Is not required if the system is well written
   (*d*) Always requires several programs

ANSWERS

1. (*c*)	2. (*c*)	3. (*a*)	4. (*a*)	5. (*a*)	6. (*d*)	7. (*d*)
8. (*d*)	9. (*d*)	10. (*a*)	11. (*a*)	12. (*b*)	13. (*b*)	14. (*b*)
15. (*d*)	16. (*a*)	17. (*a*)	18. (*d*)	19. (*b*)	20. (*d*)	21. (*b*)
22. (*a*)	23. (*d*)	24. (*a*)	25. (*b*)	26. (*b*)	27. (*d*)	28. (*a*)
29. (*a*)	30. (*a*)	31. (*a*)	32. (*b*)	33. (*d*)	34. (*a*)	35. (*c*)
36. (*a*)	37. (*a*)	38. (*b*)	39. (*a*)	40. (*d*)	41. (*d*)	42. (*b*)
43. (*a*)	44. (*d*)	45. (*d*)	46. (*a*)	47. (*a*)	48. (*a*)	49. (*c*)
50. (*d*)	51. (*a*)	52. (*a*)	53. (*b*)	54. (*a*)	55. (*c*)	56. (*a*)
57. (*a*)	58. (*d*)	59. (*b*)	60. (*a*)	61. (*d*)	62. (*a*)	63. (*b*)
64. (*a*)	65. (*c*)	66. (*c*)	67. (*a*)	68. (*c*)	69. (*b*)	70. (*a*)
71. (*b*)	72. (*c*)	73. (*a*)	74. (*d*)	75. (*c*)	76. (*d*)	77. (*b*)
78. (*a*)	79. (*a*)	80. (*b*)	81. (*c*)	82. (*c*)	83. (*a*)	84. (*c*)
85. (*a*)	86. (*a*)	87. (*a*)	88. (*a*)	89. (*d*)	90. (*b*)	91. (*c*)

92. (*b*)	93. (*d*)	94. (*c*)	95. (*b*)	96. (*a*)	97. (*a*)	98. (*b*)
99. (*a*)	100. (*a*)	101. (*c*)	102. (*d*)	103. (*b*)	104. (*d*)	105. (*c*)
106. (*b*)	107. (*c*)	108. (*d*)	109. (*b*)	110. (*a*)	111. (*d*)	112. (*d*)
113. (*d*)	114. (*a*)	115. (*b*)	116. (*a*)	117. (*b*)	118. (*b*)	119. (*b*)
120. (*a*)	121. (*a*)	122. (*a*)	123. (*d*)	124. (*d*)	125. (*a*)	126. (*a*)
127. (*b*)	128. (*a*)	129. (*a*)	130. (*a*)	131. (*b*)	132. (*a*)	133. (*a*)
134. (*b*)	135. (*a*)	136. (*a*)	137. (*a*)	138. (*b*)	139. (*b*)	140. (*c*)
141. (*d*)	142. (*c*)	143. (*b*)	144. (*b*)	145. (*a*)	146. (*a*)	147. (*c*)
148. (*b*)	149. (*d*)	150. (*a*)	151. (*a*)	152. (*a*)	153. (*a*)	154. (*b*)
155. (*a*)	156. (*b*)	157. (*a*)	158. (*a*)	159. (*a*)	160. (*a*)	161. (*a*)
162. (*a*)	163. (*b*)	164. (*d*)	165. (*a*)	166. (*a*)	167. (*a*)	168. (*a*)
169. (*a*)	170. (*a*)	171. (*a*)	172. (*a*)	173. (*b*)	174. (*b*)	175. (*a*)
176. (*a*)	177. (*a*)	178. (*b*)	179. (*a*)	180. (*a*)	181. (*a*)	182. (*b*)
183. (*b*)						

9

Computer Graphics and Multimedia

1. Which of the following is not a stage in multimedia.
   (*a*) Planning and costing
   (*b*) Designing of procedure
   (*c*) Test and implementations
   (*d*) None of the above

2. Multimedia environment is
   (*a*) Hardware and software required to run multimedia
   (*b*) The 3D presentation created by multimedia
   (*c*) Use of multimedia in the field of environment
   (*d*) None of the above

3. Capacity of DVD runs in
   (*a*) Megabytes
   (*b*) Gigabytes
   (*c*) Kilobytes
   (*d*) Terabytes

4. The pixel/line of DVD are
   (*a*) 240
   (*b*) 720
   (*c*) 1024
   (*d*) None of the above

5. The capacity and weak page of DVD is
   (*a*) 4.4 GB, 0.74 μm
   (*b*) 8.6 GB, 0.74 μm
   (*c*) 4.7 GB, 0.90 μm
   (*d*) 8.6 GB, 0.90 μm

6. Which of the following is not a feature of OCR
   (*a*) Drawing and Painting tools
   (*b*) Scalable dimensions
   (*c*) Paint tools
   (*d*) None of the above

7. Salient features of drawing tools of OCR
   (*a*) Inbuilt graphical user interface with status bar
   (*b*) Pull down menu
   (*c*) Dialog box for quite logical selection
   (*d*) All of the above

8. Antialiasing is used
   (*a*) To remove the jagged appearance of line
   (*b*) To remove the intensity of line
   (*c*) To decide pixel position
   (*d*) None of the above

9. Features of Modeling Tools are
   (*a*) Ability to drag and drop
   (*b*) Ability to add transparency and shadowing length
   (*c*) Unlimited camera with focus
   (*d*) All of the above

10. Image editing Tool features are
    (*a*) Multiple windows
    (*b*) Masking feature
    (*c*) Antializing capability
    (*d*) All of the above

11. Sonogram is
    (*a*) Method of speech recognition
    (*b*) Method of 3D display
    (*c*) Method of picture creation
    (*d*) Method of transferring data

12. VD device is used for
(*a*) Tone generation to listen to MIDI channel
(*b*) To store data
(*c*) To edit the sound
(*d*) None of the above

13. Which of the following is not vedio compression technique
(*a*) Interpolative
(*b*) Predictive
(*c*) Transform
(*d*) All of the above

14. DVI is used for
(*a*) Symmetric and asymmetric motion Video compression
(*b*) Creation of digital images
(*c*) Creation of 3D images
(*d*) None of the above

15. Which of the following is a picture layer
(*a*) Slice layer
(*b*) Macro block layer
(*c*) Block layer
(*d*) None of the above

16. Four memory chips of 16 × 4 size have their address buses connected together. The system will be of size
(*a*) 16 × 16
(*b*) 8 × 4
(*c*) 8 × 16
(*d*) None of the above

17. A 4 bit synchronous counter uses flip flop with propagation delay time 25 n seconds each. Max possible time required for change of state will be
(*a*) 25 n sec
(*b*) 0 n sec
(*c*) 50 n sec
(*d*) None of above

18. A 12 bit ADCs operating with a 1μ sec clock period and total conversion time is seen to be 14 μ sec. The ADC must be of type
(*a*) Successive approximation weights
(*b*) Register type
(*c*) Ladder type
(*d*) Any of the above type

19. Equation of a circle whose centre is (2, – 1), which passes through (3, 6) is.
(*a*) $x^2 + y^2 - 4x + 2y = 0$
(*b*) $x^2 + y^2 - 4x + 2y - 45 = 0$
(*c*) $4x^2 + 4y^2 - 4x + 2y - 45 = 0$
(*d*) None of the above

20. Equation of the circle passing through the points (5, 7), (6, 6) and (2, – 2) is.
(*a*) $x^2 + y^2 - 4x - 6y - 12 = 0$
(*b*) $x^2 + y^2 + 4x + 6y + 12 = 0$
(*c*) $4x^2 + 6y^2 - 4x - 6y - 12 = 0$
(*d*) None of the above

21. If a circle is given by equation $x^2 + y^2 - 4x - 6y - 12 = 0$, it's centre and radius is.
(*a*) (2, 3) , 5
(*b*) (3, 3) , 10
(*c*) (4, 5) , 6
(*d*) None of the above

22. Equation of a circle which touches y axis at a distance of two units from origin and cuts an intercept of three units is.
(*a*) $4x^2 + 4y^2 + 4x - 4y + 4 =0$
(*b*) $x^2 + y^2 +5x + 4x - 4 = 0$
(*c*) $x^2 + y^2 \pm 5x - 4y +4 = 0$
(*d*) None of the above

23. If y = 2x is a chord of the circle $x^2 + y^2 - 10x = 0$, the equation of a circle with this chord as a diameter is.

(*a*) $x^2 + y^2 + 2x - 4y = 0$
(*b*) $x^2 + 4y^2 - 2x - 4y = 0$
(*c*) $x^2 + y^2 + 2x + 4y = 0$
(*d*) $x^2 + y^2 - 2x - 4y = 0$

24. The ISO standard for computer graphics is.
(*a*) Graphics kernel system
(*b*) Graphics standard system
(*c*) Computer graphics standard
(*d*) None of the above

25. Which of the following is not a GKS primitive.
(*a*) Polyline
(*b*) Polymarker
(*c*) Fill area
(*d*) None of the above

26. Function of primitive polymarker is.
(*a*) Mark the points, construct a polynomial to fit the points via some fit techniques
(*b*) Fill the graphic image with multiple color
(*c*) Draw a picture in multiple dimensions
(*d*) None of the above

27. Which of the following is not a stage in multimedia.
(*a*) Planning and costing
(*b*) Designing and procedure
(*c*) Test the due
(*d*) None of the above

28. Multimedia environment is.
(*a*) Hardware and software required to run multimedia
(*b*) The 3D presentation created by multimedia
(*c*) Use of multimedia in the field of environment
(*d*) None of the above

29. In which form the drawing area contents are printed on matrix printer.
(*a*) Retrieve form
(*b*) Archive form
(*c*) Print form
(*d*) Grid spacing

30. Which are used to control the display.
(*a*) Computer protocols
(*b*) Computer communication
(*c*) Geometric model
(*d*) None

31. Which of the following can be used to link a graphic terminal with remote computer.
(*a*) Computer protocols
(*b*) Computer communication
(*c*) Geometric models
(*d*) None

32. Which of the following is used in all image generation.
(*a*) Sampling
(*b*) Line and curve generation
(*c*) Clipping
(*d*) Geometric models

33. Which algorithm require careful attention to photometry and color reproduction.
(*a*) Raster algorithm
(*b*) Shading algorithm
(*c*) Sampling algorithm
(*d*) None

34. Which technique is used to display shaded images on binary output devices.
(*a*) Computational geometry
(*b*) Shading
(*c*) Half tone
(*d*) None

35. In which form the drawing area contents are achieved under the

same name as they appear in buffer.
(*a*) Retrieve form
(*b*) Archive form
(*c*) Print form
(*d*) None

36. Which system is used to present light to eye.
(*a*) Optic system
(*b*) Feedback
(*c*) Animation
(*d*) CAD

37. Which technique is useful to teach and to entertain.
(*a*) Computer processing
(*b*) Animation
(*c*) CAD
(*d*) None

38. Which technique is used to manage large number of pictures.
(*a*) Animation
(*b*) Computer processing
(*c*) Mathematical modeling
(*d*) CAD

39. Which of the following is used to help in design automobiles, ships, aero planes, oil refineries, machine parts, etc.
(*a*) Molecular modeling
(*b*) Simulation
(*c*) Computer generated image
(*d*) None

40. Which application require extreme realism including moving images.
(*a*) Simulation
(*b*) Animation
(*c*) CAD
(*d*) None

41. Which technique depends on viewers ability to reconstruct the scene from multiple projections.
(*a*) Perspective projection
(*b*) Parallel projection
(*c*) Intensity cues
(*d*) None

42. Which technique is used to show the structure of three-dimensional object.
(*a*) Perspective projection
(*b*) Simple projection
(*c*) Parallel projection
(*d*) None

43. The technique which provides dramatic depth is.
(*a*) Stereoscopic view
(*b*) Intensities cues
(*c*) Kinetic depth
(*d*) None of the above

44. Which of the following techniques are used to brighten the parts of image closer to observer.
(*a*) Kinetic depth effect
(*b*) Hidden line elimination
(*c*) Intensity modulation
(*d*) None of the above

45. Which technique require considerable computation, but never useful for producing finished picture of scene.
(*a*) Kinetic depth effect
(*b*) Intensity cues
(*c*) Stereoscopic view
(*d*) Hidden line elimination

46. Which technique is used to convey the depth and shape of an object on raster scan display.
(*a*) 3D image
(*b*) Polarizer
(*c*) Kinetic depth effect
(*d*) Shading with hidden surface removal

47. Which of the following is used to

show the image on bottom half of CRT.
(*a*) 3D image
(*b*) Projection
(*c*) Polarizer
(*d*) None

48. Which of the following is used to combine the polarized images.
(*a*) Polarizer
(*b*) Half stones
(*c*) Horizontal half severed mirror
(*d*) None

49. Which technique gives a line drawing a more realistic appearance.
(*a*) Hidden line elimination
(*b*) Animation
(*c*) 3D imaging
(*d*) None of the above

50. Which technique is used to generate different kind of images of 3D scene, all starting from a model of a scene.
(*a*) Modeling 3D scene
(*b*) 3D imaging
(*c*) Animation
(*d*) None of the above

51. Which of the following describes the view of scene.
(*a*) Three kind of viewing parameters
(*b*) Three-dimensional images
(*c*) Three-dimensional scene
(*d*) None of the above

52. In how many classes we can divide the 3D scene.
(*a*) Two
(*b*) Three
(*c*) One
(*d*) None

53. Which of the following is a combination of geometry and topology.
(*a*) 3D image
(*b*) 3D scene
(*c*) 3D view parameter
(*d*) None of the above

54. Which of the following is used to record the structure of a scene.
(*a*) Geometry
(*b*) Topology
(*c*) Image
(*d*) None of the above

55. Which of the following are used to display the straight lines, text strings, circular arcs, and other simple graphical items.
(*a*) Graphic primitives
(*b*) Windowing functions
(*c*) Robustness
(*d*) Completeness

56. Which function is used to define the boundary visible portion of a picture.
(*a*) Graphic primitives
(*b*) Windowing function
(*c*) Robustness
(*d*) Completeness

57. The Bezier is a.
(*a*) Kind of curve
(*b*) Kind of animation services
(*c*) Kind of 3D services
(*d*) None of the above

58. Which of the following is useful to free storage allocation.
(*a*) Fragmenting effect
(*b*) Speed of allocation
(*c*) Free storage allocation
(*d*) None of the above

59. Which of the following represent circuit model.
(*a*) Data structure
(*b*) Electrical circuit

(*c*) Wire segment
(*d*) None of the above

60. Which of the following is used to train the pilot of aeroplane.
(*a*) Computer graphics
(*b*) Interactive computer graphics
(*c*) Ping pong
(*d*) None of the above

61. Which of the following is based on a video gaming technique.
(*a*) Computer graphics
(*b*) Interactive graphics
(*c*) Ping Pong
(*d*) None of the above

62. Which of the following improved requires bandwidth of a communication between user and computer.
(*a*) Multimedia
(*b*) Computer graphics
(*c*) Interactive graphics
(*d*) Ping Pong

63. Which of the following converts 0's and 1's into corresponding signal.
(*a*) Display controller
(*b*) Line drawing display
(*c*) Frame buffer
(*d*) Interactive graphics

64. Which of the following read each successive byte of data from frame buffer.
(*a*) Display controller
(*b*) Line drawing display
(*c*) Interactive graphics
(*d*) None of the above

65. Which of the following is used to represent a new pattern of pixel.
(*a*) Display controller
(*b*) Line drawing algorithm
(*c*) Frame buffer
(*d*) None of the above

66. Which of the following make the program very easy to operate.
(*a*) The user interface
(*b*) Interactive graphics
(*c*) Display controller
(*d*) None of the above

67. Which of the following need a beam accelerating potential.
(*a*) Beam penetrating CRT
(*b*) Phosphorus
(*c*) Shadow mask CRT
(*d*) None of the above

68. Which of the following use three guns, grouped in a triangle or delta.
(*a*) Beam penetration CRT
(*b*) Phosphorus
(*c*) Shadow mask
(*d*) None of the above

69. Which of the following is capable of displaying of an image measuring ¾ ft.
(*a*) Laser scan display
(*b*) Raster scan display
(*c*) Random scan display
(*d*) None of the above

70. Which of the following is useful in displaying maps, high quality text and elaborate circuit diagram.
(*a*) Laser scan display
(*b*) Raster scan display
(*c*) Random scan display
(*d*) None of the above

71. Which of the following make use of current beam position.
(*a*) Vector drawing instruction
(*b*) Line drawing instruction
(*c*) Shadow mask instruction
(*d*) None of the above

72. Which of the following display 10 bit positive integer coordinates.

(*a*) DVST
(*b*) Storage tube
(*c*) Line drawing
(*d*) None of the above

73. Which of the following uses the display file without stopping the display.
(*a*) Display controller
(*b*) DVST
(*c*) Refresh display
(*d*) None of the above

74. Which of the following changes the position of picture.
(*a*) Rotation
(*b*) Scaling
(*c*) Shading
(*d*) Translation

75. Which of the following changes the orientation of the picture.
(*a*) Rotation
(*b*) Scaling
(*c*) Shading
(*d*) Transformation

76. Which of the following changes the size of the picture?
(*a*) Rotation
(*b*) Scaling
(*c*) Shading
(*d*) Transformation

77. Which of the following is used to clear the screen or to display rectangular objects such as horizontal and vertical lines.
(*a*) Rectangle
(*b*) Mask
(*c*) Colour
(*d*) None of the above

78. Which of the following is used to display the character and implement painting program.
(*a*) Write rectangle
(*b*) Write mask
(*c*) Write colour
(*d*) Copy raster

79. Which describe painting object of varying colour into frame buffer.
(*a*) Write colour
(*b*) Copy raster
(*c*) Invert mask
(*d*) None of the above

80. Which is used for copying a rectangular region on to screen or coping a region from frame buffer into temporary raster.
(*a*) Invert mask
(*b*) Invert rectangle
(*c*) Copy raster
(*d*) Write color

81. In which of the followings a inverting function f(x) or $f^{-1}(x)$ is applied to pixels.
(*a*) Invert rectangle
(*b*) Copy raster
(*c*) Write colour
(*d*) Invert mask

82. Selection feedback is implemented using.
(*a*) Invert mask
(*b*) Write rectangle
(*c*) Invert rectangle
(*d*) Copy raster

83. By using which of the following technique, we can reduce much of the screen conversion work.
(*a*) Screen updating algorithm
(*b*) Incremental technique
(*c*) Rename segment
(*d*) None of the above

84. Which of the following can be used to update a portion of a screen.
(*a*) Screen updating algorithm

(*b*) Incremental technique
(*c*) Rename segment
(*d*) None of the above

85. Which changes position and orientation of geometrical figure.
(*a*) Geometric model
(*b*) Bezier model
(*c*) Instance of an object
(*d*) Transformation

86. What is the name of the function which is used to remove an item from a list.
(*a*) Delete cell
(*b*) Delete group
(*c*) Delete item
(*d*) None of the above

87. In a mouse, which of the following is connected to each wheel.
(*a*) Joystick
(*b*) Light pen
(*c*) Shaft – encoder
(*d*) None of the above

88. Which input device is used to work on flat surfaces.
(*a*) Tablets
(*b*) Mouse
(*c*) Stylus
(*d*) None

89. Which of the following is a pointing device.
(*a*) Tablets
(*b*) Mouse
(*c*) Light pen
(*d*) Stylus

90. Which of the following device is used for interaction with computer model.
(*a*) Input device
(*b*) Output device
(*c*) Light pen
(*d*) None of the above

91. Which provide a flat drawing area of 10 inch square.
(*a*) Tablets
(*b*) Acoustic tablets
(*c*) Electro acoustic tablets
(*d*) RAND tablets

92. Which table depends on the use of strip microphones.
(*a*) Tablets
(*b*) Acoustic tablets
(*c*) Electro acoustic tablets
(*d*) Rand tablets

93. In which a high-speed photomultiplier tube is used.
(*a*) Sensor
(*b*) Rels
(*c*) Wire
(*d*) None of the above

94. Which device is used to measure position.
(*a*) Reels
(*b*) Sensor
(*c*) Boxes
(*d*) None of the above

95. Which device uses digital reference value.
(*a*) Comparator
(*b*) Tracking hardware
(*c*) Stylus
(*d*) None of the above

96. For larger steps which key is used.
(*a*) Central key
(*b*) Stepping key
(*c*) Fifth function key
(*d*) None of the above

97. Which is used to attach a line endpoint to another line.
(*a*) Rubber band technique
(*b*) Scales
(*c*) Horizontal construct
(*d*) Gravity field

98. In a horizontal line constraint to align endpoints vertically which technique is used.
   (*a*) Modular constraints
   (*b*) Directional constraints
   (*c*) Vertical constraints
   (*d*) Horizontal line constraints

99. Which of the following technique uses digital reference values.
   (*a*) Comparator
   (*b*) Tracking hardware
   (*c*) Stylus
   (*d*) None of the above

100. Which is used to display only selected area of a figure.
   (*a*) Sampling
   (*b*) Line and curve generation
   (*c*) Clipping
   (*d*) Geometric models

101. Which is the computer software graphics.
   (*a*) Computer protocol
   (*b*) PHIGS
   (*c*) View port
   (*d*) None of the above

102. Which of the following is used to manage large number of pictures.
   (*a*) Computer protocol
   (*b*) GKIS
   (*c*) Computer processing
   (*d*) None of the above

103. Access time is defined as.
   (*a*) The amount of time taken to find and display the required information
   (*b*) Amount of time required to store some picture
   (*c*) Amount of time required to work on MS access
   (*d*) None of the above

104. Adapter cards are
   (*a*) Controller cards.
   (*b*) Expansion cards
   (*c*) Inter face cards
   (*d*) All of the above

105. AD PCM is.
   (*a*) Adaptive Differential Pulse Code Modulation
   (*b*) Adaptive Differential Phase Code Modem
   (*c*) Adaptive Doppler Pulse Code modulation
   (*d*) Adaptive Differential Phase Change Modulation

106. Antialiasing is.
   (*a*) Changing the shape of aliasing
   (*b*) Smoothing of image or sound roughness
   (*c*) Changing the quality of sound
   (*d*) None of the above

107. API stands for.
   (*a*) Application Programming Interface
   (*b*) Applied Programming Interface
   (*c*) Application Process Interface
   (*d*) Applied Proves Interface

108. Aspect ratio is .
   (*a*) Height to width ratio in PC
   (*b*) Width to height ratio in PC
   (*c*) Height to diagonal ratio in PC
   (*d*) None of the above

109. Asymmetric compression.
   (*a*) Is approach of information coding where compression and decompression are not matching in exact steps of reversal
   (*b*) Computer vision which is performed on asymmetric data
   (*c*) The compression used to generate asymmetric code
   (*d*) None of the above

110. Authoring software.
(a) The software used by authors
(b) A set of customized and preprogram elements which are used to create and organize full multimedia production
(c) The manufacturing software
(d) None of the above

111. AVI is.
(a) Audio Video Interleaved in a file format
(b) Audio Visual Interface
(c) Adaptive Voltage Interface
(d) Adaptive Voltage Inter-Connection

112. B. frame is
(a) MPEG, file format
(b) MPEG system bidirectional predictive coded frames
(c) MPEG Bit frame
(d) None of the above

113. Bi level image.
(a) It is computer image in which each pixel is represented by only one bit
(b) It is black and white image
(c) It is a satellite generated image in two phases
(d) None of the above

114. Bit map.
(a) It defines a display space color for each pixel in display space
(b) A digitized map
(c) A map consisting of bit level image
(d) None of the above

115. Blue Book.
(a) It is CD extra format specification
(b) A book printed in blue cover
(c) A book priced very high
(d) None of the above

116. CAV used in LASER stands for.
(a) Constant Angular Velocity
(b) Continuous Angular Velocity
(c) Constant Analog Voltage
(d) Continuous Analog Voltage

117. CCITT stands for.
(a) International Consultative Committee of Information Transfer
(b) International Consultative Committee for Telegraphy and Telephony
(c) Introductory Consulting Committee of Telegraphy and Telephony
(d) None of the above

118. CD I, developed by Philips, include audio, fill screen video and interactive capabilities, stand for.
(a) Compact Disk Interface
(b) Compact Disk Interference
(c) Compact Disk Interactive
(d) None of the above

119. CD-RDX stands for.
(a) CD-ROM read only data exchange standard
(b) CD Rom data exchange standard
(c) CD-Rom wise data exchange standard
(d) None of the above

120. DCT stand for.
(a) Discrete Costine Transform
(b) Digital Costive Transform
(c) Digital Constant Transformation
(v) Discrete Constant Transformation

121. Resolution supported by CGA is.
(a) 320 × 200
(b) 640 × 200

(*c*) 640 × 1024
(*d*) 1024 × 1024

122. Dithering is.
   (*a*) An attempt by a computer program to approximate a code from a mixture of other code when required color is not available
   (*b*) It is ability of display screen to project an accurate and real image
   (*c*) It is a process to translate analog data to digital data
   (*d*) None of the above

123. DPI is.
   (*a*) Measure of dots per inch
   (*b*) Digital peripheral interface
   (*c*) Dots per interface
   (*d*) None of the above

124. FSFM stands for.
   (*a*) Full Screen Motion Video, which can be displayed, back as well as broadcast TV
   (*b*) Final Screen Full Motion Video
   (*c*) Full Screen Final Motions
   (*d*) None of the above

125. Hyper media is.
   (*a*) A variant of multimedia
   (*b*) Interactive program in which information is stored in a number of different media and cross linked
   (*c*) Interactive media with name hyper
   (*d*) None of the above

126. I frame is.
   (*a*) Inter-coded frame in MPEG which does not consist reference to other frames
   (*b*) Inter coded frame form in JPEG
   (*c*) Frame Format
   (*d*) None of the above

127. Indio is
   (*a*) Compression algorithm developed by intel and used by Microsoft
   (*b*) It is new color
   (*c*) It is multimedia device
   (*d*) None of the above

128. Interleaving is.
   (*a*) Mixing of different data types, text, video, audio, graphics
   (*b*) Mixing of memory location
   (*c*) Mixing of architecture
   (*d*) None of the above

129. JBIG stands for.
   (*a*) Joint by level image experts group
   (*b*) Joint biphase Image Editor Group
   (*c*) Junior by level image expert group
   (*d*) None of the above

130. JPEG stands for.
   (*a*) Joint Photographic Experts Group
   (*b*) Junior Photographic Expert Group
   (*c*) Joint Picture Editing Group
   (*d*) Junior Picture Editing Group

131. Kiosk is.
   (*a*) Stand-alone information station that allows users to browse and retrieve information from a computer normally by touch screen mode
   (*b*) Multimedia device
   (*c*) Frame format
   (*d*) None of the above

132. MCI stands for.
   (*a*) Media Control Interface

(*b*) Memory Control Interface
(*c*) Media Consciousness Interface
(*d*) Media call of Introduction

133. Morphing is.
(*a*) A type of animation in which interpolation between specified points on two or more images create transitional effect
(*b*) It is an antialiasing technique
(*c*) it is a technique creating special sound effect
(*d*) None of the above

134. MP3 is.
(*a*) Standard technology and format for compression of sound sequence
(*b*) Technology for creating a animated picture
(*c*) Technology for creating a multimedia presentation
(*d*) None of the above

135. Open GL is.
(*a*) It is a 3D graphic programming API
(*b*) It is a 2D graphic programming API
(*c*) It is a multimedia production tool
(*d*) None of the above

136. PAL is.
(*a*) Phase Alternation specifying 768 pixel/lime, 576 lines screen and 25 frames/see
(*b*) Phase access lab
(*c*) Phase accomodation in line
(*d*) None of the above

137. PCMCIA stands for.
(*a*) Personal Computer Memory Card International Association
(*b*) Personal Computer Management Intergrated Association
(*c*) PC based Memory Management
(*d*) None of the above

138. PLU is.
(*a*) An asymmetric technique in DVI for full screen
(*b*) An symmetric technique in DVI for full screen
(*c*) A multimedia package
(*d*) None of the above

139. PNG is.
(*a*) Portable Network Graphic
(*b*) Portable News Group
(*c*) Portable New Work Generation
(*d*) None of the above

140. Polyphony is.
(*a*) It represents the total number of sounds, a sound card can reproduce at the same time
(*b*) A multimedia presentation
(*c*) An interacting computer graphic package
(*d*) None of the above

141. Refresh rate.
(*a*) Number of frames scanned per second
(*b*) Number of picture deleted per second
(*c*) Number of frames transmitted per second
(*d*) None of the above

142. RIFF.
(*a*) Refresh of Information in Frame Format
(*b*) Resource Inter Change File Format
(*c*) Refresh of Interactive File Format
(*d*) None of the above

143. Sound Editor is.

(*a*) Program that permit to edit sound files by actually audio wave form of clip
(*b*) Calling by news editor
(*c*) An interactive sound generation program
(*d*) None of the above

144. TIFF is.
(*a*) Tagged Image File Format, a cross platform file for storing high quality graphic
(*b*) Tagged Interpreter Frame Format
(*c*) Token interpreter frame format
(*d*) None of the above

145. Tweening is.
(*a*) Method where first cell of an animation and last cell of animation are selected and animation program calculates all cells in between
(*b*) It is a technique to create 3D animation
(*c*) It is new file format of multimedia creation
(*d*) It is a curve drawing technique in graphics

146. Video conferencing.
(*a*) It is transporting of real time video and voice on telecommunication
(*b*) It is conferencing done to close right video
(*c*) It is a conference organized to discuss trends in video
(*d*) None of the above

147. VRML stands for.
(*a*) Virtual Reality Markup Language
(*b*) Very Real Machine Language
(*c*) Virtually Real Machine Language
(*d*) None of the above

148. XGA stands for.
(*a*) Extended Graphics Array
(*b*) Expanded Geological Array
(*c*) Extended Graphic Adapter
(*d*) None of the above

149. Zigzag encoding.
(*a*) A technique in JPEG where low frequency components are coded first followed by high frequency components
(*b*) A technique in MPEG where coding of audio and video is performed simultaneously
(*c*) A technique is JPEG coding used for audio and text coding
(*d*) None of the above

150. MFM stands for.
(*a*) Modified Frequency Modulation
(*b*) Magnified Frequency Modulation
(*c*) Magnification Frequency of Magnetron
(*d*) None of the above

151. Integrated device electronics.
(*a*) Consists of integrated controller with the drive along with 16 bits parallel data interface
(*b*) Consists of integrated controller with the drive long with 8 bit parallel data interface
(*c*) Consists of integrated controller with the drive along with 8 bit serial data interface
(*d*) None of the above

ANSWERS

1. (*d*)	2. (*a*)	3. (*b*)	4. (*c*)	5. (*a*)	6. (*d*)	7. (*d*)
8. (*a*)	9. (*d*)	10. (*d*)	11. (*a*)	12. (*a*)	13. (*d*)	14. (*a*)
15. (*d*)	16. (*d*)	17. (*a*)	18. (*a*)	19. (*b*)	20. (*a*)	21. (*a*)
22. (*c*)	23. (*d*)	24. (*a*)	25. (*b*)	26. (*b*)	27. (*d*)	28. (*a*)
29. (*c*)	30. (*a*)	31. (*b*)	32. (*a*)	33. (*b*)	34. (*c*)	35. (*b*)
36. (*a*)	37. (*b*)	38. (*b*)	39. (*c*)	40. (*a*)	41. (*b*)	42. (*c*)
43. (*a*)	44. (*c*)	45. (*d*)	46. (*d*)	47. (*c*)	48. (*c*)	49. (*a*)
50. (*a*)	51. (*a*)	52. (*a*)	53. (*b*)	54. (*b*)	55. (*a*)	56. (*a*)
57. (*b*)	58. (*c*)	59. (*a*)	60. (*b*)	61. (*b*)	62. (*b*)	63. (*a*)
64. (*a*)	65. (*c*)	66. (*a*)	67. (*a*)	68. (*c*)	69. (*a*)	70. (*a*)
71. (*a*)	72. (*b*)	73. (*a*)	74. (*d*)	75. (*a*)	76. (*b*)	77. (*a*)
78. (*b*)	79. (*a*)	80. (*c*)	81. (*d*)	82. (*c*)	83. (*a*)	84. (*b*)
85. (*d*)	86. (*c*)	87. (*c*)	88. (*a*)	89. (*c*)	90. (*c*)	91. (*d*)
92. (*c*)	93. (*a*)	94. (*a*)	95. (*a*)	96. (*a*)	97. (*d*)	98. (*d*)
99. (*a*)	100. (*c*)	101. (*b*)	102. (*c*)	103. (*a*)	104. (*d*)	105. (*a*)
106. (*b*)	107. (*a*)	108. (*a*)	109. (*a*)	110. (*b*)	111. (*a*)	112. (*b*)
113. (*a*)	114. (*a*)	115. (*a*)	116. (*a*)	117. (*b*)	118. (*a*)	119. (*a*)
120. (*a*)	121. (*a*)	122. (*a*)	123. (*a*)	124. (*a*)	125. (*b*)	126. (*a*)
127. (*a*)	128. (*a*)	129. (*b*)	130. (*a*)	131. (*a*)	132. (*a*)	133. (*a*)
134. (*a*)	135. (*a*)	136. (*a*)	137. (*a*)	138. (*a*)	139. (*a*)	140. (*a*)
141. (*a*)	142. (*b*)	143. (*a*)	144. (*a*)	145. (*a*)	146. (*a*)	147. (*a*)
148. (*a*)	149. (*a*)	150. (*a*)	151. (*a*)			

10

Database Management System

1. Which of the following is a database element?
   (*a*) Data
   (*b*) Relationship
   (*c*) Constraints and Schema
   (*d*) All of the above

2. What are binary computer representation of stored logical entities?
   (*a*) Data
   (*b*) Relationship
   (*c*) Constraints
   (*d*) Schema

3. What represents a correspondance between various data elements?
   (*a*) Data
   (*b*) Relationship
   (*c*) Constraints
   (*d*) Schema

4. What are predicates that define correct database states and relationship with in database?
   (*a*) Data
   (*b*) Relationship
   (*c*) Constraints
   (*d*) Schema

5. What separates the physical aspect of data storage from logical aspects of data representation?
   (*a*) Data
   (*b*) Relationship
   (*c*) Constraints
   (*d*) Schema

6. What defines how and where data are organized in physical data storage?
   (*a*) Internal schema
   (*b*) External schema
   (*c*) Conceptual schema
   (*d*) None of the above

7. Which of the following define the stored data structure in term of database model used?
   (*a*) Internal schema
   (*b*) External schema
   (*c*) Conceptual schema
   (*d*) None of the above

8. What defines a view of database for a particular user?
   (*a*) Internal schema
   (*b*) External schema
   (*c*) Conceptual schema
   (*d*) None of the above

9. A collection of data design to be used for data manipulation is called
   (*a*) Database
   (*b*) DBMS
   (*c*) RDBMS
   (*d*) None of the above

10. To access information from a database, you need
    (*a*) EIS
    (*b*) DBMS
    (*c*) MIS
    (*d*) None of the above

11. Which of the following is an advantage of database?
    (*a*) Reduction in redundancy
    (*b*) Avoidance of inconsistency
    (*c*) Security enforcement
    (*d*) All of the above

12. Which of the following is a characteristic of data in database?
    (*a*) Shared
    (*b*) Secure
    (*c*) Independent
    (*d*) All of the above

13. Which of the following is an example of database application
    (*a*) Computerized library systems
    (*b*) ATMs
    (*c*) Flight reservation
    (*d*) All of the above

14. DBMS stand for
    (*a*) Data Blocking and Management System
    (*b*) Data Base Management System
    (*c*) Database Business Management System
    (*d*) None of the above

15. What is sequence of database operations that represents logical unit of work and that access a database and transform it from one state to another?
    (*a*) Logical unit of work
    (*b*) Transaction
    (*c*) Record
    (*d*) None of the above

16. What is the name of the system database that contain description of data in database?
    (*a*) Metadata
    (*b*) Data dictionary
    (*c*) Table
    (*d*) None of the above

17. IMS stands for
    (*a*) Information Management System
    (*b*) Internal Mechanical Security
    (*c*) International Managers Society
    (*d*) None of the above

18. Which of the following is hierarchial database?
    (*a*) IDMS
    (*b*) IMS
    (*c*) DBZ
    (*d*) Oracle

19. Which of the following is the oldest database model?
    (*a*) Hierarchial
    (*b*) Network
    (*c*) Relational
    (*d*) Deductive

20. SQL stands for
    (*a*) Scalable Query Language
    (*b*) Structured Query Language
    (*c*) Standard Query Language
    (*d*) None of the above

21. 4 GL stands for
    (*a*) Four General Language
    (*b*) Fourth General Language
    (*c*) Fourth Generation Language
    (*d*) Four Generation Language

22. An OODBMS holds
    (*a*) Data and text
    (*b*) Picture and image
    (*c*) Voice and video
    (*d*) All of the above

23. What is the field of data that can be used to locate a related field or record?
    (*a*) Address to pointer
    (*b*) Pointer
    (*c*) Value of pointer
    (*d*) Structure

24. What is the technique used for

physically arranging the record of a file on secondary storage device?
(*a*) Data storage
(*b*) Indexing
(*c*) Hashing
(*d*) File organization

25. Which of the following factor should be considered when choosing the file organization?
(*a*) Data retrieval speed
(*b*) Scalability
(*c*) Security
(*d*) All of the above

26. In a sequential file organization, records in the file are stored in sequence according to .... key value?
(*a*) Candidate
(*b*) Secondary
(*c*) Primary
(*d*) None of the above

27. In the index file organization, if the records are stored sequentially based on primary key value, then that file organization is called .... organization?
(*a*) Indexed primary sequence
(*b*) Index sequential
(*c*) Random sequential
(*d*) None of the above

28. Which of the following is most popular form of B-tree?
(*a*) B*tree
(*b*) B^–tree
(*c*) B+–tree
(*d*) None of the above

29. In a hashed file organization the address of each record is determined using a ....?
(*a*) Index
(*b*) Hashing algorithm
(*c*) Pointer
(*d*) None of the above

30. In which of the following file organization, sequential file processing is impractical?
(*a*) Indexed sequential
(*b*) Indexed
(*c*) B-tree
(*d*) Hashed

31. The attribute or set of attributes used to look up a record in a file is called
(*a*) Primary key
(*b*) Search key
(*c*) Candidate key
(*d*) Secondary key

32. If the file containing records is sequentially ordered, the index whose search key specifies the sequential order of file is called the .... Index?
(*a*) Primary
(*b*) Secondary
(*c*) Inverted
(*d*) None of the above

33. Which of the following is another name of primary Index?
(*a*) Secondary index
(*b*) Randomizing index
(*c*) Clustering index
(*d*) None of the above

34. Indexes whose search key specifies an order that is different from sequential order of file are called .... Index?
(*a*) Primary
(*b*) Non-key
(*c*) Secondary or Non-clustering
(*d*) None of the above

35. In case of a .... an index record appears for every search key value in the file?

(*a*) Sparse index
(*b*) Dense index
(*c*) Primary index
(*d*) None of the above

36. In the case of a .... the index record is created only for some search key values?
(*a*) Sparse index
(*b*) Dense index
(*c*) Primary index
(*d*) None of the above

37. Each node of a B+ - tree contain a .... and the associated search–key value?
(*a*) Pointer
(*b*) Chain
(*c*) Address
(*d*) None of the above

38. The number of pointers in a node is called the .... of node?
(*a*) Span
(*b*) Scope
(*c*) Fanout
(*d*) None of the above

39. What does 'B' in B-tree means?
(*a*) Better
(*b*) Binary
(*c*) Balanced
(*d*) Byte

40. Another name of hash function is ....?
(*a*) Randomizing
(*b*) Arithmetic
(*c*) Exponential
(*d*) None of the above

41. Which is hashing technique that involve applying an arithmetic function or logical function to different portion of hash field value to calculate the hash address?
(*a*) Mod hashing
(*b*) Open hashing
(*c*) Multiple hashing
(*d*) Folding

42. Which of the following is collision resolution method?
(*a*) Open addressing
(*b*) Chaining
(*c*) Multiple hashing
(*d*) All of the above

43. Which hash function maintain the record in order of hash field values?
(*a*) Malhashing
(*b*) Folding
(*c*) Order preserving hashing
(*d*) Indexed Hashing

44. Which hashing technique allocate a fixed number of buckets?
(*a*) Extensible hashing
(*b*) Linear hashing
(*c*) Static hashing
(*d*) None of the above

45. Which of the following is an example of dynamic hashing?
(*a*) Open address hashing
(*b*) Chain hashing
(*c*) Linear hashing
(*d*) All of the above

46. Which of the following dynamic hashing technique does not use directory?
(*a*) Extensible hashing
(*b*) Linear hashing
(*c*) Multiple hashing
(*d*) All of the above

47. Building a data model require answering question about ....?
(*a*) Entities
(*b*) Relationship
(*c*) Attributes

(*d*) All of the above

48. Which of the following is cause for modelling data?
    (*a*) Understand each user's perspective of data
    (*b*) Understand the nature of data itself, independent of its physical representations
    (*c*) Understand the use of data across application area
    (*d*) All of the above

49. The collection of data which can be stored as enlity is called ....
    (*a*) Record
    (*b*) Field
    (*c*) File
    (*d*) None of the above

50. To the computer, a file is nothing more than
    (*a*) Text
    (*b*) Image
    (*c*) Information
    (*d*) Series of bytes

51. A file contains .... that is needed for information processing?
    (*a*) Data
    (*b*) Knowledge
    (*c*) Instructions
    (*d*) None of the above

52. A .... is anything about which information can be stored?
    (*a*) Attribute
    (*b*) Entity
    (*c*) Instance
    (*d*) None of the above

53. Each attribute of an entity is represented in storage by .... ?
    (*a*) Data item
    (*b*) Instance
    (*c*) Field
    (*d*) None of the above

54. Which of the following is high level data model?
    (*a*) Attribute-relationship model
    (*b*) Relationship-attribute model
    (*c*) Entity-attribute model
    (*d*) Entity-relationship model

55. Which of the following criterion should be satisfied by an optimal data model?
    (*a*) Structural validity
    (*b*) Express ability
    (*c*) Shareability
    (*d*) All of the above

56. Which of the following term means the ability to distinguish between different data, data relationship and constraints?
    (*a*) Structural validity
    (*b*) Expressability
    (*c*) Shareability
    (*d*) Diagrammability

57. Which of the following is database service level?
    (*a*) External
    (*b*) Physical
    (*c*) Conceptual
    (*d*) All of the above

58. Which database level is closest to user?
    (*a*) Internal
    (*b*) Physical
    (*c*) External
    (*d*) Conceptual

59. What is RDBMS terminology for a row?
    (*a*) Tuple
    (*b*) Relation
    (*c*) Attribute
    (*d*) Domain

60. Various fields of tuple in relational schema are
   (*a*) Domain
   (*b*) Query
   (*c*) Relation
   (*d*) Sub Field

61. In a Database top to bottom relationship among items is established by
   (*a*) Relational schema
   (*b*) Hierarchical schema
   (*c*) Network schema
   (*d*) It may be performed by any of the above

62. An important feature of a query system
   (*a*) A natural language input interface
   (*b*) Access to main part of a database
   (*c*) Security from unauthentic user
   (*d*) None of the above

63. A logical schema
   (*a*) Organizes information into the accessible part
   (*b*) Can accept English language commands
   (*c*) Describes the actual storage of data on disk.
   (*d*) None of the above.

64. In database report designing, the form is used to define
   (*a*) The placement of data on the screen
   (*b*) The width of each field
   (*c*) Both (*a*) & (*b*)
   (*d*) None of the above.

65. A command which is used to change one or more fields in a record is
   (*a*) Edit
   (*b*) Rename
   (*c*) Modify
   (*d*) None of the above.

66. In order to use a record management system.
   (*a*) The low level details of information storage should be known
   (*b*) The record management system should be known
   (*c*) The field designing system should be known
   (*d*) None of the above

67. Which of the following is not a component of database environment
   (*a*) Users
   (*b*) Separate files
   (*c*) Database
   (*d*) Database Administrator

68. A characteristic of relational database model is
   (*a*) Complex logical relationship
   (*b*) Database Administrator
   (*c*) Separate files
   (*d*) None of the above.

69. Data Security threat include
   (*a*) Hardware failure
   (*b*) Privacy invasion
   (*c*) Software failure
   (*d*) (*b*) & (*c*) both

70. A software package which allows user to create retrieve and maintain record in a database
   (*a*) DBMS
   (*b*) SQL
   (*c*) ACCESS
   (*d*) FoxPro

71. Which of the following is a data dictionary software package
   (*a*) TOTAL

(*b*) DB/DC Dictionary
(*c*) Dbase 4
(*d*) None of the above

72. A schema describes
(*a*) Data element
(*b*) Records & files
(*c*) Record relationships
(*d*) All of the above

73. A important characteristic of data item is
(*a*) Good organization of fields
(*b*) Good selection of fields
(*c*) Good organization of files
(*d*) None of the above.

74. Which of the following contain a complete record of activities that affected the contents of a database during a certain period of time.
(*a*) Report writer
(*b*) Query language
(*c*) Data Manipulation language
(*d*) Transaction log

75. If a data is stored in multiple places in a database it is called
(*a*) Data redundancy
(*b*) Data inconsistency
(*c*) Data abundance
(*d*) None of the above

76 To design a DBMS the understanding of the following is important
(*a*) The physical schema
(*b*) One sub schema
(*c*) Logical schema
(*d*) File schema

76. The index consists of
(*a*) The pointers and keys of master lists
(*b*) The pointers and keys of various individual list
(*c*) The pointers and keys of various fields
(*d*) None of the above

77. Report generator is used to
(*a*) Generate the information regarding various fields
(*b*) Retrieve information from files
(*c*) Generate the information about interfaces of DBMS
(*d*) None of the above.

78. A file produced by a spread sheet
(*a*) Is stored on disk in ASCII text format
(*b*) Can be used as it is by the DBMS
(*c*) Is stored on disk in EBCDIC format
(*d*) Is stored on disk in Hollerith format

79 Which of the following information is not provided by data dictionary
(*a*) The location of data
(*b*) The size of data memory
(*c*) The length of data
(*d*) None of the above

80. The data which are related with each other from storage purpose are called
(*a*) Record
(*b*) Title
(*c*) List
(*d*) String

81. The addition and deletion in a file record is called file
(*a*) Updating
(*b*) Upgrading
(*c*) Editing
(*d*) Renewing.

82. Starting point for development of MIS is.
   (*a*) Deciding the hardware of system
   (*b*) Providing Pc's to all managers
   (*c*) Identification of business processes that are essence of all the business
   (*d*) None of the above

83. Ideally the information system objectives, should be stated in the form of.
   (*a*) Increased product sales
   (*b*) Reduced marketing cost
   (*c*) Increased product sales by 5% in the next quarter
   (*d*) All of the above

84. Environment in systems parlance refers to.
   (*a*) A sub system
   (*b*) The boundary
   (*c*) A part outside boundaries
   (*d*) None of the above

85. A report which contains values that are not in normal range of expectation, is called.
   (*a*) Exception report
   (*b*) Generation report
   (*c*) Renovation report
   (*d*) None of the above

86. Which of the following is not an organization relation.
   (*a*) Activities analysis
   (*b*) Decision analysis
   (*c*) Report analysis
   (*d*) Relationship analysis

87. The function of manager of corporate systems is.
   (*a*) To develop new systems
   (*b*) To supervise all systems analysis and programming tasks
   (*c*) To monitor performance
   (*d*) To design and develop information systems

88. Programmed decision is of type.
   (*a*) Analytic decision
   (*b*) Objective decision
   (*c*) Programmer's decision
   (*d*) None of the above

89. In MIS terminology which of the following is not a basic decision.
   (*a*) Judgmental decision
   (*b*) Adaptive decision
   (*c*) Analytic decision
   (*d*) None of the above

90. A GANTT chart is fundamentally a.
   (*a*) Bar chart
   (*b*) Reservation table
   (*c*) Pie chart
   (*d*) Log chart

91. A PERT network consists of numbered.
   (*a*) Event and activities
   (*b*) Planning and costing
   (*c*) Feasibility study element
   (*d*) None of the above

92. The MIS task force could include system analyst as well as participants from organizations belonging to
   (*a*) Prime areas
   (*b*) Functional areas
   (*c*) Political areas
   (*d*) Customer areas

93. Which of the following is not a reason for the failure of management business organization.
   (*a*) Lack of top management support and commitment
   (*b*) Over emphasis on appraisal

(*c*) Lack of clear-cut policy towards MBO
(*d*) None of the above

94. In MIS information management can be categorized into.
(*a*) Strategic planning information
(*b*) Management control information
(*c*) Operational information
(*d*) All of the above

95. Which of the following is an example of operational information.
(*a*) Scheduling work flow through a department
(*b*) Calculating direct program cost
(*c*) Financial accounting payroll
(*d*) None of the above

96. Which of the following is/are methods to check feedback of MIS.
(*a*) Modeling
(*b*) Simulation
(*c*) Test planning
(*d*) All of the above

97. Data collection is.
(*a*) The process of getting data in a form suitable for processing against master file
(*b*) The process of getting data in a form suitable for transaction file
(*c*) Storing the data in a file
(*d*) None of the above

98. Which of the following is not a stage in data collection.
(*a*) Possible conversion from one medium to another
(*b*) Input of data to computer for validation
(*c*) Sorting
(*d*) None of the above

99. The type of code, which involves the assignment of a consecutive and unique number to each item is.
(*a*) Sequence code
(*b*) Random code
(*c*) Reverse code
(*d*) None of the above

100. An alphanumeric code easy to interpret and understand is.
(*a*) Sequence
(*b*) Mnemonic
(*c*) Documentation
(*d*) None of the above

101. The main objective associated with a group code is to achieve.
(*a*) Shortest possible code
(*b*) Object code
(*c*) Internal code
(*d*) External code

102. System analysis refers to.
(*a*) Implementation of a system
(*b*) Analysis and design of a system
(*c*) Preparing a proposal for planning of a system
(*d*) None of the above

103. Reengineering is a.
(*a*) By product of good system analysis and design
(*b*) Engineering applied in research projects
(*c*) A second analysis applied to already engineered projects
(*d*) None of the above

104. Which of the following is true.
(*a*) System analysis is different than programming
(*b*) System analysis is same as programming

(*c*) System analysis and programming is partially same
(*d*) None of the above

105. Which of the following is not a part of analysis phase
(*a*) Requirement specification
(*b*) Initial feasibility study
(*c*) Evaluation of alternatives
(*d*) None of the above

106. Design stage does not include.
(*a*) Database design
(*b*) Identify hardware
(*c*) Identify software
(*d*) None of the above

107. Development stage of MIS include.
(*a*) Program coding
(*b*) Acceptance testing
(*c*) Implementation and maintenance
(*d*) All of the above

108. In the design of MIS what is appropriate amount of efforts devoted on design.
(*a*) 50% - 70%
(*b*) 10% - 15%
(*c*) 20% - 30%
(*d*) 100%

109. "Interviewing" technique for requirement specification is.
(*a*) Unstructured data gathering approach
(*b*) Structured data gathering approach
(*c*) Not a data gathering approach
(*d*) None of the above

110. Document flow diagram represent.
(*a*) Flow of data in the documents
(*b*) Flow of information
(*c*) Flow of results
(*d*) None of the above

111. A case tool generates.
(*a*) Data dictionary automatically
(*b*) Cannot generate data dictionary
(*c*) Can generate data dictionary on demand basis
(*d*) None of the above

112. Which of the following is not a phase of detailed system design.
(*a*) Functional specification
(*b*) Input output form design
(*c*) Program design
(*d*) All of the above

113. Data dictionary does not provides information about which of the following?
(*a*) Where data is located
(*b*) The size of the disk storage device
(*c*) Who owns or is responsible for the data
(*d*) How the data is used

114. Use of subschema is to
(*a*) To create very different, personalized news of same data
(*b*) Present information in different formats
(*c*) Hide sensitive information by omitting fields from the subschema's description
(*d*) All of the above

115. If data is stored redundantly then
(*a*) Storage space is wasted
(*b*) Changing data in one spot will cause data in consistency
(*c*) It can be more easily accessed
(*d*) Both (a) and (b)

116. All of following are logical data base structure except
(*a*) Tree

(*b*) Relational
(*c*) Network
(*d*) Chain

117. The physical location of a record is determined by a mathematical formula that transforms a file key into a record location in
(*a*) A tree file
(*b*) An indexed file
(*c*) A hashed file
(*d*) A sequential file

118. What is told by data dictionary about DBMS?
(*a*) What data are there in the database
(*b*) What attributes are possessed by data
(*c*) What these files contain
(*d*) All of above

119. The files stored on a secondary stage device are composed of a hierarchy a data. What does a record in a file contain?
(*a*) Bits
(*b*) Characters
(*c*) Data field
(*d*) Schema

120. Data encryption techniques are useful for
(*a*) Reducing storage space requirements
(*b*) Improving data integrity
(*c*) Protecting data in data communication systems
(*d*) All of the above

121. The best way to describe a computer file is as
(*a*) A single data item
(*b*) A general collection of data items
(*c*) an orderly collection of data items
(*d*) A random collection of data items

122. If record management allows you to edit values before they are recorded on disk, you can
(*a*) Correct spelling changes before they are recorded
(*b*) Change name of a field
(*c*) Change width of a field
(*d*) All of the above

123. Smallest unit to be processed as a single unit is called:
(*a*) Data field
(*b*) Data record
(*c*) Data file
(*d*) Data base

124. A file produced by a spreadsheet
(*a*) Is generally stored on disk in an ASCII format
(*b*) Can be used as it by the DBMS
(*c*) Can be used for graphic
(*d*) All of the above

125. Report generators can be used to
(*a*) Store data input by a user
(*b*) Retrieve information from files
(*c*) Answer queries
(*d*) Both (b) and (c)

126. The index entails
(*a*) a list of keys
(*b*) Printers to the master list
(*c*) Both (a) and (b)
(*d*) All of above

127. Which of following is true of a network structure?
(*a*) It is a physical representation of data

(*b*) It allows a many to many relationship
(*c*) It is conceptually simple
(*d*) It will be dominant database of future

128. If width of numeric field is 5.2 then value of field could be
(*a*) 23.10
(*b*) 121.83
(*c*) 143.8739
(*d*) Both (a) and (b)

129. A data dictionary contains
(*a*) Names of all fields in all files
(*b*) The data types of all fields in all files
(*c*) The width of all field in all files
(*d*) All of above

130. Batch processing is used, if
(*a*) A large computer system is available
(*b*) Only a small computer system is available
(*c*) Only a few transactions are involved
(*d*) None of above

131. Embedded pointer gives
(*a*) A secondary access path
(*b*) A physical record key
(*c*) An invested index
(*d*) All of above

132. Ist thing to be done while using DBMS is to
(*a*) Create a file
(*b*) Activate file editor
(*c*) Load the software into your micro computer
(*d*) Keep a floppy disk in readiness

133. A large computer information systems that contains many different computer files. Which of the following is called a perpetual file?
(*a*) Specialized file
(*b*) Log file
(*c*) Master file
(*d*) Update file

134. Which of the following properties is a property of a transparent DBMS?
(*a*) Cannot hide sensitive information from users
(*b*) Keep its logical structure hidden from users
(*c*) Keep its physical structure hidden from users
(*d*) Both (b) and (c)

135. What is large collections of file called?
(*a*) Fields
(*b*) Records
(*c*) Databases
(*d*) File system

136. What is language used by most of DBMS for helping their users to access data?
(*a*) High level language
(*b*) Query language
(*c*) SQL
(*d*) UGL

137. In a large DBMS
(*a*) Each user can "see" only a small part of entire database
(*b*) Each user can access every subschema
(*c*) Each subschema contains every field in the logical schema
(*d*) All of the above

138. What software package are commonly used for businesses that have to track extensive lists of clients and inventory?

(*a*) Special purpose packages
(*b*) Custom made programs
(*c*) Single function application packages
(*d*) Data base management package

139. The on-line, soft copy display of a customer's charge account to respond to an inquiry is an example of a
(*a*) Forcasting report
(*b*) Exception report
(*c*) Regularly scheduled report
(*d*) On demand report

140. Which of the following in not a RDBMS?
(*a*) dBase IV
(*b*) 4th dimension
(*c*) Foxpro
(*d*) Reflex

141. A good query system
(*a*) Can accept english language commands
(*b*) Allows non-programmers to access information stored in a database
(*c*) Can be accessed only by data processing professionals
(*d*) Both (a) and (b)

142. All of the following are true about traditional approach to information processing except:
(*a*) There is common sharing of data among the various application
(*b*) It is file oriented
(*c*) Programs are dependent on file
(*d*) None of the above

143. Administrative supervision of database activity is responsibility of
(*a*) Database administrator
(*b*) DP manager
(*c*) DB manager
(*d*) DP administration

144. The topmost level in hierarchy of data organization is called
(*a*) Data bank
(*b*) Database
(*c*) Data file
(*d*) Data record

145. Logical schema is designed because of
(*a*) Avoiding data in consistency
(*b*) Being able to construct queries easly
(*c*) Being able to access data efficiently
(*d*) All of the above

146. A serious problem with file management systems is
(*a*) Difficult to update
(*b*) Lack of data independence
(*c*) data redundancy and program dependency
(*d*) All of the above

147. A set of programs that handle a firm's data base responsibilities is called a
(*a*) DBMS (Data Base Management System)
(*b*) Data base processing system (DBPS)
(*c*) Data Management System (DMS)
(*d*) All of the above

148. The main idea behind computer files is that it is convenient to
(*a*) Arrange them
(*b*) Store information together
(*c*) Create them
(*d*) Access them

149. ADBMS
   (*a*) Allows Stmultaneous access to multiple files
   (*b*) Can do more then a record management system
   (*c*) Is a collection of programs for managing data in a single file
   (*d*) Both (a) and (b)

150. The database administration function includes
   (*a*) Application programming
   (*b*) Computer operations management
   (*c*) Database access planning
   (*d*) All of the above

151. RDBMS organizes files as
   (*a*) Tables
   (*b*) Relations
   (*c*) Tuple
   (*d*) Both (a) and (b)

152. What happens when we have finished entering information into a form?
   (*a*) The template is written to data file
   (*b*) The contents of the form are written to data file
   (*c*) The contents of the form can be printed
   (*d*) All of the above

153. A DBMS which can handle full text data image data, audio and video is called
   (*a*) Full media
   (*b*) Graphics media
   (*c*) Multi media
   (*d*) Hypertext

154. When data items are grouped together for storage purpose then those are called a
   (*a*) Record
   (*b*) Variable
   (*c*) List
   (*d*) String

155. A compound key
   (*a*) Is made up of a several pieces of imformation
   (*b*) Uniquely identifies an item in a list
   (*c*) Both (a) and (b)
   (*d*) is a combination of each unique key

156. An audit trail
   (*a*) Is used to make backup copies
   (*b*) Is the recorded history of operations performed on a file
   (*c*) Can be used to restore last information
   (*d*) All of the above

157. Which language has errantly become the defacto standard for interfacing application programs with RDBMS?
   (*a*) Oracle
   (*b*) SQL
   (*c*) dBASE
   (*d*) 4G2

158. A command used to change fields in a record is
   (*a*) Insert
   (*b*) Modify
   (*c*) Lookup
   (*d*) All of the above

159. A form defines
   (*a*) Where data is placed on the screen
   (*b*) The width of each field
   (*c*) Both (a) and (b)
   (*d*) Compilation of variables and fields

160. Location and relationships among web indicated by

(*a*) URL (Uniform Resource Locator)
(*b*) WWW
(*c*) http
(*d*) None of the above

161. A centralized and integrated database of current and historical data about an organization is
(*a*) Direct database access
(*b*) Operational database
(*c*) Data ware house
(*d*) External database

162. Databases that support the major business process of an organization are
(*a*) Direct database access
(*b*) Operational database
(*c*) Data warehouse
(*d*) External database

163. In which database, records are stored as cubes within cubes.
(*a*) Heirarchical database structures
(*b*) Relational database structures
(*c*) Multi dimensional database structures
(*d*) Sequential database access

164. A tabular structured database is called
(*a*) Hierarchical database structures
(*b*) Relational database structures
(*c*) Multi dimensional database structures
(*d*) Sequential database access

165. A tree like structure of records in a database is called
(*a*) Hierarchical database structures
(*b*) Relational database structures
(*c*) Multi dimensional database structures
(*d*) Sequential database access

166. An identification field in a record is called
(*a*) Record
(*b*) File
(*c*) Database
(*d*) A key field

167. An integrated collection of all the data of your customer is called a
(*a*) Record
(*b*) File
(*c*) Database
(*d*) A key field

168. The names, addresses and account balances of all of your customers is
(*a*) Record
(*b*) File
(*c*) Database
(*d*) A key field

169. A customer's name, address and account balances are
(*a*) Record
(*b*) File
(*c*) Database
(*d*) A key field

170. A customer's name is
(*a*) Data administration
(*b*) Data planning
(*c*) Data modeling
(*d*) Field

171. A top-down effort that ties database development to the support of basic business processes is
(*a*) Database administration
(*b*) Data planning
(*c*) Data modeling
(*d*) Field

172. The planning and control of data to support organizational objectives is

(*a*) Database administration
(*b*) Data planning
(*c*) Data modeling
(*d*) Field

173. Developing database and maintaining standards and controls for an organization's data bases is called
(*a*) End user database
(*b*) Hypermedia database
(*c*) Data resource management
(*d*) Database administration

174. The management of all the data resources of an organization is called
(*a*) End user database
(*b*) Hypermedia database
(*c*) Data resource management
(*d*) Database administration

175. Database of hyperlinked multi media documents on web is called
(*a*) End user database
(*b*) Hypermedia database
(*c*) Data resource management
(*d*) Database administration

176. The main software package that supports a database management approach is called
(*a*) Data dictionary
(*b*) Report generator
(*c*) Database management system
(*d*) Distributed database

177. Which of the following helps us in specifying and producing reports from a database?
(*a*) Data dictionary
(*b*) Report generator
(*c*) Database management system
(*d*) Distributed database

178. Which of the following defines and catalogs the data elements and data relationship in an organization's database?
(*a*) Data dictionary
(*b*) Report generator
(*c*) DBMS
(*d*) Distributed database

179. Which of the following is a DBMS feature which allows users to easily interrogate a database?
(*a*) Database management approach
(*b*) DBMS uses
(*c*) Database administrator
(*d*) Query language

180. A specialist incharge of database of an organization is
(*a*) Data management approach
(*b*) DBMS uses
(*c*) Database administrator
(*d*) Query language

181. The use of integrated collections of data records and file for data storage and processing is
(*a*) Data management approach
(*b*) DBMS uses
(*c*) Database administrator
(*d*) Query language

182. If we need to enforce resource limits for a specific profile. When command should be given to enable this enforcement for the instance?
(*a*) After system
(*b*) After profile
(*c*) After database
(*d*) After resources

183. When are redo log files applied?
(*a*) During shutdown
(*b*) During arching
(*c*) During instance startup
(*d*) During instance recovery

184. Which of the following is a oracle component that creates the memory structures and background process?
   (*a*) Instance
   (*b*) Gerner
   (*c*) Database
   (*d*) Database files

185. What is major requirement for preparing OS to create database?
   (*a*) You should have access to the root account of OS
   (*b*) You should ensure that no other processes are using any OS memory
   (*c*) You should have at least twice the disk space as will be needed to create the database
   (*d*) You should have a previleged account authenticated by OS or a passward file

186. Which of the following commands is used to regain space for an index containing deleted entries?
   (*a*) After table emp drop index;
   (*b*) After index emp_idx REBUILD;
   (*c*) After index emp_idx coalesce;
   (*d*) After index emp_idx deallocate unused;

187. When command is used to move a system data file?
   (*a*) After system bootup
   (*b*) After database startup
   (*c*) After data file
   (*d*) After table space

188. We want to create a new table based on columns in EMP table using a subquery. Which clause we should use to prevent the generation of redo log entries and speed up the creation of table?
   (*a*) CACHE
   (*b*) LOGGING
   (*c*) NO CACHE
   (*d*) NO LOGGING

189. Which of the following are logical database structures?
   (*a*) Segments
   (*b*) Data file
   (*c*) Data blocks
   (*d*) Control files

190. What is the result of following command. After table employee, move table space data.
   (*a*) The tablespace is renamed
   (*b*) Only the data is moved into a new segment
   (*c*) A copy of table is moved to new segment
   (*d*) Data is moved into a new segment presenting constraints and indexes on the table

191. Which trigger type is fired during instance startup?
   (*a*) User event
   (*b*) SQL statement
   (*c*) Database event
   (*d*) Instance event

192. Which information is stored in control file?
   (*a*) Redo log data
   (*b*) Error log information
   (*c*) Data file and redo log locations
   (*d*) Log sequence numbers since instance startup

193. Which shut down option will require instance recovery at the next startup?
   (*a*) ABORT
   (*b*) NORMAL
   (*c*) IMMEDIATE
   (*d*) TRANSACTIONAL

194. At which startup stage is the control file opened for the instance?
(*a*) Open
(*b*) Mount
(*c*) Nomount
(*d*) Shutdown

195. What is the first step we should take when transporting a tablespace?
(*a*) Make the tablespace read only
(*b*) Export the metadata from source
(*c*) Copy the data files to target system
(*d*) Transfer export files to the target machine

196. Which is script that is used to setup PL/SQ2 environment for database?
(*a*) Catadt.sql
(*b*) Atproc.sql
(*c*) Catelog.sql
(*d*) None of above

197. If we new the log file to diagnose a network error and a cause cannot be determind. What should we do next?
(*a*) Turn on tracing permanently
(*b*) View the errors logged in sqlnet.ora
(*c*) View the errors logged in transnames.ora
(*d*) Turn on tracing and re-examine the statement that produced the error message

198. A user issues a select statement against a table in their schema. If the needed data is not in the database buffer coach, what will the server process do next?
(*a*) Search the LRU list
(*b*) Look for a free buffer
(*c*) Read a data block from disk
(*d*) Move dirty buffers to the dirty list

199. Success or failure of information technology in business depends on
(*a*) Proper management of information
(*b*) Legacy system
(*c*) Globalization
(*d*) All of the above

200. Network computers that use a browser based interface for software databases provided by servers, is called
(*a*) Network computing
(*b*) Downsizing
(*c*) Legacy systems
(*d*) Ethical dimensions of IT

201. The use of groupware tools to support collaboration among networked teams is known as
(*a*) Client server computing
(*b*) Enterprise collaboration
(*c*) Electronic commerce
(*d*) Internetworked enterprise

202. A company can use the internet, corporate intranets and inter organizational extranets for
(*a*) Enterprise collaboration
(*b*) Electronic commerce
(*c*) Inter networked enterprise
(*d*) All of the above

203. Which term is used for any one who uses an information system or information it produces.
(*a*) Inter networking of computing
(*b*) End user
(*c*) Computer based information system production
(*d*) Information system

204. Which term is used for the system that uses people, hardware, software, and network resources to collect, transform and disseminate information within an organization
    (*a*) Internetworking of computing
    (*b*) End user
    (*c*) Computer based information system user
    (*d*) Information system

205. What is the term used for the fundamental rethinking and redesigning of business operations
    (*a*) Roles of information system
    (*b*) Globalization
    (*c*) Business process reengineering
    (*d*) Competitive advantage

206. Which term will be used for the statement information systems support an organization's business operations, managerial decision making and strategic competitive advantage"
    (*a*) Roles of information systems
    (*b*) Globalization
    (*c*) Business process re engineering
    (*d*) Competitive advantage

207. What is the term used for some fundamental concepts about information systems and their technology, development, applications and management
    (*a*) Knowledge needed about information needs
    (*b*) Knowledge workers
    (*c*) Global inter networked information society
    (*d*) Information technology

208. What kind of system perform transaction processing activities and also provide information to the managers of an organization
    (*a*) Integration information systems
    (*b*) Business information systems
    (*c*) Knowledge management systems
    (*d*) Expert systems

209. In which system collection, organization and dissemination of business is present within a company.
    (*a*) Integrated information systems
    (*b*) Business information systems
    (*c*) Knowledge management systems
    (*d*) Expert systems

210. Which system provide adhoc, inter action for decision making?
    (*a*) Enterprise collaboration systems
    (*b*) Management support systems
    (*c*) Management information systems
    (*d*) Decision support systems

211. Which system include management information decision support and executive information systems?
    (*a*) Enterprise information systems
    (*b*) Management support systems
    (*c*) Management information system
    (*d*) Decision support systems

212. What is the term used for control and organizing of physical process?
    (*a*) Expanding roles of information systems
    (*b*) Operating support systems
    (*c*) Transaction processing systems
    (*d*) Process control system

213. Which system include transaction processing, process control and end user collaboration systems?
    (*a*) Expanding roles of information systems
    (*b*) Operating support systems
    (*c*) Transcation processsing system
    (*d*) Process control system

214. What is being told in the statement information systems can be classified into operations, management and other categories?
    (*a*) Types of information systems
    (*b*) Control of information systems
    (*c*) Storage of information systems
    (*d*) Output of information systems

215. Saving a copy of letter on a magnetic disk is a kind of
    (*a*) Types of information systems
    (*b*) Control of information systems
    (*c*) Storage of information systems
    (*d*) Output of information systems

216. What is computation of loan payments called?
    (*a*) Procedures
    (*b*) People resources
    (*c*) Input
    (*d*) Processing

217. What are end users and information system professionals called?
    (*a*) Proceduring
    (*b*) People resources
    (*c*) Input
    (*d*) Processing

218. What is a set of instructions for a computer called?
    (*a*) Procedures
    (*b*) Media
    (*c*) Software resources
    (*d*) Program

219. Magnetic disks, optical disks and paper forms are examples of
    (*a*) Machines Hardware
    (*b*) Media
    (*c*) Software resources
    (*d*) Program

220. Machine and Media are
    (*a*) Hardware resources
    (*b*) Information system model
    (*c*) Data or information processing
    (*d*) Information

221. The act of converting data into information is called
    (*a*) Hardware resources
    (*b*) Information system model
    (*c*) Data or information processing
    (*d*) Information

222. In an information system facts or observations are used for
    (*a*) System designing
    (*b*) Feedback designing
    (*c*) Control designing
    (*d*) Data creation

223. Data about a system's performance is called
    (*a*) System
    (*b*) Feedback
    (*c*) Control
    (*d*) Data backup

224. What is the terms used for businesses who rely on their websites to sell products to other businesses for resale to consumers
    (*a*) Virtual shopping malls
    (*b*) Virtual store fronts
    (*c*) Virtual teams
    (*d*) Whole saling on the web

225. What is the term used for designing a website to look like an electronic version of a retail store or wholesale outlet?

(*a*) Virtual shopping malls
(*b*) Virtual store fronts
(*c*) Virtual teams
(*d*) Whole saling on the web

226. What is a network of online business partners who form an organization to take advantage of business opportunities?
(*a*) Supply chain
(*b*) Supply chain management
(*c*) Virtual communities
(*d*) Virtual companies

227. Which term is used for setting up a virtual store front at a website to sell products and services to networked commerce
(*a*) Security of electronic commerce
(*b*) Retailing on the web
(*c*) Push marketing
(*d*) Pull marketing

228. Which term is used for surfing the web looking for information about products and services?
(*a*) Security of electronic commerce
(*b*) Retailing on the web
(*c*) Push marketing
(*d*) Pull marketing

229. What is the term used for the ways to provide for efficient, flexible and secure payment for the purchases of products and services over the internet and other networks?
(*a*) Electronic data exchange
(*b*) Electronic funds transfer
(*c*) Electronic paying systems
(*d*) Interactive marketing

230. The computer-to-computer exchange of business transcation documents between business partners is called
(*a*) Electronic data interchange
(*b*) Electronic funds transfer
(*c*) Electronic payment systems
(*d*) Interactive marketing

231. Selling products to consumers on www is an example of
(*a*) Technology architecture
(*b*) Economic model architecture
(*c*) Business man to business man architecture
(*d*) Business to consumer architecture

232. What is being told in the statement the internet is helping companies to streng then their relationships with customers, anticipate their future needs, respond quickly to their concerns and improve their customer service and support?
(*a*) Business uses of the internet
(*b*) Business value of internet
(*c*) Customer value of internet
(*d*) Electronic commerce

233. What about is being told in statement ‘companies are using the internet for more then e-mail and website marketing”
(*a*) Business uses of internet
(*b*) Business value of internet
(*c*) customer value of internet
(*d*) Electronic commerce

234. Creating, converting and storing hyperlinked documents on web servers is called
(*a*) Web publishing
(*b*) Work group
(*c*) Virtual teams
(*d*) Voice mail

235. Who manages the task of

telephone conversations shared among several participants?
(*a*) Knowledge management
(*b*) Task and project management
(*c*) Team of software professionals
(*d*) Voice conferencing

236. Which of the following helps you in scheduling, tracking and making chart of the status of tasks within a project?
(*a*) Knowledge management
(*b*) Task of project management
(*c*) Team
(*d*) Voice conferencing

237. What is collaboration software for teams, workgroups and enterprise called?
(*a*) Electronic meeting system
(*b*) Enterprise collaboration systems
(*c*) Faxing of information
(*d*) Groupware functioning

238. Information systems that use hardware, software, data and network resources to help us work together more efficiently and effectively
(*a*) Electronic meeting systems
(*b*) Enterprise collaboration systems
(*c*) Faxing of information
(*d*) Groupware functioning

239. What is widely used to send electronic text messages between networked PCs
(*a*) Electronic mail
(*b*) Electronic conferencing tools
(*c*) Electronic communication tools
(*d*) Discussion forms

240. Which of the following includes e-mail, voice mail, faxing and web publishing?
(*a*) Electronic mail
(*b*) Electronic conferencing tools
(*c*) Electronic communication tools
(*d*) Discussion forms

241. Conferencing among participants in conference rooms or auditoriums is called
(*a*) White boarding
(*b*) Video conferencing
(*c*) Desktop conferencing
(*d*) Tele conferencing

242. Which of the following enables real time audio and video conferences?
(*a*) White boarding
(*b*) Video conferencing
(*c*) Desktop conferencing
(*d*) Tele conferencing

243. With which of the following users at networked PCs can view, markup, revise, and save changes to a shared white board of drawings and documents?
(*a*) Chat systems
(*b*) Collaboration
(*c*) Collaborative work management tools
(*d*) Data conferencing

244. Working together co-operatively on joint assignments is called
(*a*) Chat systems
(*b*) Collaboration
(*c*) Collaborative work management tools
(*d*) Data conferencing

245. Which of the following enables us to automatically check for

electronic calenders of team members to schedule a meeting

(*a*) Calendendering and scheduling
(*b*) Business value of intranets
(*c*) Business value of extranets
(*d*) Application of extranets

246. What is being told in statement 'Intranets are being used to improve communications and collaboration, publish and share information, and develop applications to support business operations and managerial decision making'?

(*a*) Intranets
(*b*) Extranets
(*c*) Intranet technology resources
(*d*) Application of intranets

247. Networks that link some of the internet resources of a company to the intranets of their customers or suppliers are called

(*a*) Intra nets resource management
(*b*) Extrants resource management
(*c*) Intrenet technology resources
(*d*) Application of intranets

248. What involves customizing, advertising and promotion methods to fit their intended audience?

(*a*) targeted marketing
(*b*) Marketing information systems
(*c*) Machine control
(*d*) None of the above

249. Transaction processing systems that can hold strong relationships with customer, and suppliers using the intranet, extranets or other networks is called

(*a*) Fault tolerant system
(*b*) Online transaction processing
(*c*) Strategic TPS networks
(*d*) Manufacturing execution systems

250. A system having a non stop transaction processing capability is

(*a*) Fault tolerant system
(*b*) Online transaction processing
(*c*) Strategic TPS networks
(*d*) Manufacturing execution systems

251. Report that identify errors occuring during transaction processing are called

(*a*) Inquiry processing
(*b*) Edit report
(*c*) Control listing
(*d*) Turn around document

252. Part of a customer's invoice which is returned for automated data entry is called

(*a*) Inquiry processing
(*b*) Edit report
(*c*) Control linking
(*d*) Turn around documents

253. A sales order form is an example of

(*a*) Batch processing
(*b*) Real time processing
(*c*) Source document
(*d*) Transaction document

254. Collecting and periodically processing transaction data is called:

(*a*) Batch processing
(*b*) Real time processing
(*c*) Source document
(*d*) Transaction document

255. Which of the following has too many activities, people, media, costs and error

(*a*) Transaction processing system
(*b*) Transaction processing cycle

(*c*) Traditional data entry
(*d*) Source data estimation

256. In which of the following process data results from business transactions?
(*a*) Transaction processing system
(*b*) Transaction processing cycle
(*c*) Traditional data entry
(*d*) Source data automation

257. Using the internet and other network for investment research and trading is done in
(*a*) General ledger
(*b*) Financial information systems
(*c*) Online investment systems
(*d*) Transaction processing system

258. Which of the following produces financial statements of a form?
(*a*) General ledger
(*b*) Financial information systems
(*c*) Online investment systems
(*d*) Transaction processing system

259. Which of the following keeps track of purchases from suppliers?
(*a*) Payroll
(*b*) Accounts payable
(*c*) Accounts receivable
(*d*) Inventory control

260. An example of using internet and extranets to calculate accounts receivable and accounts payable activities are
(*a*) Online HRM system
(*b*) Accounting information systems
(*c*) Online acconting systems
(*d*) Order processing

261. Using internet for recruitment and job hunting is an example of
(*a*) Online HRM systems
(*b*) Accounting information systems
(*c*) Online accounting systems
(*d*) Order processing

262. Which of the following translates the production schedule into a detailed plan for all materials required?
(*a*) Machine Control
(*b*) Robotics
(*c*) Material Requirement planning
(*d*) Human resource information system

263. Using computers to help operate machine tools is called
(*a*) Machine control
(*b*) Robotics
(*c*) Material requirement planning
(*d*) Human resource information systems

264. Using computers to help engineers to evaluate product and processes is
(*a*) Process control
(*b*) Computer-aided-engineering
(*c*) Computer-aided-design
(*d*) Collaborative manufacturing networks

265. In which of the following, engineers and other specialists use the internet and other networks to participate in product or process design?
(*a*) Process control
(*b*) Computer aided engineeing
(*c*) Computer aided design
(*d*) Collaborative manufacturing networks

266. Which of the following is a conceptual framework for simplifying and integrating all aspects of manufacturing automation?
(*a*) Sales force automation

(*b*) Manufacturing information systems
(*c*) Computer integrated manufacturing
(*d*) Computer-aided manufacturing

267. Using mobile computing networks to support sales people in the field is called
(*a*) Sales force automation
(*b*) Management information systems
(*c*) Computer integrated manufacturing
(*d*) Computer-aided manufacturing

268. Information systems for sales management, product management and promotion management is called
(*a*) Interactive marketing
(*b*) Marketing information systems
(*c*) Cross-sectional information systems
(*d*) Business information

269. Information systems that support marketing, production, accounting, finance and human resource management is called
(*a*) Interactive marketing
(*b*) Marketing information systems
(*c*) Cross-functional information systems
(*d*) Business information

270. Software that uses mathematical functions to simulate an evolutionary process is called
(*a*) Neural network
(*b*) Fuzzy logic
(*c*) Intelligent agent
(*d*) Genetic algorithms

271. AI systems that use approximate reasoning to process ambiguous data is called
(*a*) Neural network
(*b*) Fuzzy logic
(*c*) Intelligent agent
(*d*) Genetic algorithms

272. An analyst who intervews experts to develop a knowledge base about a specific application area is
(*a*) Knowledge engineer
(*b*) System development
(*c*) Expert system shell
(*d*) Inference engine

273. A software package consisting of an inference engine and user interface programs used as an expert system development tools is
(*a*) Knowledge engineer
(*b*) System development
(*c*) Expert system shell
(*d*) Inference engine

274. A collection of efforts and reasoning procedures in a specific subject area is called
(*a*) Expert system
(*b*) Applications
(*c*) Benefits and limitations
(*d*) Knowledge base

275. Application such as diagnosis, design, prediction interpretation and repair are
(*a*) expert system
(*b*) Application
(*c*) Benefits and limitation
(*d*) Knowledge base

276. An information system that integrates computer graphics, geographic databases and DSS capabilities as called
(*a*) Geographic information system
(*b*) Virtual reality
(*c*) Robotics
(*d*) Artificial intelligence application area

277. Development of computer based machines that posses capabilities such as sight, hearing, dexterity and movement is
   (*a*) Geographic information systems
   (*b*) Virtual reality
   (*c*) Robotics
   (*d*) Artificial intelligence application area

278. Information technology that focuses on the development of computer functions is normally associated with
   (*a*) Optimization analysis
   (*b*) Executive information system
   (*c*) Online analytical processing
   (*d*) Artificial intelligence

279. Information systems used for strategic information needs of top and middle managers is
   (*a*) Optimization analysis
   (*b*) Executive information system
   (*c*) Online analytical processing
   (*d*) Artificial intelligence

280. Changing revenues and expenses to find how you could achieve a specified amount of net profit after taxes is called
   (*a*) Analytical modelling
   (*b*) What if analysis
   (*c*) Sensitivity analysis
   (*d*) Goal seeking analysis

281. The process of changing revenues and tax rates to see the effect on net profit after taxes is called
   (*a*) Analytical modelling
   (*b*) What if analysis
   (*c*) Sensitivity analysis
   (*d*) Goal seeking analysis

282. A collection of mathematical models and analytical techniques is called
   (*a*) Model base
   (*b*) Decision support versus management reporting
   (*c*) Decision support systems
   (*d*) Reporting alternatives

283. Which provides an interactive modelling capability tailored to the specific information needs of managers?
   (*a*) Model base
   (*b*) Decision support versus management reporting
   (*c*) Decision support systems
   (*d*) Report alternatives

284. Systems that produce predefined reports for management is
   (*a*) Level of management decision making
   (*b*) Decision structure
   (*c*) Management support system
   (*d*) Management information system

285. Ensuring the accuracy integrity and safety of information system activities and resources is called
   (*a*) Information system security
   (*b*) Information system controls
   (*c*) Computer virus
   (*d*) None of the above

286. Controls totals, error signals, backup files and security codes are examples of
   (*a*) Information system security
   (*b*) Information system controls
   (*c*) Computer virus
   (*d*) None of the above

287. Documentation and authorization requirements are examples of
   (*a*) Privacy laws
   (*b*) Software piracy

(*c*) Procedural controls
(*d*) None of the above

288. Fire and access detection systems are examples of
(*a*) System security monitor
(*b*) Software piracy
(*c*) Facility controls
(*d*) Fault tolerant

289. Software that can control access and use of a computer system is
(*a*) System security monitor
(*b*) Software piracy
(*c*) Facility controls
(*d*) Fault tolerant

290. A computer system can continue to operate even after a major system failure if it has the following capability
(*a*) System security monitor
(*b*) Software piracy
(*c*) Facility controls
(*d*) Fault tolerant

291. A computer system that serves as a filter for access to and from other networks by a company's networked computers is
(*a*) Controls for end user computing
(*b*) Audit trail
(*c*) Auditing information systems
(*d*) Firewall

292. Which of the following periodically examine the accuracy and integrity of computer processing?
(*a*) Controls for end user computing
(*b*) Audit trail
(*c*) Auditing information systems
(*d*) Firewalls

293. The presence of documentation that allows a transaction to be traced through all stages of information processing
(*a*) Controls for end user computing
(*b*) Audit trail
(*c*) Auditing information systems
(*d*) Firewalls

294. Using your voice or fingerprints to identify you electronically is called
(*a*) Encryption
(*b*) Control totals
(*c*) Disaster recovery
(*d*) Biometric controls

295. A plan to continue a operation during an emergency is called
(*a*) encryption
(*b*) Control totals
(*c*) Disaster recovery
(*d*) Biometric controls

296. What is the term used for statement 'the sum of subtotals must equal a grand total'.
(*a*) Encryption
(*b*) Control totals
(*c*) Disaster recovery
(*d*) Biometric controls

297. Scrambling data during transmission is called
(*a*) Encryption
(*b*) Control totals
(*c*) Disaster recovery
(*d*) Biometric controls

298. Passwords user IDs and account codes are examples of
(*a*) Security codes
(*b*) Network security
(*c*) Ethical philosophies
(*d*) Ethical models

299. Protection of network resources using network fire walls and security moniters is called
(*a*) Security codes
(*b*) Network security
(*c*) Ethical philosophies
(*d*) Ethical models

300. Whose examples include egoism, natural law, utilitarianism and respect for person?
(*a*) Security codes
(*b*) Network security
(*c*) Ethical philosophies
(*d*) Ethical models

301. 'Ethical choices may result from decision-making processes, cultural values or behavioural stages. The term used for this is
(*a*) Security codes
(*b*) Network security
(*c*) Ethical philosophies
(*d*) Ethical methods

302. Managing must confront numerous ethical questions in their business. This is
(*a*) Individuality
(*b*) Employment
(*c*) Spanning
(*d*) Business ethics

303. Sending unsolicited email indescriminately is involved in
(*a*) Individuality
(*b*) Employment
(*c*) Spanning
(*d*) Business ethics

304. Constant long-term use of computers at work may cause health problem. This statement is associated with
(*a*) Working conditions
(*b*) Societal solutions
(*c*) Privacy
(*d*) Health

305. With which of the following the statement is associated—personal information in computer accessible files
(*a*) Working conditions
(*b*) Societal solutions
(*c*) Privacy
(*d*) Health

306. Computer based monitoring of environmental quality is an example of
(*a*) Working conditions
(*b*) Societal solutions
(*c*) Privacy
(*d*) Health

307. Using computers to identify individuals that fit a certain profile is called
(*a*) Computer matching
(*b*) Privacy laws
(*c*) Computer monitoring
(*d*) Human factors

308. Regulation of collection, access and use of personal data is
(*a*) Computer
(*b*) Privacy laws
(*c*) Computer monitoring
(*d*) Human factors

309. Using computers to monitor activities of workers is
(*a*) Computer
(*b*) Privacy laws
(*c*) Computer monitoring
(*d*) Human factors

310. Using computers to steal money, services, software or data is called
(*a*) Computer crime
(*b*) Computer laws
(*c*) Shoftware piracy

(*d*) Hacking

311. Legislation makes it illegal to access a computer with intension to defraud is a
    (*a*) Computer
    (*b*) Privacy laws
    (*c*) Computer law
    (*d*) Human factors

312. Unauthorized copying of software is called
    (*a*) Computer
    (*b*) Software piracy
    (*c*) Computer monitoring
    (*d*) Hacking

313. Electronic breaking and entering into a computer system is called
    (*a*) Computer
    (*b*) Privacy laws
    (*c*) Computer monitoring
    (*d*) Hacking

314. A program which makes copies of itself and destroys data and programs is called
    (*a*) Responsible end user
    (*b*) Ergonomics
    (*c*) Flaming
    (*d*) Computer virus

315. Sending extremely critical, derogatory and vulger e-mail messages is called
    (*a*) Responsible end user
    (*b*) Ergonomics
    (*c*) Flaming
    (*d*) Computer virus

316. Designing computer hardware, software and workstation that are safe, comfortable and easy to use is
    (*a*) Responsible end user
    (*b*) Ergonomics
    (*c*) Flaming
    (*d*) Computer virus

317. An organization should create a shared business vision and mission and plan how it will achieve its strategic goals and objectives is called
    (*a*) Operating systems planning
    (*b*) Factical systems planning
    (*c*) Strategic systems planning
    (*d*) Organizational planning

318. Which of the following outlines a business vision, business/IT strategies and technical architecture of the information systems function?
    (*a*) Operating systems planning
    (*b*) Factical systems planning
    (*c*) Strategic systems planning
    (*d*) Organizational planning

319. Which of the following priortizes and schedules the development and implementations of major information systems projects for an organization?
    (*a*) Operating systems planning
    (*b*) Factical systems planning
    (*c*) Strategic systems planning
    (*d*) Organizational planning

320. Which of the following develops operating budgets for the information system function?
    (*a*) Operating systems planning
    (*b*) Factical systems planning
    (*c*) Strategic systems planning
    (*d*) Organizational planning

321. Evaluating strategic IT opportunities based on their business impact and company's ability to use IT is a
    (*a*) Planning for competitive advantage

(*b*) Scenario approach
(*c*) End user involvement
(*d*) Change management

322. Planning team to simulate role of information technology in various hypothetical business situations
(*a*) Planning for competitive advantage
(*b*) Scenario approach
(*c*) End user involvement
(*d*) Change management

323. End users should be part of organizational change and IS project teams. That is
(*a*) Planning for competitive advantage
(*b*) Scenario approach
(*c*) End user involvement
(*d*) Change management

324. Companies should try to minimize the risks and costs and maximize the benefits of major changes in business and technology. This is
(*a*) Planning for competitive advantage
(*b*) Scenario approach
(*c*) End user involvement
(*d*) Change management

325. The source of hardware, software and IS services for end users is
(*a*) Computer industry
(*b*) Implementation process
(*c*) Hardware
(*d*) Software

326. Which of the following includes acquisition, testing, training and conversion to a new system?
(*a*) Computer industry
(*b*) Implementation process
(*c*) Hardware
(*d*) Software

327. Performance, list, reliablity, technology and ergonomics are examples of
(*a*) Computer industry
(*b*) Implementation process
(*c*) Hardware
(*d*) Software

328. Maintenance, conversion, training and business portion are examples of
(*a*) IS service
(*b*) End user resistance
(*c*) Conversion methods
(*d*) System testing

329. End user frequently resist the introduction of new methods. This is
(*a*) IS service
(*b*) End user resistance
(*c*) Conversion methods
(*d*) System testing

330. Which of the following operate in parallel with old system use a test site, switch in stages or cut over immediately to a new system?
(*a*) IS service
(*b*) End user resistance
(*c*) Conversion methods
(*d*) System testing

331. Checking whether hardware and software work properly for end users. This is included in
(*a*) IS service
(*b*) End user resistance
(*c*) Conversion methods
(*d*) System testing

332. A user manual communicates the design and operating procedures of a system. This is associated with
(*a*) Documentation
(*b*) Systems maintenance

(*c*) Systems development
(*d*) None of the above

333. Modifying an operational system by adding internet website access is an example of
(*a*) Documentation
(*b*) Systems maintenance
(*c*) Systems development
(*d*) None of the above

334. Managers may have a lot of information, processing power and responsibility for information systems. This is
(*a*) Operation and management
(*b*) Information system
(*c*) Impact of IT on organization
(*d*) Impact of IT on management

335. Information system resources can be distributed throughout an organization or consolidated in corporate data centers. This is
(*a*) Operation and management
(*b*) Information system
(*c*) Impact of IT on organization
(*d*) Impact of IT on management

336. Information system can help management increase the number of regional and branch offices for consolidated operations.
(*a*) Operation and management
(*b*) Information system
(*c*) Impact of IT on organization
(*d*) Impact of IT on management

337. The management of data, information, hardware software and IS personal as organizational resources. This statement is associated with
(*a*) Management involvement
(*b*) Information system performance
(*c*) Five dimensions of IRM
(*d*) Information resource management

338. Managing information technology is a distributed responsiblity focussing on the strategic manager of IS resources and technology. This statement is associated with
(*a*) Management involvement
(*b*) Information system performance
(*c*) Five dimensions of IRM
(*d*) Information resistance management

339. Information systems have not been used efficiently, effectively, economically. This is associated with
(*a*) Management involvement
(*b*) Information system performance
(*c*) Five dimensions of IRM
(*d*) Information requirement management

340. A management steering committee is an example of
(*a*) Management involvement
(*b*) Information system performance
(*c*) Five dimensions of IRM
(*d*) Information resource management

341. End users need an end user services group or other forms of liaison, consulting and training support. This is
(*a*) End user services
(*b*) Information services functions
(*c*) Chief information officer
(*d*) System development management

342. Which of the following includes. The basic functions of system

development, operations and technical services?
(a) End user services
(b) Information services functions
(c) Chief information officer
(d) System development management

343. Which of the following includes an executive that oversees all information systems technology for an organization?
(a) End user services
(b) Information services functions
(c) Chief information officer
(d) System development management

344. Which of the following includes management system analysis and design, computer programming and systems maintenance activities?
(a) End user services
(b) Information services functions
(c) Chief information officer
(d) System development management

345. Which of the following includes planning and controlling data center operations?
(a) Operations Management
(b) Data Center management
(c) Development Center
(d) Information Centre

346. Which of the following includes corporate locations for computer system operations?
(a) Operations Management
(b) Data Center management
(c) Development Center
(d) Information Centre

347. Which of the following includes a support group for organization's professional programmers and system analysis?
(a) Operations Management
(b) Data Center
(c) Development Center
(d) Information Centre

348. Which of the following includes a support group for an organization's end users?
(a) Operations Management
(b) Data Center
(c) Development Center
(d) Information Centre

349. In which of the following rapid changing technological development must be anticipated, identified and maintained?
(a) Technology Management
(b) Outsourcing IS Operation
(c) Telecommunications Network Management
(d) System Performance Monitor

350. Which of the following includes using outside contractors to provide and manage IS operations?
(a) Technology Management
(b) Outsourcing IS Operation
(c) Telecommunications Network Management
(d) System Performance Monitor

351. In which of the following a company's use of internet, intranets and extranets must be developed, administered and maintained?
(a) Technology Management
(b) Outsourcing IS Operation
(c) Telecommunications Network Management
(d) System Performance Monitor

352. The cost of IS services may be allocated back to end users. This is

(*a*) Global company
(*b*) Downsizing
(*c*) Human resource management of IT
(*d*) Charge back systems

353. Which of the following includes recruting and development information services employees?
(*a*) Global company
(*b*) Downsizing
(*c*) Human resource management of IT
(*d*) Charge back systems

354. Many business forms are replacing their mainframe systems with networked PCs and servers. This is
(*a*) Global company
(*b*) Downsizing
(*c*) Human resource management of IT
(*d*) Charge back systems

355. A business that is driven by a global strategy is
(*a*) Global company
(*b*) Downsizing
(*c*) Human resource management of IT
(*d*) Charge back systems

356. Using IT to support company's international business operations is included in
(*a*) Global business drivers
(*b*) Cultural, political and geo economic challenges
(*c*) Transactional stratergy
(*d*) Global information technology

357. Integrating global business activities through co-operation among international subsidiaries and corporate headquaters is included in
(*a*) Global business drivers
(*b*) Cultural, political and geo economic challenges
(*c*) Transactional stratergy
(*d*) Global information technology

358. Differences in customers, governmental regulations, and cost of liasoning are examples of
(*a*) Global business drivers
(*b*) Cultural, political and geo economic challenges
(*c*) Transactional stratergy
(*d*) Global information technology

359. Global customers, products, operations, resources and collaboration all are included in
(*a*) Global business drivers
(*b*) Cultural, political and geo economic challenges
(*c*) Transactional stratergy
(*d*) Global information technology

360. Applying IT to global transaction processing systems is an example of
(*a*) Global IT management applications
(*b*) Business/IT strategies
(*c*) Data issues
(*d*) IT platforms

361. The goal of some organizations is to develop integrated worldwide networks for global electronic commerce. That is
(*a*) Global IT management applications
(*b*) Business/IT strategies
(*c*) Data issues
(*d*) IT platforms

362. Transborder data flows and security of personal databases are top concerns of

(*a*) Global IT management applications
(*b*) Business/IT strategies
(*c*) Data issues
(*d*) IT platforms

363. Standardizing computer system, software package, telecommunication networks and computing facilities is considered
(*a*) Global IT management applications
(*b*) Business/IT strategies
(*c*) Data issues
(*d*) IT platforms

364. Agreement is needed on common user interface and other design features in global IT. This is a part of
(*a*) System development
(*b*) Transborder data flows
(*c*) System flows
(*d*) All of the above

365. Global telecommunication networks like the internet move data across national boundaries. This is
(*a*) System development
(*b*) Transborder data flows
(*c*) System flows
(*d*) All of the above

366. A business must deal with customers, suppliers, competitors, new entrants and substitues. These are
(*a*) Competitive forces
(*b*) Competitive strategies
(*c*) Raising barriers to entry
(*d*) Locking in customers and suppliers

367. Using investment in technology to keep firms out of an industry included as
(*a*) Competitive forces
(*b*) Competitive strategies
(*c*) Raising barriers to entry
(*d*) Locking in customers and suppliers

368. Making it unattractive for a firm's customers or suppliers to watch to its competitors. This is
(*a*) Competitive forces
(*b*) Competitive strategies
(*c*) Raising barriers to entry
(*d*) Locking in customers

369. Time, money and effort needed for customers or suppliers to change to a firm's competitors. This is
(*a*) Improving business processes
(*b*) Promoting business invocation
(*c*) Stratigic information systems
(*d*) Creating switching costs

370. Information systems that improve operational efficiency or promote business invocation are examples of:
(*a*) Improving business processes
(*b*) Promoting business invocation
(*c*) Stratigic information systems
(*d*) Creating switching costs

371. Information systems can help a business to develop new products, services and processes. This is
(*a*) Improving business processes
(*b*) Promoting business invocation
(*c*) Stratigic information systems
(*d*) Creating switching costs

372. Information systems can help a business significantly reduce costs and improve productivity. This is
(*a*) Improving business processes
(*b*) Promoting business invocation
(*c*) Strategic information systems
(*d*) Creating switching costs

373. Information system can help a business develop a strategic base of information. This is
   (*a*) Developing a strategic information base
   (*b*) Building a strategic IT platform
   (*c*) Inter organizational information systems
   (*d*) Value chain

374. A business can develop strategic capabilities in IT skills and resources. This is
   (*a*) Developing a strategic information base
   (*b*) Building a strategic IT platform
   (*c*) Inter organizational information systems
   (*d*) Value chain

375. Information systems can help a business develop electronic links to its customers and suppliers. This is
   (*a*) Developing a strategic information base
   (*b*) Building a strategic IT platform
   (*c*) Inter organizational information systems
   (*d*) Value chain

376. Which of the following highlights how strategic information system can be applied to firm's business processes and support activities for competitive advantage?
   (*a*) Developing a strategic information base
   (*b*) Building a strategic IT platform
   (*c*) Inter organizational information systems
   (*d*) Value chain

377. A business can find strategic uses for the computing and telecommunication capabilities it has acquired to run its operations. This is
   (*a*) Leveraging investment in IT
   (*b*) Strategic roles of information systems
   (*c*) Breaking business barriers
   (*d*) Business process re-engineering

378. A business can use information systems to build barriers to entry, promote innovation, create switching costs and so on. This is
   (*a*) Leveraging investment in IT
   (*b*) Strategic roles of information systems
   (*c*) Breaking business barriers
   (*d*) Business process re-engineering

379. A business can use information technology to develop low cost ways to build close, conventional business relationships with global customers. This is
   (*a*) Leveraging investment in IT
   (*b*) Strategic roles of information systems
   (*c*) Breaking business barriers
   (*d*) Business process re-engineering

380. Information technology can help a business make radical improvements in business processes. This is
   (*a*) Leveraging investment in IT
   (*b*) Strategic roles of information systems
   (*c*) Breaking business barriers
   (*d*) Business process re-engineering

381. Programs of continual improvement in meeting or exceeding customer requirements or expectations. This is
(*a*) Strategic business use of internet techniques
(*b*) Virtual company
(*c*) Agile competitor
(*d*) Total quality management

382. A business can prosper in rapidly changing markets while offering its customers individualized solutions to their needs. This is
(*a*) Strategic business use of internet techniques
(*b*) Virtual company
(*c*) Agile competitor
(*d*) Total quality management

383. A network of business partners formed to take advantage of rapidly changing market opportunities. This is
(*a*) Strategic business use of internet techniques
(*b*) Virtual company
(*c*) Agile competitor
(*d*) Total quality management

384. Many companies use the internet, intranets and extranets to achieve strategic gains in their competitive position. This is
(*a*) Strategic business use of internet techniques
(*b*) Virtual company
(*c*) Agile competitor
(*d*) Total quality management

385. The internet and extranet have reduced or eliminations reach/richners trade offs in the content and dissemination of information products. This is
(*a*) New economies of information
(*b*) Knowledge creating company
(*c*) Knowledge management systems
(*d*) Sustaining competitive advantage

386. Learning organizations that focus on creating, disseminating and managing business knowledge is
(*a*) New economies of information
(*b*) Knowledge creating company
(*c*) Knowledge management systems
(*d*) Sustaining competitive advantage

387. Information systems that manage the creation and dissemination of organizational knowledge are
(*a*) New economies of information
(*b*) Knowledge creating company
(*c*) Knowledge management systems
(*d*) Sustaining competitive advantage

388. The competitive advantages of IT will disappear unless management implements strategies such as exploiting knowledge management. This is
(*a*) New economies of information
(*b*) Knowledge creating company
(*c*) Knowledge management systems
(*d*) Sustaining competitive advantage

389. A CEO and a production team may have different information needs for decision making. This is
(*a*) Level of management decision making
(*b*) Decision structure
(*c*) Management support system

(*d*) Management information system

390. Decision making procedures can be specified in advance for some complex decision situations. This is
(*a*) Level of management decision making
(*b*) Decision structure
(*c*) Management support system
(*d*) Management information system

391. An information category which includes management information systems, decision support systems and executive information systems is
(*a*) Level of management decision making
(*b*) Decision structure
(*c*) Management support system
(*d*) Management information system

392. Systems that produce predefined reports for management are called
(*a*) Level of management decision making
(*b*) Decision structure
(*c*) Management support system
(*d*) Management information system

393. According to which of following, managers can receive reports periodically, on an exception basis or on demand
(*a*) Model base
(*b*) Decision support versus management reporting
(*c*) Decision support systems
(*d*) Reporting alternatives

394. Which of the following provide an interactive modelling capability tailored to the specific information needs of managers?
(*a*) Model base
(*b*) Decision support versus management reporting
(*c*) Decision support systems
(*d*) Reporting alternatives

395. Which of the following provide interactive responses to adhoc queriesversus prespecified information
(*a*) Model base
(*b*) Decision support versus management reporting
(*c*) Decision support systems
(*d*) Reporting alternatives

396. A collection of mathematical models and analytical techniques is called:
(*a*) Model base
(*b*) Decision support versus management reporting
(*c*) Decision support systems
(*d*) Reporting alternatives

ANSWERS

1. (*d*)	2. (*a*)	3. (*b*)	4. (*c*)	5. (*d*)	6. (*a*)	7. (*a*)
8. (*b*)	9. (*a*)	10. (*b*)	11. (*d*)	12. (*d*)	13. (*d*)	14. (*b*)
15. (*b*)	16. (*b*)	17. (*a*)	18. (*b*)	19. (*a*)	20. (*b*)	21. (*c*)
22. (*d*)	23. (*b*)	24. (*d*)	25. (*d*)	26. (*c*)	27. (*b*)	28. (*c*)
29. (*b*)	30. (*d*)	31. (*b*)	32. (*a*)	33. (*c*)	34. (*c*)	35. (*b*)

36. (*a*)	37. (*a*)	38. (*c*)	39. (*c*)	40. (*a*)	41. (*d*)	42. (*a*)
43. (*b*)	44. (*c*)	45. (*c*)	46. (*b*)	47. (*d*)	48. (*b*)	49. (*c*)
50. (*d*)	51. (*d*)	52. (*a*)	53. (*a*)	54. (*d*)	55. (*d*)	56. (*b*)
57. (*d*)	58. (*c*)	59. (*c*)	60. (*c*)	61. (*b*)	62. (*b*)	63. (*a*)
64. (*c*)	65. (*a*)	66. (*b*)	67. (*b*)	68. (*a*)	69. (*d*)	70. (*a*)
71. (*b*)	72. (*d*)	73. (*b*)	74. (*d*)	75. (*a*)	76. (*d*)	77. (*a*)
78. (*a*)	79. (*b*)	80. (*a*)	81. (*c*)	82. (*c*)	83. (*c*)	84. (*c*)
85. (*a*)	86. (*c*)	87. (*b*)	88. (*a*)	89. (*d*)	90. (*a*)	91. (*a*)
92. (*b*)	93. (*d*)	94. (*d*)	95. (*a*)	96. (*d*)	97. (*a*)	98. (*d*)
99. (*a*)	100. (*b*)	101. (*a*)	102. (*b*)	103. (*a*)	104. (*a*)	105. (*d*)
106. (*d*)	107. (*d*)	108. (*b*)	109. (*a*)	110. (*a*)	111. (*a*)	112. (*d*)
113. (*c*)	114. (*a*)	115. (*d*)	116. (*b*)	117. (*a*)	118. (*c*)	119. (*c*)
120. (*c*)	121. (*c*)	122. (*d*)	123. (*a*)	124. (*a*)	125. (*c*)	126. (*b*)
127. (*d*)	128. (*a*)	129. (*d*)	130. (*a*)	131. (*a*)	132. (*c*)	133. (*c*)
134. (*d*)	135. (*d*)	136. (*c*)	137. (*a*)	138. (*d*)	139. (*d*)	140. (*a*)
141. (*d*)	142. (*a*)	143. (*a*)	144. (*b*)	145. (*d*)	146. (*c*)	147. (*a*)
148. (*b*)	149. (*c*)	150. (*b*)	151. (*d*)	152. (*b*)	153. (*c*)	154. (*a*)
155. (*c*)	156. (*b*)	157. (*b*)	158. (*b*)	159. (*c*)	160. (*a*)	161. (*c*)
162. (*b*)	163. (*a*)	164. (*c*)	165. (*a*)	166. (*d*)	167. (*c*)	168. (*b*)
169. (*a*)	170. (*d*)	171. (*b*)	172. (*a*)	173. (*d*)	174. (*c*)	175. (*b*)
176. (*c*)	177. (*b*)	178. (*a*)	179. (*d*)	180. (*c*)	181. (*a*)	182. (*b*)
183. (*a*)	184. (*b*)	185. (*d*)	186. (*a*)	187. (*c*)	188. (*c*)	189. (*c*)
190. (*d*)	191. (*d*)	192. (*d*)	193. (*a*)	194. (*a*)	195. (*d*)	196. (*b*)
197. (*c*)	198. (*a*)	199. (*d*)	200. (*a*)	201. (*b*)	202. (*d*)	203. (*b*)
204. (*c*)	205. (*c*)	206. (*a*)	207. (*d*)	208. (*b*)	209. (*b*)	210. (*d*)
211. (*c*)	212. (*d*)	213. (*d*)	214. (*a*)	215. (*c*)	216. (*d*)	217. (*b*)
218. (*a*)	219. (*a*)	220. (*a*)	221. (*c*)	222. (*d*)	223. (*b*)	224. (*a*)
225. (*d*)	226. (*a*)	227. (*b*)	228. (*d*)	229. (*c*)	230. (*b*)	231. (*d*)
232. (*b*)	233. (*d*)	234. (*a*)	235. (*d*)	236. (*b*)	237. (*b*)	238. (*a*)
239. (*a*)	240. (*c*)	241. (*b*)	242. (*d*)	243. (*a*)	244. (*c*)	245. (*a*)
246. (*d*)	247. (*c*)	248. (*a*)	249. (*c*)	250. (*b*)	251. (*b*)	252. (*d*)
253. (*a*)	254. (*a*)	255. (*a*)	256. (*a*)	257. (*b*)	258. (*a*)	259. (*d*)
260. (*c*)	261. (*a*)	262. (*c*)	263. (*a*)	264. (*a*)	265. (*b*)	266. (*d*)
267. (*b*)	268. (*b*)	269. (*c*)	270. (*d*)	271. (*b*)	272. (*a*)	273. (*c*)
274. (*a*)	275. (*a*)	276. (*a*)	277. (*d*)	278. (*a*)	279. (*b*)	280. (*a*)

281. (*d*)	282. (*c*)	283. (*b*)	284. (*c*)	285. (*a*)	286. (*b*)	287. (*a*)
288. (*b*)	289. (*a*)	290. (*d*)	291. (*d*)	292. (*b*)	293. (*a*)	294. (*d*)
295. (*c*)	296. (*b*)	297. (*a*)	298. (*a*)	299. (*b*)	300. (*c*)	301. (*c*)
302. (*d*)	303. (*c*)	304. (*a*)	305. (*c*)	306. (*b*)	307. (*d*)	308. (*c*)
309. (*c*)	310. (*a*)	311. (*c*)	312. (*b*)	313. (*d*)	314. (*d*)	315. (*c*)
316. (*a*)	317. (*d*)	318. (*c*)	319. (*d*)	320. (*a*)	321. (*a*)	322. (*a*)
323. (*b*)	324. (*a*)	325. (*a*)	326. (*b*)	327. (*a*)	328. (*a*)	329. (*b*)
330. (*c*)	331. (*d*)	332. (*a*)	333. (*c*)	334. (*d*)	335. (*c*)	336. (*a*)
337. (*d*)	338. (*c*)	339. (*c*)	340. (*a*)	341. (*a*)	342. (*d*)	343. (*b*)
344. (*d*)	345. (*b*)	346. (*a*)	347. (*a*)	348. (*d*)	349. (*a*)	350. (*b*)
351. (*c*)	352. (*d*)	353. (*b*)	354. (*a*)	355. (*a*)	356. (*a*)	357. (*a*)
358. (*c*)	359. (*d*)	360. (*a*)	361. (*b*)	362. (*a*)	363. (*d*)	364. (*b*)
365. (*b*)	366. (*d*)	367. (*c*)	368. (*a*)	369. (*b*)	370. (*a*)	371. (*b*)
372. (*a*)	373. (*a*)	374. (*a*)	375. (*d*)	376. (*d*)	377. (*d*)	378. (*c*)
379. (*a*)	380. (*a*)	381. (*d*)	382. (*c*)	383. (*a*)	384. (*a*)	385. (*a*)
386. (*c*)	387. (*c*)	388. (*c*)	389. (*d*)	390. (*a*)	391. (*b*)	392. (*b*)
393. (*d*)	394. (*b*)	395. (*b*)	396. (*a*)			

11

Object Oriented Programming

1. Server Context Information is available at any time through
   (*a*) Serv-context object
   (*b*) Serv-let config object
   (*c*) Serv-let info object
   (*d*) None of the above

2. The 'GET' method
   (*a*) Requests information from a web server
   (*b*) Requests the header information from web server
   (*c*) Allows a client to send data to the server
   (*d*) None of the above

3. The HEAD method
   (*a*) Requests information from a web server
   (*b*) Requests the header information from server
   (*c*) Allows the client to send data to the server
   (*d*) None of the above

4. The 'POST' method
   (*a*) Allows a client to send data to the server
   (*b*) Allows a server to send data to client
   (*c*) Allows a client to send data to another client
   (*d*) None of the above

5. The HEAD method does not check which of the following
   (*a*) Last modification date of a document
   (*b*) Size of document before downloading
   (*c*) Server type allowing the client to customize requests for that server
   (*d*) None of the above

6. Java is a
   (*a*) Object oriented language
   (*b*) Structured language
   (*c*) Unstructured language
   (*d*) Type cast language

7. The syntax of conditioned assignment operator is
   (*a*) Variable = (condition)? Value 1: Value 2;
   (*b*) Constant = (condition)? Value 1: Value 2;
   (*c*) Variable = Value 1: Value 2: (condition)?
   (*d*) Constant = Value 1: Value 2: (condition)?

8. Format of 'Do........While' control structure is
   (*a*) Do {........} while (condition)
   (*b*) While {.......} Do (condition)
   (*c*) Do {while (condition)}
   (*d*) None of the above

9. Reusability means
   (*a*) Reuse of properties of base class in the derived class

(*b*) Creating a new class from one or more existing classes
(*c*) Creating a new derived class
(*d*) None of the above

10. Which of the following is not a type of inheritance?
(*a*) Hierarchical
(*b*) Derived
(*c*) Multipath
(*d*) Multilevel

11. Multilevel inheritance means
(*a*) Procedure of deriving a class from derived class
(*b*) Deriving a class from single base class
(*c*) Single base class deriving two class
(*d*) None of the above

12. Virtual function is.
(*a*) A function which is not physically present
(*b*) A member function that can be changed at runtime
(*c*) A function whose name is virtual
(*d*) None of the above

13. Which of the following is not a property of pure virtual function?
(*a*) A pure virtual function has no implementation in the base class, hence a class with pure virtual function cannot be instantiated.
(*b*) It acts as empty bucket that derived class is supposed to fill
(*c*) A pure virtual member function can be invoked by its derived class
(*d*) None of the above

14. The dereferencing of pointer means
(*a*) Process of accessing and manipulating data stored in memory location pointed by pointer
(*b*) Passing parameter using call by reference method
(*c*) It is defining pointer as dereference data type
(*d*) None of the above

15. Void pointer is
(*a*) It is a pointer which cannot be defined
(*b*) Specific data type and it couldn't hold the address of some other type of variable
(*c*) A pointer pointing to an array
(*d*) None of the above

16. The arithmetic operator that can be used with pointer.
(*a*) Increment and decrement
(*b*) Modulus
(*c*) Multiply
(*d*) Divide

17. The correct syntax to define pointer to pointer is
(*a*) ** ptr
(*b*) * ptr
(*c*) ptr
(*d*) *** ptr to ptr

18. Pointer to a function can be defined as
(*a*) It holds the starting address of a function, and it can be used to invoke a function
(*b*) It is a pointer used in functions
(*c*) It is a function used in pointer
(*d*) None of the above

19. Static binding is
    (*a*) Resolving the function call at compile time
    (*b*) Defining the binding statically
    (*c*) resolving a function call at run time
    (*d*) None of the above

20. Dynamic binding is
    (*a*) Resolving the function call at compile time
    (*b*) Defining binding statically
    (*c*) Resolving function call at run time
    (*d*) None of the above

21. Stream library is
    (*a*) Collection of classes or objects which can be used to build a powerful system or modified and extended to handle user defined data type
    (*b*) Series of bytes which acts as source or destination
    (*c*) Function already stored in library
    (*d*) None of the above

22. The streams that are automati-cally opened before function main ( ),
    (*a*) Cin
    (*b*) Cout
    (*c*) Clog
    (*d*) All of the above

23. Function defined by Istream class.
    (*a*) get ( ) , getline ( ), read ( )
    (*b*) get ( ) , istream ( ),read ( )
    (*c*) Get ( ) , read ( ) , write ( )
    (*d*) None of the above

24. The purpose of getline ( ) function is
    (*a*) To read whole line of text
    (*b*) To read a character from next line
    (*c*) To write a character in new line
    (*d*) None of the above

25. The IOS class member function used for formatting IO are.
    (*a*) width ( ), precision ( ), setf ( )
    (*b*) getch ( ), width ( ), Io ( )
    (*c*) width ( ), precision ( ),read ( )
    (*d*) unsetf ( ), setf ( ) ,write ( )

26. Function fill ( ) is used to.
    (*a*) Specify character to be displayed in unused portion of display width
    (*b*) Specify line in a fill format
    (*c*) Fill a portion with specified color
    (*d*) None of the above

27. Which of the following function do not have bit field?
    (*a*) Ios : : showbase
    (*b*) Ios : : showpoint
    (*c*) Ios : : skipws
    (*d*) None of the above

28. Manipulators w.r.t. object oriented programming are defined as
    (*a*) These are special functions designed to modify working of stream
    (*b*) They are arithmetic operator
    (*c*) They are used to manipulate functions
    (*d*) None of the above

29. Two types of manipulators are.
    (*a*) Static and dynamic
    (*b*) Parameterized and non parameterized
    (*c*) Single valued and multivalued

(*d*) Compile time and run time

30. Non parameterized manipulators are
    (*a*) Setw ( )
    (*b*) Ends
    (*c*) Set base
    (*d*) Set precision

31. Parameterized manipulator is.
    (*a*) Dec
    (*b*) Flush
    (*c*) Setiosflags ( )
    (*d*) Ends

32. The classes for handling file are.
    (*a*) If stream
    (*b*) Of stream
    (*c*) F stream
    (*d*) All of the above

33. Functions used to manipulate file pointer is.
    (*a*) Seekg ( )
    (*b*) Eof ( )
    (*c*) Fail ( )
    (*d*) Good

34. Function used to handle error during file manipulation.
    (*a*) Seekg ( )
    (*b*) Seekp ( )
    (*c*) Tellg ( )
    (*d*) Rdstate ( )

35. Code to detect end of file is.
    (*a*) While (! infile, eof ( ))
    (*b*) For (i = 1 ; i ≤ eof ( ), i ++)
    (*c*) Do { } while ! eof))
    (*d*) None of the above

ANSWERS

1. (*b*)	2. (*a*)	3. (*b*)	4. (*a*)	5. (*d*)	6. (*a*)	7. (*a*)
8. (*a*)	9. (*a*)	10. (*b*)	11. (*a*)	12. (*b*)	13. (*d*)	14. (*a*)
15. (*b*)	16. (*a*)	17. (*a*)	18. (*a*)	19. (*a*)	20. (*c*)	21. (*a*)
22. (*d*)	23. (*a*)	24. (*a*)	25. (*a*)	26. (*a*)	27. (*d*)	28. (*a*)
29. (*b*)	30. (*b*)	31. (*c*)	32. (*d*)	33. (*a*)	34. (*d*)	35. (*a*)

12

Computer Networks

1. The .... is the physical path over which message travels.
   (*a*) Protocol
   (*b*) Signal
   (*c*) Medium
   (*d*) All of the above

2. The information to be communicated in a data communication system is the.
   (*a*) Medium
   (*b*) Message
   (*c*) Protocol
   (*d*) Transmission

3. Checking an unauthorized user in a network is a .... issue.
   (*a*) Performance
   (*b*) Security
   (*c*) Reliability
   (*d*) All of the above

4. Which topology requires a central controller or hub.
   (*a*) Mesh
   (*b*) Bus
   (*c*) Star
   (*d*) Ring

5. Communication between computer and a keyboard involves.
   (*a*) Simplex transmission
   (*b*) Full duplex transmission
   (*c*) Half duplex transmission
   (*d*) Automatic transmission

6. A .... provides a dedicated link between two devices.
   (*a*) Point to point
   (*b*) Primary
   (*c*) Multipoint
   (*d*) Secondary

7. In a .... connection more than two devices can share a single link.
   (*a*) Point to point
   (*b*) Primary
   (*c*) Multipoint
   (*d*) Secondary

8. In .... transmission the channel capacity is shared by both communication devices at all times.
   (*a*) Simplex
   (*b*) Full duplex
   (*c*) Half duplex
   (*d*) Half simplex

9. In .... topology if cable breaks, it will stops all transmission.
   (*a*) Mesh
   (*b*) Star
   (*c*) Bus
   (*d*) Primary

10. Which organisation has authority over interstate and international commerce in the communication field.
    (*a*) ITU-T
    (*b*) FCC
    (*c*) IEEE

(*d*) ISO

11. The internet model consists of .... layers.
    (*a*) Three
    (*b*) Seven
    (*c*) Five
    (*d*) Eight

12. The process to process delivery of the entire message is the responsibility of the .... layer.
    (*a*) Network
    (*b*) Application
    (*c*) Transport
    (*d*) Physical

13. The .... layer is the closest to the transmission medium.
    (*a*) Physical
    (*b*) Network
    (*c*) Data link
    (*d*) Transport

14. Mail services are available to the network user through the .... layer.
    (*a*) Data link
    (*b*) Physical
    (*c*) Transport
    (*d*) Application

15. As the data packet moves from the upper to the lower layers, headers are ....
    (*a*) Added
    (*b*) Rearranged
    (*c*) Subtracted
    (*d*) Modified

16. The .... lies between the network layer and application layer.
    (*a*) Physical
    (*b*) Transport
    (*c*) Data link
    (*d*) Session

17. The .... layer changes bits into electromagnetic signal.
    (*a*) Physical
    (*b*) Transport
    (*c*) Data link
    (*d*) None of the above

18. What is the main function of transport layer.
    (*a*) Node to node delivery
    (*b*) Process to process delivery
    (*c*) Synchronization
    (*d*) Updating and maintenance of routing tables

19. Which of the following is a application layer service.
    (*a*) Remote login
    (*b*) Mail service
    (*c*) File transfer
    (*d*) All of the above

20. OSI model was designed by.
    (*a*) ISO
    (*b*) ITU-T
    (*c*) IEEE
    (*d*) FCC

21. Which layers has the network support layer and the user support layer.
    (*a*) Network
    (*b*) Application
    (*c*) Transport
    (*d*) Session

22. Transmission media are usually categorized as.
    (*a*) Fixed or unfixed
    (*b*) Guided or inguided
    (*c*) Determinate or indeterminate
    (*d*) Metallic or nonmetallic

23. BNC connectors are used by .... cables.
    (*a*) UTP coaxial
    (*b*) Coaxial

(*c*) STP
(*d*) Fibre optic

24. In fiber optics, the signal source is .... waves.
(*a*) Light
(*b*) Infrared
(*c*) Radio
(*d*) Very low frequency

25. What is the major factor that makes coaxial cable less susceptible to noise than twisted pair cable.
(*a*) Inner conductor
(*b*) Diameter of cable
(*c*) Outer conductor
(*d*) Insulating material

26. The RG number gives us information about ....
(*a*) Twisted pair
(*b*) Coaxial cable
(*c*) Optic fibre
(*d*) None of the above

27. The inner core of an optical fibre is .... in composition.
(*a*) Glass or plastic
(*b*) Bimetallic
(*c*) Copper
(*d*) Liquid

28. Which propagation method is subjected to greatest distortion.
(*a*) Multimode step index
(*b*) Multimode graded index
(*c*) Multimode single index
(*d*) Single mode

29. Radio waves and microwave frequencies range from ....
(*a*) 3 to 300 khz
(*b*) 300 kHz to 300 GHz
(*c*) 3 kHz to 300 GHz
(*d*) 3 kHz to 3000 GHz

30. Category 1 UTP cable is most often used in .... network.
(*a*) Fast Ethernet
(*b*) Traditional Ethernet
(*c*) Infrared
(*d*) Telephone

31. In an optical fibre, the inner core is .... than the cladding.
(*a*) Denser
(*b*) Less dense
(*c*) Same density
(*d*) None of the above

32. A parabolic dish antenna is a .... antenna.
(*a*) Omnidirectional
(*b*) Bidirectional
(*c*) Unidirectional
(*d*) Horn

33. The .... is an association that sponsors the use of infrared waves.
(*a*) Infrared data association
(*b*) EIA
(*c*) FCC
(*d*) PUD

34. Which device or switch connects n inputs to m outputs.
(*a*) 2 × 2 switch
(*b*) Modem
(*c*) Cross bar
(*d*) RAM

35. In which type of circuit switching, delivery of data is delayed because data must be stored and retrieved from RAM.
(*a*) Space division
(*b*) Virtual
(*c*) Time division
(*d*) Packet

36. To create a ...., combine crossbar switches in stages.

(*a*) Multistage switch
(*b*) Packet switch
(*c*) Cross point
(*d*) TSI

37. Which of the following is a time division switch.
(*a*) TSI
(*b*) TDM bus
(*c*) Cross point
(*d*) Both (*a*) and (*b*)

38. A telephone network is an example of .... network.
(*a*) Packet switched
(*b*) Circuit switched
(*c*) Message switched
(*d*) None of the above

39. The local loop has .... cable that connects the subscriber tele-phone to the nearest end office.
(*a*) Twisted pair
(*b*) Ca-axial
(*c*) Fibre optic
(*d*) (*b*) and (*c*)

40. A traditional telephone line has a bandwidth of ....
(*a*) 2000 Hz
(*b*) 2000 MHz
(*c*) 4000 Hz
(*d*) 4000 MHz

41. Which of the following is a connecting device.
(*a*) Bridge
(*b*) Hub
(*c*) Repeater
(*d*) All of the above

42. A bridge can ....
(*a*) Filter a frame
(*b*) Forward a frame
(*c*) Extend a frame
(*d*) All of the above

43. Repeaters function in the .... layers.
(*a*) Physical (MAC)
(*b*) Network
(*c*) Data link
(*d*) (*a*) and (*b*)

44. Bridges function in the .... layers.
(*a*) Physical (MAC)
(*b*) Network
(*c*) Data link
(*d*) (*a*) and (*b*)

45. A repeater takes the weakened and corrupted signal and .... it.
(*a*) Amplifies
(*b*) Resample
(*c*) Regenerates
(*d*) Reroutes

46. Which connecting device use spanning tree algorithm to create a loop less technology.
(*a*) Repeater
(*b*) Router
(*c*) Bridge
(*d*) Hub

47. Which bridge has smallest ID.
(*a*) Root
(*b*) Forwarding
(*c*) Designated
(*d*) Blocking

48. In a VLAN stations are separated into groups by ....
(*a*) Physical methods
(*b*) Software methods
(*c*) Locations
(*d*) Switch

49. VLAN technology divides a LAN into .... groups.
(*a*) Physical
(*b*) Multiplexed

(*c*) Logical
(*d*) Frame

50. A bridge never forwards a frame out to the .... port.
(*a*) Root
(*b*) Forwarding
(*c*) Designated
(*d*) Blocking

51. Frame relay operates in the ....
(*a*) Physical layer
(*b*) Data link layer
(*c*) Physical and data link layer
(*d*) Physical data link and network layer

52. In data communication, ATM is an acronym for ....
(*a*) Automated Teller Machine
(*b*) Automated Transmission Model
(*c*) Asynchronous Telecommunication Method
(*d*) Asynchronous Transfer Mode

53. A .... is a computerized centre, that is responsible for connecting calls, recording call information and billing.
(*a*) Base station
(*b*) Mobile switching centre
(*c*) Cell
(*d*) Mobile station

54. In a ...., a mobile station always communicates with just one base station.
(*a*) Messaging hand off
(*b*) Hard hand off
(*c*) Soft hand off
(*d*) Roaming hand off

55. Which is first generation cellular phone system.
(*a*) AMPS (Advance Mobile Phone System)
(*b*) DAMPS (Digital AMPS)
(*c*) GSM (Global System for mobile communication)
(*d*) IS-95

56. Which is a second generation cellular phone system.
(*a*) D-AMPS
(*b*) GSM
(*c*) IS-95
(*d*) All of the above

57. AMPS uses .... for modulation.
(*a*) FM
(*b*) PM
(*c*) FSK
(*d*) Both (*a*) and (*b*)

58. A GEO satellite has .... orbit.
(*a*) An equatorial
(*b*) A polar
(*c*) An inclined
(*d*) An equilateral

59. Which orbit has the highest altitude.
(*a*) GEO
(*b*) LEO
(*c*) MEO
(*d*) HEO

60. Which is the low earth orbit satellite that provides universal broadband internet access.
(*a*) Teledesic
(*b*) Iridium system
(*c*) Global star
(*d*) All of the above

61. Which layer in ATM protocol formats the data received from other networks.

(*a*) Physical
(*b*) Application adaptation
(*c*) ATM
(*d*) Data adaptation

62. On a network that uses NAT (Address Translation), the .... has translation table.
(*a*) Switch
(*b*) Server
(*c*) Router
(*d*) None of the above

63. An IP address consists of how many bits.
(*a*) 4
(*b*) 32
(*c*) 8
(*d*) All of the above

64. The portion of the IP address that identifies the network is called as.
(*a*) Host id
(*b*) Mask
(*c*) Netid
(*d*) None of the above

65. Name the dynamic mapping protocol in which a physical address is found for a given IP address.
(*a*) ARP (Address Resolution Protocol)
(*b*) RARP (Reverse ARP)
(*c*) ICMP (Internet control message protocol)
(*d*) None of the above

66. An ARP request is made from ....
(*a*) Broadband: all host
(*b*) Multicast: one host
(*c*) Unicast: to all hosts
(*d*) Unicast: to one host

67. What is the maximum size of a data portion of the IP diagram..
(*a*) 65535 bytes
(*b*) 65515 bytes
(*c*) 65375 bytes
(*d*) 65460 bytes

68. The IP header size is ....
(*a*) 20 to 60 bytes long
(*b*) 20 bytes long
(*c*) 60 bytes long
(*d*) Depends upon the MDU

69. Packet in the IP layer are called ....
(*a*) Datagram
(*b*) Message
(*c*) Fragments
(*d*) None of the above

70. One method to alert a source host of congestion is the .... message.
(*a*) Redirection
(*b*) Echo request
(*c*) Source quench
(*d*) Destination unreachable

71. A time exceeded message is generated if ....
(*a*) The round trip time between hosts is close to zero
(*b*) The time to live field has zero value
(*c*) Fragments of the message don't arrive within a set time
(*d*) Both (*b*) and (*c*)

72. RIP (Routing Information Protocol) is based on ....
(*a*) Link state routing
(*b*) Distance routing
(*c*) Dijkstra's algorithm
(*d*) Part vector routing

73. The routing table contains ....
(*a*) The destination network ID
(*b*) The hop count to reach the network

(*c*) The router ID of next hp
(*d*) All of the above

74. Which of the following is a multicasting application.
(*a*) Teleconferencing
(*b*) Distance learning
(*c*) Information dissemination
(*d*) All of the above

75. UDP and TCP are both .... layer protocol.
(*a*) Physical
(*b*) Network
(*c*) Data link
(*d*) Transport

76. Which of the following function does UDP performs.
(*a*) Process to process communication
(*b*) Host to host communication
(*c*) End to end reliable data delivery
(*d*) All of the above

77. UDP needs .... address to deliver the data gram to the correct application program.
(*a*) Port
(*b*) Application
(*c*) Physical
(*d*) Network

78. Which is a legal port address.
(*a*) 0
(*b*) 65535
(*c*) 513
(*d*) All of the above

79. Which field is used for error detection.
(*a*) Urgent pointer
(*b*) Checksum
(*c*) Sequence number
(*d*) Acknowledgement number

80. Connection establishment involves a .... handshake.
(*a*) One way
(*b*) Two way
(*c*) Three way
(*d*) None of the above

81. Which mechanism is used by TCP for flow control.
(*a*) Sliding window
(*b*) Checksum
(*c*) Keep alive timer
(*d*) None of the above

82. The maximum length of time that traffic is generated at the peak rate is called the ....
(*a*) Average data rate
(*b*) Maximum burst size
(*c*) Effective bandwidth
(*d*) Constant bit rate

83. In .... queuing the first packet into the queue is the first packet out of the queue.
(*a*) FIFO
(*b*) Priority
(*c*) LIFO
(*d*) Weighted fair

84. Which traffic shaping method gives a host credit for it's idle time.
(*a*) Leaky bucket
(*b*) Traffic bucket
(*c*) Token bucket
(*d*) Bursty bucket

85. Which of the following can request a service.
(*a*) A socket interface
(*b*) A client
(*c*) A port
(*d*) A server

86. Which of the following can provide a service.
(*a*) An interactive server

(*b*) A concurrent server
(*c*) A client
(*d*) Both (*a*) and (*b*)

87. A client program is .... because it terminate after it has been served.
(*a*) Active
(*b*) Passive
(*c*) Finite
(*d*) Infinite

88. The server program is .... because it is always, available waiting for a client request.
(*a*) Active
(*b*) Passive
(*c*) Finite
(*d*) Infinite

89. Which of the following processes requests one at time.
(*a*) An iterative client
(*b*) An iterative server
(*c*) A concurrent client
(*d*) A concurrent server

90. Which socket is used with a connection oriented protocol.
(*a*) Stream
(*b*) Datagram
(*c*) Raw
(*d*) Remote

91. Which socket is used with a connection less protocol.
(*a*) Stream
(*b*) Datagram
(*c*) Raw
(*d*) Remote

92. Which socket is used with a protocol that directly uses the services of IP.
(*a*) Stream
(*b*) Datagram
(*c*) Raw
(*d*) Remote

93. A DNS .... server gets its data from another NDS server.
(*a*) Primary
(*b*) Secondary
(*c*) Root
(*d*) All of the above

94. A DNS .... creates, maintains and updates the zone file.
(*a*) Primary
(*b*) Secondary
(*c*) Root
(*d*) All of the above

95. A DNS .... servers zone is the entire DNS tree.
(*a*) Primary
(*b*) Secondary
(*c*) Root
(*d*) All of the above

96. To find the IP address of the host when domain name is known the .... can be used.
(*a*) Inverse domain
(*b*) Generic domain
(*c*) Country domain
(*d*) None of the above

97. A resolver is the ....
(*a*) DNS client
(*b*) DNS server
(*c*) Host machine
(*d*) Root server

98. The purpose of user agent.
(*a*) Message preparation
(*b*) Envelope creation
(*c*) Transfer of message across Internet
(*d*) All of the above

99. The purpose of MTA is ....
(*a*) Message preparation

(b) Envelope creation
(c) Transfer of message across Internet
(d) All of the above

100. In the E_MAIL address Mackenzie@pic.arc.gov. what is the domain name.
(a) Mackenzie
(b) Pic.arc.gov
(c) Mackenzie@pic.arc.gov.
(d) None of the above

101. Before a message is encrypted, it is called ....
(a) Plaintext
(b) Cipher text
(c) Crypto text
(d) Kryptonite

102. A JPEG image is sent as email. What is the content type.
(a) Multipart/mixed
(b) Multipart/image
(c) Image/JPEG
(d) Image ? basic

103. In FTP, there are three types of ....: stream, block, and compressed.
(a) Files
(b) Data structure
(c) Transmission modes
(d) All of the above

104. In FTP, ASCII, EBCDIC, and image define an attribute called ....
(a) File type
(b) Data structure
(c) Transmission modes
(d) All of the above

105. In anonymous FTP, the user can usually ....
(a) Retrieve file
(b) Navigate through directories
(c) Store files
(d) All of the above

106. HTTP (Hyper Text Transfer protocol) has similarities to both .... and ....
(a) FTP:SNMP
(b) FTP:SMTP
(c) FTP: MTV
(d) FTP: URL

107. Which of the following is a retrival method:
(a) HTTP
(b) Telnet
(c) FTP
(d) All of the above

108. Hypertext documents are linked through ....
(a) DNS
(b) TELNET
(c) Pointers
(d) Homepages

109. An applet is a small application program written in ....
(a) C
(b) C++
(c) Shell script
(d) Java

110. .... is used to enable the use of active document.
(a) HTML
(b) JAVA
(c) CGI
(d) All of the above

111. Name the transport layer security protocol.
(a) TLS
(b) IP sec
(c) PGP
(d) AH

112. A method to provide secure transport of email is called ....
(*a*) TLA
(*b*) PGP (Prettey Good Privacy)
(*c*) SA
(*d*) IP sec

113. Which of the following network is totally isolated from the global internet.
(*a*) Private
(*b*) Virtual private
(*c*) Hybrid
(*d*) Any of the above

114. An .... is a private network with limited external access that uses the TCP/IP suite.
(*a*) Internet
(*b*) Intranet
(*c*) Extranet
(*d*) None of the above

115. The path that a satellites makes around the world is called ....
(*a*) A period
(*b*) An orbit
(*c*) A foot print
(*d*) An uplink

116. Which of the following is not used for voice communication.
(*a*) IS-95 system
(*b*) Global star system
(*c*) GPS
(*d*) Iredium system

117. What is the operational speed for traditional Ethernet.
(*a*) 10 Mbps
(*b*) 10 kbps
(*c*) 100 mbps
(*d*) 100 kbps

118. Which of the following is most widely used local area network protocol.
(*a*) ARP
(*b*) RARP
(*c*) Ethernet
(*d*) UDP

119. Which connecting device can raise the bandwidth & separate the collision domain on an Ethernet LAN.
(*a*) Repeater
(*b*) Router
(*c*) Bridge
(*d*) Hub

120. What standard of IEEE has specification for a wireless LAN.
(*a*) IEEE 820.11
(*b*) IEEE 831
(*c*) IEEE 1011
(*d*) IEEE 101

121. Which technique is designed to provide communication between two moving units called mobile station.
(*a*) Cellular technology
(*b*) Mobile switching
(*c*) Paging
(*d*) Advanced mobile phone system

122. Which network is a combination of nodes that provides communication from one point on the earth to another.
(*a*) Mobile network
(*b*) Satellite network
(*c*) Wide area network
(*d*) Metropolitan area network

123. Global positioning system (GPS) is an example of.
(*a*) Low earth orbit (LEO)
(*b*) Medium earth orbit (MEO)

(*c*) Geosynchronous earth orbit (GEO)
(*d*) Higher earth orbit (HEO)

124. Which of the following is a virtual circuit wide area network
(*a*) Frame relay
(*b*) ATM
(*c*) PPP
(*d*) Ethernet

125. .... is the interface between two ATM switches.
(*a*) User to network interface
(*b*) User-user interface
(*c*) Network to network interface
(*d*) None of the above

126. In ...., a network is divided into several smaller groups with each sub network having it's own sub network address.
(*a*) Subnetting
(*b*) Masking
(*c*) Internetworking
(*d*) Addressing

127. Which process extracts the network address from an IP address.
(*a*) Subnet masking
(*b*) Addressing
(*c*) Default masking
(*d*) Internetworking

128. Internet control message protocol (ICMP) message are encapsulated in ....
(*a*) Packets
(*b*) IP datagrams
(*c*) User datagram
(*d*) None of the above

129. .... defines the amount of data a source can send before receiving an acknowledgement from the destination.
(*a*) Flow control
(*b*) Error control
(*c*) Segmentation
(*d*) Checksum

130. The first component of an electronic system is the ....
(*a*) User agent
(*b*) Mail transfer agent
(*c*) Domain name
(*d*) Address

131. Name the supplementary protocol that allows non-ASCII data to be sent through SMTP.
(*a*) HTTP
(*b*) HTML
(*c*) MIME
(*d*) Telnet

132. .... is the art of transforming message to make them secure and immune to attack.
(*a*) Decryption
(*b*) Substitution
(*c*) Cryptography
(*d*) Transformation

133. Which of the following is a multiple access method in which one channel carries all transmission simultaneously.
(*a*) CDMA
(*b*) Token ring
(*c*) CD
(*d*) Congestion

134. Name the ITU standard that defines the interface between a data terminal device and a packet switching network.
(*a*) X.509
(*b*) X.35
(*c*) X.25
(*d*) None of the above

135. Which of the following OSI layer is concerned with transmitting raw

bits over a communication channel.
(*a*) Session layer
(*b*) Application layer
(*c*) Data link layer
(*d*) Physical layer

136. A collection of interconnected network is ....
(*a*) Gateways
(*b*) Internetwork
(*c*) Intranet
(*d*) Extranet

137. Point to point transmission with one sender and one receiver is called ....
(*a*) Unicasting
(*b*) Broadcasting
(*c*) Multicasting
(*d*) Addressing

138. Various topologies are possible for which network.
(*a*) MAN
(*b*) WAN
(*c*) LAN
(*d*) Satellite network

139. Which switching technique uses the mechanism of store and forward.
(*a*) Circuit switching
(*b*) Packet switching
(*c*) Message switching network
(*d*) Virtual switching

140. Which scheme allows mobile stations to send and receive IP packet in a cell running voice system.
(*a*) GPRS
(*b*) AMPS
(*c*) D_AMPS
(*d*) GSM

141. Telephone system may be classified as:
(*a*) Duplex and asymmetrical
(*b*) Simplex and asymmetrical
(*c*) Simplex and symmetrical
(*d*) Duplex and symmetrical

142. The Internet is an example of a:
(*a*) Circuit switched network
(*b*) Packet switched network
(*c*) Cell switched network
(*d*) None of the above

143. A LAN.
(*a*) Always contains more than 5 PCs
(*b*) Connects PCs to telephones
(*c*) Connects PCs to other computer devices within a small geographical area
(*d*) Always contain a server which houses a centralized file

144. Any electronic device on a network is called a.
(*a*) Node
(*b*) Hub
(*c*) Router
(*d*) Cable

145. A peer to peer network.
(*a*) Is ideal for transmitting large files
(*b*) Always requires a router
(*c*) Only functions with fiber optic cable
(*d*) Requires no special operating system other than windows 95 or 98.

146. On a client server network:
(*a*) Files can be stored on server computer and can be stored on individual PCs
(*b*) No special operating system is needed
(*c*) When one node goes down, entire network malfunctions

(*d*) 20 nodes is the absolute maximum allowed.

147. Ethernet is:
    (*a*) An internal company's internet, not accessible by outside server
    (*b*) Requires it's own OS
    (*c*) One of several methods by which information travels through a network
    (*d*) Not available for peer to peer network.

148. Which piece of equipment installs on a PC and allows the PC to connect to a network.
    (*a*) Hub
    (*b*) Access router
    (*c*) Accelerator card
    (*d*) NIC

149. A network can have all the following devices except:
    (*a*) Printers
    (*b*) Lights
    (*c*) Laptops
    (*d*) Macintosh computers

150. Modems ....
    (*a*) Stands for modulator/demodulator
    (*b*) Connects to multiple computers
    (*c*) Broadcast wireless signals
    (*d*) Only work with AOL

151. What is a router.
    (*a*) A device that makes sure all devices on your network get power
    (*b*) A device that manages data flow on a network
    (*c*) A device having firewall for security
    (*d*) None of the above

152. Wireless adaptors are ....
    (*a*) Found in all laptops made after 1998
    (*b*) Always needed to connects to wireless networks
    (*c*) None of the above

153. What is a file server.
    (*a*) A computer that performs services for other computers
    (*b*) A computer that controls the printers on the network
    (*c*) A computer that stores files that are created by network users
    (*d*) None of the above

154. What is the protocol used for the internet.
    (*a*) IPX/SPX
    (*b*) TCP/IP
    (*c*) Net BIOS
    (*d*) None of the above

155. Social network sites uses which media for communication.
    (*a*) Video
    (*b*) Audio
    (*c*) Text
    (*d*) All of the above

156. Which standard is a thoroughly tested specification adhered to those who work with Internet.
    (*a*) Internet standard
    (*b*) IEEE standard
    (*c*) ITU-T standard
    (*d*) None of the above

157. What term is used for transfer of data from one device to other via some form of transmission media.
    (*a*) Addressing
    (*b*) Data communication
    (*c*) Switching
    (*d*) None of the above

158. Name the term used for set of rules that governs data communication.
   (*a*) Standard
   (*b*) Protocol
   (*c*) Internet
   (*d*) Network

159. Which topology requires a multipoint connection.
   (*a*) Mesh
   (*b*) Bus
   (*c*) Star
   (*d*) Ring

160. The processes on each machine that communicate at a given layer are called ....
   (*a*) Peer to peer processes
   (*b*) Communication processes
   (*c*) Network processes
   (*d*) None of the above

161. Which OSI layer is responsible for source to destination delivery of packet.
   (*a*) Data link
   (*b*) Network
   (*c*) Transport
   (*d*) Session

162. Which of the following layers enables the users to access the network.
   (*a*) Presentation
   (*b*) Network
   (*c*) Application
   (*d*) Session

163. For the purpose of transmission the data must be converted to .... signals.
   (*a*) Electrical
   (*b*) Electromagnetic
   (*c*) Magnetic
   (*d*) Digital

164. Human voice is an example of .... signal.
   (*a*) Analog
   (*b*) Digital
   (*c*) Electrical
   (*d*) Synchronous

165. Attenuation refers to the loss of ....
   (*a*) Signal
   (*b*) Energy
   (*c*) Data
   (*d*) Time

166. .... is the process of converting binary data, a sequence of bits to a digital signal.
   (*a*) Line coding
   (*b*) Masking
   (*c*) Conversion
   (*d*) Multiplexing

167. In which transmission bits are send one after another without start/stop bits or gaps.
   (*a*) Asynchronous
   (*b*) Synchronous
   (*c*) Digital
   (*d*) Periodic

168. A telephone line has a bandwidth of almost .... for data transmission.
   (*a*) 1000 Hz
   (*b*) 24 Hz
   (*c*) 10 Hz
   (*d*) 2400 Hz

169. .... is the process of changing the characteristics of an analog signal based on the information on a digital signal.
   (*a*) Digital to analog modulation
   (*b*) Analog to digital modulation

(*c*) Digital to digital modulation
(*d*) Analog to analog modulation

170. Which technique allows the simultaneous transmission of multiple signals across a single data link.
(*a*) Broadcasting
(*b*) Networking
(*c*) Multiplexing
(*d*) None of the above

171. Telephone companies use .... to combine voice channels into successively larger groups for efficient transmission.
(*a*) TDM
(*b*) FDM
(*c*) WDM
(*d*) None of the above

172. Which medium provides a physical connection from one device to another.
(*a*) Guided
(*b*) Unguided
(*c*) Satellite
(*d*) None of the above

173. Which of the following is an error correction method using redundant bits.
(*a*) Redundancy
(*b*) Hamming code
(*c*) LRC
(*d*) VRC

174. HDLC is an acronym for.
(*a*) High duplex line communication
(*b*) Half duplex digital link communication
(*c*) High lavel data control
(*d*) Host double label service

175. .... is a set of control proto-cols to allow the encapsulation of data coming from network protocol.
(*a*) Network control protocol (NCP)
(*b*) Inter network control protocol (IPCP)
(*c*) Internet protocol
(*d*) None of the above

176. To minimize the chance of collision .... method was developed.
(*a*) ALOHA
(*b*) CSMA
(*c*) Multiple access
(*d*) None of the above

177. In which method a station sends data when it receives a special frame called a token.
(*a*) Polling
(*b*) Token passing
(*c*) Collision
(*d*) CDMA

178. Which is the wireless LAN technology that connects devices in a small area.
(*a*) Bluetooth
(*b*) Hub
(*c*) Router
(*d*) Multiplexing

179. Which LAN is configured by software not by physical wiring.
(*a*) Backbone LAN
(*b*) Virtual LAN (VLAN)
(*c*) Wireless LAN
(*d*) All of the above

180. .... is a repository of information spread all over the world and linked together.
(*a*) World wide web
(*b*) Hypertext
(*c*) Hyperlink
(*d*) HTML

181. In .... cryptography same secret key is used by the sender and the receiver.
   (*a*) Public key
   (*b*) Private key
   (*c*) Symmetric key
   (*d*) Asymmetric key

182. .... is the method to authenticate the sender of a message.
   (*a*) Digital signature
   (*b*) Encryption/decryption
   (*c*) Password
   (*d*) None of the above

183. Transmission of a message to all nodes in network is called ....
   (*a*) Multiplexing
   (*b*) Broadcasting
   (*c*) Unicasting
   (*d*) Demultiplexing

184. A group of bits representing a block of data is called ....
   (*a*) Frame
   (*b*) Packet
   (*c*) Data unit
   (*d*) None of the above

185. Sending a local file or data to a remote site is called.
   (*a*) Downlinking
   (*b*) Uploading
   (*c*) Uplinking
   (*d*) All of the above

186. Protocol in which stations listen for a carrier and act accordingly are called.
   (*a*) Carrier sence protocol
   (*b*) Persistent protocol
   (*c*) Broadcasting protocol
   (*d*) None of the above

187. SMTP is an acronym of.
   (*a*) Simple Message Transfer Privacy
   (*b*) Sample Message Transport Protocol
   (*c*) Simple Mail Transfer Protocol
   (*d*) Simple Mail Transfer Packet

188. Each webpage is assigned .... that effectively serves as the pages worldwide name.
   (*a*) URL
   (*b*) WWW
   (*c*) Http
   (*d*) Address

189. Which of the following is search engine.
   (*a*) Google
   (*b*) Yahoo search
   (*c*) Gopher
   (*d*) All of the above

190. Java applets are small Java programs compiler to stack oriented machine language called as ....
   (*a*) Java virtual machine
   (*b*) Universal resource network
   (*c*) Servers
   (*d*) None of the above

191. .... are the Pentium binary program that can be embedded in a web page.
   (*a*) Servlets
   (*b*) Hyperlink
   (*c*) Hypertext
   (*d*) Active X controls

192. Which of the following internet protocol are related to internet.
   (*a*) HTTP
   (*b*) NNTP
   (*c*) Hyperlinks
   (*d*) All of the above

193. Type of software that can be downloaded by FTP are.
   (*a*) Freeware
   (*b*) Shareware
   (*c*) Demo ware
   (*d*) All of the above

194. .... is external energy that corrupts a signal.
   (*a*) Wavelength
   (*b*) Amplitude
   (*c*) Noise
   (*d*) Frequency

195. In which transmission there is only one line and bits are sent sequentially.
   (*a*) Serial
   (*b*) Analog
   (*c*) Parallel
   (*d*) Digital

196. Which theorem says that the sampling rate must be at least twice the highest frequency component is the original signal.
   (*a*) Fourier signal
   (*b*) Polar
   (*c*) Nyquist
   (*d*) None of the above

197. In ...., the bandwidth of modulated signal must be 10 times the bandwidth of modulating signal.
   (*a*) FM radio
   (*b*) SW radio
   (*c*) AM radio
   (*d*) None of the above

198. .... is a multiple access method in which the available bandwidth of a link is shared in time frequency between different stations.
   (*a*) CSMA
   (*b*) CDMA
   (*c*) TDMA
   (*d*) Channelization

199. The number of signal elements transmitted per second are called as ....
   (*a*) Bit rate
   (*b*) Baud rate
   (*c*) Bit interval
   (*d*) Bit stuffing

200. An application program that displays a WWW document is called.
   (*a*) Applet
   (*b*) Hypertext
   (*c*) Browser
   (*d*) Web server

201. What is meant by fabrication w.r.t computer networks.
   (*a*) When unauthorized party inserts counterfeit objects into the system
   (*b*) It is creation of a new protocol
   (*c*) It is unauthorized creation of a internet

202. The passive attack on computer security is.
   (*a*) Traffic analysis
   (*b*) Masquerade
   (*c*) Denial of service
   (*d*) None of the above

203. Active attack on network security is.
   (*a*) Release of message context
   (*b*) Traffic analysis
   (*c*) Modification of message
   (*d*) None of the above

204. Vigenere cipher is.
   (*a*) Stream cipher
   (*b*) Data cipher

(*c*) I/O cipher
(*d*) None of the above

205. Block cipher is defined as.
(*a*) One that encrypts a digital data system one bit at a time
(*b*) Which treats block of plaintext as a whole
(*c*) Which treats complete file as whole
(*d*) None of the above

206. Anlanche effect in encryption is.
(*a*) Desirable
(*b*) Undesirable
(*c*) Cannot be said
(*d*) Depends upon the context

207. The formula of RAS algorithm is.
(*a*) c = Me mod w
(*b*) c = Me mod w
(*c*) c = nM mod e
(*d*) c = M ne MOD x

208. Which of the following is not a method of public key distribution.
(*a*) Publicaly available directory
(*b*) Public key certificate
(*c*) Public announcement
(*d*) None of the above

209. OSI network architecture, the routing is performed by
(*a*) Network layer
(*b*) Data link layer
(*c*) Transport layer
(*d*) Session layer

210. Which of the following signals is not standard RS-232-C signal?
(*a*) VDR
(*b*) RTS
(*c*) CTS
(*d*) DSR

211. The transmission signal coding method of TI carrier is called
(*a*) Bipolar
(*b*) NRZ
(*c*) Manchester
(*d*) Binary

212. In a synchronous modem, the digital-to-analog converter transmits signals to the
(*a*) Equalizer
(*b*) Modulator
(*c*) Demodulator
(*d*) Terminal

213. In communication satellite, multiple repeaters are known as
(*a*) Detector
(*b*) Modulator
(*c*) Stations
(*d*) Transponders

214. The receive equalizer reduces delay distortions using a
(*a*) Tapped delay lines
(*b*) Gearshift
(*c*) Descrambler
(*d*) Difference engine

215. Which of the following is an example of bounded medium?
(*a*) Coaxial cable
(*b*) Wave guide
(*c*) Fiber optic cable
(*d*) All of above

216. The amount of uncertainty in a system of symbol is called?
(*a*) Bandwidth
(*b*) Entropy
(*c*) Loss
(*d*) Quantum

217. Coaxial cable has condutors with
(*a*) Equal resistance
(*b*) Same diameter
(*c*) (a) and (b) both
(*d*) A common axis

218. How much power (roughly) a light-emitting diode can couple into

an optical fiber?
(*a*) 100 microwatts
(*b*) 440 microwatts
(*c*) 100 picowatts
(*d*) 10 milliwatts

219. The loss in signal power as light travels down the fiber is called
(*a*) attenuation
(*b*) Propagation
(*c*) Scattering
(*d*) Interruption

220. Which data communication method is used to transmit the data over a serial communication link
(*a*) Simplex
(*b*) Half-duplex
(*c*) Full-duplex
(*d*) Both (b) and (c)

221. Avalanche photodiode receivers can detect bits of transmitted data by receiving
(*a*) 100 photons
(*b*) 200 photons
(*c*) 300 photons
(*d*) None of the above

222. Which of the following transmission systems provides the highest data rate to an individual device.
(*a*) Computer bus
(*b*) Telephone bus
(*c*) Voice band modem
(*d*) Leased lines

223. Which of the following is not a standard synchronous communication protocol?
(*a*) SDLC
(*b*) SMTP
(*c*) SLIP
(*d*) PAS

224. The cheapest modems can transmit
(*a*) 300 bits per second
(*b*) 1200 bits per second
(*c*) 2400 bits per second
(*d*) None of above

225. A device that can convert digital signals to analog signals is
(*a*) Packet
(*b*) Modem
(*c*) Block
(*d*) None of the above

226. If you get both local and remote echoes, every character you type will appear on the screen.
(*a*) Once
(*b*) Twice
(*c*) Three times
(*d*) Never

227. All of the parts in a computer talk to each other by sending
(*a*) digital signals
(*b*) Analog signals
(*c*) Smoothly vary
(*d*) None of the above

228. A network that requires human intervention to route signals is called a
(*a*) Bus network
(*b*) Ring network
(*c*) Star networking
(*d*) T-switched network

229. How many pairs of stations can simultaneously communicate on Ethernet LAN
(*a*) 1
(*b*) 2
(*c*) 3
(*d*) Multiplexer

230. Which of the following is used for modulation and demodulation?
(*a*) Modem
(*b*) Protocols

(*c*) Gateway
(*d*) Multiplexer

231. Devices on one network can communicate with devices on another network via a
(*a*) File server
(*b*) Utility server
(*c*) Printer server
(*d*) Gateway

232. A software that allows a dumb personal computer to pretend that it is a terminal is
(*a*) Auto-dialing
(*b*) Bulletin board
(*c*) Modem
(*d*) Terminal emulation

233. Which of the following divides the high speed signal into frequency bands?
(*a*) T-switch
(*b*) Modem
(*c*) Frequency-division multiplexer
(*d*) Time-division multiplexer

234. The slowest transmission speeds are those of
(*a*) Twisted-pair wire
(*b*) Coaxial cable
(*c*) Microwaves
(*d*) None of the above

235. To avoid transmission errors, a check sum figure is calculated by the
(*a*) Transmitting computer
(*b*) Receiving computer
(*c*) Both (a) and (b)
(*d*) None of above

236. Error detection at the data link layer is achieved by?
(*a*) Bit stuffing
(*b*) Hamming codes
(*c*) Cyclic redundancy codes
(*d*) Equalization

237. End-to-end connectivity is provided from host-to-host in:
(*a*) Network layer
(*b*) Session layer
(*c*) Data link layer
(*d*) Transport layer

238. Packet Switch Stream (PSS) was introduced in
(*a*) The US in 1961
(*b*) The UK in 1981
(*c*) The UK in 1971
(*d*) The US in 1961

239. How many digits of the DNIC (Data Network Identification Code) identify the country?
(*a*) First three
(*b*) First four
(*c*) First five
(*d*) First fix

240. Which of the following digits are known as the terminal number of the Network User Address (NUA)?
(*a*) 5-7
(*b*) 1-4
(*c*) 8-12
(*d*) 13-14

241. The size or magnitude of a voltage or current waveform is
(*a*) Amplitude
(*b*) Aloha
(*c*) Angle modulation
(*d*) Attenuation

242. A medium access control technique for multiple access transmission media is
(*a*) Aloha
(*b*) Amplitude
(*c*) Angle modulation
(*d*) Attenuation

243. Which layer of OSI determines the interface of the system with the user?
(*a*) Network
(*b*) Application
(*c*) Data-link
(*d*) Session

244. A devices that links two homogeneous packet-broadcast local network, is
(*a*) hub
(*b*) bridge
(*c*) Repeater
(*d*) Gateway

245. The simultaneous transmission of data to a number of stations is known as
(*a*) Broadcast
(*b*) Band width
(*c*) Aloha
(*d*) Analog transmission

246. Which of the following medium is used for broadband local networks?
(*a*) Coaxial cable
(*b*) Optic fiber
(*c*) CATV
(*d*) UTP

247. Which of the following condition is encountered if two packets are transmitted over a medium at the same time?
(*a*) Contention
(*b*) Collision
(*c*) Synchronous
(*d*) Asynchronous

248. Which of the following device is used to connect two system, especially if the system use different protocols?
(*a*) Gateway
(*b*) Hub
(*c*) Bridge
(*d*) Repeater

249. Which device is used with an X.25 network to provide service to asynchronous terminals.
(*a*) Repeater
(*b*) bridges
(*c*) Gateway
(*d*) Paket assembler/disassembler

250. Which communication service provides message preparation and transmission facilities?
(*a*) Teletex
(*b*) Telemetery
(*c*) X400
(*d*) Fax

251. Which medium access control technique is used for bus/tree?
(*a*) Token bus
(*b*) Token ring
(*c*) CSMA
(*d*) MAC

252. How many hosts are attached to each of the local area networks at your site?
(*a*) 128
(*b*) 254
(*c*) 256
(*d*) 64

253. Which TCP/IP internet protocol a diskless machine uses to obtain IP address from a server?
(*a*) RDP
(*b*) RARP
(*c*) X.25
(*d*) RIP

254. Which TCP/IP protocol is used for file transfer with minimal capability and minimal overhead?

(*a*) RARP
(*b*) FTP
(*c*) TFTP
(*d*) TELNET

255. How many class A, B and C network IDs can exist?
(*a*) 2113658
(*b*) 16382
(*c*) 126
(*d*) 128

256. Which device copies electrical signals from one ethernet to another?
(*a*) Bridge
(*b*) Repeater
(*c*) Hub
(*d*) Passive hub

257. What is the minimum number of wires required for sending data over a serial communications links?
(*a*) 1
(*b*) 2
(*c*) 3
(*d*) 4

258. Working of the WAN generally involves.
(*a*) Telephone lines
(*b*) Satellites
(*c*) Microwaves
(*d*) All of the above

259. A modem is connected between a telephone line and a
(*a*) Network
(*b*) Computer
(*c*) Communication adapter
(*d*) Serial port

260. Modem (used in data transmission) was invented when and in which country?
(*a*) 1963, USA
(*b*) 1965, Germany
(*c*) 1960, USA
(*d*) 1950, Japan

261. Different computers are connected to a LAN by a cable and a/an
(*a*) Modem
(*b*) Interface card
(*c*) Special wire
(*d*) Telephone lines

262. The word telematics is a combination of
(*a*) Computer
(*b*) Telecommunication
(*c*) Informatics
(*d*) (b) and (c)

263. "Store and forward" applies to
(*a*) Distributed processing
(*b*) Time sharing
(*c*) Both (a) and (b)
(*d*) None of the above

264. An example of digital communication is
(*a*) DDD
(*b*) DDS
(*c*) WATS
(*d*) DDT

265. The term "remote job entry" relates to
(*a*) Distributed processing
(*b*) Realtime processing
(*c*) Batch processing
(*d*) Transaction processing

266. A baud is always equivalent to
(*a*) 0 byte
(*b*) 9 bit
(*c*) 100 bits
(*d*) 16 bits

267. A hard copy would be prepared on a
(*a*) Typewrite terminal

(*b*) Line printer
(*c*) Plotter
(*d*) All of the above

268. Data communication monitors available on the software market incude
(*a*) ENVIRON/1
(*b*) TOTAL
(*c*) BPL
(*d*) Telenef

269. Video text is a combination of
(*a*) Television
(*b*) Communication
(*c*) Computer technology
(*d*) All of the above

270. Which of the following does not allow multiple users or devices to share one communications line?
(*a*) Doubleplexer
(*b*) Multiplexer
(*c*) Concentrator
(*d*) Controller

271. Which of the following items is not used in local area networks?
(*a*) Modem
(*b*) Cable
(*c*) Computer
(*d*) Printer

272. Communication between computer is almost always
(*a*) Serial
(*b*) Parallel
(*c*) Series parallel
(*d*) Direct

273. Identify the odd term amongst the following group.
(*a*) Microwaves
(*b*) Optical fibre
(*c*) Coaxial cable
(*d*) Twisted pair wire

274. Terminals are required for
(*a*) Batch processing
(*b*) Realtime processing
(*c*) Both (a) and (b)
(*d*) None of above

275. The dialogue techniques for terminal use do not include.
(*a*) Question and answers
(*b*) Open-ended questions
(*c*) Form filling
(*d*) Menu display

276. An example of an analog communication method is
(*a*) Laser beam
(*b*) Microwave
(*c*) Voice grade telephone line
(*d*) All of the above

277. A data terminal serves as a (n)
(*a*) Effector
(*b*) Sensor
(*c*) Both (a) and (b)
(*d*) Neither (a) nor (b)

278. An example of a medium-speed, switched communications service is
(*a*) Series 1000
(*b*) DDD
(*c*) Data phone 50
(*d*) All of the above

279. Which of the following performs modulation and demodulation?
(*a*) Fiber optic
(*b*) Satellite
(*c*) Coaxial cable
(*d*) Modem

280. Which of the following is not a transmission medium?
(*a*) Telephone lines
(*b*) Coaxial cable
(*c*) Modem

(*d*) Microwave systems

281. What is the commonly used unit for measuring the speed of data transmission
(*a*) Bytes per second
(*b*) Baud
(*c*) Bits per second
(*d*) Either (b) or (c)

282. What is the name of the network topology in which there are bi-directional links between each possible node?
(*a*) Ring
(*b*) Star
(*c*) Mesh
(*d*) Tree

283. The transfer of the data from a CPU to peripheral devices of a computer is achieved through
(*a*) Modems
(*b*) Computer ports
(*c*) Interfaces
(*d*) Buffer memory

284. Which of the following is a voice band channel?
(*a*) Telephone line
(*b*) Telegraph line
(*c*) Coaxial cable
(*d*) Microwave systems

285. Typewriter terminals can print computer-generated data at a rate of
(*a*) 10 characters per second
(*b*) 120 characters per second
(*c*) 120 characters per minute
(*d*) None of the above

286. The OCR reading unit attached to a POS terminal is called a
(*a*) Light pen
(*b*) Wand
(*c*) Cursor
(*d*) All of the above

287. A communication device that combines transmissions from several I/O device into one line is a:
(*a*) Concentrator
(*b*) Modifier
(*c*) Multiplexer
(*d*) Full-duplex line

288. Which might be used by a company to satisfy its growing communication needs?
(*a*) Controller
(*b*) Concentrator
(*c*) Multiplexer
(*d*) None of the above

289. Operating system functions may include
(*a*) I/O control
(*b*) Virtual storage
(*c*) Multi programming
(*d*) None of the above

290. Which type of channel moves data relatively slowly?
(*a*) Wide band
(*b*) Voice band
(*c*) Narrow band
(*d*) Broad band

291. The digits 8 to 12 are known as the terminal number of the (NUA)
(*a*) True
(*b*) False
(*c*) Varies from situation to situation
(*d*) None of the above

292. The second layer of communication is
(*a*) Data link layer
(*b*) Network layer
(*c*) Application layer
(*d*) None of the above

293. The network layer is also known as packet layer
(*a*) True
(*b*) False
(*c*) Can't be said
(*d*) None of the above

294. RTS signal is a standard RS-232-C signal
(*a*) True
(*b*) False
(*c*) Partially true
(*d*) None of the above

295. Teleprinter have a printer for output and a keyboard for input
(*a*) True
(*b*) False
(*c*) Can't be said
(*d*) None of the above

296. Buffering is a method to reduce cross-talks
(*a*) True
(*b*) False
(*c*) Partially true
(*d*) None of the above

297. The basic Ethernet design does not provide addressing
(*a*) True
(*b*) False
(*c*) Partially true
(*d*) None of the above

298. Protocol converters are the same as multiplexers
(*a*) True
(*b*) False
(*c*) In certain situation
(*d*) None of the above

299. Synchronous protocols transmit characters one at a time
(*a*) True
(*b*) False
(*c*) Partially true
(*d*) None of the above

300. T-switched networks route messages automatically among devices
(*a*) True
(*b*) False
(*c*) Depends upon the devices
(*d*) None of the above

301. All personal computers are dumb terminals
(*a*) True
(*b*) False
(*c*) Partially true
(*d*) None of the above

302. In OSI netwrok architecture, the dialogue control and token management are responsibilities of
(*a*) Session layer
(*b*) Network layer
(*c*) Transport layer
(*d*) Data link layer

303. Micro programming is
(*a*) Assembly language programming
(*b*) Programming of mini-computers
(*c*) Control unit programming
(*d*) Macro programming of micro-computer

304. A LAN designed for "long-haul data communications".
(*a*) True
(*b*) False
(*c*) Partially true
(*d*) None of the above

305. Packet Switch Stream (PSS) was introduced in
(*a*) US, 1961
(*b*) UK, 1981
(*c*) UK, 1971
(*d*) UK, 1989

306. The fundamental requirements of private-to-public network interconnection methods, which need to be provided in gateway is/are
   (*a*) Universal accessibility for private network Data Terminal Equipment
   (*b*) Adequate cost control mechanisms for administration of the private networks
   (*c*) Both (*a*) and (*b*)
   (*d*) None of the above

307. Which of the following digits are known as the sub-address digits of the Network User Address
   (*a*) 5-7
   (*b*) 13-14
   (*c*) 8-12
   (*d*) 1-4

308. IP address can be used to specify a broadcast and map to hardware broadcast if available. By convention, broadcast address has host id with all bits
   (*a*) 0
   (*b*) 1
   (*c*) Both (*a*) and (*b*)
   (*d*) None of the above

309. The 32 bit internet address 10000000 00001010 00000010 00011110 will be written in dotted decimal notation as
   (*a*) 148.20.2.30
   (*b*) 210.20.2.64
   (*c*) 164.10.2.61
   (*d*) 128.10.2.30

310. Which of the following TCP/IP protocol is used for transferring e-mail messages from one machine to another
   (*a*) FTP
   (*b*) SNMP
   (*c*) SMTP
   (*d*) RPC

311. Which of the following TCP/IP protocol is used to monitor IP gateways and the networks to which they are attached
   (*a*) SGMP
   (*b*) SUMP
   (*c*) FTP
   (*d*) Both A and B

312. To make a group window active
   (*a*) Open group window
   (*b*) Minimize a window
   (*c*) Maximize a window
   (*d*) Restore a window

313. To shrink a window to an icon
   (*a*) Open group window
   (*b*) Minimize a window
   (*c*) Maximize a window
   (*d*) Restore a window

314. To enlarge a window to its greatest size
   (*a*) Open group window
   (*b*) Minimize a window
   (*c*) Maximize a window
   (*d*) Restore a window

315. To return a maximized window to its previous size
   (*a*) Open group window
   (*b*) Minimize a window
   (*c*) Maximize a window
   (*d*) Restore a window

316. To move through information in a window in order to review parts that are beyond window's borders
   (*a*) Arrange icons
   (*b*) Arrange window
   (*c*) Scroll through a window
   (*d*) Size window

ANSWERS

1. (*c*)	2. (*b*)	3. (*b*)	4. (*c*)	5. (*a*)	6. (*a*)	7. (*c*)
8. (*b*)	9. (*c*)	10. (*b*)	11. (*c*)	12. (*c*)	13. (*a*)	14. (*d*)
15. (*a*)	16. (*b*)	17. (*a*)	18. (*b*)	19. (*d*)	20. (*a*)	21. (*c*)
22. (*b*)	23. (*b*)	24. (*a*)	25. (*c*)	26. (*b*)	27. (*a*)	28. (*b*)
29. (*c*)	30. (*d*)	31. (*b*)	32. (*c*)	33. (*a*)	34. (*c*)	35. (*c*)
36. (*a*)	37. (*d*)	38. (*b*)	39. (*a*)	40. (*c*)	41. (*d*)	42. (*d*)
43. (*a*)	44. (*d*)	45. (*c*)	46. (*c*)	47. (*a*)	48. (*d*)	49. (*a*)
50. (*d*)	51. (*c*)	52. (*d*)	53. (*b*)	54. (*b*)	55. (*a*)	56. (*d*)
57. (*d*)	58. (*a*)	59. (*a*)	60. (*c*)	61. (*b*)	62. (*c*)	63. (*b*)
64. (*c*)	65. (*a*)	66. (*b*)	67. (*a*)	68. (*a*)	69. (*a*)	70. (*c*)
71. (*d*)	72. (*b*)	73. (*d*)	74. (*d*)	75. (*d*)	76. (*a*)	77. (*a*)
78. (*d*)	79. (*b*)	80. (*c*)	81. (*a*)	82. (*b*)	83. (*a*)	84. (*c*)
85. (*b*)	86. (*d*)	87. (*a*)	88. (*b*)	89. (*d*)	90. (*a*)	91. (*b*)
92. (*c*)	93. (*b*)	94. (*a*)	95. (*c*)	96. (*a*)	97. (*a*)	98. (*d*)
99. (*c*)	100. (*b*)	101. (*a*)	102. (*c*)	103. (*c*)	104. (*a*)	105. (*a*)
106. (*b*)	107. (*a*)	108. (*c*)	109. (*d*)	110. (*b*)	111. (*a*)	112. (*b*)
113. (*a*)	114. (*b*)	115. (*c*)	116. (*c*)	117. (*a*)	118. (*c*)	119. (*c*)
120. (*a*)	121. (*a*)	122. (*b*)	123. (*b*)	124. (*a*)	125. (*c*)	126. (*a*)
127. (*c*)	128. (*b*)	129. (*a*)	130. (*a*)	131. (*c*)	132. (*c*)	133. (*a*)
134. (*c*)	135. (*d*)	136. (*b*)	137. (*a*)	138. (*c*)	139. (*c*)	140. (*a*)
141. (*d*)	142. (*b*)	143. (*c*)	144. (*a*)	145. (*d*)	146. (*a*)	147. (*c*)
148. (*d*)	149. (*b*)	150. (*a*)	151. (*b*)	152. (*b*)	153. (*c*)	154. (*b*)
155. (*d*)	156. (*a*)	157. (*b*)	158. (*b*)	159. (*a*)	160. (*a*)	161. (*b*)
162. (*c*)	163. (*b*)	164. (*a*)	165. (*b*)	166. (*a*)	167. (*b*)	168. (*d*)
169. (*a*)	170. (*c*)	171. (*b*)	172. (*a*)	173. (*b*)	174. (*c*)	175. (*a*)
176. (*b*)	177. (*b*)	178. (*a*)	179. (*b*)	180. (*a*)	181. (*c*)	182. (*a*)
183. (*b*)	184. (*a*)	185. (*b*)	186. (*a*)	187. (*c*)	188. (*a*)	189. (*d*)
190. (*a*)	191. (*d*)	192. (*d*)	193. (*d*)	194. (*c*)	195. (*a*)	196. (*c*)
197. (*a*)	198. (*d*)	199. (*b*)	200. (*c*)	201. (*b*)	202. (*b*)	203. (*a*)
204. (*b*)	205. (*b*)	206. (*a*)	207. (*a*)	208. (*c*)	209. (*a*)	210. (*b*)
211. (*c*)	212. (*c*)	213. (*d*)	214. (*d*)	215. (*d*)	216. (*b*)	217. (*d*)
218. (*b*)	219. (*c*)	220. (*d*)	221. (*c*)	222. (*d*)	223. (*d*)	224. (*b*)
225. (*b*)	226. (*c*)	227. (*a*)	228. (*d*)	229. (*a*)	230. (*a*)	231. (*b*)
232. (*b*)	233. (*c*)	234. (*d*)	235. (*a*)	236. (*c*)	237. (*b*)	238. (*a*)

239. (*a*)	240. (*c*)	241. (*a*)	242. (*a*)	243. (*b*)	244. (*d*)	245. (*a*)
246. (*b*)	247. (*b*)	248. (*a*)	249. (*d*)	250. (*b*)	251. (*a*)	252. (*a*)
253. (*b*)	254. (*b*)	255. (*b*)	256. (*b*)	257. (*b*)	258. (*b*)	259. (*d*)
260. (*a*)	261. (*b*)	262. (*d*)	263. (*a*)	264. (*d*)	265. (*a*)	266. (*d*)
267. (*d*)	268. (*a*)	269. (*c*)	270. (*a*)	271. (*d*)	272. (*a*)	273. (*a*)
274. (*b*)	275. (*c*)	276. (*c*)	277. (*c*)	278. (*c*)	279. (*d*)	280. (*c*)
281. (*d*)	282. (*a*)	283. (*b*)	284. (*a*)	285. (*c*)	286. (*b*)	287. (*c*)
288. (*b*)	289. (*c*)	290. (*c*)	291. (*a*)	292. (*a*)	293. (*a*)	294. (*a*)
295. (*b*)	296. (*b*)	297. (*a*)	298. (*b*)	299. (*a*)	300. (*b*)	301. (*b*)
302. (*a*)	303. (*c*)	304. (*b*)	305. (*c*)	306. (*c*)	307. (*c*)	308. (*b*)
309. (*d*)	310. (*c*)	311. (*d*)	312. (*d*)	313. (*b*)	314. (*c*)	315. (*a*)
316. (*c*)						

13

Artificial Intelligence and Neural Network

1. AI can be defined as.
   (*a*) A branch of computer science concerned with creating computer systems exhibiting intelligence
   (*b*) A branch of computer science used for creating a databases
   (*c*) A branch of computer science dealing with graph theory
   (*d*) A branch of computer science dealing with artificial data structures

2. Intelligence can be defined as.
   (*a*) Ability to acquire, understand and apply knowledge
   (*b*) Ability to immitate somebody
   (*c*) Ability to cure a person
   (*d*) None of the above

3. GPS stands for.
   (*a*) Generalized Problem Solver
   (*b*) Generate Problem Solution
   (*c*) Generate Present State
   (*d*) None of the above

4. Cognitive science is a.
   (*a*) Combination of AI and psychology
   (*b*) Combination of AI and sociology
   (*c*) Combination of AI and medicine
   (*d*) None of the above

5. Knowledge can be defined as.
   (*a*) Possession of facts and principles gathered for a specific task
   (*b*) Combination of state and facts
   (*c*) Gathering of new information
   (*d*) None of the above

6. Procedural knowledge is
   (*a*) Compiled knowledge to perform some task
   (*b*) Passive knowledge expressed as statements or facts
   (*c*) Knowledge about steps
   (*d*) None of the above

7. Declarative knowledge is.
   (*a*) Compiled knowledge to perform some task
   (*b*) Passive knowledge represented as statements or facts expressed
   (*c*) Knowledge about steps
   (*d*) None of the above

8. Hypothesis is a.
   (*a*) Justified belief that is not known to be true
   (*b*) Belief that is known to be true
   (*c*) Evidence that is known to be true
   (*d*) None of the above

9. Epistemology is.
   (*a*) Study of nature of knowledge
   (*b*) Knowledge about knowledge
   (*c*) Study of types of knowledge
   (*d*) None of the above

10. Meta knowledge is
    (*a*) Study of nature of knowledge
    (*b*) Knowledge about knowledge
    (*c*) Study of types of knowledge
    (*d*) None of the above

11. Which of the following is not level of knowledge representation.
    (*a*) Mental image
    (*b*) Written text
    (*c*) Character string
    (*d*) None of the above

12. Indexing is a method used for.
    (*a*) Knowledge organization
    (*b*) Knowledge acquisition
    (*c*) Knowledge manipulation
    (*d*) Knowledge conclusion

13. Basic building blocks of LISP are.
    (*a*) Character string
    (*b*) Atom, list and string
    (*c*) Atom, character and structure
    (*d*) Character, structure and integer

14. String is defined as.
    (*a*) Group of characters enclosed in double quotation marks
    (*b*) Group of characters
    (*c*) Group of statements
    (*d*) None of the above

15. Which of the following is an invalid atom, in LISP
    (*a*) This_is_a symbolic_atom
    (*b*) Bill
    (*c*) 100004352
    (*d*) (ab)

16. Which of the following is a valid atom, in LISP
    (*a*) (abc)
    (*b*) 123 abc
    (*c*) Mountain_top
    (*d*) above

17. Which of the following is a valid string.
    (*a*) This is not a string
    (*b*) "neither is this
    (*c*) "a b c d e # $ @"
    (*d*) None of the above

18. The top elements of the list (ab (cd) e (+1) are.
    (*a*) a,b (cd), e, (f)
    (*b*) (ab), (cd), e, (f)
    (*c*) ab (cd) e (f)
    (*d*) None of the above

19. In LISP 'S' expressions consists of.
    (*a*) Atoms, lists and strings
    (*b*) Arrays, atoms and lists
    (*c*) Arrays, atoms and lists
    (*d*) None of the above

20. The interpreted code is called.
    (*a*) Read Evaluate Print
    (*b*) Evaluate, Read, Print
    (*c*) Read, Print, Evaluate
    (*d*) None of the above

21. To add three numbers 5 6 9, correct LISP formula is.
    (*a*)⟶ (+5 6 9)
    (*b*) ⟶ (5 6 9)
    (*c*) ⟶ + (5 6 9)
    (*d*) ⟶ + 5 6 9

22. LISP uses.
    (*a*) Infix notation
    (*b*) Prefix notation
    (*c*) Suffix notation
    (*d*) None of the above

23. LISP code to covert Centigrade to Fahrenheit is.
    (*a*) (+(*(/95)50)32)
    (*b*) (+ * / 95 50 32
    (*c*) (((* * / 95) 50) 32)
    (*d*) None of the above

24. Function Setq
    (*a*) Assigns the value of second argument to first argument
    (*b*) Assigns the value of first argument to second argument
    (*c*) Assigns the value of third argument to first argument
    (*d*) None of the above

25. Value returned by (car' (abc)) is.
    (*a*) b
    (*b*) a
    (*c*) c
    (*d*) (abc)

26. (cdr' (abc)) returns.
    (*a*) (bc)
    (*b*) cdr' (abc)
    (*c*) a
    (*d*) None of the above

27. (cons 'a' (bc)) returns.
    (*a*) (abc)
    (*b*) a
    (*c*) (bc)
    (*d*) None of the above

28. (list 'a' (bc)) returns.
    (*a*) (a(bc))
    (*b*) a
    (*c*) (bc)
    (*d*) None of the above

29. The output of ⟶ cons '(*23)'(1) is.
    (*a*) 6
    (*b*) (6 1)
    (*c*) 231
    (*d*) None of the above

30. Output of (car (cdr' (abcd)" is.
    (*a*) A
    (*b*) B
    (*c*) C
    (*d*) D

31. Output of (cdr car '((ab) cd)) is.
    (*a*) A
    (*b*) B
    (*c*) (B)
    (*d*) C

32. ⟶ (append'(*a*)" (bc)' (*d*)) gives output.
    (*a*) A(BC)DE)
    (*b*) A B C D E
    (*c*) (A(BC)DE)
    (*d*) None of the above

33. ⟶ (append'(*a*)' (bc)' (*d*)) gives output.
    (*a*) (ABCD)
    (*b*) A (BC) D E)
    (*c*) (A (BC) (DE)
    (*d*) None of the above

34. ⟶ reverse '(ab(cd)e) gives output
    (*a*) (E(CD)(BA)
    (*b*) (BA(AC)E)
    (*c*) (ABCD)
    (*d*) (EDCBA)

35. The array in LISP can be defined using function.
    (*a*) Make array
    (*b*) Create array
    (*c*) Def array
    (*d*) Int array

36. The function ⟶ (set f my array (make-array '(q))) returns
    (*a*) # (NIL NIL NIL NIL)
    (*b*) # A (NIL NIL NIL NIL)
    (*c*) A (NIL NIL NIL NIL)
    (*d*) None of the above

37. The output of following code⟶(set f (are f my array 2) (samsule) will be.
    (*a*) SAM SUE
    (*b*) My array

(*c*) SAM
(*d*) SUE

38. A mapping function of LISP is.
(*a*) Mapcar
(*b*) Carmap
(*c*) Car
(*d*) Cdr

39. Output of following code will be ⟶ mapcar '1+'(5 10 15)).
(*a*) (6 11 16)
(*b*) (7 11 17)
(*c*) 27
(*d*) None of the above

40. Output of following code ⟶ map car '+' (1234)' (123)).
(*a*) (1 2 3 4)
(*b*) (2 4 6)
(*c*) 1 2 3 4
(*d*) 1 2 3

41. Lambda functions are used for writing.
(*a*) Unnamed functions
(*b*) Named functions
(*c*) Mathematical functions
(v) None of the above

42. Output of following code⟶ define cubelist (lst)
(mapcar # (lambda (x) (*xxx) lst))
CUBELIST → cubelist (1 2 3 4)) will be.
(*a*) (1 8 27 64)
(*b*) (1 4 3 16)
(*c*) (100)
(*d*) None of the above

43. The storage representation of (a(be (*d*))ef) is given by

(*a*) 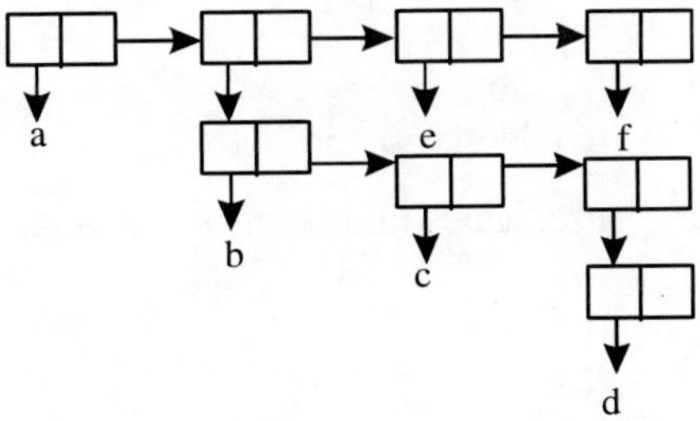

(*b*) 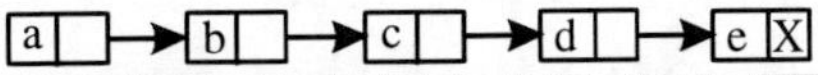

(*c*) 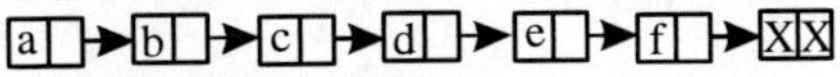

(*d*) None of the above.

44. Prolog rule.
Grandfather (x, z) : parent (x, y), parent (y, z), male (x) defines conditions for
(*a*) x is grandfather of z
(*b*) x is grandfather of y
(*c*) y is grandfather of z
(*d*) None of the above

45. Output of following: code?
[Head/Tail] = [tom, sue, joe, mary] will be.
(*a*) Head = tom
Tail = [sue, joe, mary]
(*b*) Head = tom, sue
Tail = joe, mary
(*c*) Head = tom, sue, mary
Tail = joe
(*d*) None of the above

46. The predicate (atom 'aabb) returns.
(*a*) False
(*b*) True
(*c*) aabb
(v) Illegal

47. Predicate (equal' a (car (ab)) returns.
(*a*) False
(*b*) True

(*c*) ab
(*d*) None of the above

48. Predicate (number p 10ab) returns.
(*a*) Nil
(*b*) 10ab
(*c*) 10
(*d*) None of the above

49. (Odd p 3) returns.
(*a*) False
(*b*) True
(*c*) Nil
(*d*) None of the above

50. Predicate (zeop.000001).
(*a*) Nil
(*b*) Zerop
(*c*) .000001
(*d*) None of the above

51. Predicate (lessp 5312) returns.
(*a*) Nil
(*b*) 1
(*c*) 1 2 3 5
(*d*) None of the above

52. Setq X' (abc) returns.
(*a*) (A B C)
(*b*) X
(*c*) X' a b c
(*d*) None of the above

53. Predicate member (C,[abcd)] returns.
(*a*) Yes
(*b*) No
(*c*) Undefined predicate
(*d*) None of the above

54. Which of the following is not a list manipulation function.
(*a*) Car
(*b*) Cdr
(*c*) *
(*d*) None of the above

55. First order predicate calculus has.
(*a*) Sound mathematical proof
(*b*) Does not have mathematical proof
(*c*) Does not require any proof
(*d*) None of the above

56. The FOPL conversion of statement "All employees of AI software company are programmer is.
(*a*) ∀ X: AI-Soft-co-Emp (x) ⟶ programmer (x))
(*b*) (Ai-soft-Emp(x)⟶ programmer (x)
(*c*) Programmer (x) ⟶ ∀ X:AI-soft-Emp (x)
(*d*) None of the above

57. Prepositions are.
(*a*) Atomic formulas having sentences
(*b*) Valid numbers
(*c*) Nuclear formulas
(*d*) None of the above

58. "It is raining and the wind is blowing" is.
(*a*) Compound proposition
(*b*) Simple proposition
(*c*) Atomic formula
(*d*) None of the above

59. If T and F are formulas, then which of the following is not a valid formula.
(*a*) ((P ↔ Q))
(*b*) (P ⇒ Q)
(*c*) (P V Q)
(*d*) (P & Q)

60. (CP&(>Q∨R)→(Q → S) is
(*a*) Compound formula
(*b*) Simple formula
(*c*) Atomic formula
(*d*) None of the above

61. A statement is satisfiable if.
    (*a*) There is no interpretation for which is ture
    (*b*) There is some interpretation for which is true
    (*c*) For all interpretations it is true
    (*d*) None of the above

62. A sentence has contradiction, if.
    (*a*) There is no interpretation for which it is true
    (*b*) For all interpretations it is true
    (*c*) For some interpretations it is true
    (*d*) None of the above

63. A sentence is a logical consequence of another,
    (a) If it is satisfied for all interpretations
    (*b*) If it is not satisfied for all interpretations
    (*c*) If it is satisfied for few interpretations
    (*d*) None of the above

64. A sentence S is a logical consequence of S_1......... S_n if and only if.
    (*a*) s_1 & s_2 &.....& s_n ——→ s is invalid
    (*b*) s_1 & s_2 &......& s_n ——→ s is valid
    (*c*) s_1 & s_2 &......& s is contradictory
    (*d*) None of the above

65. The rule of distributivity says P & (Q V R) is equivalent (±) to.
    (*a*) (P & Q)V(P & R)
    (*b*) (P & R)∧(P & Q)
    (*c*) (P & Q & R)
    (*d*) (PVQVR)

66. P ↔ Q is equivalent to.
    (*a*) (P → Q) & (Q → P)
    (*b*) (P → P) & (Q → Q)
    (*c*) (P → Q) V (P → Q)
    (*d*) (P → P) Λ (Q → R)

67. ¬(P V Q) is equivalent to.
    (*a*) ¬P & ¬Q
    (*b*) ¬PV¬Q
    (*c*) P & Q
    (*d*) None of the above

68. Modus Ponen rule is.
    (*a*) $\dfrac{\begin{matrix}P\\ P \to Q\end{matrix}}{Q}$
    (*b*) $\dfrac{\begin{matrix}Q\\ P \to Q\end{matrix}}{P}$
    (*c*) $\dfrac{\begin{matrix}P \to Q\\ Q\end{matrix}}{Q}$
    (*d*) $\dfrac{\begin{matrix}P \to Q\\ P\end{matrix}}{P}$

69. According to conjunction rule from P and from Q.
    (*a*) Infer P & Q
    (*b*) Infer ¬P & ¬Q
    (*c*) Infer ¬P V ¬Q
    (*d*) None of the above

70. Which of the following is not a valid wff.
    (*a*) Man (john)
    (*b*) ∀P: P(x) → Q(x)
    (*c*) Man (¬john)
    (*d*) Father of (Q(x))

71. Which of the following is valid wff.
    (a) ∀P : P(x) → Q(x)
    (*b*) Man (¬john)
    (*c*) $\forall X \exists y (P(x) \& Q | y)) \to$

$(R(a) \vee Q(b))$

(*d*) Married (man, woman)

72. A ground atom is.
(*a*) A predicate that has no variable
(*b*) A predicate having only constant values
(*c*) A predicate having only variables
(*d*) None of the above

73. Expression (F∨G) ∨ H is equivalent to.
(*a*) (F∨(G∨H)
(*b*) (F∨G) & (F∨H)
(*c*) P & G
(*d*) None of the above

74. ~[∀x] F[x] is equivalent to.
(*a*) $\exists x\ (\neg F[x])$
(*b*) $\forall x\ (F[x])$
(*c*) ~ F(x)
(*d*) None of the above

75. A wff Q is said to be logical consequence of wffs $P_1, P_2 \ldots\ldots P_n$.
(*a*) If $P_1, P_2\ P_n$ is always true
(*b*) If and only if P_1, P_2, P_n is true under one interpretation and Q is also true
(*c*) Q is always false
(*d*) None of the above

76. Non monotonic reasoning is.
(*a*) When new fact contradict with previous facts
(*b*) When new facts does not contradict with previous knowledge
(*c*) When old facts are not preserved
(*d*) None of the above

77. Truth maintenance system does not have which component.
(*a*) Inference engine
(*b*) Knowledge base
(*c*) Problem solver
(*d*) None of the above

78. Default reasoning is a form of.
(*a*) Non monotonic reasoning
(*b*) Monotonic reasoning
(*c*) Pro-monotonic reasoning
(*d*) None of the above

79. Closed word assumption says.
(*a*) If a proposition cannot be proved it is assumed to be false
(*b*) If a proposition is always false
(*c*) If a proposition is always true
(*d*) If a proposition cannot be prove it is assumed to be true

80. According to closed world assumption, if CONNECT (boston, van horn) cannot be derived from KB, it can be assumed that which is true.
(*a*) CONNECT (Van Horn, Boston)
(*b*) ¬CONNECT (Van Horn, Boston)
(*c*) ¬CONNECT (Boston, Van Horn)
(*c*) None of the above

81. Horn clause is a clause having.
(*a*) At most one positive literal
(*b*) All literal as +ve literal
(*c*) At most one –ve literal
(*d*) None of the above

82. In modal logic R is reflexive, if.
(*a*) $(W_i, W_j) \in R$ for each $W_i \in W$
(*b*) $(W_i, W_j) \in R$ for each $W_i \in W$
(*c*) if $(W_i, W_j) \in R$ than each $(W_j, W_i) \in R$
(*d*) None of the above

83. The intersection operator on fuzzy set is.

(*a*) $\tilde{A} = \tilde{B}$ if and only if $\mu_A(X) = \mu_B(X)$ for all $X \in R$
(*b*) $\mu_{A \cap B}(x) = \min_x \{\mu_A(x), \mu_B(x))]$
(*c*) $\mu_{A \cup B}(x) = \max_x\{\mu_A(x), \mu_B(x)\}$
(*d*) None of the above

84. Over a fuzzy set the identity $\tilde{A} \Lambda \tilde{A} = \tilde{A}$ is called
(*a*) Distributivity
(*b*) Associativity
(*c*) Indempotency
(*d*) None of the above

85. For two events H and E the conditional probability of event H, give that event E has occurred is defined as.
(*a*) P (E/H) = P (H&E)/P(E)
(*b*) P (H/E) = P (H&E)/P(E)
(*c*) P (H,E) = P (H&E)/P(E)
(*d*) None of the above

86. Dampster Shafer theory is used for.
(*a*) Uncertain reasoning
(*b*) Certain reasoning
(*c*) Probabilistic reasoning
(*d*) Statistical reasoning

87. According to Dampster Shafer theory.
(*a*) $P(A) + P(\sim A) = 1$
(*b*) $P(A) + P(\sim A) \leq 1$
(*c*) $P(A) + P(\sim A) \geq 1$
(*d*) $P(A) + P(\sim A) = 0$

88. MYCIN is developed for.
(*a*) Blood pressure
(*b*) Underground minerals
(*c*) Meningitis and infectious blood diseases
(*d*) Ferrite identification

89. Certainty factor is defined as.
(*a*) Major of belief–major of disbelief
(*b*) Major of disbelief–major of belief
(*c*) Major of evidence–major of belief
(*d*) Major of belief–major of evidence

90. The range of CF is.
(*a*) – 1 to 0
(*b*) 0 to 1
(*c*) – 1 to + 1
(*d*) – 00 to +00

91. Adhoc methods are used in.
(*a*) Formal systems
(*b*) Informal systems
(*c*) Outformal systems
(*d*) None of the above

92. Heuristic methods are used to.
(*a*) Reduce the search space
(*b*) To increase the search space
(*c*) To go in a DFS search
(*d*) To go in a BFS search

93. The valid relations of semantic network is.
(*a*) ISA
(*b*) Member – of
(*c*) Subset – of
(*d*) All of the above

94. Which of the following is generic –generic relationship.
(*a*) Subset – superset
(*b*) Set membership
(*c*) Prediction
(*d*) Abstraction

95. Which of the following is generic individual relationship.
(*a*) Conceptual containment
(*b*) Predication
(*c*) Sets and their type
(*d*) Role value restriction

96. The data structure used for semantic network is.
(*a*) Tree

(b) Graph
(c) Array
(d) Queue

97. Conceptual graphs are used for.
(a) Representing concepts
(b) Representing time
(c) Representing space
(d) None of the above

98. The representation of sentence "Every car has an engine" is
(a) ∀x∃ Y: (CAR (x)→(ENGINE (y) & PART (x, y)))
(b) ∃x∀ Y: (CAR(x)→(ENGINE (y) & PART (x, y)))
(c) ∀x∀ Y: (CAR (x)→(ENGINE (x) & PART (x, y)))
(d) None of the above

99. "Restrict" graph formation operator.
(a) Produces a duplicate copy CG
(b) Modifies a graph by replacing a type lable of a concept
(c) Combines two identical graphs
(d) None of the above

100. "Simplify" graph formation operator.
(a) Eliminates one of two identical relations in a conceptual graph
(b) Combines two identical graphs
(c) Produces a duplicate copy of conceptual graph
(d) None of the above

101. Frame structures are used to.
(a) Represent a mental model of stereotypical situation
(b) Temporal concept
(c) Spatial concept
(d) None of the above

102. Frames consists of.
(a) Collection of slot and slot values
(b) Collection of nodes and arcs
(c) Collection of arrays
(d) None of the above

103. Property list is a method to implement.
(a) Frames
(b) Conceptual graphs
(c) Scripts
(d) None of the above

104. 'EXPEL' primitive action indicates.
(a) Build information
(b) Expulsion of any thing from body
(c) Transfer of abstract entity
(d) Transfer of mental information

105. PTRANS represents.
(a) Physical transfer of one location to another
(b) Focusing attention of an object
(c) Grasping object tightly
(d) None of the above

106. Which of the following is not a valid conceptual case.
(a) Objective case
(b) Instrumental case
(c) Recipient case
(d) None of the above

107. Conceptual dependency structure of "bird flew" is.
(a) PP ⇔ ACT
(b) PP ⇔ PP
(c) ACT ⇔ PP
(d) None of the above

108. Which of the following is not a valid conceptual tense.
(a) Interrogative
(b) Conditional
(c) Negative
(d) None of the above

109. Combinatorial explosion problem is encountered in.
    (*a*) Chess
    (*b*) Traveling salesman
    (*c*) 8 Queen
    (*d*) None of the above
110. In uninformed search.
    (*a*) No preference is given to the order of successor node generation
    (*b*) Heuristic identifies next node
    (*c*) The best node is explored first
    (*d*) None of the above
111. In informed search.
    (*a*) Information about the problem space is used to compute a preference among children for exploration
    (*b*) No preference is given to find order of successor node generation
    (*c*) Depth first search technique is used
    (*d*) None of the above
112. For a 'n' city travelling salesman problem, the order of traverses would be
    (*a*) 0(n)
    (*b*) 0 (log n)
    (*c*) 0 (n log n)
    (*d*) (2^n)
113. The travelling salesman problem can be solved using.
    (*a*) Hill climbing
    (*b*) Means ends analysis
    (*c*) Constraint satisfaction
    (*d*) None of the above
114. The time complexity of breadth first search is.
    (*a*) $O(b^d)$
    (*b*) $O(d^b)$
    (*c*) O(bd)
    (*d*) O(b/d)
115. "Shopping in a supermarket" concept can be represented by.
    (*a*) Frame
    (*b*) Script
    (*c*) Conceptual dependency
    (*d*) None of the above
116. In A* algorithm the algorithm is said to be admissible:
    (*a*) If it is guaranteed to return an optimal solution
    (*b*) If it always terminates with a solution
    (*c*) If a good heuristic function is used
    (*d*) None of the above
117. The algorithm is said to be complete if.
    (*a*) It always terminates with a solution
    (*b*) If it guarantees to return optimal solution
    (*c*) If it uses a good heuristics
    (*d*) None of the above
118. An algorithm is optimal if.
    (*a*) A dominates all members of the class
    (*b*) If it guarantees a good heuristics
    (*c*) If it returns optimal solution
    (*d*) None of the above
119. An algorithm is said to be more informed if.
    (*a*) It returns the solution in least number of steps
    (*b*) If it returns the solution in more number of steps
    (*c*) If it does not return a solution
    (*d*) None of the above
120. Distance between two fuzzy sets $\tilde{A}$ and $\tilde{B}$ is defined as.

(a) $d(\tilde{A},\tilde{B}) = 1/n\left[\sum_{i=1}^{n}\mu_A(x_i) - \mu_B(X_i))^2\right]^{1/2}$

(b) $d(\tilde{A},\tilde{B}) = \left[\sum_{i=1}^{n}(\mu_A(x_i) - \mu_B(X_1))^2\right]^{1/2}$

(c) $d(\tilde{A},\tilde{B}) = 1/n^2\sum_{i=1}^{n}\mu_A(x_i) - \mu_B(X_i))^2]^{1/2}$

(d) None of the above.

121. In Neural Network, the network capacity is defined as
(a) The traffic carrying capacity of network
(b) The number of patterns that can be stored and recalled in a net
(c) The number of nodes in a net
(d) None of the above

122. The competitive n/w is defined as
(a) It is a group of input patterns clustered in a way inherent to input data
(b) Two parallel networks having competitive edges
(c) Network designed for online competitive exams
(d) None of the above

123. Is BPN an example of competitive network
(a) Yes
(b) No
(c) Cannot be determined
(d) Sometimes

124. Learning vector quantization method is related with
(a) Supervised learning
(b) Unsupervised learning
(c) Hope field learning
(d) None of the above

125. Self organizing networks can be defined as
(a) These are the systems in which system is not given any external indication as to what correct responses should be
(b) Network used for an organization
(c) Network privately used by group of people
(d) None of the above

126. Which of the following is not a buffering strategy
(a) Finite bound buffer
(b) Single message buffer
(c) Unbounded capacity buffer
(d) None of the above

127. The top down design approach
(a) Provides the solution of a problem starting from main
(b) Starts solution starting from bottom
(c) Is an integrated approach of problem solving
(d) None of the above

128. Which of the following is not a good learning method
(a) Learning from an instructor
(b) Learning with a computer
(c) Learning with a manual
(d) None of the above

129. Cognitive schema is
(a) Mental pattern that a person uses to interpret future experience of a reading program

(*b*) It is a recent art about designing of program
(*c*) It is an expert system shell
(*d*) None of the above

130. Open ended questionnaires are advantageous because
(*a*) They give prescribed reaction to the user
(*b*) They gather the user's actual feedback through questionnaries
(*c*) They are not useful
(*d*) Cannot be said

131. Job security, compensation, independence are
(*a*) External motivations that affect the software users
(*b*) Internal motivations that affect the software users
(*c*) Do not affect software user
(*d*) None of the above

132. Task list can be defined as.
(*a*) Lists the features in task oriented languages that represents the uses of program by intended users
(*b*) It is professional group managing the tasks
(*c*) It is list defining tasks
(*d*) None of the above

133. What is alpha draft in document production process.
(*a*) It represents first complete document, including all font matter, test, graphics, appendixes, indexes
(*b*) It is a draft prepared before beta draft
(*c*) It is draft prepared in greek language
(*d*) None of the above

134. Main advantages of document review plan is.
(*a*) It encourages to think the process through by making it a goal driven process
(*b*) It acts as a communication device for review meeting, opens up the process to colleagues
(*c*) Both (*a*) and (*b*) above
(*d*) None of the above

ANSWERS

1. (*a*)	2. (*a*)	3. (*a*)	4. (*a*)	5. (*a*)	6. (*a*)	7. (*b*)
8. (*a*)	9. (*a*)	10. (*b*)	11. (*c*)	12. (*a*)	13. (*b*)	14. (*a*)
15. (*d*)	16. (*c*)	17. (*a*)	18. (*a*)	19. (*a*)	20. (*a*)	21. (*a*)
22. (*b*)	23. (*a*)	24. (*a*)	25. (*b*)	26. (*a*)	27. (*a*)	28. (*a*)
29. (*b*)	30. (*b*)	31. (*c*)	32. (*a*)	33. (*a*)	34. (*a*)	35. (*a*)
36. (*b*)	37. (*a*)	38. (*a*)	39. (*a*)	40. (*a*)	41. (*a*)	42. (*d*)
43. (*a*)	44. (*a*)	45. (*a*)	46. (*b*)	47. (*b*)	48. (*a*)	49. (*b*)
50. (*a*)	51. (*a*)	52. (*a*)	53. (*a*)	54. (*d*)	55. (*a*)	56. (*a*)
57. (*c*)	58. (*a*)	59. (*a*)	60. (*a*)	61. (*b*)	62. (*a*)	63. (*a*)
64. (*b*)	65. (*a*)	66. (*a*)	67. (*a*)	68. (*a*)	69. (*a*)	70. (*a*)
71. (*c*)	72. (*a*)	73. (*a*)	74. (*a*)	75. (*b*)	76. (*b*)	77. (*d*)

78. (*a*)	79. (*a*)	80. (*b*)	81. (*a*)	82. (*a*)	83. (*b*)	84. (*c*)
85. (*b*)	86. (*a*)	87. (*b*)	88. (*c*)	89. (*a*)	90. (*c*)	91. (*a*)
92. (*a*)	93. (*d*)	94. (*a*)	95. (*b*)	96. (*b*)	97. (*a*)	98. (*a*)
99. (*b*)	100. (*a*)	101. (*a*)	102. (*a*)	103. (*a*)	104. (*b*)	105. (*a*)
106. (*a*)	107. (*a*)	108. (*c*)	109. (*a*)	110. (*a*)	111. (*a*)	112. (*a*)
113. (*b*)	114. (*a*)	115. (*b*)	116. (*c*)	117. (*b*)	118. (*a*)	119. (*a*)
120. (*a*)	121. (*b*)	122. (*a*)	123. (*a*)	124. (*a*)	125. (*a*)	126. (*d*)
127. (*a*)	128. (*d*)	129. (*a*)	130. (*a*)	131. (*a*)	132. (*a*)	133. (*a*)
134. (*c*)						

14

Internet Technology

1. Which of the following is not an example of a non-commercial Spam?
   (*a*) Blog Spam
   (*b*) Hobbit Spam
   (*c*) Spam as denial of service
   (*d*) Gaming Spam

2. Commercial spamming started in armed forces on March 5, 1994, when a pair of lawyer, Laurence Canter and Martha Siegel begin using Usenet posting. The particular incident was commonly termed after the subject line of the posting as?
   (*a*) Flooding
   (*b*) Green card Spam
   (*c*) Monty python Spam Sketch
   (*d*) Excessive multiple posting

3. The Spam cost such as low productivity, opportunity cost and fraud etc. are borne by?
   (*a*) Public
   (*b*) Spammers
   (*c*) Internet Service Provider
   (*d*) A and C both

4. In the context of Spam, which of the following is a computer system that contains Email address created specifically for the purpose of collecting Spam?
   (*a*) Blackist
   (*b*) Inbox shield
   (*c*) Honey pot
   (*d*) None of the above

5. Which one of the following Anti-Spam filtration technology is not an example of inbound protection schemes?
   (*a*) URL – based filter
   (*b*) Heuristics scheme
   (*c*) Web traffic filtration
   (*d*) End point filtration

6. Which one of these is a rule-based problem solving techniques, looking for tellatale signs in email message that indicates the message is spam or phishing?
   (*a*) Finger printing scheme
   (*b*) Bayesian Filter
   (*c*) IP address blacklist
   (*d*) Heuristic scheme

7. In which of the following form of media, Spammer makes use of instant messaging system such as AOL, instant messenger or ICQ?
   (*a*) Mobile Phone Spam
   (*b*) Messaging Spam
   (*c*) Spamdexing
   (*d*) Hobbit Spam

8. Which of the following does not represent a form of spamming?
   (*a*) Blog Spam
   (*b*) Chat Spam
   (*c*) Spam Bully
   (*d*) Newsgroup Spam

9. Which of the following represent the emerging classes of messaging abuse in the mobile environment.
   (*a*) Smishing
   (*b*) Phising
   (*c*) Viruses
   (*d*) Spamming

10. The innocent E-mail that get mistakenly identified as Spams, while applying Spam filtering techniques are known as?
   (*a*) Legitimate e mail
   (*b*) True positives
   (*c*) False positives
   (*d*) None of the above

11. "Spam is prevalent on the Internet because that transaction cost of electronic communication is racially less than any alternate form of communication". Is the given statement?
   (*a*) True
   (*b*) False
   (*c*) Irrelevant
   (*d*) None of the above

12. Using a slightly tweaked Bayesian filter, one can filter present-day spam acceptably well using nothing more than a Bayesian combination of the Spam probabilities of?
   (*a*) Individual words
   (*b*) Special Character
   (*c*) List of address
   (*d*) False positives

13. The real advantage of using Bayesian approach to filter Spam is?
   (*a*) You have top read thousand of Spam
   (*b*) You don't know what you are measuring
   (*c*) You know what you are measuring
   (*d*) None of the above

14. Which one of these is an ADHOC, All volunteer organization created by Netizens to advocate for a legislative solution to the problem of UCL (Spam).
   (*a*) ISPA (International Society of Bayesian Analysis)
   (*b*) CAUCE (Coalition Against Unsolicited Commercial email)
   (*c*) WORD PRESS
   (*d*) CAN – Spam

15. Select the right option:
   (*a*) Spam is unsolicited bulk E mail
   (*b*) Spam is an extremely efficient and cost-effective way to distribute message
   (*c*) Cancelable Usenet Spam is a type of Spam
   (*d*) Spam is not is the subject of legislation in any jurisdiction
      (*a*) Only (*a*) is true
      (*b*) Only (*d*) is false
      (*c*) (*a*),(*b*) and (*d*) are true
      (*d*) All are true

16. The practice on the world wide web of modifying HTML pages to increase the chance of them being placed high on search engine relevancy list is commonly known as?
   (*a*) Spamdexing
   (*b*) Wiki Spam
   (*c*) Chat Spam
   (*d*) Spam as denial of service

17. There are several free and commercial security solutions on the market that plug into the users Email software and filter Spam/ Phising message from incoming

mails. One of the solutions is invoked when a user reads their email and is called?
(*a*) Forgery Detection
(*b*) End point filtration
(*c*) Policy consideration
(*d*) Out bound protection

18. With reference to spamming what is the full form of UCE?
(*a*) Unsolicited Common Email
(*b*) Undesired Commercial Email
(*c*) Underline Common Email
(*d*) Unsolicited Commercial Email

19. For Spammers to best Bayesian filter, they would require?
(*a*) To make their email unique
(*b*) To stop using individual offense word
(*c*) To make their mail indistinguishable from ordinary mails
(*d*) All of the above

20. Which one of these terms are used to define Spamming on Web logs, which takes advantage of the open nature of comments in the bogging software?
(*a*) Mobile phone spasm
(*b*) Blam
(*c*) Hobbit Spam
(*d*) In Gaming

21. Internet is.
(*a*) Network of network that connects computers all over the world
(*b*) Connection of two PCs situated in two countries
(*c*) Network restricted within an area
(*d*) None of the above

22. Web page is.
(*a*) A page of the book on web technology
(*b*) Is a HTML document that is stored in web server
(*c*) A hard copy of server pages print out
(*d*) None of the above

23. www.annauniv.com is.
(*a*) Webpage
(*b*) Website
(*c*) Can be anything depending upon the context
(*d*) None of the above

24. Index.html is a.
(*a*) Webpage
(*b*) Website
(*c*) Depends upon the context
(*d*) None of the above

25. Which of the following is not type of website.
(*a*) Portal
(*b*) Web guides
(*c*) Search engine
(*d*) None of the above

26. Portal is.
(*a*) Website providing web categories
(*b*) Website that provides numerous free service that enhances web experience
(*c*) Website to search some keyword
(*d*) None of the above

27. Web guide is.
(*a*) Website, which is a system of categories and sub categories that organizes links to the web pages
(*b*) A guidebook explaining web concept
(*c*) A guidebook explaining Java concept

(*d*) None of the above

28. Search engine is.
(*a*) Website used by intelligence agencies
(*b*) Website to find out any specific information
(*c*) Website used by universities
(*d*) None of the above

29. The tag in HTML means.
(*a*) It is a signal to browser that it should throw text upon the screen
(*b*) It give signal to server
(*c*) Both (*a*) and (*b*)
(*d*) None of the above

30. Cookies is.
(*a*) Mechanism for storing persistent data on client in the file called cookies
(*b*) A product made in bakery
(*c*) Mechanism for storing a information on the net
(*d*) None of the above

31. The use of 'This' operator keyword is.
(*a*) It returns current object
(*b*) It creates a new object
(*c*) It kills an object
(*d*) None of the above

32. Use of "new" operator is.
(*a*) It can be used to create an instance of a user defined object type of one that built in object type array
(*b*) It returns the current object
(*c*) Used for running a new program
(*d*) None of the above

33. URL is.
(*a*) Uniform Resource Locator
(*b*) Universal Resource Locator
(*c*) Unified Register Language
(*d*) Unified Resource Language

34. Web browser is.
(*a*) Software tool that computers used for communication with server on Internet
(*b*) Hardware tool used to browse the internet
(*c*) Software tool used to configure a web server
(*d*) None of the above

35. ISDN stand for.
(*a*) Integrated Society Discreet Network
(*b*) Integrated Services Digital Network
(*c*) Integrated Society Digital Network
(*d*) None of the above

36. Basic data rate of ISDN has.
(*a*) Two 64 kbps B channels and 1 D channel
(*b*) Two D channel and one B channel
(*c*) 2, B channel and 32 D channel
(*d*) None of the above

37. Two categories of DSL are.
(*a*) a symmetric and asymmetric DSL
(*b*) Unidirectional and Bidirectional DSL
(*c*) Broadband and Baseband DSL
(*d*) None of the above

38. Mail Server.
(*a*) Move and store mail over corporate network
(*b*) Software designed to enable users to collaborate
(*c*) Used for distribution and delivery of news
(*d*) None of the above

39. Web server.
(*a*) Computer system that delivers web pages

(*b*) Delivery news
(*c*) Provide option for those seeking real time discussion capabilities
(*d*) None of the above

40. SMTP protocol.
(*a*) Sends email message between servers
(*b*) Sits between client and server
(*c*) Transmits news to all clients
(*d*) None of the above

41. Router.
(*a*) Controls the red light of crossing
(*b*) Determines path of travel for a datagram in TCP/IP
(*c*) Connects multiple computers in a network
(*d*) None of the above

42. In Windows NT the IP address of router is determined by.
(*a*) WINI PCFE•EXE
(*b*) WIN, NT•EXE
(*c*) WINADD•EXE
(*d*) WINIPADD•EXE

43. WAP stands for.
(*a*) Wireless Application Protocol
(*b*) Wired Application Protocol
(*c*) Wireless Access Protocol
(*d*) None of the above

44. Bluetooth is.
(*a*) Short-range radio technology used to perform synchronization between net devices and other devices
(*b*) It is a VLSI chip making technique
(*c*) An AI technique
(*d*) None of the above

45. SOAP, a Microsoft designed protocol, stands for
(*a*) Serial Object Access Protocol
(*b*) Simple Object Access Protocol
(*c*) Synchronized Object Access Protocol
(*d*) Single Object Access Protocol

46. The IP address has.
(*a*) 3 separate fields
(*b*) 2 separate fields
(*c*) 4 separate fields
(*d*) None of the above

47. Depending upon the traffic handling capacity of class A,B,C network which of the following is true.
(*a*) Large, moderate, small
(*b*) Small, moderate, large
(*c*) Moderate, small, large
(*d*) Moderate, large, small

48. 50.150.H1..H2 is a.
(*a*) Class A network
(*b*) Class B network
(*c*) Class C network
(*d*) None of the above

49. In the URL http://www.stxavie.com/index.html the domain name is.
(*a*) http
(*b*) www
(*c*) stxavier
(*d*) index

50. Gopher Service.
(*a*) Designed to act as a distributed document delivery system
(*b*) Is a multiple access portal
(*c*) Is a email service
(*d*) None of the above

51. Instant messaging.
(*a*) Enables to create private chat room
(*b*) Sends an sms instantly

(*c*) Sends a call instantly
(*d*) None of the above

52. Bulletin Board system.
(*a*) Is electronic message centre which provides information about electronic goods
(*b*) Is news creating agency
(*c*) Is a message board display system
(*d*) None of the above

53. Usenet news Group service.
(*a*) A service related with Internet relay chat
(*b*) Worldwide bulletin board system that can be accessed through Internet
(*c*) An instant messaging service
(*d*) None of the above

54. MAPI
(*a*) Multiple Application Programming Interface
(*b*) Messaging Application Programming Interface
(*c*) Multiple Access Protocol Interface
(*d*) All of the above

55. A web page cannot be created using.
(*a*) Java Server pages
(*b*) Active Server pages
(*c*) Active USP pages
(*d*) Java services

56. Cookie are.
(*a*) Messages that a web server transmits to a web browser
(*b*) A bakery product
(*c*) A message that client transmits to server
(*d*) None of the above

57. Which of the following is not a reason to create cookies.
(*a*) To collect demographic information
(*b*) To personalize users experience on the web site
(*c*) To keep track of what advertisements it lets you see
(*d*) None of the above

58. Which of the following is not a valid cookie parameter.
(*a*) Name of cookie
(*b*) Expiration date of cookie
(*c*) Domain
(*d*) None of the above

59. URL starting with https: require.
(*a*) Secure socked layer connection
(*b*) URL cannot start with https
(*c*) A www security
(*d*) Indicates a website starting with 'S'

60. Public key cryptography was invented by.
(*a*) Whitfield Diffie and Martin Hellman
(*b*) Network team of Motorola engineers
(*c*) Microsoft.team
(*d*) None of the above

61. Electronic data interchange.
(*a*) Indicates transfer to data between different companies using network
(*b*) Data interchange done at electronic level
(*c*) The data used in electronics industry
(*d*) None of the above

62. Digital cash.
(*a*) Is a system that allows a person to pay for goods by transmitting a number from one computer to another

(*b*) Cash in the chained form
(*c*) Cash in credit card format
(*d*) Cash in smart card format

63. Key difference between digital cash and credit cash system is.
(*a*) The digital cash bears serial number similar to on real dollar numbers
(*b*) Digital cash certificates can be reused
(*c*) Both (*a*) and (*b*)
(*d*) Digital cash and credit cards systems are same

64. Digital signature.
(*a*) A digital code that can be attached to an electronically transmitted message that uniquely identifies the sender
(*b*) It is a scanned code in digital form
(*c*) It is signature done using digital device
(*d*) None of the above

65. In HTML the links are not used
(*a*) To inform the browser about previous document
(*b*) To inform the browser about the next document
(*c*) To inform the location of base document location
(*d*) None of the above

66. Banner is.
(*a*) Fixed part of page that will stay out the screen when we scroll the text of the page
(*b*) An advertisement displayed on the roadside
(*c*) A software that is used to create a poster
(*d*) None of the above

67. In HTML src attributes specifies.
(*a*) Sequences of picture
(*b*) Sources of picture
(*c*) Serial order of picture
(*d*) None of the above

68. In Nested frame sets.
(*a*) First the window is row-wise divided into two frames then bottom frame is column wise divided into frames
(*b*) Bit is frames inside frame
(*c*) The window is not divided
(*d*) None of the above

69. Which of the following is not a attribute of form tag.
(*a*) Action
(*b*) Method
(*c*) Exe type
(*d*) None of the above

70. Which of the following is not a valid Java integer?
(*a*) 25
(*b*) True
(*c*) 0 × 2A
(*d*) None of the above

71. String is.
(*a*) Any list of characters given within single or double quotes
(*b*) The ASCII value character
(*c*) Is a user defined data structure
(*d*) None of the above

72. A variable having global scope means.
(*a*) It can be accessed within function
(*b*) It can be accessed from any function on the page
(*c*) It can be accessed by other files
(*d*) It can be accessed by other language program

73. A Java script object is composition of.
(*a*) Methods and properties
(*b*) Functions and procedures
(*c*) Methods and operands
(*d*) Instructions and properties

74. Which of the following is a valid Java event.
(*a*) HTML document is loaded to the browser
(*b*) A button on web page is clicked
(*c*) A radio button is selected
(*d*) All of the above

75. The purpose of method focus () is.
(*a*) To set the cursor focus to the desired object
(*b*) To create the Java Applet for a function
(*c*) To provide a focus for functionality of an object
(*d*) None of the above

76. Select () method is used for.
(*a*) Select the text in a text field
(*b*) Select the file from Java script
(*c*) Select an operand from the database
(*d*) None of the above

77. Parse Int. () function.
(*a*) Converts text input into integer
(*b*) Outputs the equivalent float value of the number
(*c*) Output the equivalent character value
(*d*) None of the above

78. Constructor is a.
(*a*) Special type of function used to create an object
(*b*) Special type of operator to construct a program
(*c*) Special type of compiler
(*d*) None of the above

79. Consider the code

```
radius = 1;
   area = PI* radius * radius;
```

it is a
(*a*) Circumference construction
(*b*) Area of a circle construction
(*c*) Area of a polygon code
(*d*) None of the above

80. Which of the following is a client responsibility of JSP.
(*a*) Business process
(*b*) Data validation
(*c*) Service request to server
(*d*) None of the above

81. Which of the following is a server side responsibility.
(*a*) Business process
(*b*) Data validation
(*c*) Service request to server
(*d*) None of the above

82. JSP.
(*a*) Provides a simplified way to create a web page that display dynamically generated control
(*b*) Technology to create a HTML script
(*c*) Both (*a*) and (*b*)
(*d*) None of the above

83. JSPs are.
(*a*) HTML page with special JSP tags embedded
(*b*) Server side page
(*c*) Java code written in C sharp
(*d*) None of the above

84. Which of the following is not a JSP tag.
(*a*) Declaration tag
(*b*) Expression tag
(*c*) Directive tag
(*d*) None of the above

85. JSP tag.
<%
Private int counter = 0
Private string get account (int account no):
% > is
(*a*) Expression tag
(*b*) Declaration tag
(*c*) Action tag
(*d*) Script let tag

86. JSP tag.
Data: <% = new Java.util.Date ()%> is
(*a*) Declaration tag
(*b*) Expression tag
(*c*) Script tag
(*d*) None of the above

87. <%@ page auto flush = "true"%>
This code performs the function of
(*a*) Flush the output buffer when full
(*b*) Does the page make use of sessions
(*c*) Developer uses to inform attribute to add information
(*d*) None of the above

88. Include directive.
(*a*) Allows JSP developer to include contents of a file inside other
(*b*) Includes the client coding into server
(*c*) Include the preprocessor directive
(*d*) None of the above

89. JDBC stands for.
(*a*) Java Data Business Connectivity
(*b*) Java Data Base Connectivity
(*c*) Joint Data Base Connectivity
(*d*) Joint Data Business Company

90. Servlet is a.
(*a*) Java component that can be plugged into Java enabled web server to provide custom services
(*b*) Java code written and stored in library to be used by others
(*c*) Database of Java
(*d*) Protocol designed to the code of Java

91. Servlet work on.
(*a*) Request/response processing model
(*b*) Client/server model
(*c*) Three tier architecture
(*d*) None of the above

92. Servlet API provides.
(*a*) Link between server and servlet
(*b*) Provide link between servlet and Java code
(*c*) Provide link between Java and JDMC
(*d*) Provide interface between JDBC and JMBC

93. CGI is.
(*a*) Common Gateway Interface
(*b*) Computer Generated interface
(*c*) Computer Gateway Interface
(*d*) Computer Generated Interruption

94. In which of the following fields API does not provide support.
(*a*) Servlet life cycle management
(*b*) Access to servlet context
(*c*) Utility classes
(*d*) None of the above

95. Int () method is.
(*a*) Invoked when a servlet is first loaded
(*b*) Invoked to edit a Java code

(*c*) Invoked at the starting of a function
(*d*) None of the above

96. Destroy () method, is
(*a*) Called to allow your servlet to clean up any resources
(*b*) Called to edit a Java code
(*c*) Called to destroy Java code
(*d*) None of the above

97. A HTML file starts with the tag.
(*a*) <TITLE>
(*b*) <BODY>
(*c*) <HEAD>
(*d*) <HTML>

98. Computers owned and operated by business organization form a part of the.
(*a*) .Com domain
(*b*) .Edu domain
(*c*) .Mil domain
(*d*) .Gov domain

99. FTP is.
(*a*) A person
(*b*) A file
(*c*) A program for copying files from one computer to another
(*d*) An operating system

100. The internet protocol (IP).
(*a*) Ensures that connections are maintained between computers
(*b*) Handles software computer address
(*c*) Finds the quickest route between two computers
(*d*) None of the above

101. Main protocol used in Internet.
(*a*) IPX/SPX
(*b*) TCP/IP
(*c*) Token bus
(*d*) X.25

102. Web pages are uniquely defined using.
(*a*) IP addresses
(*b*) URL
(*c*) Domain
(*d*) Filename

103. For IP addresses which of the following is false
(*a*) May be written as four decimal numbers separated
(*b*) May be static
(*c*) May be dynamic
(*d*) May be random

104. Which one of the following statement is not correct for digital signature.
(*a*) It is a mechanism for authentication
(*b*) It is the scanned image of ones' signaturs
(*c*) It is created by encrypting information
(*d*) It cannot be duplicated

105. Indicate which is correct statement.
(*a*) Real Audio is plugged in multimedia
(*b*) Web casting is one kind of firewall
(*c*) ASP is a protocol
(*d*) There is no difference between UDP and TCP

106. Search engine help user.
(*a*) Find web pages on a given subject
(*b*) Find queries on a given subject.
(*c*) Send the email
(*d*) Chatting over computer

107. Search engine is a.
(*a*) Hardware
(*b*) Software

(*c*) Both
(*d*) None of the above

108. Which of the following is not a component of search engine.
(*a*) Search engine software
(*b*) Spider software
(*c*) Algorithm
(*d*) Stack

109. Web Browser search for information using.
(*a*) Keywords
(*b*) Phrase and Boolean logic
(*c*) Logic Gates
(*d*) None of the above

110. Search engine works using.
(*a*) Querying
(*b*) Ranking
(*c*) Indexing
(*d*) All of the above

111. Meta data is.
(*a*) Data about data
(*b*) Data with symbolic name "Meta".
(*c*) It is a special data type
(*d*) Structure called meta

112. Which is next job search engine.
(*a*) Jobfoxter.com
(*b*) Simply hired.com
(*c*) Monster.com
(*d*) Ask me now

113. SEO stands for
(*a*) Search Engine Optimization
(*b*) Search Engine Opcode
(*c*) Search Engineering Operation
(*d*) Search Engine Operation

114. SEO functions for
(*a*) Process of improving the ranking of a website
(*b*) Process of visibility of website
(*c*) Both (a) and (b)
(*d*) None of the above

115. SEO is mainly categorised into following types
(*a*) 2
(*b*) 3
(*c*) 4
(*d*) 5

116. Search engine software use algorithm.
(*a*) For determining rank of a website
(*b*) For sending message over computer
(*c*) For performing operation on computer
(*d*) None of the above

117. Crawlers are also known as.
(*a*) Spiders
(*b*) Robots
(*c*) Both (*a*) and (*b*)
(*d*) None of the above

118. Gateway pages improve.
(*a*) A website search engine placement
(*b*) A semantic accuracy
(*c*) Syntactic accuracy
(*d*) Resolution of page

119. Bridge pages are also known as
(*a*) Doorway pages
(*b*) Gateway pages
(*c*) Both (a) and (b)
(*d*) None of the above

120. HTML stands for.
(*a*) Hypertext Makeup Language
(*b*) Hypertext Markup Level
(*c*) Hypertext Markup Language
(*d*) Typotext Makeup level

121. Metatag is.
(*a*) Element of HTML

(*b*) Element of 'c'
(*c*) Element of Operating System
(*d*) Element of assembler

122. Meta search engine.
(*a*) Allow user to conduct a search across 2 or more search engine and directories in one go.
(*b*) Search performed by Keyword 'Meta'
(*c*) Search performed in many steps
(*d*) It is a search performed by Police to find criminal

123. Search engine marketing is
(*a*) Practice of marketing and advertising through the search engine
(*b*) Marking of search engine
(*c*) Mark chains with name search engine
(*d*) None of the above

124. Bot is another word for.
(*a*) Spider
(*b*) Spammer
(*c*) Cloaker
(*d*) None of the above

125. Cloaking is situation where.
(*a*) Contents of web page differ depending on who is asking for the content
(*b*) Two computers are connected
(*c*) The time is told using clock
(*d*) An automated time generator

126. Ctr stands for.
(*a*) Click through rate
(*b*) Clock tick rate
(*c*) It is control key
(*d*) Click tick rate

127. Cpc stands for.
(*a*) Cost per clock
(*b*) Cost per click
(*c*) Cost per computer
(*d*) Cost per check

128. KEI
(*a*) Keyword effectiveness index
(*b*) Keyword Expressiveness
(*c*) Keyword Excess Interest
(*d*) Keyword Excess Intrusion

129. Rank means
(*a*) A web page position in search results
(*b*) A web page position in computer display
(*c*) A rank given to student in online examination
(*d*) None of the above

130. RSS stands for.
(*a*) Rich site summary
(*b*) Real simple syndication
(*c*) Both (*a*) and (*b*)
(*d*) None of the above

131. SEM stands for
(*a*) Search Engine Marketing
(*b*) Search Engine Markup Language
(*c*) Search Effective Means
(*d*) Search Engine Means

132. Search string means.
(*a*) Words entered to do search
(*b*) Words returned by search
(*c*) Strings allowed in Java
(*d*) Strings allowed in computer Languages

133. SERPS stands for
(*a*) Search Engine Result Pages
(*b*) Search End Result Produced
(*c*) Search Effective Results Produced
(*d*) Search Effective Result page

134. URL
    (*a*) Uniform Resource Locator
    (*b*) Unified Resource Locator
    (*c*) Unified Resource Locomotive
    (*d*) Uniform Rate Location

135. Spamming is.
    (*a*) Technique used to trick search engines into ranking a website high up in their research results
    (*b*) Technique to perform formatting in e-mail
    (*c*) Technique to perform On line automotion
    (*d*) Technique to perform search over Internet

136. Is there simple solution to top placement, in search result
    (*a*) It can be done using spamming
    (*b*) It can be done using normal algorithm
    (*c*) It can not be done
    (*d*) None of the above

137. What is search engine.
    (*a*) It is a railway engine
    (*b*) It is a hardware
    (*c*) It is a software
    (*d*) It is a kind to steam engine

138. Are all search engines the same.
    (*a*) Yes
    (*b*) No
    (*c*) In some aspects
    (*d*) Can't be said

139. What is directory?
    (*a*) It is a repository of information regarding file structure
    (*b*) It contains data
    (*c*) It contains program
    (*d*) None of the above

140. What is ppc?
    (*a*) Program Pay check
    (*b*) Program performance cost
    (*c*) Pay per click
    (*d*) Process performing code

141. How does search engine find websites?
    (*a*) Using their URL
    (*b*) Using HTML program
    (*c*) Using their content
    (*d*) None of the above

142. SEO stands for
    (*a*) Search Engine optimisation
    (*b*) System Efficiency optimisation
    (*c*) System Effective Operation
    (*d*) Search Effective Operation

143. What do you mean by search engine friendly Webpage
    (*a*) Webpage displaying
    (*b*) a friendship Webside friendly content
    (*c*) A Webpage prepared according to search engine guidelines
    (*d*) None of the above

144. Each search engine has its.
    (*a*) Own indexing algorithm
    (*b*) Own portal
    (*c*) Own protocol
    (*d*) Own passoword

145. Better SEO means.
    (*a*) Higher the ranking
    (*b*) Lower ranking
    (*c*) Higher effeciency
    (*d*) Higher accuracy

146. Website is a collection of.
    (*a*) HTML documents
    (*b*) Graphics files
    (*c*) Audio and visual files
    (*d*) All of the above

147. Internet is governed by.
    (*a*) IETF
    (*b*) Gnternic
    (*c*) IVB
    (*d*) None of the above

148. Internet is.
    (*a*) Complex system
    (*b*) Decentralized system
    (*c*) Dynamic system
    (*d*) All of the above

149. First page that you normally view at a website is its.
    (*a*) Home page
    (*b*) Master page
    (*c*) First page
    (*d*) Banner page

150. Take the add item out.
    (*a*) Yahoo
    (*b*) Lycoss
    (*c*) Hot Bot
    (*d*) Win 2000

151. Which out of the following retrieves and indexes web documents using a robot called slurp and a parallel network of workstations.
    (*a*) Hot Bot
    (*b*) Excite
    (*c*) Yahoo
    (*d*) None of the above

152. To which of the following a search engine continuously sends out the start on a home page of a server and pursue all links stepwise?
    (*a*) Spiders
    (*b*) Cookies
    (*c*) Packets
    (*d*) None of the above

153. Which out of the following has been created by research facility of digital electronic corporation of USA?
    (*a*) Yahoo
    (*b*) Web crawler
    (*c*) Alta vista
    (*d*) All of the above

154. Objective of SEO is to.
    (*a*) Increase web visitor counts by ranking very high is results of searches.
    (*b*) Increase search efficiency
    (*c*) Increase search speed
    (*d*) Decrease page rank

155. Cloaking is a
    (*a*) Black hat SEO
    (*b*) White hat SEO
    (*c*) Red hat SEO
    (*d*) Green hat SEO

156. During cloaking.
    (*a*) Content presented to search engine spider is different from that presented to user's browser
    (*b*) Content presented to search engine spider and browser are same
    (*c*) Contents of website are changed
    (*d*) None of the above

157. During cloaking content is delivered on the basis of.
    (*a*) IP address
    (*b*) HTML address
    (*c*) Portal address
    (*d*) URL

158. Purpose of cloaking is to deceive.
    (*a*) System program
    (*b*) Website
    (*c*) Search engine
    (*d*) Operating system

159. Cloaking is also known as.
    (*a*) Stealth

(*b*) Steal
(*c*) Steel
(*d*) Still

160. Cloaking represent.
(*a*) Something different to a search engine rather than hiding something from it
(*b*) the clock inside the system
(*c*) the Website creation technique
(*d*) None of the above

161. Reason of cloaking.
(*a*) Increase search engine ranking
(*b*) Protect pages from SEO
(*c*) Both (*a*) and (*b*)
(*d*) None of the above

162. Component for SEO are.
(*a*) Link tracking
(*b*) Combine keywords
(*c*) Both (*a*) and (*b*)
(*d*) None of the above

163. SEO efforts.
(*a*) Can be made after website is launched
(*b*) is made before website is created
(*c*) is automatically incorporated inside Webpage
(*d*) None of the above

164. Tool used to find products information on web is
(*a*) Search Engine
(*b*) Operating System
(*c*) E-mail
(*d*) Chatting

165. Spamming is a
(*a*) Ethical Technique
(*b*) Unethical Technique
(*c*) Illegal technique
(*d*) Legal technique

166. Search engine.
(*a*) Never disclose their proprietary inner workings
(*b*) Certain algorithms are made public
(*c*) always discloses their functioning
(*d*) None of the above

167. Search engine consists of
(*a*) Thousands of complex interconnected algorithms
(*b*) Thousands of small computers
(*c*) Thousands of procedures
(*d*) None of the above

168. Is link equity has same value as URL equity.
(*a*) No
(*b*) Yes
(*c*) In some situations
(*d*) These are not related

169. If context is moved to a new URL, old URL is removed from search engine index.
(*a*) No
(*b*) Yes
(*c*) In some situations
(*d*) These are not related

170. Page Rank.
(*a*) a rate of computer stationary
(*b*) a rank given to Internet
(*c*) a rating associated with Webpage
(*d*) None of the above

171. All the page on a dynamic site should have
(*a*) Unique name
(*b*) Different Name
(*c*) Dynamic Name
(*d*) Static Name

172. Factors affecting search engine

ranking are
(*a*) Four
(*b*) Three
(*c*) Two
(*d*) Ten

173. Anchor test is
(*a*) Off page factor
(*b*) On page factor
(*c*) Home page factor
(*d*) End page factor

174. Page copy is
(*a*) Visible on page factor
(*b*) Transparent to page factor
(*c*) Transparent to website
(*d*) None of the above

175. Meta keywords are
(*a*) Invisible on page factors
(*b*) Visible on page factor
(*c*) Reversible on page factors
(*d*) Transparent to page factors

176. Black hat technique help
(*a*) Webmaster to protect his web site.
(*b*) to create a Website
(*c*) to copy a Website
(*d*) to load a Website on Internet

177. Black Hat
(*a*) Do not follow the rules of search Engine.
(*b*) Works according to search engine guidelines
(*c*) Disturbs a Website
(*d*) None of the above

178. White Hat
(*a*) Follow the rules of search engine
(*b*) Do not follow the rules of search engine
(*c*) Is used to decorate a Website
(*d*) None of the above

179. Cloaking is implemented through.
(*a*) IP delivery
(*b*) HTTP delivery
(*c*) Email
(*d*) System clock

180. Geo targeting is same like.
(*a*) Cloaking
(*b*) Clocking
(*c*) Chatting
(*d*) Portal

181. IP delivery use.
(*a*) Network address
(*b*) Website address
(*c*) Webpage address
(*d*) None of the above

182. Apache is
(*a*) Open source web server
(*b*) Webpage creation program
(*c*) Website creation software
(*d*) Main frame Computer

183. Delist means
(*a*) To remove a website from search engine index
(*b*) To list the contents of doubly linked list
(*c*) To delete data from list
(*d*) None of the above

184. Conversation rate means.
(*a*) Ratio of conversions
(*b*) Sales per no. of visitors
(*c*) Both (a) and (b)
(*d*) None of the above

185. Content theft is.
(*a*) Practice of stealing another individuals web contents
(*b*) Malpractice of loading wrong sites on net
(*c*) sending wrong emails
(*d*) None of the above

186. SERP means
(*a*) Search Engine Result Page

(*b*) Search Engine Response Page
(*c*) Search Efficient Result Program
(*d*) Search Engine Rank Page

187. Web syndication.
(*a*) Permits and facilitates other websites to publish your web content
(*b*) Permits groupmails to send your messages
(*c*) allows creation of synchronised websites
(*d*) None of the above

188. Spoofing.
(*a*) Sending of incorrect information
(*b*) Sending of illegal information
(*c*) Sending of mixed information
(*d*) None of the above

189. Spider.
(*a*) Computer program that perform the process of spidering
(*b*) An insect
(*c*) A name of TV program
(*d*) An operating system

190. SEO copywriting.
(*a*) Present content to be read well for surfer
(*b*) Present content for programmer
(*c*) Present content for Webpage developer
(*d*) None of the above

191. Spidering, is
(*a*) Process of string context of website
(*b*) Process of traversing of website
(*c*) Both (*a*) and (*b*)
(*d*) None of the above

192. Site map is a.
(*a*) File
(*b*) Program
(*c*) Web page
(*d*) Web site

193. Spam.
(*a*) Contain no valuable content
(*b*) Contains valuable content
(*c*) Contains content about Website and is an Operating System
(*d*) None of the above

194. Spider Trap Collect.
(*a*) Infinite number of requests
(*b*) Finite number of requests
(*c*) I request
(*d*) Web request

195. Supplemental index is.
(*a*) Secondary index
(*b*) Primary index
(*c*) Indirect index
(*d*) Direct index

196. Supplemental index is.
(*a*) Provided by Google
(*b*) Provided by Internet Service provider
(*c*) Provided by operating system
(*d*) None of the above

197. SWF fills are referred to
(*a*) Flash movies
(*b*) Paint Software
(*c*) Corel Draw
(*d*) Page Maker

198. URL Rewriting.
(*a*) Translate incoming URL requests to other URLS
(*b*) Writes URL in different language
(*c*) Adds more features to URL
(*d*) None of the above

199. Usability of search engine
 (*a*) Ease of use exhibited by a website
 (*b*) The tendency to use a software
 (*c*) The preparation of data
 (*d*) None of the above

200. User agent is.
 (*a*) Web spider
 (*b*) Any user
 (*c*) String sent by user
 (*d*) All of the above

201. XML is used to.
 (*a*) Transport information in a structured format
 (*b*) Write program in machine language
 (*c*) Name of MACRO ASSEMBLER
 (*d*) Software testing tool.

202. Web analytics.
 (*a*) Track website data
 (*b*) Writes a Webpage
 (*c*) Internet Service provider
 (*d*) None of the above

203. Web feed provides.
 (*a*) Access to content contained by a website
 (*b*) Protocol format
 (*c*) Web server content
 (*d*) None of the above

204. Viral marketing.
 (*a*) Spread a message through help replication
 (*b*) It is a viral discease
 (*c*) A medicine marketing strategy
 (*d*) A computer virus

205. SEA for
 (*a*) Search Engine Advertising
 (*b*) Search Effective Algorithm
 (*c*) Search Engine Algorithm
 (*d*) System Effective Algorithm

206. ROI stands for
 (*a*) Return On Investment
 (*b*) Return On Internet
 (*c*) Retyping Of Instruction
 (*d*) Redesigning Of Interpreter

207. Robot is a
 (*a*) Spider
 (*b*) Sphinx
 (*c*) Web server
 (*d*) Web publisher

208. ROI is
 (*a*) Metric for benefit attained by particular investment
 (*b*) Efforts made in an investment
 (*c*) Web development metric
 (*d*) Health quotient

209. Screen scraping.
 (*a*) Produces information from HTML document
 (*b*) Write HTML document
 (*c*) Redesign HTML document
 (*d*) None of the above

210. Redirect moves.
 (*a*) Request from a web page to another
 (*b*) Generates new protocol
 (*c*) Creates new Webserver
 (*d*) None of the above

211. Referer is
 (*a*) Header
 (*b*) Footer
 (*c*) Trailer
 (*d*) Sailor

212. Referer indicate.
 (*a*) From where is the header is generated
 (*b*) Where the header referred to
 (*c*) Both (*a*) and (*b*)

(*d*) It is name of a XML procedure

213. PR stands for
(*a*) Page Rank
(*b*) Popularity Rating
(*c*) Page Rate
(*d*) Personal Rank

214. Page Rank measures
(*a*) Importance of a particular page
(*b*) Importance of a particular person
(*c*) Page Transfer Rate
(*d*) Web page creation rate

215. Outbound link
(*a*) Link from a web page to external website
(*b*) Link from a web page to internal website
(*c*) Link a website to server
(*d*) Link a website to search engine

216. OOP stands for
(*a*) Object Oriented Programming
(*b*) Object Oriented Procedure
(*c*) Output Oriented Procedure
(*d*) Output Oriented Programming

217. Inbound link
(*a*) A link to your website from an external website
(*b*) A link from your website
(*c*) A type of link in doubly linked list
(*d*) Link created by Webserver

218. Content theft
(*a*) Practise of stealing another individual web content
(*b*) A theft performed in male
(*c*) A programming theft
(*d*) None of above

219. Directory, with respect to Internet technologies stands for:
(*a*) Catalog of websites
(*b*) Catalog of books
(*c*) Catalog of publishers
(*d*) Catalog of webpages

220. Dats escaping
(*a*) Do not damage the message
(*b*) Damages the message
(*c*) Creates new message
(*d*) Destroys new message

221. DOM stands for
(*a*) Document Object Model
(*b*) Data Object Model
(*c*) Document Oriented Model
(*d*) Data Oriented Model

222. Web application use.
(*a*) Document Object Model
(*b*) Data Specific Model
(*c*) Machine Specific Model
(*d*) None of the above

223. Domain name server
(*a*) Store data about domain names
(*b*) Stores data about programs
(*c*) Webpage creation facility
(*d*) Webpage uploading facility

224. Domain name server
(*a*) Translate domain name to IP address
(*b*) Trnslates HTTP to IP
(*c*) Creates a new web page for uploading
(*d*) None of the above

225. Duplicate content.
(*a*) Identical content located on different web pages
(*b*) Multiple web pages with the

same name
(*c*) Different Procedures performing same work
(*d*) None of the above

226. Feed reader.
(*a*) Reads and display web feeds for human
(*b*) Feeds the orphans
(*c*) A kind of input device
(*d*) A type of book reading device program.

227. Florida program occurred in
(*a*) 2003
(*b*) 2005
(*c*) 2000
(*d*) 1900

228. Florida is
(*a*) Google ranking updation algorithm
(*b*) Google garbage collection algorithm
(*c*) Place of googles head office
(*d*) Please of gooles branch office

229. Bread crumb navigation
(*a*) Show path from one web page to another web page
(*b*) Translates one protocol to another
(*c*) Transfers website to another server
(*d*) None of the above

230. Blog
(*a*) Presents articles in reverse chronological order
(*b*) Special partition in web server
(*c*) Title of a book
(*d*) Name of a search engine

231. Big daddy occurred in.
(*a*) Early 2006
(*b*) Early 2005
(*c*) Early 2004
(*d*) Early 2003

232. Big Daddy is
(*a*) A Website on parenting
(*b*) A popular TV Program
(*c*) Google ranking updation algorithm
(*d*) A popular book

233. AJAX is acronym for.
(*a*) Asynchronous java script XML
(*b*) Asynchronous Java screen XML
(*c*) Asynchromous Jack Send Message
(*d*) None of the above

234. The Mod – Rewrite function
(*a*) Perform URL rewriting
(*b*) Perform mod operation
(*c*) Performs Rewrite function
(*d*) None of the above

235. Escaped data.
(*a*) Provides free links to spammers
(*b*) Provides free webspace
(*c*) Does not provide free links to spammers
(*d*) Creates website free of cost

236. Google trends
(*a*) A tool from google
(*b*) A search algorithm of Google
(*c*) The main webserver of Google
(*d*) None of the above

237. Google trends provides
(*a*) Volumes of keywords it handles over various time periods
(*b*) The number of visited

websites
(*c*) The paid links of google
(*d*) None of the above

238. Alexa rankings
(*a*) Rank all websites globally by quantity of traffic
(*b*) Rank the webservers
(*c*) Perform ranking in Alexa Software
(*d*) None of the above

239. Web analytics
(*a*) Track user behaviour on a particular website
(*b*) Track user behaviour on internet
(*c*) Group of people analyzing web content
(*d*) None of the above

240. For improving the ranking duplicating of a webpage the contents should be avoided
(*a*) True
(*b*) False
(*c*) Partially true
(*d*) None of the above

241. Reciprocal links.
(*a*) Belongs to internal factors
(*b*) Belongs to linked lists
(*c*) Belongs to external factors.
(*d*) None of the above

ANSWERS

1. (*c*)	2. (*c*)	3. (*a*)	4. (*b*)	5. (*b*)	6. (*c*)	7. (*a*)
8. (*b*)	9. (*b*)	10. (*c*)	11. (*b*)	12. (*d*)	13. (*a*)	14. (*b*)
15. (*a*)	16. (*a*)	17. (*b*)	18. (*b*)	19. (*c*)	20. (*c*)	21. (*a*)
22. (*b*)	23. (*b*)	24. (*a*)	25. (*d*)	26. (*b*)	27. (*a*)	28. (*b*)
29. (*a*)	30. (*a*)	31. (*a*)	32. (*a*)	33. (*b*)	34. (*a*)	35. (*b*)
36. (*a*)	37. (*a*)	38. (*a*)	39. (*a*)	40. (*a*)	41. (*b*)	42. (*a*)
43. (*a*)	44. (*a*)	45. (*a*)	46. (*c*)	47. (*a*)	48. (*a*)	49. (*d*)
50. (*a*)	51. (*a*)	52. (*a*)	53. (*b*)	54. (*b*)	55. (*c*)	56. (*a*)
57. (*d*)	58. (*d*)	59. (*a*)	60. (*a*)	61. (*a*)	62. (*a*)	63. (*c*)
64. (*a*)	65. (*d*)	66. (*a*)	67. (*b*)	68. (*a*)	69. (*c*)	70. (*b*)
71. (*a*)	72. (*b*)	73. (*d*)	74. (*d*)	75. (*a*)	76. (*a*)	77. (*a*)
78. (*a*)	79. (*b*)	80. (*a*)	81. (*a*)	82. (*a*)	83. (*a*)	84. (*d*)
85. (*b*)	86. (*b*)	87. (*a*)	88. (*a*)	89. (*b*)	90. (*a*)	91. (*a*)
92. (*a*)	93. (*a*)	94. (*d*)	95. (*a*)	96. (*a*)	97. (*a*)	98. (*a*)
99. (*c*)	100. (*a*)	101. (*b*)	102. (*b*)	103. (*d*)	104. (*b*)	105. (*b*)
106. (*a*)	107. (*b*)	108. (*d*)	109. (*b*)	110. (*d*)	111. (*a*)	112. (*d*)
113. (*a*)	114. (*c*)	115. (*a*)	116. (*a*)	117. (*c*)	118. (*a*)	119. (*c*)
120. (*c*)	121. (*a*)	122. (*a*)	123. (*a*)	124. (*a*)	125. (*a*)	126. (*a*)
127. (*b*)	128. (*a*)	129. (*a*)	130. (*c*)	131. (*a*)	132. (*a*)	133. (*a*)
134. (*a*)	135. (*a*)	136. (*a*)	137. (*c*)	138. (*c*)	139. (*a*)	140. (*c*)
141. (*a*)	142. (*a*)	143. (*c*)	144. (*a*)	145. (*a*)	146. (*d*)	147. (*d*)

148. (*d*)	149. (*a*)	150. (*d*)	151. (*a*)	152. (*a*)	153. (*b*)	154. (*a*)
155. (*a*)	156. (*a*)	157. (*a*)	158. (*c*)	159. (*a*)	160. (*a*)	161. (*c*)
162. (*c*)	163. (*a*)	164. (*a*)	165. (*b*)	166. (*a*)	167. (*a*)	168. (*b*)
169. (*c*)	170. (*c*)	171. (*a*)	172. (*a*)	173. (*a*)	174. (*a*)	175. (*a*)
176. (*a*)	177. (*a*)	178. (*a*)	179. (*a*)	180. (*a*)	181. (*a*)	182. (*a*)
183. (*a*)	184. (*c*)	185. (*a*)	186. (*a*)	187. (*a*)	188. (*a*)	189. (*a*)
190. (*a*)	191. (*c*)	192. (*a*)	193. (*a*)	194. (*a*)	195. (*a*)	196. (*a*)
197. (*a*)	198. (*a*)	199. (*a*)	200. (*d*)	201. (*a*)	202. (*a*)	203. (*a*)
204. (*a*)	205. (*a*)	206. (*a*)	207. (*a*)	208. (*a*)	209. (*a*)	210. (*a*)
211. (*a*)	212. (*c*)	213. (*a*)	214. (*a*)	215. (*a*)	216. (*a*)	217. (*a*)
218. (*a*)	219. (*a*)	220. (*a*)	221. (*a*)	222. (*a*)	223. (*a*)	224. (*a*)
225. (*a*)	226. (*a*)	227. (*a*)	228. (*a*)	229. (*a*)	230. (*a*)	231. (*a*)
232. (*c*)	233. (*c*)	234. (*a*)	235. (*c*)	236. (*a*)	237. (*a*)	238. (*a*)
239. (*a*)	240. (*a*)	241. (*a*)				

15

Software Engineering

1. Following software process model can be represented schematically as a series of major technical activities, and there associated state?
   (*a*) Incremental model
   (*b*) Component assembly model
   (*c*) Concurrent development model
   (*d*) All of the above

2. A data model consists of the following information?
   (*a*) Data object
   (*b*) The attributes that describe data object
   (*c*) Relationship that connect data object to one another
   (*d*) All of the above

3. What is the modality of relationship, if there is no explicit need for relationship to occur?
   (*a*) One
   (*b*) Two
   (*c*) Three
   (*d*) Four

4. The object relationship pair of data model is represented graphically by using
   (*a*) Data flow diagram
   (*b*) Flow chart
   (*c*) Entity relationship diagram
   (*d*) All of the above

5. In which life cycle model a working version of program will not be available?
   (*a*) Waterfall model
   (*b*) RAD model
   (*c*) Prototyping model
   (*d*) None of the above

6. Which architecture provide framework for information needs of a business function?
   (*a*) Application architecture
   (*b*) Technology infrastructure
   (*c*) Data architecture
   (*d*) All of the above

7. Which life cycle model suggests a systematic, sequential, approach to software development that begins at system level and processes through analysis, design, coding and maintenance.
   (*a*) Waterfall model
   (*b*) Prototype model
   (*c*) Sequential model
   (*d*) RAD model

8. Which of the life cycle model is high-speed adaptation of linear sequential model in which faster development is achieved by using a component based construction approach
   (*a*) Waterfall model
   (*b*) Prototype model
   (*c*) RAD model
   (*d*) None of the above

9. Name the evolutionary software

process model that couples the interactive nature of prototyping with controlled and systematic aspects of linear sequential model
(*a*) Incremental model
(*b*) Spiral model
(*c*) RAD model
(*d*) None of the above

10. Which software package model composes application from prepackaged software components
(*a*) Component assembly model
(*b*) Concurrent development model
(*c*) Incremental model
(*d*) None of the above

11. The primary aim of software engg. is to provide
(*a*) Reliable software
(*b*) According to requirement a complete software
(*c*) Cost-effective software
(*d*) All of the above

12. A good requirement specification should be
(*a*) Unambiguous
(*b*) Distinctly specific
(*c*) Functional
(*d*) None of the above

13. Related to object oriented design of software, which of the following is not true
(*a*) Object inherit the properties of a class
(*b*) Classes are defined based on attributes of objects
(*c*) An object can belong to two classes
(*d*) None of the above

14. Design phase include
(*a*) Data architectural and procedural design only
(*b*) Architectural, procedural, and interface design only
(*c*) Data, architectural and interface design only
(*d*) Data, architectural, interface, and procedural design only

15. In a software engg. approach, the design phase is,
(*a*) Top down
(*b*) Bottom up
(*c*) Random
(*d*) Centre fringing

16. Assuming the existence of a start and end nodes for a program graph, total number of patterns required in a set of data to test the software is
(*a*) Minimum
(*b*) Optimum
(*c*) Maximum
(*d*) None of the above

17. If x is a CASE statement in a program graph with n cases, and each case leading to only one path to and from the node, total number of paths through x is
(*a*) $x + n$
(*b*) x^n
(*c*) $x \log n$
(*d*) xn

18. Following are the categories of the automated system
(*a*) Online system
(*b*) Real time system
(*c*) Decision support system
(*d*) None of the above

19. Which of the following are the categories of the real time system
(*a*) Many processing activities goes on simultaneously
(*b*) Interruption of processing tasks

(*c*) Dynamic use of resources of computer system
(*d*) All of the above

20. Decision support systems are used to
(*a*) Evaluate and analyse the mission of organization
(*b*) Perform multiple activities simultaneously
(*c*) To perform accounting
(*d*) None of the above

21. Who are supervisory user
(*a*) They are normal user
(*b*) Thay are employed in a supervisory category usually to manage a group of operation users
(*c*) They are clients
(*d*) None of the above

22. The static and dynamic views are created for
(*a*) Objected oriented system
(*b*) Natural system
(*c*) Molecular system
(*d*) None of the above

23. What are the qualities of a good S/W
(*a*) Reliability
(*b*) Portability
(*c*) Interoperability
(*d*) All of the above

24. A zero level DFD describes
(*a*) That the system design cannot be split further
(*b*) Overview of the processes input and output
(*c*) Fully blown up system design
(*d*) None of the above

25. Software maintenance includes
(*a*) Bug fixing
(*b*) Setting preventive maintenance policy for servers
(*c*) Installation of software at site
(*d*) Designing of software for maintenance purposes

26. The role of an integrated CASE tool in system analysis and design project is
(*a*) Providing a case study for software development
(*b*) To provide an environment that automate key tasks throughout software development process
(*c*) To provide a tool for creating a word file.
(*d*) None of the above

27. Cross reference checking with respect to data dictionary refers to
(*a*) linking of documents through hypertext in case system deals with document imaging
(*b*) Finding that there is no inconsistency between the way a reference is quoted in a text file, and therefore reference is listed in reference file
(*c*) Determination of where data are stored in the system
(*d*) None of the above

28. Error correction is minimum expensive at
(*a*) Feasibility study stage
(*b*) Requirement analysis stage
(*c*) Development stage
(*d*) Testing stage

29. Difference between menu interface and question answer dialogue is
(*a*) In menu driven system user files a form, whereas in latter user responds to questions.

(*b*) Menu driven system is difficult and question answer system is easy
(*c*) Their difference varies according to application
(*d*) None of the above

30. Main difference between primary testing and system testing is
(*a*) Program testing is more comprehensive than system testing
(*b*) System testing focuses on testing the interface between program and program testing focuses on individual programs
(*c*) System testing is tough and program testing is easy
(*d*) None of the above

31. Which of the following is not a major design consideration of the system
(*a*) Response time required
(*b*) Frequency of record updates
(*c*) Availability of technically qualified personnel to carry out design and development
(*d*) Data integrity constraints

32. The largest percentage of total life cycle cost of software is
(*a*) Design cost
(*b*) Maintenance cost
(*c*) Coding cost
(*d*) Testing cost

33. A shared collection of logically related data designed to meet information needs of multiple users in an organization is
(*a*) Database
(*b*) Level – 1 diagram
(*c*) Transposition diagram
(*d*) None of the above

34. Database administrator
(*a*) Designs database for administration
(*b*) Manages database
(*c*) Implements database
(*d*) None of the above

35. The static system model exhibits which type of relationship
(*a*) Time cost
(*b*) Activity time
(*c*) Quantity cost
(*d*) None of the above

36. A decision table consists of two parts
(*a*) Stub and entry
(*b*) Pros and cons
(*c*) Condition and result
(*d*) None of the above

37. In parallel run of software testing
(*a*) Both physical system and computerized system work simultaneously.
(*b*) Only physical system runs
(*c*) Only computerized system runs
(*d*) None of the above.

38. Coupling is a measure of
(*a*) Relative functional strength
(*b*) Interdependence among modules
(*c*) Both of the above
(*d*) None of the above

39. Intangible costs refer to
(*a*) Costs those have financial values, which are not easily measured
(*b*) Costs those can be easily measured
(*c*) Are not required to be measured
(*d*) None of the above

40. Structure chart is the documentation tool for
    (*a*) Physical design
    (*b*) Logical design
    (*c*) Structure design
    (*d*) None of the above

41. In which testing system is run with live data by actual user
    (*a*) Acceptance testing
    (*b*) Unit testing
    (*c*) System testing
    (*d*) None of the above

42. In a unit testing of a module, 90% of the code was tested with probability of success 0.9. The reliability of module is
    (*a*) At least greater than 0.9
    (*b*) Equal to 0.9
    (*c*) At most 0.81
    (*d*) At least 1/0.81

43. Which of the following methods is normally used as acceptance test for
    (*a*) Software system
    (*b*) Regression test
    (*c*) Unit test
    (*d*) Functional test

44. Which of the following is not an assertion.
    (*a*) P is true, P and Q are true and K or not(Q) is true implies K is true
    (*b*) P is true, P and Q are true and K or Q is true implies K is true
    (*c*) P is true, P and Q are false and K or (Q) is true implies K is true
    (*d*) P is true, P and Q are true and K or not (K) is true implies K is true

45. Consider a source code with 10 operators, including 6 unique operators, 6 operands including 2 unique operands. The program volume is
    (*a*) 48
    (*b*) 100
    (*c*) 512
    (*d*) cannot be determined

46. With help of what kind of symbols flowcharts are drawn
    (*a*) Non-standard symbols
    (*b*) General symbols
    (*c*) Abbreviated symbols
    (*d*) Specific symbols

47. First step in a system study project is to
    (*a*) Define system performance criteria
    (*b*) Describe information needs
    (*c*) Staff for the study project
    (*d*) Announce the study project

48. How do analysts determine manager's information needs?
    (*a*) conducting tours of a nearly computer center
    (*b*) Asking questions
    (*c*) Showing samples of computer reports
    (*d*) Teaching short courses in programming language

49. What is condition for storing the outstanding invoice file on pardon access storage device?
    (*a*) Invoice data entry is online
    (*b*) Payment recording is done in a batch role
    (*c*) Inquires concering payments are to be answered online
    (*d*) Last record points to be first record

50. Data can be collected through
    (*a*) Questionnaires

(*b*) Interviews
(*c*) Onsite observations
(*d*) All of the above

51. Coding and testing can be done in a
(*a*) Top-down manner
(*b*) Bottom-up manner
(*c*) Adhoc manner
(*d*) Gross-sectional manner

52. In which phase procedure development occurs?
(*a*) Structured design phase
(*b*) Conversion phase
(*c*) System building phase
(*d*) Maintenance

53. What is the purpose of implementing backup and recovery procedures?
(*a*) To handle contingency which file gets corrupted
(*b*) To provide data redundancy
(*c*) To show different versions of data and programs
(*d*) All of the above

54. Nassi-schneiderman charts
(*a*) Are being replaced by flowcharts
(*b*) Often describe overlapping control structures
(*c*) Are made up of boxes within boxes
(*d*) Both a and c

55. An example of a hierarchical data structure is
(*a*) An array
(*b*) Link list
(*c*) Tree
(*d*) Ring

56. How does a system analyst designs a new system?
(*a*) By identifying subsystems and interfaces between subsystems
(*b*) Adopting a developed system to present environment
(*c*) Developing system as a large, single unit
(*d*) Propose alternatives to the current system

57. On what assumption the black box concept is based on
(*a*) The supersystem of it is stable
(*b*) Black boxes are dependent on environments
(*c*) The relationships between inputs and outputs is stable
(*d*) All of the above

58. Which of the following tools is not used for process description
(*a*) Structured English
(*b*) Decision tables
(*c*) Pseudo code
(*d*) Data dictionaries

59. In data flow diagrams, how an originator or receiver of data is represented?
(*a*) By circle
(*b*) By arrow
(*c*) By a square box
(*d*) By a rectangle

60. What is the first thing to be defined for a new system?
(*a*) Inputs
(*b*) Outputs
(*c*) Storage
(*d*) Processing

61. The packaged design includes all of the following except
(*a*) Program flow charts
(*b*) System configuration
(*c*) Module descriptions
(*d*) All of the above

62. The black-box concepts
    (*a*) Is invoked by describing a systems in terms of inputs and oututs, easing the transformation process a black box
    (*b*) Assumes that black box is independent
    (*c*) Assumes that inputs and output will remain stable
    (*d*) None of the above

63. The technique of system conversion in which existing system is totally removed and immediately new system is implemented is called a
    (*a*) Pilot conversion
    (*b*) Crash conversion
    (*c*) Phased converion
    (*d*) Parallel run

64. Some firms have created a combination position called
    (*a*) Manager/analyst
    (*b*) Programmer/operator
    (*c*) Analyst/programmer
    (*d*) Manager/operator

65. Conditions immediately outside a system are called
    (*a*) The boundary
    (*b*) The interface
    (*c*) The environment
    (*d*) The protocols

66. What is done in top down analysis and design
    (*a*) Each succeeding phase is more detailed than phase before it
    (*b*) Each succeeding phase is as detailed as the phase before it
    (*c*) Each succeeding phase is less detailed than the phase before it
    (*d*) All of the above

67. What is a word processor designed for programmer called
    (*a*) A formatter
    (*b*) A compiler
    (*c*) An editor
    (*d*) A debugger

68. Indian Railways reservation system is an example of
    (*a*) Transcation processing system
    (*b*) Interactive decision support system
    (*c*) Management controls system
    (*d*) Expert system

69. What is a structural chart?
    (*a*) A document of what has to be accomplished
    (*b*) A hierarchical partioning of the program
    (*c*) A statement of information processing requirements
    (*d*) All of the above

70. Which of the following is not true of the conversion phase of the development life cycle?
    (*a*) The user and systems personnel must work cosely together
    (*b*) steps must be taken to phase out the old system
    (*c*) Documentation should be emphasized
    (*d*) The non-machine corresponding component of system should be considered

71. All of the following tools are used for process descriptions excepts
    (*a*) Pseudocodes
    (*b*) Decision tables
    (*c*) Structured english
    (*d*) Data dictionaries

72. All of the following are part of a data flow diagram except

(*a*) Disk storage
(*b*) Arrow
(*c*) Data store
(*d*) Process represented by a circle

73. Which of the following does not occur in phase-4 of the system development life cycle (SDLC)?
(*a*) Conduct interviews
(*b*) Train users
(*c*) Acquire hardware and software
(*d*) Test the new system

74. In functional composition, what is done with data flow diagrams
(*a*) Is ignored
(*b*) Is partioned according to the "closeness" of datagrams and data storages items
(*c*) Is partitioned according to the logical "closeness" of the actigrams
(*d*) Both a and c

75. Department representatives serve as
(*a*) Ready source of information on feasibility committee
(*b*) Liason to their departments on feasibility committee
(*c*) Direct users of the new system in feasibility committee
(*d*) Both a and c

76. A decision table facilitates conditions to be related to
(*a*) Actions
(*b*) Programs
(*c*) Tables
(*d*) Operation

77. All of the following are requirements of a structured design except
(*a*) It should be made up of a hierarchy of modules
(*b*) It should use many GOTO statements
(*c*) The code should be executed in a top-to-bottom fashion within each module
(*d*) Each module should be as independent as possible of all other modules, except its parent

78. A statement by statement description of a procedure is detailed in a
(*a*) Written narrative
(*b*) Procedure's log
(*c*) System flow chart
(*d*) Record layout

79. In data flow diagrams, the processes at the most detailed level are called
(*a*) transform descriptions
(*b*) Functional primitives
(*c*) Data flows
(*d*) Interfaces

80. A decision table is
(*a*) A way of representing the information flow
(*b*) A way of representing multiple conditions
(*c*) A way to get an accurate picture of system
(*d*) All of the above

81. The characteristic of good test data is following except
(*a*) users do not participate at this preliminary stage
(*b*) Should be comprehensive
(*c*) Every statement should be executed
(*d*) All of the above

82. Which of the following affect extent to which you are involved

with system development life cycle in your company?
(*a*) Your job description
(*b*) Size of the organization
(*c*) Your relevant experience
(*d*) None of the above

83. System study involves
(*a*) Study of an existing system
(*b*) Documenting of existing system
(*c*) Identifying current deficiencies and establishing new goals
(*d*) All of the above

84. Which of the following is (are) the characteristics of a system?
(*a*) Organization
(*b*) Interaction
(*c*) Inter dependence
(*d*) All of the above

85. Intergration (in terms of system concepts)
(*a*) Implies structure and order
(*b*) Refers to manner in which each component functions with other components of the system
(*c*) Means that parts of the computer system depends on one another
(*d*) Refers to holis of systems

86. What is advantage of database system?
(*a*) Storage space duplication is eliminated
(*b*) All application share centralized files
(*c*) Data are stored once in database and are easily accessible when needed
(*d*) All of the above

87. A square symbol in flow chart
(*a*) Defines a source or destination of system data
(*b*) Identifies data flow
(*c*) Represents a process that transforms incoming data flow into outgoing data flows
(*d*) Is a data store-data at rest, or a temporary repository of data

88. What should be consideration of analyst while constructing a data dictionary?
(*a*) Each data flow in DFD should be considerd as one data dictionary entry
(*b*) definitions must be readly acessible by name
(*c*) There should be no redundancy in the data definition
(*d*) All of the above

89. When are mistakes made in requirement analysis visible?
(*a*) System design
(*b*) System development
(*c*) System testing
(*d*) Systems implementation

90. What is a pseudocode?
(*a*) A machine-level code
(*b*) A random number
(*c*) A flow chart
(*d*) Structured english to communicate logic of a program

91. Management's decision to rent a computer system may be based upon
(*a*) Tax advantages
(*b*) desire to avoid a large one time payment
(*c*) Operational flexibility in changing hardware
(*d*) None of above

92. Relational database management

systems have the following advantage
(*a*) Flexibility of relating different logical files
(*b*) Security controls which can be more easily implemented
(*c*) Data independence since it allows the database grow by adding new attributes and relations
(*d*) All of the above

93. Reverse video is a technique of
(*a*) Showing data with half brightness
(*b*) Showing data upside down on the screen
(*c*) Hiding confidential data on the screen
(*d*) Emphasizing data by reverging the foreground background

94. A data element which is used to distinguish between different records is called
(*a*) Response time
(*b*) Key
(*c*) System review
(*d*) Test data

95. An appraisal, of a system performance after it has been installed system
(*a*) Planning
(*b*) Review
(*c*) Maintenance
(*d*) Batch processing

96. Earlier trend of computer stage was
(*a*) Batch processing
(*b*) Parallel processing
(*c*) Random processing
(*d*) Multi-task processing

97. What is graphic representation of the control logic of processing function or modules representing a system called?
(*a*) Structured analysis
(*b*) Structured chart
(*c*) Structured english
(*d*) System flow chart

98. Which of the following statement is false except
(*a*) As parallel run involves two different terminals accessing a common database
(*b*) Computers are essential for systems analysis
(*c*) Flow of information in an organization is always vertical
(*d*) Alpha testing is the verification process a system goes through for the first time

99. The process to refine data structure, is called
(*a*) Structuring process
(*b*) Hierarchical structure
(*c*) Normalization
(*d*) Relation structure

100. Rental option has following advantage
(*a*) No financing is required. The risk of system chsolescence is less.
(*b*) The flexibility of modifying the system at will
(*c*) Insurances, maintenance and other expenses are the rental charge
(*d*) All of the above

101. What is prepared by a programmer?
(*a*) General system flow chart
(*b*) Specific system flow chart
(*c*) General program flow chart
(*d*) Specific program flow chart

102. All of the following is factor in the failure of a systems developing project except
    (*a*) Inadequate user involvement
    (*b*) Failure of system integration
    (*c*) Size of company
    (*d*) Continuation of a project that should have been cancelled

103. Ist step of SDLC is
    (*a*) Database design
    (*b*) System design
    (*c*) Preliminary investigation and analysis
    (*d*) Graphical user interface

104. What is the responsibility of executive vice-president and other manager during the system study?
    (*a*) Planning
    (*b*) Controlling
    (*c*) Directing
    (*d*) Organizing

105. What is included in system study project?
    (*a*) System analysis
    (*b*) System design
    (*c*) Implementation
    (*d*) Both a and b

106. What is used by analyst to learn manager's information needs?
    (*a*) Mail survey
    (*b*) In depth interview
    (*c*) Controlled experiment
    (*d*) Observation

107. The document which is used to list all procedure and regulations that generally govern an organization is
    (*a*) Personal policy bank
    (*b*) Organization manual
    (*c*) Administration policy manual
    (*d*) Procedures log

108. A feasibility study
    (*a*) Includes a statement of the problems
    (*b*) Considers a single solution
    (*c*) Both a and b
    (*d*) A list of alternative solution considered

109. In decision trees
    (*a*) Nodes represent the condition, with the right side of tree highligting the actions to be taken
    (*b*) The root is drawn on the left and is the starting point on the decision sequence
    (*c*) The branch depends on the condition and decisions to make
    (*d*) All of the above

110. The method used for collecting information regarding user's requirements is (are)
    (*a*) Asking questions
    (*b*) Obtaining information from the present system
    (*c*) Prototyping
    (*d*) All of the above

111. What is monthly scheme?
    (*a*) The relationship service bureau database
    (*b*) A map of overall structure of a database
    (*c*) A parent with no owners
    (*d*) Two-dimensional table

112. What is most suitable use of on-line data entry?
    (*a*) In case of updating payroll master
    (*b*) In case of entering monthly journal entries
    (*c*) In case of processing payment of cheque in a bank
    (*d*) All of the above

113. The term parallel run refers to
   (*a*) The same job run on two different computers to test their speeds
   (*b*) The processing of two different jobs initiated from two terminals
   (*c*) The concurrent operation of an operating system and a new system
   (*d*) All of the above

114. System implementation phase consists of
   (*a*) System check outs
   (*b*) Pilot run
   (*c*) Parallal runs
   (*d*) All of the above

115. All of the following are characteristic of good test data except
   (*a*) Should be comprehensive
   (*b*) Users do not participate at this preliminary stage
   (*c*) Every statement should be executed
   (*d*) Expected output from the module's execution should be determined manually

116. The computer programs produced by structured design are
   (*a*) Easily maintained
   (*b*) Easily understood
   (*c*) Tested in a bottom-up fashion
   (*d*) a and b only

117. An indexed file organisation offers access method to a
   (*a*) Sequential file
   (*b*) Indexed file
   (*c*) Direct access file
   (*d*) Random access file

118. A hierarchical chart that divides a large program into modules, in which greater details are designed in successibely lower programming levels, is called a
   (*a*) Scheme
   (*b*) Sub-schema
   (*c*) Structure
   (*d*) All of the above

119. The turn around time is
   (*a*) The elapsed time between the receipt of input and availability of output
   (*b*) A group of related fields
   (*c*) The key information of programming
   (*d*) A program statement that violates one or more rules of the language in which it is written

120. Which of the following statements is true?
   (*a*) Entity relationship diagrams are used to design files
   (*b*) Systems overview can be prescribed by data flow diagrams
   (*c*) Phases, in a systems life cycle, are fixed and invariant
   (*d*) Only a programmer can conduct a system study

121. What is a group of related fields, called?
   (*a*) Tuple
   (*b*) Schema
   (*c*) Records
   (*d*) File

122. Declining sales is a symptom of an underlying problem. Select best fit for this statement
   (*a*) Systems approach
   (*b*) Problem versus symptions
   (*c*) Systems thinking

(*d*) Post implementation review

123. The costs of acquring computer hardware, software and specialists. Select the best fit for this answer
(*a*) Cost/benefit analysis
(*b*) Costs
(*c*) Feasibility
(*d*) Benefits

124. Increase in profits caused by a new system. Select the best fit for this answer
(*a*) Cost/benefit analysis
(*b*) Costs
(*c*) regrets
(*d*) Benefits

125. A multistep process to conceive, design and implement an information system. Select best fit for this answer
(*a*) Benefits
(*b*) System development life cycle
(*c*) System investigation
(*d*) Feasibility study

126. Determines the organization's economic, technical and operational feasibility of a proposed information system. Select the best fit for this answer.
(*a*) Benefits
(*b*) Systems development life cycle
(*c*) Systems investigation
(*d*) Feasibility study

127. Reliable hardware and software are available to implement a proposed system. Select the best fit for this answer.
(*a*) Economic feasibility
(*b*) Technical feasibility
(*c*) Operational feasibility
(*d*) Organizational feasibility

128. The proposed system support strategic plan of the business. Select the best fit for this answer
(*a*) Economic feasibility
(*b*) Technical feasibility
(*c*) Operational feasibility
(*d*) Organizational feasibility

129. A detailed description of user information needs and the input, processing, outputs storage and control capabilities required to meet those needs. It is related with
(*a*) Systems analysis
(*b*) Functional requirement
(*c*) Systems design
(*d*) User interface, data and process design

130. Systems design should focus on developing end user input/output methods, data structures, and programs and procedures. Select best fit for this answer:
(*a*) Systems analysis
(*b*) Functional requirement
(*c*) Systems design
(*d*) User interface, data and process design

131. Acquiring hardware and software, testing and documenting a proposed system and training people to use it. Select the best fit for this answer:
(*a*) Systems specifications
(*b*) Systems implementation
(*c*) Systems maintenance
(*d*) Computer aided systems engineering

132. Using software packages to computerize many of the activities in system development process. Select best fit for this answer:
(*a*) Systems specifications
(*b*) Systems implementation

(*c*) Systems maintenance
(*d*) Computer aided systems engineering

133. An interactive and iterative process of developing and refining information system prototypes. Select the best fir for this answer:
(*a*) Incrementing
(*b*) Prototyping
(*c*) End user development
(*d*) All of the above

134. The main characteristic of "ring" used in data structure, is
(*a*) Last record, points to the first record
(*b*) First record points only to the last record
(*c*) Many records point to one record
(*d*) All of the above

135. The term organization
(*a*) Implies structure and order
(*b*) Refers to manner in which each component functions with other components of the system
(*c*) Means that parts of the computer system depend on one another
(*d*) Refer to holism of systems

136. The characteristics of an open system are (is):
(*a*) Input from outside
(*b*) Entropy and differntiation
(*c*) Process, output and cycles
(*d*) All of the above

137. Database has following drawback (s):
(*a*) The cost of specialized document is more
(*b*) The need to protect sensitive data from unauthorized access
(*c*) All applications share centralized files
(*d*) Both a and b

138. What does an open rectangle represent?
(*a*) A source or destination of system data
(*b*) Data flow
(*c*) A process that transforms incoming data flow into outgoing data flows
(*d*) A data store at rest, or a temporary repository of data

139. What is the term used for referring to the checkings of outputs of a computer, with corresponding input documents, is called?
(*a*) Auditing around the computer
(*b*) Auditing through the computer
(*c*) Process control
(*d*) Beta-test

140. File type having smallest life is
(*a*) Master file
(*b*) Program file
(*c*) Transaction file
(*d*) Work file

141. The technique which is used to totally remove existing system and immediatly implementing new system is called
(*a*) Crash conversion
(*b*) Phased conversion
(*c*) Pilot conversion
(*d*) Parallel run

142. Which is a function in process step of data processing
(*a*) Protect
(*b*) Index
(*c*) Retrieval
(*d*) Update

143. Primarly, system design aid provide

(*a*) Help analyse both data and activities
(*b*) Help in documentation
(*c*) Help in programming
(*d*) Generate code

144. A menu driven system
(*a*) Can be used only for computer professionals
(*b*) Is required only for on line systems
(*c*) Increases operator's work
(*d*) Presents options and allows users to make selections

145. The time elapsed between processes of entering input and getting appearance of Ist character output on screen, is called
(*a*) Key
(*b*) System review
(*c*) Response time
(*d*) Batch processing

146. What are the changes made periodically to a system after development called
(*a*) Analysis
(*b*) Design
(*c*) Development
(*d*) Maintenance

147. What is the structure called, in which last element refers to Ist element in chain?
(*a*) Addressing
(*b*) Location
(*c*) Printer
(*d*) Loop

148. All of following statements are true except
(*a*) A structured chart is a sequential representation of program design
(*b*) The real-time system is a particular case of an on-line-system
(*c*) Batch totals are not incorporated while designing real-time applications
(*d*) UGI's are used for application prototyping

149. What is true for direct-access organization?
(*a*) Means storing records in contiguous blocks according to a key
(*b*) Stores records sequentially but uses an index to locate records
(*c*) Uses an index for each key type
(*d*) Has records placed randomly throughout the file

150. Purchase option's advantage (s) is (are)
(*a*) No financing is required. The risk of system obsolescence is shifted to the lessor
(*b*) The flexibility of modifying the system at work
(*c*) Insurances, maintenance and other expenses which are included in the rental charge
(*d*) All of the above

151. What is ensured by "user friendly" computers
(*a*) Management requires no system analysis and design
(*b*) Programmers are no longer needed
(*c*) Structured programming is not needed
(*d*) None of the above

152. Environment is
(*a*) A subsystem
(*b*) The boundary
(*c*) A part outside the boundaries

(*d*) All of above

153. What is provided by a system design aid?
(*a*) Help analyse both data and activities
(*b*) Help in documentation
(*c*) Generate code
(*d*) Use a GUI

154. What is task of managers in MIS?
(*a*) Select the optimum equipment configurations
(*b*) Evaluate alternate equipment configurations
(*c*) Describe information needs
(*d*) None of the above

155. What is combination of top-down and bottom-up approach called?
(*a*) Integrative approach
(*b*) Interpretative approach
(*c*) Interactive approach
(*d*) Both b and c

156. Which tool is not used to model new system?
(*a*) Decision tables
(*b*) Data dictionary
(*c*) Data flow diagram
(*d*) All of the above

157. During which process errors can be found by "outsiders"
(*a*) Alpha testing
(*b*) Beta testing
(*c*) Structured walk through
(*d*) Debugger

158. What is the use of system specifications?
(*a*) To describe system flows
(*b*) To get an accurate picture of the system
(*c*) To avoid an ambiguity
(*d*) All of the above

159. A turnkey package includes
(*a*) Software
(*b*) Hardware
(*c*) Training
(*d*) All of the above

160. Structured designing is an approach to design that adheres to rules based on principles such as
(*a*) Top-down retirement
(*b*) Bottom-up design
(*c*) Data flow analysis
(*d*) All of the above

161. What is a DFD?
(*a*) The modern version of flowchart
(*b*) Mainly used at systems specification stage
(*c*) The primary output of the systems design phase
(*d*) All of the the above

162. The system should provide which thing, to avoid error in transcription and transposition, during data entry
(*a*) A check digit
(*b*) A hash totals
(*c*) Batch totals
(*d*) All of the above

163. DFD shows
(*a*) The flow of data
(*b*) The processes
(*c*) The areas where they are stored
(*d*) All of the above

164. How are information system and capability related to each other?
(*a*) Improved processing speed
(*b*) Increased volume of activities
(*c*) Faster retrieval of information
(*d*) All of the above

165. Which of the following is not considered a tool at system design phase?
 (*a*) Data flow diagram
 (*b*) Decision table
 (*c*) Pie chart
 (*d*) System flow chart

166. Controls must be established in a system in order to
 (*a*) Prohibit tampering with information by unauthorized person
 (*b*) Verify that all data have been processed
 (*c*) The concurrent operation of an existing system and a new system
 (*d*) All of the above

167. What is done during maintenance phase?
 (*a*) System requirements are established
 (*b*) System analysis is carried out
 (*c*) Programs are tested
 (*d*) None of the above

168. Coding and testing is done in following manner:
 (*a*) Adhoc
 (*b*) Cross sectional
 (*c*) Bottom-up
 (*d*) Top-down

169. Which is primary tool used in structured design?
 (*a*) Data flow diagram
 (*b*) Module
 (*c*) Structure chart
 (*d*) Program flow chart

170. The best file orgaization in which one has to process all data records in a file called
 (*a*) Indexed
 (*b*) Sequential
 (*c*) Direct access
 (*d*) Randon access

171. The mistakes, comitted by intercharging two digits in a numeric field, during data entry, is called
 (*a*) Transposition error
 (*b*) Transcription error
 (*c*) Beta testing error
 (*d*) Alpha testing error

172. The time lag, between initiating a query and receiving a response is called
 (*a*) Response time
 (*b*) Waiting time
 (*c*) Processing time
 (*d*) Turn around time

173. HIPO is
 (*a*) A forms driven technique in which standard forms are used to document the information
 (*b*) Consists of a hierarchy chart and an associated set of input/process/output charts
 (*c*) Captures essence of top down decomposition
 (*d*) All of the above

174. Checking quality of software in both simulated and live environments is known as
 (*a*) Checking
 (*b*) Usability
 (*c*) Validity
 (*d*) Validation

175. Using an organized sequence of activities to study a problem or opportunity using systems thinking. Select the best fit for answer:
 (*a*) Systems approach
 (*b*) Problem versus symbols
 (*c*) Systems thinking

(*d*) Post implementation review

176. Trying to recognize systems and the new inter relationships and components of systems in any situation. Select the best fit for answer:
(*a*) Systems approach
(*b*) Problem versus symbols
(*c*) Systems thinking
(*d*) Post implementation review

177. Your evaluation shows the benefits out weigh costs for a proposed system. Select the best fit for answer:
(*a*) Cost/benefit analysis
(*b*) Feasibility study
(*c*) Feasibility
(*d*) Benefits

178. Loss of customer goodwill caused by errors in a new system. Select the best fit for answer:
(*a*) Cost/benefit analysis
(*b*) Feasibility study
(*c*) Feasibility
(*d*) Benefits

179. Improved employee morale caused by efficiency and effectiveness of a new system. Select the best fit for this answer:
(*a*) Benefits
(*b*) SDLC
(*c*) Systems investigation
(*d*) Feasibility study

180. Cost savings and additional profits will exceed the investment required. Select the best fit for this statement
(*a*) Economic feasibility
(*b*) Technical feasibility
(*c*) Operational feasibility
(*d*) Organizational feasibility

181. Customers will not have trouble using a proposed system. Select the best fit for answer:
(*a*) Economic feasibility
(*b*) Technical feasibility
(*c*) Operational feasibility
(*d*) Organizational feasibility

182. Studying in detail the information needs of users and any information systems presently used.
(*a*) Systems analysis
(*b*) Functional requirement
(*c*) Systems design
(*d*) User interface, data and process design

183. In above program (Question 182) the length of a program is.
(*a*) 80
(*b*) 48
(*c*) 46
(*d*) 52

184. In object oriented design of software, objects have.
(*a*) Operations and name only
(*b*) Attributes, name and operation
(*c*) Attributes and name only
(*d*) None of the above

185. An example of natural system is.
(*a*) Stellar system
(*b*) Hospital management system
(*c*) Bank management system
(*d*) None of the above

186. An example of man-made social system is.
(*a*) Accounting
(*b*) Organization of laws
(*c*) Telephone
(*d*) None of the above

187. Which of the following is not a communication system?

(*a*) Telephone
(*b*) Telex
(*c*) Hand signals
(*d*) None of the above

188. Knowledge-based system is an example of.
(*a*) Automated system
(*b*) Communication system
(*c*) Molecular system
(*d*) None of the above

189. Following are the categories of automated system.
(*a*) Online system
(*b*) Real-time system
(*c*) Decision support system
(*d*) All of the above

190. Which of the following is a charcteristic of real-time system.
(*a*) Many processing activities going on simultaneously
(*b*) Interruption of processing task
(*c*) Dynamic use of resources of computer system
(*d*) All of the above

191. Decision support systems are used to.
(*a*) Evaluate and analyze the mission of organization
(*b*) Perform multiple activities simultaneously
(*c*) To perform accounting
(*d*) None of the above

192. Who are supervisory user.
(*a*) They are the normal users
(*b*) They are employed in a supervisor capacity level usually to manage a group of operational users
(*c*) They are clients
(*d*) None of the above

193. The static and dynamic views are created for.
(*a*) Object oriented system
(*b*) Natural system
(*c*) Molecular system
(*d*) None of the above

194. What are the qualities of a good s/w?
(*a*) Reusability
(*b*) Portability
(*c*) Inter operability
(*d*) All of the above

195. A zero level DFD describes.
(*a*) That the system design cannot be split further
(*b*) Fully blown up system design
(*c*) Overview of processes input and output
(*d*) None of the above

196. Prototype is a
(*a*) Working model of existing system
(*b*) Mini model of existing system
(*c*) Mini model of processed system
(*d*) None of the above

197. Which of the following is not an important characteristics of useful and effective information.
(*a*) Completeness
(*b*) Timeliness
(*c*) Economy
(*d*) Accuracy

198. A sequential access file is not a file.
(*a*) In which the last record is retrieved in the same time as the first record
(*b*) In which a record cannot be

accessed unless the predecessor records are accessed
(*c*) Usually stored on magnetic tape
(*d*) In which new copy of a file is created to insert a record

199. Cost of error correction is least at.
(*a*) Implementation stage
(*b*) Design stage
(*c*) Development stage
(*d*) Requirement analysis stage

200. A starting point in the design phase of a system design project is.
(*a*) Benchmarking
(*b*) Preparation of a purchase contract
(*c*) The determination of size and capacity requirements for hardware
(*d*) Calling quotation from hardware vendors

201. The most creative and challenging phase of system life cycle is.
(*a*) Feasibility study
(*b*) Maintenance
(*c*) Design
(*d*) None of the above

202. The database design activity deals with the design of.
(*a*) Logical database
(*b*) Physical database
(*c*) Both (*a*) and (*b*)
(*d*) None of the above

203. The static system model exploit which type of relationship.
(*a*) Time cost
(*b*) Activity time
(*c*) Quality cost
(*d*) None of the above

204. In parallel run of s/w testing.
(*a*) Both physical system and computerized system work simultaneously
(*b*) Only physical system runs
(*c*) Only computerized system runs
(*d*) None of the above

205. Coupling is a measure of
(*a*) Relative functional strength
(*b*) Interdependence among module
(*c*) Both of the above
(*d*) None of the above

206. The MAR register.
(*a*) Stores address of memory location
(*b*) Stores contents of memory location
(*c*) Stores address of C.P.U
(*d*) Stores address of I/O device

207. Which of the following is not a component of object oriented software engg.
(*a*) Process
(*b*) Method
(*c*) Architecture
(*d*) None of the above

208. System development is a.
(*a*) Process of successive changes of systems from new and changed requirement
(*b*) It is a development of SRS of a system
(*c*) Both (*a*) and (*b*)
(*d*) None of the above

209. Delta requirement stands for.
(*a*) The SRS document prepared in delta from
(*b*) Where specification of desired changes is sent to earlier version of a system

(*c*) The delta version of a system
(*d*) None of the above

210. The advantages of creating a prototype are.
(*a*) It allows developers to experiment with number of different design options
(*b*) It can serve as a means of communication between developers and customers
(*c*) Both (*a*) and (*b*)
(*d*) None of the above

211. One demerit of functional model is.
(*a*) It is complex to build
(*b*) If we change data structure we must modify all functions related to it
(*c*) It is difficult to implement
(*d*) None of the above

212. In a system design project hardware design starts from.
(*a*) Identification of size and capacity requirements of hardware
(*b*) Cataloging price from hardware vendors
(*c*) Finding compatibility between hardware and software
(*d*) None of the above

213. Software maintenance includes.
(*a*) Bug fixing
(*b*) Settling preventing maintenance policy for servers
(*c*) Installation of software at site
(*d*) Designing of software for maintenance purposes

214. The role of an integrated CASE tool in system analysis and design project is.
(*a*) Providing a CASE study for software development
(*b*) To provide an environment that automate key tasks throughout software development process
(*c*) To provide tool for creating a word file
(*d*) None of the above

215. Cross reference checking w.r.t data dictionary refers to.
(*a*) Linking of documents through hypertext, in case system deals with document imaging
(*b*) Finding that there is no inconsistency between the way a reference is quoted in a text file, and therefore reference is listed in reference file
(*c*) Determination of where data are used in the system
(*d*) None of the above

216. Main difference between program testing and system testing is.
(*a*) Program testing is more comprehensive than system testing
(*b*) System testing focuses on testing the interfaces between programs, program testing focuses on individual programs
(*c*) System testing is tough and program testing is easy
(*d*) None of the above

217. Which of the following is not a major design consideration of the system.

(*a*) Response time required
(*b*) Frequency of record updates
(*c*) Availability of technically qualified personnel to carry out design and development
(*d*) Data integrity constraint

218. The largest percentage of total life cycle cost of software is.
(*a*) Design cost
(*b*) Maintenance cost
(*c*) Coding cost
(*d*) Testing cost

ANSWERS

1. (*c*)	2. (*d*)	3. (*a*)	4. (*c*)	5. (*a*)	6. (*a*)	7. (*a*)
8. (*c*)	9. (*a*)	10. (*b*)	11. (*d*)	12. (*a*)	13. (*c*)	14. (*d*)
15. (*a*)	16. (*a*)	17. (*d*)	18. (*c*)	19. (*d*)	20. (*a*)	21. (*b*)
22. (*a*)	23. (*d*)	24. (*b*)	25. (*b*)	26. (*b*)	27. (*b*)	28. (*b*)
29. (*a*)	30. (*b*)	31. (*c*)	32. (*a*)	33. (*b*)	34. (*b*)	35. (*b*)
36. (*c*)	37. (*b*)	38. (*b*)	39. (*a*)	40. (*b*)	41. (*a*)	42. (*c*)
43. (*b*)	44. (*d*)	45. (*a*)	46. (*d*)	47. (*b*)	48. (*a*)	49. (*a*)
50. (*d*)	51. (*a*)	52. (*c*)	53. (*a*)	54. (*d*)	55. (*c*)	56. (*a*)
57. (*c*)	58. (*d*)	59. (*a*)	60. (*a*)	61. (*c*)	62. (*a*)	63. (*b*)
64. (*b*)	65. (*c*)	66. (*a*)	67. (*c*)	68. (*b*)	69. (*b*)	70. (*a*)
71. (*d*)	72. (*b*)	73. (*a*)	74. (*d*)	75. (*d*)	76. (*a*)	77. (*d*)
78. (*d*)	79. (*a*)	80. (*b*)	81. (*b*)	82. (*b*)	83. (*d*)	84. (*b*)
85. (*b*)	86. (*d*)	87. (*c*)	88. (*d*)	89. (*d*)	90. (*d*)	91. (*b*)
92. (*d*)	93. (*d*)	94. (*d*)	95. (*b*)	96. (*a*)	97. (*d*)	98. (*c*)
99. (*c*)	100. (*c*)	101. (*a*)	102. (*b*)	103. (*c*)	104. (*a*)	105. (*d*)
106. (*d*)	107. (*c*)	108. (*d*)	109. (*a*)	110. (*d*)	111. (*d*)	112. (*d*)
113. (*a*)	114. (*b*)	115. (*d*)	116. (*d*)	117. (*b*)	118. (*d*)	119. (*a*)
120. (*b*)	121. (*c*)	122. (*d*)	123. (*a*)	124. (*a*)	125. (*b*)	126. (*d*)
127. (*d*)	128. (*d*)	129. (*a*)	130. (*b*)	131. (*a*)	132. (*b*)	133. (*b*)
134. (*a*)	135. (*b*)	136. (*c*)	137. (*d*)	138. (*c*)	139. (*d*)	140. (*d*)
141. (*a*)	142. (*c*)	143. (*a*)	144. (*d*)	145. (*c*)	146. (*c*)	147. (*d*)
148. (*d*)	149. (*b*)	150. (*d*)	151. (*b*)	152. (*c*)	153. (*a*)	154. (*b*)
155. (*a*)	156. (*b*)	157. (*b*)	158. (*d*)	159. (*d*)	160. (*c*)	161. (*c*)
162. (*d*)	163. (*a*)	164. (*c*)	165. (*a*)	166. (*d*)	167. (*d*)	168. (*b*)
169. (*c*)	170. (*b*)	171. (*a*)	172. (*d*)	173. (*b*)	174. (*b*)	175. (*a*)
176. (*d*)	177. (*a*)	178. (*d*)	179. (*c*)	180. (*a*)	181. (*c*)	182. (*b*)

183. (*c*)	184. (*c*)	185. (*a*)	186. (*b*)	187. (*d*)	188. (*a*)	189. (*d*)
190. (*d*)	191. (*a*)	192. (*b*)	193. (*a*)	194. (*d*)	195. (*d*)	196. (*a*)
197. (*a*)	198. (*a*)	199. (*a*)	200. (*d*)	201. (*c*)	202. (*c*)	203. (*c*)
204. (*a*)	205. (*b*)	206. (*a*)	207. (*c*)	208. (*c*)	209. (*b*)	210. (*c*)
211. (*b*)	212. (*a*)	213. (*a*)	214. (*b*)	215. (*b*)	216. (*b*)	217. (*c*)
218. (*a*)						

16

Data Communication

1. Which of the following is ture for data communication?
   (*a*) The transfer of information between two locations
   (*b*) Transfer of encoded data between two locations
   (*c*) Transfer of encoded information using communication
   (*d*) Use of telecommunication

2. Attenuation is a measure of.
   (*a*) Speed at which signal travels down a communication medium
   (*b*) Amount of loss of signal when it travels down a communication medium
   (*c*) Amount of phase shift as signal travels down a communication medium
   (*d*) Cost of communication medium

3. PTN stands for
   (*a*) Public Transport Network
   (*b*) Private Transport Network
   (*c*) Public Telephone Network
   (*d*) Private Telephone Network

4. In synchronization ETX stands for.
   (*a*) Extra terrestrial exploration
   (*b*) End of text
   (*c*) End of file
   (*d*) None of the above

5. Bisync protocol is
   (*a*) Bit oriented protocol
   (*b*) Byte oriented protocol
   (*c*) Frame oriented protocol
   (*d*) None of the above

6. ISDN stands for
   (*a*) Integrated Services Digital Network
   (*b*) Input Source Data Network
   (*c*) Integrated Source Destination Nework
   (*d*) None of the above

7. Switched multimegabit data service is.
   (*a*) Cell based transmission technology
   (*b*) Computer based transport technology
   (*c*) Computerization of data network
   (*d*) None of the above

8. A data communication system consists of.
   (*a*) DTE
   (*b*) DCE
   (*c*) Medium
   (*d*) All of the above

9. Bandwidth of cable TV is approximately.
   (*a*) 6 MHz
   (*b*) 8MHz
   (*c*) 10MHz
   (*d*) None of the above

10. Public telephone switched network.
    (*a*) Uses open wires circuits to

cable subscribers
(*b*) Interconnects satellite stations
(*c*) Is used only for the transmission of computer digital data
(*d*) Interconnects dial up users

11. The basic telephone channel has a bandwidth of.
(*a*) 2700 Hz
(*b*) 2400 Hz
(*c*) 1200 Hz
(*d*) 3100 Hz

12. Multiplexing is a technique which.
(*a*) Permits a single conversation per wire
(*b*) Allows the user of more than one wire for a single conversation
(*c*) Permits more than one conversation on a single wire
(*d*) Permits multiple conversations and each conversations on a separate wire.

13. The maximum data rate that a medium of 10 KHz and signal to noise ratio of 30 dB is roughly.
(*a*) 10 Kbps
(*b*) 30 Kbps
(*c*) 100 Kbps
(*d*) 300 Kbps

14. An ISDN circuit is of which category type.
(*a*) Dial-up
(*b*) Permanent
(*c*) Non-switched
(*d*) Leased line

15. Analog signals can be .... by combining them with a carrier frequency.
(*a*) Carried
(*b*) Transported
(*c*) Multiplexed
(*d*) Mixed

16. The interface between a computer and a modem usually employs.
(*a*) Synchronous connection
(*b*) Asynchronous connection
(*c*) Direct wire connection
(*d*) None of the above

17. In binary synchronous, communication .... code is used by the receiver to check the validity of the message recovered.
(*a*) OK
(*b*) ACK
(*c*) BCC
(*d*) SOH

18. Signal transitions per second is defined as.
(*a*) Bit rate
(*b*) Byte rate
(*c*) Baud rate
(*d*) All of the above

19. Connectionless network processes are often referred to as.
(*a*) Network switched
(*b*) Circuit switched
(*c*) Packet switched
(*d*) Routed switched

20. A switched virtual circuit (SVC) is.
(*a*) Similar to permanent virtual circuit but allows users to dial into the network of virtual circuit
(*b*) A virtual circuit implemented using switches
(*c*) A circuit made up of virtual switches
(*d*) None of the above

21. To transmit electrical digital signal over regular telephone line, we

require.

(a) Multiplexer
(b) Modem
(c) Cluster controller
(d) Front end processor

22. In the distributed system most of the processing is done.
(a) At user computer
(b) At some centralized computer
(c) Distributed among all computers in the LAN
(d) All of these

23. The most reliable network topology is.
(a) Fully connected
(b) Star topology
(c) Ring topology
(d) Bus topology

24. Broadband LAN supports.
(a) Multichannel services
(b) Multimedia services
(c) Greater bandwidth
(d) All of these

25. Baseband LAN does not use.
(a) Modulated digital channel
(b) Unmodulated digital channel
(c) RF signal only
(d) None of the above

26. A device that links several separate LAN'S and provides packet filtering between them is called.
(a) Token
(b) Protocol
(c) Switch
(d) None of the above

27. CSMA/CD is used in.
(a) Bus topology
(b) Ring network
(c) Star network
(d) All of the these

28. Which of the following is not a LAN hardware.
(a) Gateway
(b) Memory access unit
(c) Network interface card
(d) None of the above

29. Which network resource provide service for users.
(a) Local host
(b) Server
(c) Workstation
(d) ISDN

30. A high speed communication system designed to link computers and other data processing devices together with a small geographic area called.
(a) Wide area network
(b) Ring network
(c) Local area network
(d) Bus network

31. Which network topology is most fault tolerant and has most redundancy?
(a) Bus
(b) Ring
(c) Mesh
(d) Star

32. What IEEE specification is used by CSMA/CD
(a) 802.5
(b) 802.3
(c) 802.4
(d) 802.6

33. Ethernet frame format contains information filled up to length.
(a) 1500 bytes
(b) 1500 Kbytes
(c) 1500 bits
(d) 1500 Kbits

34. Token passing is a method implemented to.
    (*a*) Transmit two messages simultaneously to line
    (*b*) Control access to the line such that two messages are not transmitted simultaneously
    (*c*) Control the correct destination of the message
    (*d*) None of the above

35. IEE 802.5 is.
    (*a*) Token bus
    (*b*) Ethernet
    (*c*) Token ring
    (*d*) Voice data transmission

36. Operating speed of token ring is.
    (*a*) 12 Mbps
    (*b*) 16 Mbps
    (*c*) 100 Mbps
    (*d*) 10 Mbps

37. Which is true for character oriented protocol.
    (*a*) Each bit means something
    (*b*) Each bit is preceded by start flag sequence
    (*c*) Groups of 16 bits represents control codes
    (*d*) Each character has meaning

38. An information frame is used to .... in HDLC.
    (*a*) Acknowledge data frames
    (*b*) Set up a link circuit
    (*c*) Perform error control
    (*d*) Send data

39. Which is true for binary synchronous data transmission
    (*a*) Each bit is sent over a separate wire
    (*b*) Each character is prefixed with DLF
    (*c*) Characters are used for control purposes
    (*d*) Sequence numbers are sent in unnumbered frame

40. The character ETX belongs to .... protocol.
    (*a*) HDLC
    (*b*) X.25
    (*c*) Bisync
    (*d*) SNA

41. Protocol is ....
    (*a*) Implicit rules governing the communication.
    (*b*) A type of layer
    (*c*) An open system interconnector reference model
    (*d*) A complex internetworking device

42. Prime difference between network and distributed operating system is.
    (*a*) In contrast to user of a distributed system, users of a network operating system are aware of individual m/c on a network
    (*b*) A distributed operating system makes it look like as though every resource is local while network O/S allows to specify which resource they want to use
    (*c*) A distributed O/S can move and allocate any processes to several processors on network
    (*d*) All of the above

43. BNC connector is used to connect.
    (*a*) Cable and terminal
    (*b*) Terminator and cable
    (*c*) Both (*a*) and (*b*)
    (*d*) None of the above

44. Fast LAN can offer maximum bandwidth.
    (*a*) 10 Mbps
    (*b*) 16 Mbps
    (*c*) 20 Mbps
    (*d*) None of the above

45. ARC net.
    (*a*) Is low cost token bus system
    (*b*) Employs broadband network
    (*c*) Uses bit oriented protocol
    (*d*) None of the above

46. A terminator is connected at the end of line because.
    (*a*) It avoids the reflection of signal on segment
    (*b*) It allows reflections to occur on segment
    (*c*) It is customary to identify one segment with presence of it
    (*d*) None of the above

47. Repeater acts like a ....
    (*a*) Amplifier
    (*b*) Rectifier
    (*c*) Bridge
    (*d*) None of the above

48. Routers and bridges are same in terms of ———.
    (*a*) Encapsulation and filtering
    (*b*) Self-learning
    (*c*) Both (*a*) and (*b*)
    (*d*) None of the above

49. Router uses network layer. This means.
    (*a*) It may support different network topologies such as TCP/IP and SNA
    (*b*) It provides addressing, data connectivity and switching
    (*c*) They are not protocol sensitive
    (*d*) None of the above

50. Difference between hub and a switch is
    (*a*) Hub works on point to point topology and switch works on bus topology
    (*b*) Hub works on bus topology while switch provides point to point communication
    (*c*) Hub is multiport and switch is single port
    (*d*) There is no difference

51. Gateways are used to connect.
    (*a*) Different networks together such as TCP/IP and DEC net
    (*b*) Main frame computer to network
    (*c*) Overseas network
    (*d*) None of the above

52. Which layer of OSI reference model provides inter network connectivity.
    (*a*) Physical
    (*b*) Network
    (*c*) Data link
    (*d*) Transport

53. A workstation placed 105 meter away from server uses 10 base T wiring but it cannot be connected to network. How this can be connected to server with faster connection and easier access for users.
    (*a*) By using 100 base FX NIC, this can be connected to server with faster connection and easier access for users
    (*b*) By using 100 base FX NIC, this may be connected to server only
    (*c*) By using 100 base FX NIC,

only faster connection and easier access for users may be provided but not the connection to server

(*d*) This does not solve the purpose

54. Which hub boosts the signal strength.
   (*a*) Passive
   (*b*) Active
   (*c*) Hybrid
   (*d*) Token

55. LAN to LAN connection may be provided with.
   (*a*) Leased line
   (*b*) ISDN
   (*c*) Frame relay
   (*d*) All of the above

56. What factors contribute to a quality of WAN implementation.
   (*a*) Employee involvement
   (*b*) Cost
   (*c*) Customer service
   (*d*) Both (*b*) and (*c*)

57. Which OSI reference model provides for internetwork connectivity?
   (*a*) Data link
   (*b*) Physical
   (*c*) Session
   (*d*) Network

58. ARP is converting the.
   (*a*) IP address into physical address
   (*b*) Physical address into domain name
   (*c*) Domain name into IP address
   (*d*) IP address into domain name

59. Which routing method is costliest?
   (*a*) Bridging
   (*b*) Static
   (*c*) Dynamic
   (*d*) Relay

60. Advantage of ISDN over PSTN is that ....
   (*a*) ISDN is cheaper
   (*b*) PSTN is cheaper
   (*c*) ISDN is faster
   (*d*) None of the above

61. Conventional WAN's are built using.
   (*a*) Multiple dial up links interconnecting each office location
   (*b*) Short leased line circuit connecting each office to its closest neighbour
   (*c*) Expansive, distance sensitive leased line circuit
   (*d*) In expensive wireless network transmission technologies

62. X.25 is for
   (*a*) Connection oriented networking
   (*b*) Connectionless networking
   (*c*) Both of these
   (*d*) None of the above

63. Modulation refers to
   (*a*) The distance between the uplink and downlink frequencies
   (*b*) The separation between adjacent carrier frequency
   (*c*) The process of changing the characteristics of carrier frequency
   (*d*) The number of cycles per unit of time

64. Which of the following are not telephony services supported by GSM.

(*a*) Dual tone multi frequency
(*b*) Fax mail
(*c*) Voice mail
(*d*) Call waiting

65. In cellular communication technology larger cells are preferred in.
(*a*) Densely populated urban areas
(*b*) Rural areas
(*c*) Lightly populated urban areas
(*d*) Mountainous areas

66. Which of the following does not provide a physical link between terminal & computer?
(*a*) Optical fibre
(*b*) Microwave
(*c*) Telephone lines
(*d*) Coaxial cable

67. Which of the following transmission medium is immune from electromagnetic interference.
(*a*) Category 3 shielded cable
(*b*) Optical fibre
(*c*) Coaxial cable
(*d*) Category 5 twisted cable

68. Which is not the advantage of fibre optic cable over copper cable.
(*a*) Less expensive
(*b*) Non-flammable
(*c*) Higher data carrying capacity
(*d*) Low power

69. Fibre optics is immune to.
(*a*) All kinds of interference
(*b*) Chemical interference
(*c*) Lightning interference
(*d*) Soil interference

70. The highest data rate is provided by transmission medium.
(*a*) Coaxial cable
(*b*) Microwave
(*c*) Optical fibre
(*d*) Twisted pair

71. Digitization is a combination of sampling and.
(*a*) Pulse coding
(*b*) Shift keying
(*c*) Quantization
(*d*) None of the above

72. In distance vector routing the path.
(*a*) Upto destination is allocated before transmission of packets begins
(*b*) Upto next intermediate node is allocated before transmission of packet begins
(*c*) To be followed depends on the length of packets
(*d*) None of the above

73. A Conventional LAN bridge specifies only the functions of.
(*a*) Layers 1 and 2
(*b*) Lay 1 through 3
(*c*) All layers
(*d*) None of the above

74. X.25 protocol consists of
(*a*) Physical and frame level
(*b*) Frame and packet level
(*c*) Physical frame and packet level
(*d*) None of the above

75. Signal becomes weak with increase in distance travelled because of.
(*a*) Modulation
(*b*) Attenuation
(*c*) Switching
(*d*) None of the above

76. Channel coding is used to.
(*a*) Secure the channel
(*b*) Minimize interference in the channel

(*c*) Protect the information against channel noise
(*d*) Protect against unnecessary tapping of signal from the channel

77. GSM/CDMA systems
(*a*) Are limited to very low speed data
(*b*) Require no local loop wires
(*c*) Are predominantly used for voice
(*d*) All of the above

78. A high performance switching and multiplexing technology that utilizes fixed length packets to carry different types of traffic.
(*a*) ATM
(*b*) ADSL
(*c*) SONET
(*d*) None of the above

79. The character ETX belongs to .... protocols.
(*a*) SNA
(*b*) HDLC
(*c*) X.25
(*d*) Bisyne

80. .... code is used to implement data transparency in the binary synchronous protocol.
(*a*) DLE
(*b*) NAK
(*c*) EOH
(*d*) EOT

81. .... is a binary synchronous data transmission.
(*a*) Each bit is sent over a separate wire
(*b*) Sequence numbers are sent in unnumbered frames
(*c*) Each character is prefixed with DLE
(*d*) Characters are used for control purpose

82. Data in a full duplex circuit
(*a*) Travel in both directions but not at the same time
(*b*) Travel in one direction only
(*c*) Travel in both directions at the same time
(*d*) None of the above

83. .... modulation technique provides the fastest transmission speed.
(*a*) Amplitude
(*b*) Frequency
(*c*) Phase
(*d*) Phase plus amplitude

84. For separating channels in FDM, it is necessary to use ....
(*a*) Time slots
(*b*) Bandpass filters
(*c*) Differentiation
(*d*) None of the above

85. For separating channels in TDM, it is necessary to use ....
(*a*) Time slots
(*b*) Differentiation
(*c*) Bandpass filters
(*d*) None of the above

86. Coaxial cable ....
(*a*) Requires a special receiving dish to receive signals
(*b*) Is easily bent
(*c*) Is made from silica glass
(*d*) Supports hundreds of thousands of telephone conversions

87. .... is a larger transmission line that carries data gathered from smaller lines that interconnect with it.
(*a*) Optical fibre

(*b*) Coaxial cable
(*c*) Backbone
(*d*) Truck

88. Satellites system ....
(*a*) Use fibre cable to send signal
(*b*) Are cheap to implement
(*c*) Are suited to small numbers of users located close together
(*d*) Send signals high above the earth to ground stations

89. Light remains confined within core of simple optical fibre because of.
(*a*) Refraction
(*b*) Total internal reflection from insulation
(*c*) Total internal reflection from core cladding boundary
(*d*) None of the above

90. The device that permits electrical digital signal to be transmitted to a server over regular telephone line is a
(*a*) Multiplexer
(*b*) Modem
(*c*) Cluster controller
(*d*) Front end processor

91. What is not true w.r.t channel capacity
(*a*) It is related to maximum data rate for a transmission medium
(*b*) It is concerned with quality of communication channel
(*c*) It is measured in dB
(*d*) None of the above

92. The purpose of cladding is.
(*a*) To avoid the cross talk during transmission
(*b*) To increase information transmission rate
(*c*) To reduce transmission error
(*d*) To reduce computation error

93. Which is not true for packet switching.
(*a*) Works at different line speeds
(*b*) Faster than circuit switching
(*c*) Greater line efficiency
(*d*) It is most popular method in internet

94. Half duplex data transmission is defined as.
(*a*) Either party can send data to other at same time
(*b*) Either party can send data to other alternately
(*c*) Both parties can send and receive data but not at the same time
(*d*) Only one party can send data to other

95. A shared collection of logically related data designed to meet information needs of multiple users in an organization is.
(*a*) Database
(*b*) Level-1 diagram
(*c*) Transposition document
(*d*) None of the above

96. How many OSI layers are covered in the x.25 standard?
(*a*) Two
(*b*) Three
(*c*) Seven
(*d*) Six

97. The x.25 standard specifies a.
(*a*) Technique for representing a start and stop of data
(*b*) Data bit rate
(*c*) Technique for dial access
(*d*) DIE/DCE interface

98. A protocol is a set of rules governing a time sequence of. events that must take place.
    (*a*) Between modems
    (*b*) Between interface
    (*c*) Across an interface
    (*d*) None of the above

99. One important characteristic of the hub architecture of ARC network is.
    (*a*) Directionalized transmission
    (*b*) Unlimited number of stations
    (*c*) Multiple virtual networks
    (*d*) Alternative routing

100. FDDI is a
    (*a*) Ring network
    (*b*) Star network
    (*c*) Mesh network
    (*d*) Bus based network

101. To connect a computer with a device in the same room, you can use
    (*a*) C coaxial cable
    (*b*) A dedicated link
    (*c*) A ground station
    (*d*) All of the above

102. The slowest transmission speed are those of
    (*a*) Twisted pair wire
    (*b*) Coaxial cable
    (*c*) Fiber-optic cable
    (*d*) Microwaves

103. A protocol is a set of rules governing a time sequence of events that must take place
    (*a*) Between peers
    (*b*) Between modems
    (*c*) Between interface
    (*d*) Across interface

104. Which of the following is an important characteristic of LAN
    (*a*) Application independent interfaces
    (*b*) Unlimited expansion
    (*c*) Low cost access for low bandwidth channels
    (*d*) Parallel transmission

105. Which of the following is possible in a token passing bus network
    (*a*) In-service expansion
    (*b*) Unlimited number of stations
    (*c*) (*a*) and (*b*) both
    (*d*) Unlimited distance

106. Which of the following statment is correct
    (*a*) Protocol converters are same as multiplexers
    (*b*) Protocol converters are same as TDMs
    (*c*) Protocol converters are usually not operated in pairs
    (*d*) Protocol converters are usually operated in pairs

107. Which of the following statements is correct
    (*a*) Teleprinters are used for printing at remote locations, not for input
    (*b*) Teleprinters are same as teletype
    (*c*) Teleprinters are same as x400
    (*d*) Teleprinters have a printer for output and keyboard for input

108. The main difference between synchronous and asynchronous tranmission is
    (*a*) The clocking is derived from the data in synchronous transmission
    (*b*) The clocking is mixed with the data in asynchronous transmission

(*c*) The pulse height is different
(*d*) the bandwidth required is different

109. Synchronous protocols
(*a*) Transmit characters one at a time
(*b*) Allow faster transmission than asynchronous protocols do
(*c*) Are generally used by personal computers
(*d*) Are more reliable

110. The physical layer of a network
(*a*) Defines the electrical characteristics of signals passed between the computer and communication devices
(*b*) Controls error detection and correction
(*c*) Constructs packets of data and send them across the network
(*d*) All of the above

111. The application layer of a network
(*a*) Establishes, maintains and terminates virtual circuits
(*b*) Defines the users' port into the network
(*c*) Consists of software being run on the computer connected to the network
(*d*) All of the above

112. A distributed network configuration in which all data/information pass through a central computer is
(*a*) Bus network
(*b*) Star network
(*c*) Ring network
(*d*) Point to point network

113. A communication network which is used by large organization over regional, national or global area is called
(*a*) LAN
(*b*) WAN
(*c*) MAN
(*d*) Internet

114. Now a days computers all over the world can talk to each other, which is one of the special accessories essential for this purpose
(*a*) Keyboard
(*b*) Modem
(*c*) Scanner
(*d*) FAX

115. A smart modem can dial, hang up and answer incoming calls automatically. Can you tell who provides appropriate instructions to the modem for this purpose
(*a*) Communication software
(*b*) Error detecting protocols
(*c*) Link access procedure (LAP)
(*d*) Telecommunications

116. Which of the following data transmission media has the largest terrestrial range without the use of repeaters and other devices
(*a*) Hard wiring
(*b*) Microwave
(*c*) Satellite
(*d*) Laser

117. What are the data transmission channels available for carrying data from one location to another
(*a*) Narrow band
(*b*) Voice band
(*c*) Broad band
(*d*) All of the above

118. What function does a serial interface perform in data communication
(*a*) Convert serial data into audio signals

(*b*) Convert analog signals into digital signals
(*c*) Convert parallel data into a stream of bits
(*d*) Decodes incoming data into computer data

119. Which of the following is not a transmission medium
(*a*) Telephone lines
(*b*) Coaxial cable
(*c*) Modem
(*d*) Microwave system

120. Which of the following is an advantage to using fiber optics data tranmission
(*a*) Resistance to data theft
(*b*) Fast data transmission rate
(*c*) Low noise level
(*d*) Few trasmission errors

121. Which of the following performs modulation and demodulation
(*a*) Fiber optic
(*b*) Satellite
(*c*) Coaxial cable
(*d*) Modem

122. We can receive data either through our television aerial or down our telephone lines and display this data on our television screen. What is the general name given to this process
(*a*) Viewdata
(*b*) Teletext
(*c*) Telesoftware
(*d*) Videotex

123. Processors of all computers, micro, mini or mainframe must have
(*a*) ALU
(*b*) Primary storage
(*c*) Control Unit
(*d*) All of the above

124. The term memory applies to which one of the following
(*a*) Logic
(*b*) Storage
(*c*) Control
(*d*) Input Device

125. The ascending order of a data Hierarchy is
(*a*) Bit-bytes-field-record-file-database
(*b*) Bit-bytes-record-field-file-database
(*c*) Bytes-bit-field-record-file-database
(*d*) Bytes-bit-record-field-file-database

126. The Central Processing Unit (CPU) consists of :
(*a*) Input, Output and processing unit
(*b*) Control unit,primary and secondary storage
(*c*) Control unit, ALU and primary storage
(*d*) Control unit, processing and primary storage

127. Which of the following is an example of non-volatile memory
(*a*) ROM
(*b*) SRAM
(*c*) Cache memory
(*d*) RAM

128. Which of the following holds the ROM, CPU, RAM and expansion cards
(*a*) Hard disk
(*b*) Cache Memory
(*c*) Motherboard
(*d*) All of the above

129. Which of the following is the fastest

(*a*) CPU
(*b*) Magnetic tape
(*c*) Video terminal
(*d*) Sensors

130. Which of the following is the user programmed semiconductor memory
(*a*) SRAM
(*b*) DRAM
(*c*) EROM
(*d*) All of the above

131. A floppy disk contains
(*a*) Circular tracks only
(*b*) Sectors only
(*c*) Tracks and sectors
(*d*) All of the above

132. Average access time in the magnetic disk is of the order of
(*a*) 50 millisecond
(*b*) 50 microsecond
(*c*) 50 second
(*d*) All of the above

133. What was the computer conceived by Babbage
(*a*) Analytical Engine
(*b*) Earthmetic Machine
(*c*) Donald Knuth
(*d*) All

134. The organized set of instructions to direct the computer in solving a problem is called
(*a*) Program
(*b*) Flow chart
(*c*) Algorithm
(*d*) All of the above

135. The memory which is programmed at the time it is manufactured
(*a*) ROM
(*b*) RAM
(*c*) PROM
(*d*) EPROM

ANSWERS

1. (*a*)	2. (*b*)	3. (*c*)	4. (*b*)	5. (*a*)	6. (*a*)	7. (*a*)
8. (*d*)	9. (*a*)	10. (*d*)	11. (*d*)	12. (*d*)	13. (*b*)	14. (*d*)
15. (*a*)	16. (*a*)	17. (*b*)	18. (*c*)	19. (*c*)	20. (*a*)	21. (*b*)
22. (*c*)	23. (*a*)	24. (*d*)	25. (*c*)	26. (*c*)	27. (*b*)	28. (*b*)
29. (*b*)	30. (*c*)	31. (*c*)	32. (*c*)	33. (*a*)	34. (*b*)	35. (*a*)
36. (*b*)	37. (*c*)	38. (*d*)	39. (*a*)	40. (*a*)	41. (*a*)	42. (*d*)
43. (*a*)	44. (*b*)	45. (*a*)	46. (*a*)	47. (*a*)	48. (*c*)	49. (*b*)
50. (*a*)	51. (*a*)	52. (*b*)	53. (*a*)	54. (*b*)	55. (*a*)	56. (*d*)
57. (*d*)	58. (*a*)	59. (*c*)	60. (*a*)	61. (*d*)	62. (*a*)	63. (*c*)
64. (*a*)	65. (*c*)	66. (*b*)	67. (*b*)	68. (*b*)	69. (*d*)	70. (*c*)
71. (*c*)	72. (*b*)	73. (*c*)	74. (*b*)	75. (*b*)	76. (*d*)	77. (*d*)
78. (*a*)	79. (*b*)	80. (*a*)	81. (*b*)	82. (*c*)	83. (*c*)	84. (*b*)
85. (*a*)	86. (*a*)	87. (*a*)	88. (*c*)	89. (*c*)	90. (*b*)	91. (*c*)
92. (*a*)	93. (*d*)	94. (*b*)	95. (*b*)	96. (*d*)	97. (*d*)	98. (*c*)

99. (*c*)	100. (*a*)	101. (*b*)	102. (*a*)	103. (*d*)	104. (*a*)	105. (*c*)
106. (*d*)	107. (*a*)	108. (*a*)	109. (*b*)	110. (*a*)	111. (*a*)	112. (*b*)
113. (*b*)	114. (*b*)	115. (*c*)	116. (*c*)	117. (*d*)	118. (*d*)	119. (*c*)
120. (*c*)	121. (*d*)	122. (*c*)	123. (*d*)	124. (*b*)	125. (*a*)	126. (*c*)
127. (*a*)	128. (*c*)	129. (*a*)	130. (*c*)	131. (*c*)	132. (*a*)	133. (*a*)
134. (*a*)	135. (*a*)					

17

Information Technology

1. An information system that supplies information specifically to aid managers with decision-making responsibilities is called a
(*a*) DBMS
(*b*) MIS
(*c*) DSS
(*d*) DBA

2. A management information system is composed of
(*a*) Data
(*b*) Software
(*c*) Hardware
(*d*) All of the above

3. A .... decision routine is one that's made following the completion of a preplanned series of steps.
(*a*) Strategic
(*b*) Structured
(*c*) Simulation
(*d*) Tactical

4. Top-level managers are responsible for .... plans and decisions
(*a*) Strategic
(*b*) Structured
(*c*) Simulation
(*d*) Tactical

5. Middle-level managers are responsible for making the .... decisions to allocate recources and establish controls.
(*a*) Strategic
(*b*) Structured
(*c*) Simulation
(*d*) Tactical

6. Lower-level managers make day-to-day .... decisions to schedule and control specific tasks.
(*a*) Operational
(*b*) Decision
(*c*) Success
(*d*) Simulation

7. A MIS provides
(*a*) Past information
(*b*) Present information
(*c*) Future information
(*d*) All of the above

8. Which of the following is a component of an expert system?
(*a*) Explanation module
(*b*) Knowledge base
(*c*) Natural language interface
(*d*) All of the above

9. The online hotel reservation system having database capabilities are a good example of
(*a*) Database management system (DBMS)
(*b*) Marketing information system
(*c*) Manual information system
(*d*) Managerial information system

10. A characteristic of MIS is
(*a*) User-oriented information

(*b*) Restriction on the system's size to inhibit future growth
(*c*) Priority for data handling over the output of decision-oriented information
(*d*) All of the above

11. A primary use of decision support system (DSS) is to simulate and experiment over by using different parameters and assumptions.What is it called?
(*a*) Artificial intelligence
(*b*) "What is analysis"
(*c*) Exception report
(*d*) Computer assisted

12. The four major corporate recources are money, materials, information and ....
(*a*) People
(*b*) Icons
(*c*) Information system
(*d*) On-line

13. Management uses information for two purposes: planning and ....
(*a*) Programmable
(*b*) Control
(*c*) Predictive reports
(*d*) Relevant

14. Duplicate copies of the database are stored at all locations under:
(*a*) Partitioning
(*b*) Polling
(*c*) Replication
(*d*) Data sharing

15. Which of the following is not one of the major components of decision-support system?
(*a*) Language system
(*b*) Knowledge system
(*c*) Expert system
(*d*) Problem-processing system

16. A programmer would most likely prepare a
(*a*) General system flow chart
(*b*) Specific system flow chart
(*c*) General program flow chart
(*d*) Specific program flow chart

17. "User-friendly" computers have insured that
(*a*) Management requires no system analysis design
(*b*) Programmer no longer needed
(*c*) Structured programming is not needed
(*d*) None of the above

18. Which of the following might be output as a result of using a CASE tool?
(*a*) Programming code
(*b*) Flow charts and data flow diagram
(*c*) Prototypes and cost/benifits analysis
(*d*) All of the above

19. Announcement of MIS implementation is made by
(*a*) Operational level managers
(*b*) Tactical level managers
(*c*) The president of organisation
(*d*) All of the above

20. The first step of the implementation phase is
(*a*) Implementation planning
(*b*) Select the computer
(*c*) Announce the implementation project
(*d*) Prepare physical facilities

21. Which of the following is used when a company goes outside its organisation to develop a new system?

(a) Request for proposal
(b) Data flow diagram
(c) System flow chart
(d) Project directory

22. At the time of system study, flowcharts are drawn using
(a) Non-standing symbols
(b) General symbols
(c) Abbreviated symbols
(d) Specific symbols

23. During system study, data can be collected through
(a) Questionnaires
(b) Interviews
(c) On-site observations
(d) All of the above

24. In prototyping
(a) BASIC is used
(b) COBOL is used
(c) 4GLs are used
(d) System is documented

25. In prototyping the following are used
(a) Screen generators
(b) Input generators
(c) Application generators
(d) All of the above

26. The first step to system study project is
(a) Define system performance criteria
(b) Describe information needs
(c) Staff for the study project
(d) Announce the study project

27. During the system study, analysts determine manager's information needs by
(a) Conducting tours of a nearby computer center
(b) Asking questions
(c) Showing samples of computer reports
(d) Teaching short courses in programming languages

28. Which of the following is not a factor in the failure of a systems development project
(a) Inadequate user involvement
(b) Failure of sytems integration
(c) Size of company
(d) Continuation of a project that should have been cancelled

29. Environment in systems parlance refers to
(a) A sub-system
(b) The boundary
(c) A part outside the boundaries
(d) All of the above

30. Which of the following are the tools not used for System Analysis
(a) System-test data
(b) Decision table
(c) Data Flow Diagram
(d) Flow charts

31. A feasibility study should focus on
(a) Technical feasibility
(b) Economic feasibility
(c) Operational feasibility
(d) All of the above

32. The 'big picture' diagram of a system is the
(a) Block diagram
(b) Logic diagram
(c) System flow chart
(d) Program flow chart

33. An announcement of the MIS project is made to
(a) Appeal to the employees for cooperation
(b) Prevent strikes by organized factory workers
(c) Inform the marginally-

productive employees that they should begin looking for new job
(*d*) Boost stock prices

34. Cost benefit analysis
(*a*) Evaluates the tangible and non- tangible factors
(*b*) Compares the cost, with the benefits of introducing a computer based system
(*c*) Estimates the hardware and software costs
(*d*) All of the above

35. The four icons used in building Data Flow Diagram are
(*a*) Flow, Source, Store, Process
(*b*) Flow, Process, Source, Store
(*c*) Flow, Process, Source/ Destination, Store
(*d*) Source, Process, Destination, Store

36. Digital convergence implies that different kinds of data (voice, sound and video) can be delivered via a single medium, such as;
(*a*) CD-ROM or Internet
(*b*) Only CD-ROM
(*c*) Only internet
(*d*) None of these

37. Which is the best consumer of multimedia technology
(*a*) Marketing
(*b*) Training
(*c*) Education
(*d*) All of the above

38. A CD to the Red Book specification could hold up to 80 minutes of full motion video, using .....compression
(*a*) MP3
(*b*) MPEG-1
(*c*) Both a and b
(*d*) None of the above

39. In 1993, which UK Company demonstrated the ability to playback video from a compact disk on a special decoder
(*a*) HP
(*b*) Nimbus
(*c*) Apple Computers
(*d*) IBM

40. When freelance worker or outside companies are hired for a project rather than full-time employees, the project is known as
(*a*) Outsourcing
(*b*) Project Management
(*c*) Both a and b
(*d*) None of the above

41. Who is responsible for providing possible solution, when an Information System needs to be updated
(*a*) Programmer
(*b*) System Analyst
(*c*) DBA
(*d*) Network Manager

42. Department responsible for creating and maintaining information systems in a company
(*a*) IS Department
(*b*) HR Department
(*c*) O/P department
(*d*) None of the above

43. .... job is to create computer programs either as commercial products or as separate parts of a company's information system
(*a*) System Manager
(*b*) DBA
(*c*) Programmer
(*d*) System Analyst

44. Who creates the network administrators guide
   (*a*) Technical Writer
   (*b*) Marketing and Sales Department
   (*c*) S/W Engineer
   (*d*) All

45. Who is responsible for keeping information systems up and running
   (*a*) Network Manager
   (*b*) Technician only
   (*c*) System Analyst
   (*d*) Technical writer

46. Technicians are needed to maintain the ..... components of an Information System
   (*a*) Hardware Components
   (*b*) S/W Components
   (*c*) Both a and b
   (*d*) None

47. IS personnel can contact ..... if they can't find out the solution of a problem
   (*a*) Help Desk
   (*b*) Programmer
   (*c*) None
   (*d*) Both (*a*) and (*b*)

48. ..... choose suppliers for system components and negotiate the necessary items
   (*a*) Purchasing agents
   (*b*) Top Level Management only
   (*c*) CEO
   (*d*) None

49. Size of a company's information system department typically correlates with the .... it supports
   (*a*) Size of Company
   (*b*) CEO
   (*c*) Projects Handled
   (*d*) Annual Turnover

ANSWERS

1. (*b*)	2. (*b*)	3. (*d*)	4. (*a*)	5. (*c*)	6. (*a*)	7. (*d*)
8. (*d*)	9. (*a*)	10. (*a*)	11. (*b*)	12. (*a*)	13. (*b*)	14. (*c*)
15. (*c*)	16. (*c*)	17. (*d*)	18. (*d*)	19. (*c*)	20. (*a*)	21. (*a*)
22. (*c*)	23. (*d*)	24. (*a*)	25. (*c*)	26. (*b*)	27. (*b*)	28. (*c*)
29. (*d*)	30. (*a*)	31. (*d*)	32. (*c*)	33. (*b*)	34. (*d*)	35. (*c*)
36. (*a*)	37. (*d*)	38. (*a*)	39. (*b*)	40. (*a*)	41. (*b*)	42. (*a*)
43. (*a*)	44. (*a*)	45. (*a*)	46. (*a*)	47. (*d*)	48. (*a*)	49. (*d*)